**Forgotten Horrors 2:
Beyond the Horror Ban**

Forgotten Horrors 2
Beyond the Horror Ban

by Michael H. Price
with
George E. Turner
Authors of a Great Many Things

With a Foreword
by Josh Alan Friedman

Luminary Press
Baltimore, Maryland

Also by Michael H. Price and George E. Turner:

The Ancient Great Plains and *The Palo Duro Story* (In Preparation)
Forgotten Horrors: The Definitive Edition
Southern-Fried Homicide
Aw-Shucks Suspense Stories: Mo' Southern-Fried Homicide
Human Monsters: The Bizarre Psychology of Movie Villains
V.T. Hamlin's Collected Alley Oop, Vols. No. 2 & 3
The Cinema of Adventure, Romance & Terror
The Spider
Roy Crane's Collected Wash Tubbs & Captain Easy, Vol. No. 10
Al Capp's Collected Li'l Abner, Vol. No. 6
Forgotten Horrors: Early Talkie Chillers from Poverty Row (Two Prior Editions)

Also by Michael H. Price:

Selected Volumes in the Midnight Marquee Actors Series
(Contributing Author)
It's Christmas Time at the Movies
(Contributing Author)
Lon Chaney, Jr.: Midnight Marquee Actors Series
(Contributing Author)
Lex Eicon and the Numerologist
(With Jerome McDonough)
The A-to-Z Encyclopedia of Serial Killers
(Contributing Illustrator)
Krime Duzzin't Pay!
The Guitar in Jazz
(Contributing Author)
R. Crumb: The Musical
(With Robert Crumb & Johnny Simons)
The 50 Greatest Cartoons
(Contributing Author)
Michael H. Price's Hollywood Horrors Electrified!
(With Timothy Truman)
Bloody Visions, Vols. I-III

Cover Design: Susan Svehla
Copyright © 2001 Michael H. Price

Portions of this book have appeared, in markedly different form, in *The Cinema of Adventure, Romance & Terror* (A.S.C. Press; 1989); in *Human Monsters: The Bizarre Psychology of Movie Villains* (Kitchen Sink Press; 1996); in *The American Cinematographer* and *Psychotronic Video* magazines; and in Michael H. Price's talk-radio broadcasts and dispatches via the New York Times News Service.

Without limiting the rights reserved under the copyright above, no part of this publication may be reproduced, stored in or introduced into a retrieval system, or transmitted, in any form, or by any means (electronic, mechanical, photocopying, recording, or otherwise), without the prior written permission of the copyright owner or the publishers of this book.

ISBN: 1-887664-43-2
Library of Congress Catalogue Card Number 2001117794
Manufactured in the United States of America
Second Printing by Luminary Press, an imprint of Midnight Marquee Press, Inc., April 2004

Dedication

In Memory of
Jerome McDonough
(1946-1999)

...Who Inspired Two
Generations of Aspiring
Actors and Dramatists—
And Somehow Made the
Time To Practice Everything
Good That He Preached

"Give me the good old days of early American indie filmmaking—where the directors acted like producers and the actors took on the role of writers."
—The *Evil Dead* Films' Bruce Campbell

"Naturally, we cannot expect all weird tales to conform to any theoretical model... [M]uch of the choicest weird work is unconscious, appearing in memorable fragments scattered through material whose massed effect may be of a very different cast."
—H.P. Lovecraft (*Supernatural Horror in Literature*)

Table of Contents

9	Foreword by Josh Alan Friedman
10	Author's Preface
14	Prologue: Beyond the Horror Ban
17	Acknowledgments

1930-35

18	Annotations, Marginalia & Addenda to Forgotten Horrors: The Definitive Edition

1936-37

28	The Lion Man
29	Thunderbolt
30	The Leavenworth Case
31	I Conquer the Sea!
32	Prison Shadows
33	It Couldn't Have Happened (But It Did)
35	Kliou (The Tiger)
36	Robinson Crusoe of Clipper Island
37	African Holiday
37	Blake of Scotland Yard
38	The Fighting Deputy
39	Larceny on the Air
40	The Devil Diamond
40	Hit the Saddle
41	The Girl from Scotland Yard
43	It Happened Out West
43	Killers of the Sea
44	Angkor, or Forbidden Adventure
46	Dr. Jekyll & Mr. Hyde
47	The 13th Man
48	Rod La Rocque's "Shadow"
	•The Shadow Strikes
	•International Crime
50	Paradise Isle: A Romance of the South Seas
51	Shadows of the Orient
51	Outlaws of the Orient
52	S O S Coast Guard
55	Sky Racket
56	Special Agent K-7
57	Safari on Wheels
57	Wallaby Jim of the Islands
58	Love Life of a Gorilla
59	Vu Iz Mayn Kind? (Where Is My Child?)
60	Telephone Operator
61	Orphan of the Pecos

1938

62	Wolves of the Sea
62	The Black Doll
64	Hollywood Stadium Mystery
65	Forbidden Adventure
66	It's All in Your Mind
69	Fury Below
69	The Adventures of Chico
70	Zamboanga
71	Topa Topa
72	Wajan
72	Life Returns
74	"Dick Tracy" Redactus: In Appreciation of the Republic Serials
76	Durango Valley Raiders
77	It Happened in Chicago
77	The Night Hawk
78	The Karloff "Mr. Wong" Pictures
	•Mr. Wong, Detective
	•The Mystery of Mr. Wong
	•Mr. Wong in Chinatown
	•The Fatal Hour
	•Doomed To Die
82	Shadows over Shanghai
82	Titans of the Deep
83	Gun Packer
83	Marusia

1939

84	Mystery Plane
85	The Mystic Circle Murders
86	Exile Express
87	Across the Plains
88	S.O.S.—Tidal Wave
89	Death Goes North
91	Daughter of the Tong
91	Irish Luck
93	The Fighting Renegade
94	Adventures of the Masked Phantom
95	Torture Ship

97	Hitler—Beast of Berlin
100	Buried Alive
101	The Devil's Daughter

1940

103	Hidden Enemy
103	Chasing Trouble
104	The Invisible Killer
105	Frankenstein
107	Son of Ingagi
111	Phantom Rancher
112	Drums of Fu Manchu
115	Mr. Washington Goes to Town
117	Sky Bandits
118	On the Spot
120	The Leopard Men of Africa: An Exposé of Unrecorded Savage Rituals in the Congo
121	The Last Alarm
122	Boys of the City
124	Haunted House
125	Billy the Kid Outlawed
127	The Ranger and the Lady
128	Laughing at Danger
129	The Range Busters
129	Marked Men
130	Up in the Air
132	The Ape
134	Midnight Shadow
136	Who Killed Aunt Maggie?
138	Phantom of Chinatown
139	The Devil Bat

1941

142	The Blood of Jesus
143	The Lone Rider Rides On
144	You're Out of Luck
145	The Great Train Robbery
146	The Forgotten Village
147	Mr. District Attorney
149	City of Missing Girls
150	Adventures of Captain Marvel
152	Federal Fugitives
153	Bride of Buddha
154	Invisible Ghost
157	King of the Zombies
160	The Shark Woman
160	The Gang's All Here
161	Murder by Invitation
164	Criminals Within
164	The Deadly Game
165	Peer Gynt
168	Up Jumped the Devil
168	Saddle Mountain Roundup
169	Mercy Island
172	Jungle Man
173	Spooks Run Wild
174	The Devil Pays Off
177	I Killed That Man
178	Four Shall Die
179	Mr. District Attorney in the Carter Case

1942

181	The "Strange Holiday" of "This Precious Freedom"
184	Private Snuffy Smith
185	Law of the Jungle
186	Lucky Ghost
187	Professor Creeps
190	Black Dragons
194	The Man with Two Lives
195	Spy Smasher
196	House of Errors
197	The Panther's Claw
199	Home in Wyomin'
200	The Corpse Vanishes
205	The Mad Monster
210	Prisoner of Japan
211	Jungle Siren
213	Tomorrow We Live
215	Phantom Killer
216	The Devil with Hitler
219	Criminal Investigator
220	Bowery at Midnight
222	Outlaws of Boulder Pass
222	Hitler—Dead or Alive
223	Valley of Hunted Men
224	The Living Ghost
227	Secrets of the Underground
229	Afterword
231	Recommended Video Sources
233	About the Authors
235	Index

Foreword by Josh Alan Friedman: Ah, To Be Young, Gifted and Mantan Moreland

Michael H. Price and the late George E. Turner have taken film criticism into an altruistic realm which has come to be known as "moving-picture archaeology." They cornered a truly forgotten outer landscape in film history, lending dignity to the potboilers of Poverty Row—which Price considers the true repository of the Common Man's cinema—not the elite domain of Hollywood or the national film studios of pre-war Europe. The years covered in this volume represent a time when Joe Palooka, America's Common Man, had better taste. At least, what was then considered junk has come to be art today.

Perhaps Price relates to the Poverty Row spookers as an analogy to his own career. He produces R&B albums, literary comic books and theatre productions (like *R. Crumb Comix*, the stage revue), all from down-home Fort Worth, Texas. Frighteningly prolific, he *gets things done*, doesn't wait for corporate sponsorship. Price, the 9-to-5 newspaper editor, published the most perceptive film criticism I've ever read, during 19 incorruptible years at the Fort Worth *Star-Telegram* (with *New York Times* News Service syndication). Price and Turner were the type of scholars who literally dug into volatile nitrate film-stock canisters, risking life and limb, like bomb-squad detectives. They have helped to discover and restore silents and talkies not seen since the heyday of Vaudeville. They are too modest to take credit.

Also tops on Mike Price's agenda is his breakthrough take on colored movies—as in forgotten Negro cinema. He points out the missing link between Spencer Williams and Somerset Maugham; is the first to give Pigmeat Markham his screenwriting due; and waxes poetic on the film acting of Mantan Moreland. (Price is Moreland's posthumous patron saint. No mere Negro comedian, Moreland was a deceptively brilliant comic actor who could have easily joined the Three Stooges, had Columbia Pictures offered him the gig instead of the two Joes.)

Like a certain Victor Frankenstein, Price and Turner breathe life into forgotten horror movies, reviving these precious, chilling artifacts of old American showbiz. They can thread my 16mm film projector any time.
—Josh Alan Friedman

(Josh Alan Friedman is the composer and librettist of The Worst!*, a musical dramatization of the life of the Poverty Row filmmaker Edward D. Wood, Jr.; the author of* Tales of Times Square*; and the singer-songwriter-producer of such albums as* Famous and Poor *and* Blacks 'n' Jews.*)*

Author's Preface

So what's to do but carry it on? George Turner's death in June 1999 came only three days after George had received the first copies of our *Forgotten Horrors: The Definitive Edition* and pronounced the book the beginning of an aggressive new phase of research and opinionizing for our long-standing partnership in film archaeology.

We had already begun compiling this sequel and planning additional volumes yet, and George spoke delightedly of the bold packaging and straightforward, accessible interior design that Midnight Marquee Press had brought to our revamp of the original *Forgotten Horrors*.

"Yessiree—we've finally found a publisher that understands what we're about," George said. "Looks like we're about ready to raise some hell!"

And so we will. *Yessiree*. We had been pushing toward such a readiness since 1968, when as a college-boy cub reporter at the Texas newspaper where George had become a phenomenally popular illustrator and writer, I imposed myself upon his good graces and volunteered myself into the service of a book George was developing. The book would be called *The Making of King Kong*. My assignment, which felt a great deal like a cherished hobby, found me proofreading early drafts, filing research notes and transcribing pertinent press notices from microfilm. *King Kong* (1933) was George's hands-down favorite movie—run a close second and third by *Bride of Frankenstein* and *East of Java* (both from 1935)—and he was plotting to honor *Kong* as no one else had done by reconstructing its story from the vantage of every surviving participant. I became acquainted with the likes of Fay Wray, Bruce Cabot, co-director Ernest B. Schoedsack and his wife, the scenarist Ruth Rose, among many others, and spent hours at a stretch with George and his co-author, the *Kong* techno-artisan and all-'round documentary filmmaker Orville Goldner.

In the meantime, George taught me to refine my raw movie-buff enthusiasm into a focused productivity. We pooled our respective collections of 16-millimeter feature films—consumer-video technology was yet a ways off from any practical reality—into the archive that would become the basis for *Forgotten Horrors*. The year was now 1975, right after *The Making of King Kong* had been published.

"Collaboration is really the ideal way to work," George said, "but legitimate collaboration is a hard thing to come by. Usually, one party does all the real work while the other contributes the kibitzing and kvetching and the 'brilliant' ideas." He spoke from immediate experience, though without rancor, for even while his well-matched teaming with Dr. Goldner was in progress, George had let himself be snookered into ghost-writing a paperback novel for a fellow journalist who insisted upon calling the project a "collaboration." At about the same time, I had struck up a correspondence with a hero of George's and mine, the Wisconsin author and publisher August W. Derleth, who detailed for me a working partnership he and Mark Schorer had fashioned during the 1930s. Derleth and Schorer had built a formidable batch of short stories for *Weird Tales* magazine—one of George's and my favorite pulps—by batting their manuscripts back and forth in a game of cordial one-upsmanship until both pronounced this yarn or that fit for submission. George and I developed a modified version of the Derleth-Schorer system and used it right on through the writing of *Forgotten Horrors* and our second book, *Human Monsters*, and any number of magazine articles, essays for volumes of comic-strip history and even our own original comic strips. The tactic continues to serve, in the manuscripts and fragments that George had delivered as late as the week prior to his unexpected demise. I am reminded here of why I prefer Texas Draw Poker over Solitaire.

George had resettled in Hollywood in 1978 at the behest of the master cinematographer Linwood Dunn. I have remained in Texas for the long stretch. While our projects continued apace despite the distance—and it helps to have a colleague within shouting distance of the Motion Picture Academy's archive—I found myself learning at first hand the truth of George's *caveat* about collaboration: Simple editing assignments, from a history of a provincial junior college to a sweeping, scholarly survey of political cartooning in Texas, have turned into full-scale ghost-writing ordeals by abrupt, infuriating default. Fresh talents from the college-kid/cub-reporter ranks, amply aware of my indebtedness to George, had calculated that I can do for their careers what George has done for mine—but have proved more keenly interested in the practice that our cartoonist friend, Robert Crumb, calls "ripping off your energy" than in bringing to the table anything of weight or interest. And people wonder why I finally abandoned the newspaper business; say, I was just following George's lead, 20 years late. As George would often say, appropriating a line from his dad's Depression-era golfing buddy, Oliver Hardy: "'Twas evah *thus!*"

And meanwhile, here sits George Turner, 'way the hell off in California, burdened to the limit with *American Cinematographer* deadlines and *Friends* storyboarding assignments, asking me if he's pulling his weight on our own books and apologizing for "running late" on labor-of-love comics art for which no deadline even exists. All

Michael H. Price (left) and George E. Turner on an early tour promoting the first *Forgotten Horrors*.

this time since his passing, and that genteel Texas drawl, faintly garnished with a British affectation, remains a vivid presence, although I oftener find it exhorting me to get cracking on this unfinished business of ours.

An Acute Case of Sequelitis

George and I scarcely expected, back in mid-1977 when we wrapped the manuscript for the first *Forgotten Horrors*, ever to be developing a sequel to what had become a daunting project. We worked largely in a vacuum of our own choosing, researching information from scratch and not giving much of a hang about published opinions, and consulting only selectively with such acknowledged experts as William K. Everson and Dr. Bill G. "Buck" Rainey. We seldom received feedback from the readership that we knew the book must have found, but we were delighted to learn of its designation as a Standard Reference of the American Film Institute, and to be invited to help compile *The American Film Institute Catalogues*.

In the final resolve, however, the book that originally was called *Forgotten Horrors: Early Talkie Chillers from Poverty Row* turned out pretty much to suit us—even though its sluggish first publisher took another couple of years to bring it to market—and it left us feeling more pleased that we'd done the thing than if we'd taken a Pasadena on it. We had already launched into another project for that same publisher, A.S. Barnes & Co., with a movie-villain anthology called *Human Monsters*. But although we lacked the gumption to switch publishing houses, we still had the good sense to pack the *Human Monsters* playlist with pictures of our own choosing, rather than tackle anew the encyclopedic scope of *Forgotten Horrors*.

We had unwittingly set ourselves up, however, for a *Forgotten Horrors II* in our original preface to *Forgotten Horrors*. Invoking the British-European horror ban that effectively put the kibosh on this genre for a stretch, we had chosen the earlier months of 1937 as a cutting-off point for releases and remarked thusly: "Three years later, the genre rose from the grave for another go at it. Which is a story for another day."

A generation later, that other day has arrived. George and I spent 1995-1999 compiling a 20th-anniversary edition of *Forgotten Horrors* for Midnight Marquee Press, and while that expanded and jazzed-up volume was in final edits we began talking about picking up where we had left off. Another attempt at near-encyclopedic thoroughness still struck us as a horrific prospect—but then, interpretive research has come increasingly easy in the intervening years (mainly because of relentless practice). Too, such credentials as *Forgotten Horrors* and *Human Monsters* (finally published, but not by Barnes & Co.); the Turner-Goldner *The Making of King Kong*; my own *Hollywood Horrors* portfolio (Shel-Tone Publications; 1993) and the CD-ROM encyclopedia *A Century of Fantastic Cinema* (Knowledge

Scott Nollen and Michael H. Price present the Laemmle Award to Sara Karloff, accepting for her father Boris Karloff, at Monster Rally, Arlington, Virginia, 1999.

Media; 1995); and our multiple-author *The Cinema of Adventure, Romance & Terror* (A.S.C. Press; 1989) have opened many a door.

And so here we have it: The ground rules remain the same—weird mysteries and patent oddities, if not outright chillers, from low-rent, independent, North American filmmaking companies—but the playing field at this Depression-into-wartime juncture has been so leveled that the companies are fewer, the adventurous approach to subject matter and technique less prevalent and the aesthetic values in drastic flux. (Many latter-day genre scholars nowadays get a charge out of unearthing some "forgotten horror that *Forgotten Horrors* forgot to remember," and of extending that "forgotten horrors" distinction to such *major*-studio hair-raisers as Fox's *Almost Married* and Universal's *Cross Country Cruise*. More power to them; the more the players, and the keener their zeal for rediscovery, the likelier the lot of us are to whip that old devil obscurity. We may be the proprietors of the franchise, but anybody can play.)

We have, as with the first *Forgotten Horrors*, made some exclusions based upon economic realities: The Pine-Thomas production company, for example, turned out many respectable B-as-in-budget thrillers but enjoyed too secure a distribution arrangement with big-league Paramount Pictures to rank as a true Poverty Row outfit. A name-brand company will figure now and again in the dealings of Poverty Row, as witness Hal Roach's descent to the rank of a struggling independent in the long and unforgiving wake of a pre-war political indiscretion. Veteran indie/exploitation producer Walter Futter even crops up at big Universal Pictures at one fleeting juncture, helping to launch a long-running *Crime Club* series with a comedy-spooker called *The Black Doll*.

Among the true Poverty Row studios that would forge on, obediently or subversively, through the horror ban or crop up in its wake, we find such developments as these:

• A *Dr. Jekyll & Mr. Hyde* (1937) and a *Frankenstein* (1940), scarcely known today even to have existed, came virtually out of nowhere, via a Texas schoolboy's production company that actually secured some commercial theatrical play. While the search goes on for surviving footage, we present herewith the first detailed accounts of these pictures since their scattered trade-magazine coverage of the 1940s.

• Was Republic Pictures' *The Leavenworth Case* (1936) the final straw toward provoking the international embargo on Hollywood's chillers? Maybe so, maybe not—but Republic's extraordinary pains to placate the British censors certainly set an alarming precedent that the U.S. film capital could never have sustained.

• Psychological horror emerges to give the old standbys of man-made monsters and supernatural predators a run for their money. By no coincidence, the film noir style begins finding its way.

• Outright fershlugginer weirdness crops up in such out-of-the-way places as the adaptations of some popular newspaper cartoons. Nothing unexpected to find a science-fictional element in a *Tailspin Tommy* picture—but *Barney Google & Snuffy Smith*? We would be remiss to deny the bizarre merely because its strays from its known precincts.

• The Third Reich becomes a convenient metaphor for monstrousness—as exaggerated in such tarnished finery as *Black Dragons*—but also proves suitably horrifying in contexts more true-to-life. *I Escaped the Gestapo* and *Prisoner of Japan* draw more literally from the realities of the day.

• Bela Lugosi finds a permanent home in the studio slums as a bankable name-above-the-title for Producers Releasing Corp. and Monogram Pictures Corp. Boris Karloff goes slumming, as a matter of career strategy, on Poverty Row.

•Weird Westerns, those phantoms of the horse opera, keep cropping up even though the cowboy picture as a class turns unnaturally cheery and tuneful. Our Western selections here are meant to be representative more so than comprehensive, and most often subjective: Even Gene Autry and Roy Rogers made the occasional frontier spooker—sez us—and a display of cold malevolence from the right bad-guy actor can be as unsettling as a ghost or a maniac.

The bearer of this unused WWII-era ticket should have exhibited better sense than to let it go to waste. For the pasteboard passport held the promise of not only a gander at some low-budget horror movie, and on a Halloween night, yet—but also an on-stage extravaganza to chill the blood and tickle the gizzard. The lapsed tradition of the midnight spook-show pageant is one of the culture's more troubling losses.

•Elsewhere within the 1940s, Mantan Moreland emerges as a deft and commanding scene-stealer, rendering remarkable many pictures that otherwise might better remain forgotten. With Moreland and Spencer Williams as its guiding lights, the black independent cinema takes on a newfound assurance, adapting even horror and hellfire religion to its concerns.

Unearthed rarities abound, putting such better-known fare as Monogram Pictures' "Lugosi Nine" and the *Mr. Wong* detective series (starring Boris Karloff and, at the very end, Keye Luke) in a sturdier historical context than most movie buffs have known. We're particularly delighted to have a vehicle with which to track the progress of an ahead-of-its-time buddy-picture series starring Frankie Darro and Mantan Moreland, and to be able to sort out all the title-vs.-contents confusion that has entangled such mock-safari pictures as *Angkor*, *Forbidden Adventure* and *Love Life of a Gorilla*. To flesh things out further, I have dredged up from George's Hollywood files our originally proposed contents list for the 1975-77 *Forgotten Horrors* project and given an airing to quite a few pictures that did not make the cut.

For those Constant (if not Constipated) Readers who have been haranguing me since 1987 that they "must know more" about a legendary picture called *On the Prowl*, supposedly from the war years, I must now put paid to the issue: *On the Prowl* is a fakerooney—a fabrication concocted within the pages of Timothy Truman's and my *Prowler* comic books of 1987-90, as back-story for the title character. That much had been made plain within the very magazine, where we published a *Forgotten Horrors*-like text feature about *On the Prowl*. But even so, I've been accosted off and on ever since by well-intentioned fans who believe that I hold their only hope of ever seeing this "lost" thriller. Now that we're up into the WWII period of *Forgotten Horrors*, I can only anticipate a renewed outcry. So listen up, already: There ain't no *On the Prowl*. Never was. Except in the *Prowler* funnybooks.

There are, meanwhile, a great many genuine *Forgotten Horrors*—some, genuinely horripilating; some, genuinely horrendous; and most, genuinely forgotten—just waiting right here to be remembered, if not to be discovered outright for the first time in their impoverished existence. The entire point of George Turner's career was to render distant history both accessible and fascinating to as many people as he could reach, and he'd be plumb tickled to know that we've finally reached enough of a readership to require this encore volume.

—Michael H. Price

Prologue
Beyond the Horror Ban

Just as Universal Pictures' *Dracula* and *Frankenstein* had laid a foundation for the modern horror film in 1931, so those very properties returned late in the decade to rescue the genre from a long stretch of near-abandonment.

Because of an embargo on horror movies by British and European censors, drastically fewer such films were made from 1936 until well along into 1939. The foreign market was lucrative enough that it actually could influence what U.S. moviegoers were allowed to see. Careers suffered: Bela Lugosi was particularly hard-hit, and Boris Karloff enjoyed just about all he could stand of impersonating Mr. James Lee Wong, popularly regarded as a poor man's Charlie Chan. Despite the occasional subversive exception, impatience swelled among the paying customers.

In an inspired moment that proved to be the turning point, a showman named Emil Umann, of the Regina Theatre (later known as the Fine Arts) in Beverly Hills, sensed a phenomenon that the marketing strategists of a later generation would call "pent-up demand." The Regina was incapable of booking first-run pictures because of the monopolistic dominance of studio-owned theatre chains, and thus depended upon revival showings. Umann, the manager, found some long-neglected prints of *Dracula* and *Frankenstein* at a film warehouse. He had trailers made up for advance ballyhoo and opened a "Mammoth Horror Show" double feature on August 4, 1937, daring people to give it a try. The theatre was packed for four weeks running. In Seattle, the Blue Mouse Theatre picked up the same bill, which broke the house record for paid attendance.

The ban persisted, but eventually Universal Pictures got wise to the Regina's success and ordered new prints struck for a national reissue. The master negatives of both *Dracula* and *Frankenstein* had

Lifting a page from the unwritten law book of carnival showmanship, Beverly Hills' independent Regina Theatre "dared" the masses to look in on the resurrected attractions. They took the bait—hook, line, bobber and sinker.

become somewhat battered. They would sustain further damage when submitted anew to the Hays Office. The Production Code Administration had become considerably more severe in the intervening years, and several small but telling cuts were demanded. These included Colin Clive's line from *Frankenstein*, "Oh! In the name of God! Now I know what it feels like to *be* God!" along with the more violent action from the first fight with Boris Karloff's Monster; several close-ups from the sequence where Dwight Frye torments the Monster with a torch; and a close-up of Edward Van Sloan's Dr. Waldman jabbing the Monster with a hypodermic needle.

The Regina bolstered the fourth week of its historic 1938 revival with a guest appearance from Bela Lugosi.

The new release prints were made on Eastman's Aquagreen Colortone stock, partly because negative damage is less noticeable in a tinted print, but also because the green stock used throughout the Universal serial *Flash Gordon's Trip to Mars*, released on March 22, 1938, had caused a popular sensation. The color proved equally right for the 1938 editions of *Dracula* and *Frankenstein*, which were released on May 15.

The official resurrection echoed and amplified the success of the Regina Theatre's revival: All seats were sold by 10 a.m. on opening day at the Victory Theatre in Salt Lake City, and police lines held back a mob of 4,000 souls who had surrounded the place by noon. The crowd crushed the box-office and caved in the doors. The manager hastily rented a vacant theatre across the street and had it filled within 20 minutes, keeping the program constant by bicycling the reels back and forth. A 3,800-seat house in Waterbury, Connecticut played to 6,500 admissions on opening day. The Warners Theatre in Fresno, California, did the biggest business in its history. Six policemen were on hand to control the crowds at the Fox Uptown in Kansas City. The St. Louis Theatre in St. Louis, Missouri did double the business of its nearest competitor for a week and held the program over for another week. On October 17, the double feature opened on Broadway to huge crowds.

From this gradual progress came the sudden realization that Hollywood did not need the foreign market to make big profits on a good horror show. Universal announced production on *Son of Frankenstein*, which commenced on October 24, and immediately sent out prints of other vintage chillers to fill the void. Other studios followed suit with reissues and new projects, and the ban found itself beaten. The foreign censors might have rationalized with the standard rejoinder that there is no accounting for taste—a so-what-else-is-new? truism—even though they had been trying their damnedest to account for everyone else's tastes by dictatorial means.

Much of that renewed activity, of course, took place within the independent studios of Hollywood's Poverty Row, which is the province of our *Forgotten Horrors* volumes. We had cut off the first book—*Forgotten Horrors: The Definitive Edition*—with 1936-37, at the beginning of the ban, and now we overlap with the original trail during 1936-37 to show how the littler studios were faring, through the ban and on into the early 1940s.

Now, we've caught some folks in the act of declaring that "no horror movies" got made during that long dry spell. Which is a naive and simplistic view, inasmuch as there can be no absolutes in art, or in artifice. Others acknowledge only a scant few such pictures, hewing to definitions more rigid than we care to use. Easy graders that we are with regard to what constitutes a horror movie, we remain as keen as ever upon looking beyond the conventional and convenient pigeonholes. Horrific serials con-

The dual bill that broke the ban: One theatre with a bit of gumption was all it took.

tinued apace—including a notably sadistic star vehicle for Bela Lugosi, *S O S Coast Guard*—because the chapter-a-week cliffhangers were considered kid stuff and generally went overlooked by the censors. Black-ensemble films, likewise ignored within the mainstream, dealt generously with the bizarre as a matter of their documenting the folkways of religion and/or superstition. Crime melodramas were often naturalistic horror pictures that no one cared to acknowledge as such. And as to gallows comedies, we've seldom met one we didn't like. (We once would have used the perfectly okay term *black comedy* to describe an exercise in grim humor. But the same foolish compulsions that once snookered Hollywood into backing away from horror pictures continue to compromise the culture. Take, for example, the recent occasion on which a well-intentioned but fundamentally harebrained editor changed the phrase *black comedy* to read, instead, "African-American comedy," in a newspaper article on a stage production of *Arsenic and Old Lace*. The entirely Caucasian ensemble cast scarcely knew what to make of the published review.)

Be that as it may. Here we have a picture-by-pic-ture accounting of what was going down in the independent sector during that long-ago period of crippling Political Correctness, when the fear of offending a nebulous and ill-understood mass audience scared the American movie-making establishment away from the very idea of creating anything that might generate a welcome thrill of terror. We—as in We, the People—owe a hand to big-league Universal's *Frankenstein* and *Dracula* for booting the industry off high-center, but we also owe thanks to the unassuming little Regina Theatre for testing the waters to find out what folks *really* wanted to be watching.

And here's to Poverty Row, whose struggling independent studios kept a light burning against the day that unadulterated, unapologetic horror movies could come charging back home with a vengeance.

—Price & Turner
Somewhere between Vasquez Rocks
and the Llano Estacado;
Somewhere between 1989 and 2001 A.D.

Acknowledgments

A grateful nod to John Wooley, Josh Alan Friedman, Jan Alan Henderson, Gary Don Rhodes and Steve Brigati for their Contributions Beyond the Call; and to these additional sources of information, encouragement and assistance:

Forrest J Ackerman; Paul Adair; Al Adamson, Ben & Buck Altman; Anthony Ambrogio; Don & Jim Ameche; Samuel Z. Arkoff; Robert Armstrong; Gene Autry; Vince Barnett; Billy Barty; Dan Bates; Spencer Gordon Bennet; Stephen R. Bissette; Robert Bloch; Wm. V. & Toni Boecker; Ron Borst; Pat Brady; Ryan Brennan; Mel Brooks; T. Sumter Bruton III; Larry Buchanan; Bob Burns; Bruce Cabot; Sam Calvin; Yakima Canutt; Roger Corman; Frank Coughlan, Jr.; Gene Clardy; Mark Clark; Jim & Marian Clatterbaugh; Jim Colegrove; Cindy Collins; Bob Colman; Ray "Crash" Corrigan; Buster Crabbe; Robert Crumb; Frankie Darro; Kim Dietch; Guillermo del Toro; Reginald Denny; August W. Derleth; G. Michael Dobbs; Linwood P. Dunn, A.S.C.; Bob Dylan; William K. Everson; Bill Fairchild; David F. Friedman; Kinky Friedman; John Gallaudet; Andrew Gallina; Kerry Gammill; Jimmy Gilmer; Whoopi Goldberg; Martin Grams, Jr.; Louis "Buddy" Hale; Robert Heinlein; Charlton Heston; Bob Hope; Arthur Housman; Amy Iverson; Burl Ives; James Janis; Herb Jeffries; I. Stanford Jolley; Charley Jones; Dr. G. William Jones; James Earl Jones; Boris Karloff; Sam Katzman; Benjamin Keck; Tom Keene; John Keeyes; Cy Kendall; Edgar Kennedy; Larry King; Fuzzy Knight; Steve Kronenberg; Mark Lamberti; Jonathan Lampley; Baxter Lane; Herschell Gordon Lewis; Jerry Lewis; Weldon Edwin "Big Bill" Lister; Greg Luce; Bela G. Lugosi [Jr.]; Keye Luke; Arthur Lundquist; Scott MacQueen; Bob Madison; Gregory William Mank; Kermit Maynard; Mark Martin; Jerome McDonough; George "Spanky" McFarland; Rudy Ray Moore; Earl Moseley; Brad Musick; Edwin Neal; Terry Pace; John E. Parnum; Bill Paxton; Gregory Peck; Samuel A. Peeples; Robin Pen; Nat Pendleton; Barbara Pepper; Richard Peterson; Norman Petty; Wilson Pickett; John Pierson; Michael R. Pitts; Roland C. Price; Lucien Prival; Dr. Bill G. "Buck" Rainey; Tom Rainone; Fred Olen Ray; Otis Redding; Duncan Renaldo; Gary Don Rhodes; Paul T. Riddell; Tex & Dorothy Fay Ritter; Roy & Dale Evans Rogers; Angelo Rossitto; Reb Russell; Vivian Salazar; John Saxon; Martin Scorsese; Harry Semels; Johnny Sheffield; Lawrence Adam Shell; Sam Sherman; Wayne Shipley; Dennis Spies; Larry D. Springer; Frank Stack; James Stephenson; Brinke Stevens; Patrick Stewart; Billy Gene Stull; Gary & Susan Svehla; Dee Lee Thomas, Jr.; Jeff Thompson; Fred & Mary Kate Tripp; Timothy Truman; Big Joe Turner; Mario Van Peebles; Melvin Van Peebles; Steve Vertlieb; Andrew & Carlela Vogel; Vanessa Vogel; George Waggner; Loudon Wainwright III; Aaron "T-Bone" Walker; Linda J. Walter; Pierre Watkin; John & Pilar Wayne; Dawn Weiner; Bart Weiss; Buddy Weiss; Michael Weldon; Ian Whitcomb; Chill Wills; Grady L. Wilson; Joanna Wiskowski; Grant Withers; Fay Wray; Carleton Young; and Terry Zwigoff

And on the Institutional Front: The Academy of Motion Picture Arts & Sciences; The American Film Institute; The American Society of Cinematographers; The American Society of Composers, Authors & Publishers; the Billy Barty Foundation; the British Film Institute; the Hoblitzelle Theatre Arts Library at the University of Texas; the Dallas–Fort Worth Film Commission; the Dallas Museum of Art; the Dallas Video Festival; Independent-International Pictures; the Library of Congress, KRLD NewsRadio 1080, Dallas–Fort Worth; Little People of America; *Mad about Movies* Magazine; *Midnight Marquee Monsters* Magazine; *Monsters from the Vault* Magazine; the National Association of Theatre Owners; Photofest; the Screen Directors Guild; the Screen Writers Guild; Sinister Cinema; Southwest Film & Video Archive at Southern Methodist University

Annotations, Marginalia & Addenda to
Forgotten Horrors: The Definitive Edition

This field we call film archaeology, being a fusion of information and critical interpretation, is a plastic, even organic, medium: New material keeps coming to light that calls for amendment and even expansion, especially if one has exhibited the arrogance to pronounce a job of work "definitive." One of the niftier things about mounting one's own sequel is that one can use a portion of it to backtrack and make adjustments.

Just a few weeks before his unexpected demise, George Turner had remarked, "Well, hockey! Y'know, I just watched Republic's [*Robinson*] *Crusoe* [*on Clipper Island*] for the first time in years, and damned if I'm not thinking we might ought to've given it a chapter." So *voila*, already: That serial, still obscure despite a generalized popular rediscovery of the Republics, graces the 1936-37 section following, prefaced herewith by assorted flotsam and jetsam from the earlier Depression years.

A recurring motif in my conversations with the readers—*you* know, those loyal souls who keep us in business—is that they'd like to know more about the films that George and I had only *considered* for discussion in the original *Forgotten Horrors*. Delighted to oblige, I drew the following laundry-list of Cine McNuggets from the broader range of titles we had compiled during 1975-76. I can only reckon there'll be more tweaking and amplifying in store after *this* book is put to bed, but I also reckon that there'll be another sequel or three, inasmuch as George and I had long since started laying a foundation for new volumes of *Forgotten Horrors* right on up past the mid-century (20th Century, I mean) mark.
—M.H.P.

1930

The Voice from the Sky (Ben Wilson Productions)—Once one of the more elusive titles in the original *Forgotten Horrors*, this still-obscure madman-at-large serial proves at last to have been shown in commercial theatrical engagements. Star player Wally Wales had doubted the film's very release. The Indiana-based regional historian Michael R. Pitts provided the crucial documentation of a newspaper advertisement. Just like we said: film archaeology.

1931

Hell Bound (James Cruze Productions/Tiffany Productions)— Hidden passageways, mistaken identities and a prevailing sense of preordained doom inform this gangster melodrama from the pioneering producer-director James Cruze. With Leo Carillo and Lola Lane.

Monsters of the Deep (Talking Picture Epics)—Documentary account of an expedition off Baja California ends with a struggle with a 17-foot manta ray, known among superstitious seafarers as a devilfish.

Mystery of Life: A Drama of Life as Told by Clarence Darrow (Classic Productions, Inc.)—Released by big-time Universal Pictures, this sensationalized educational documentary takes the form of a lecture by Clarence Darrow and Prof. H.M. Parshley of Smith College, advancing evolutionary arguments. The sequence of key interest here—demonstrating, like a 1923 short subject called "Monsters of the Past," that filmmakers outside the Willis O'Brien camp were at least dabbling in dinosaurs—portrays fancifully sculpted, scientifi-

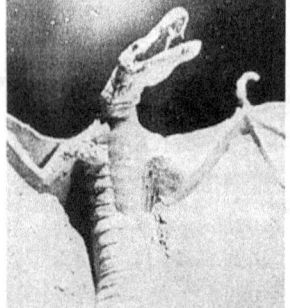

Fancy a *crocodilian* pterosaur! One of the perversions of natural history that compromise the well-intentioned *Mystery of Life*.

cally suspect replicas of such creatures in a "prehistoric habitat" setting. One "bird as big as an elephant" suggests an effigy of Sebek, the crocodile-god of Ancient Egypt, more so than any Pterosaur known to science. No creature-effects artisans are identified. The *Variety* review identifies much of the nature footage as coming from productions of the German company, UFA. *Mystery of Life* was issued just half a dozen years after Darrow had defended classroom teacher John Scopes against charges of lecturing on matters Darwinian in defiance of Tennessee state law.

Hell Bent for Frisco (Sono Art–World Wide Pictures/ Thrill-O-Dramas) — *The Death Kiss*'s Edmund Burns is a banker whose involvement with gangsters leads to serial murder.

Alice in Wonderland (Bud Pollard Productions/Unique-Cosmos Pictures) — Lewis Carroll's *Alice* tales, first published in 1865, have always struck us as more horror than fantasy, what with all those nightmarish creatures and a prevailing obsession with trans-mogrifications and beheadings. Shoddy costume pageant is the work of Bud Pollard, who also is responsible for the most fascinatingly elusive film in the original *Forgotten Horrors* — 1933's *The Horror*. Pollard reissued his *Alice* in 1933 to make hay on a popular anticipation of Paramount's all-star version.

Ralph Ince and William Farnum in *Law of the Sea*.

Law of the Sea (Monogram Pictures Corp.) — Revenge thriller starts off with a rampage of rape, torture and murder committed by schooner captain Ralph Ince. A generation later, the victims' surviving son (Rex Bell) recognizes Ince's cold-blooded laughter. An unattributed remake is 1934's *West of the Divide*, an entry in John Wayne's extended rehearsals-for-stardom sojourn on Poverty Row.

1932

Hell's House (B.F. Ziedman Productions, Ltd.) — Sadistic abuses at a boys' detention hall. Civic leader Pat O'Brien moonlights as a bootlegger and exploiter of youth. Early star vehicle for Bette Davis, whose interference provokes reform. Not properly a horror picture, but acknowledged by E.C. Comics publisher Bill Gaines as an influence on the *Tales from the Crypt* and *SuspenStories* yarns.

Thirteen Steps (Congress Pictures Corp.) — The Yellow Peril, that pulp-fictional assumption of malice among the Oriental populace, stalks a crusading newspaper publisher, who is in further danger from a treacherous colleague. Presumably a lost film, but likelier just misplaced. In a society where even the long-lost 1912 version of *The Life and Death of King Richard III* can come to light from unlikely quarters, any rediscovery is possible.

Border Devils (Supreme Features/Weiss Bros./Artclass) — The Yellow Peril again, stalking the Southwestern frontier. Japanese actor Tetsu Komai (of *Island of Lost Souls*) plays a Chinese bandit who poisons the local water supply, frames Harry Carey for murder and grabs surrounding ranchlands for the sake of smuggling explosives into Mexico.

Lone Trail (Webb-Douglas Productions/Syndicate Pictures) — Predatory outlaw known as the Tiger (Jack Mower) makes life miserable for lawman Rex Lease. A heroic dog shoves Mower over a cliff.
Aloha (Rogell Productions, Ltd./Tiffany Productions, Inc.) — Albert Rogell (of that groundbreak-

Raquel Torres is the doomed South Seas beauty in *Aloha*. (Photofest)

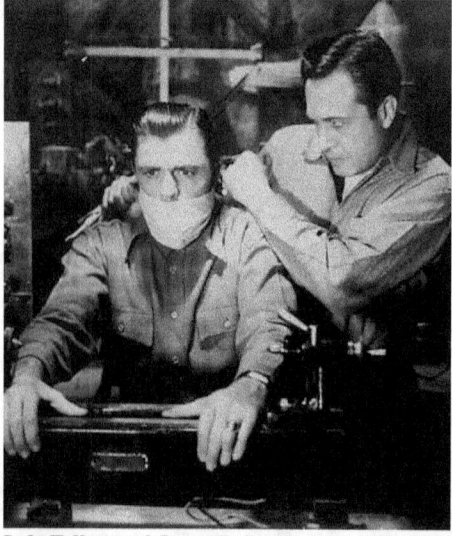

Lyle Talbot and Jason Robards star in *Klondike* (Photofest)

ing jungle thriller *Mamba*) directs, with Edgar G. Ulmer as assistant director. Soap-operatics involving a forbidden romance between Ben Lyon and South Seas beauty Raquel Torres. She cancels out the agonies with a self-sacrificial leap into a volcano.

Hell's Headquarters (Action/Mayfair) — Frank Mayo, as an embittered jungle explorer, commits murder while stalking a trove of ivory. With Jack Mulhall and Phillips Smalley.

Joseph in the Land of Egypt (Guaranteed Pictures Co.) — Yiddish Biblical drama, as laden with supernatural terrors as with honest piety. Jacob Greenberg plays Joseph, visionary infiltrator of the House of Pharaoh.

Devil of the Matterhorn, a.k.a. ***The Devil's Rope*** (Harry Revier) — The title seems but figurative, a superstition surrounding the mortal difficulties of climbing the highest peak in the Swiss Alps — until at last, the Matterhorn is seen to transform into the image of a laughing Satan.

Yiskor (Gloria Films, Inc./Judische Kunstfilm) — Legend of Jewish martyr, laden with torture, suicide, debauchery and burial alive. Pious to a fault, but dour and sadistic in the extreme. Re-edited, expanded and talkie-fied version of a 1924 Austrian silent of the same title.

Gorilla Ship (Ralph M. Like, Ltd./Mayfair Pictures Corp.) — Not to be taken literally. The gorilla here, figuratively speaking, is brutal sea captain Ralph Ince. The real villain is mutinous Wheeler Oakman, who provokes an uprising that brings out the captain's more heroic nature.

Isle of Paradise (Adolph Pollak Productions) — Goona-goona travelogue sets sail for Dutch East Indies, whose exotic diversions include a Balinese cremation ceremony.

The Last Mile (K.B.S. Film Co./World Wide Pictures, Inc.) — Prison-break massacre, engineered by condemned killer Preston Foster. Shattering finale finds Foster walking deliberately into a guardsmen's barrage.

Klondike (Monogram Pictures Corp.) — Madness and romantic intrigues in — where else? — Alaska: Ill-fated Thelma Todd plays a beauty known as Klondike, fiancée of invalid genius Jason Robards. Robards conspires to murder disgraced surgeon Lyle Talbot with an electrical device.

Exposure (Premiere Attractions/Tower Productions, Inc.) — Big-city newspaper rivalries fuel this melodrama. Wavers between domestic tensions and an indictment of the tabloids' voyeuristic scandal-mongering habits. Hard-drinking reporter Walter Byron's failure to keep up with a maniac-at-large case (marginal to the plot) costs him his job. Tough guy Nat Pendleton plays the maniac.

The King Murder (Chesterfield Motion Pictures Corp.)—Sturdy Conway Tearle as a homicide squad chief who has an awkwardly personal interest in the mysterious slaying of blackmailing gold-digger Dorothy Revier. Murder by poison-coated phonograph styluses. Or is it *styli*? You know what we mean: record-player needles. Or does anybody out there even remember record players?

Goona-Goona: An Authentic Melodrama of the Isle of Bali (Andre Roosevelt & Arm-and Denis)—And yes, there is a perfectly okay reason why we refer to all those Third World expeditionary thrillers as "goona-goona pictures." This is it. *Goona-Goona* is hardly the first of its kind, but it is definitive in the sense of having, like 1930's *Ingagi*, a title that registered strongly within the popular vocabulary. In this context, goona-goona is a powerful stimulant administered by a tribal sorcerer. The story concerns out-of-caste romantic intrigues and a chronic-to-acute case of hatred unto death between a laborer and a member of the royal household.

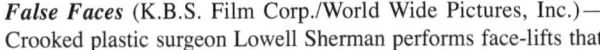

False Faces (K.B.S. Film Corp./World Wide Pictures, Inc.)—Crooked plastic surgeon Lowell Sherman performs face-lifts that lead to paralyzing complications. Maimed patient Nance O'Neil murders the quack after he is acquitted in court.

The Face on the Barroom Floor (Aubrey Kennedy Pictures Corp./Criterion Pictures Corp.)—Hugh Antoine D'Arcy's sentimental narrative poem about the toll of drunkenness gets a severe re-interpretation in this melodrama of human wreckage and blood vengeance. *Svengali*'s Bramwell Fletcher, as a derelict befriended by the tipplers in a speakeasy, relates the grisly, heart-wrenching tale in flashback.

Young Blood (Trem Carr Pictures, Ltd./Monogram Pictures Corp.)—Bob Steele is Nick the Kid, a genial outlaw framed for the murder of a highfalutin' French showgirl (Neoma Judge). Steele is saved from a lynching by the victim's pet monkey, which turns up crucial evidence. Charles King is a crooked sheriff whom Steele pursues smack into a fatal fall from atop a cliff.

The Unwritten Law (Majestic Pictures Corp.)—Backstage Hollywood murder thriller, with Lew Cody as a scheming producer menaced by a vengeful electrician wielding a high-wattage sun-arc lamp. Practically everyone on hand has some score to settle with Cody, whose eventual murder generates any number of suspects.

Beyond the Horror Ban

With Williamson beneath the Sea: Adventures among the Mysteries and Monsters of the Deep (Principal Distributing Corp.) — J. Ernest Williamson (1881-1966), pioneer of undersea photography, launched the Submarine Film Corp. in 1915 with a production called *Thirty Leagues under the Sea*, in which he could be seen knifing a shark to death. Williamson filmed a breathtaking adaptation of Jules Verne's *Twenty Thousand Leagues under the Sea* in 1916, followed by *The Submarine Eye*, from his own story, in 1917. Other original pictures about shipwrecks, sunken treasure and fantastic creatures led to a frustrating three years of work-for-hire on MGM's *The Mysterious Island* (1929), another Verne takeoff that wound up using none of Williamson's scenes. For *With Williamson beneath the Sea: Adventures among the Mysteries and Monsters of the Deep*, the artist-inventor took along his wife, Lilah, and their 3-year-old daughter, Sylvia, on a seabottom excursion in the Bahamas. Documentary includes pieces of Williamson's earlier fact-and-fictional productions, including the first undersea color footage, from 1920. An attack on a crew member by a gigantic octopus climaxes the film. A restoration of *With Williamson beneath the Sea* was completed during the 1990s by the Library of Congress.

The Jungle Killer (Century Productions, Inc.) — Forward-thinking explorer Carveth Wells, using cameras instead of guns, positions this well-assembled documentary as an indictment of big-game hunting. Zulus are shown mutilating their lips for cosmetic effect. Trigger-happy hunters are killed, here, by an elephant and there, by a lion.

Virgins of Bali (Imperial Distributing Corp.) — Purely educational, of course. *Variety* called it a "bust picture," alluding to ogler appeal. Balinese cremation ceremony lends morbid interest.

1933

The Horror (Rajah Raboid) — The placement of this title under 1933 is purely arbitrary. The picture is a persistent rumor, nothing more, and that rumor might even amount to a simple case of confusion with Bud Pollard's like-titled *The Horror*, from 1933. But the popular stage magician Maurice Kitchen (1896-1962), a.k.a. Rajah Raboid, is reported by the historian Mark Walker to have made "his own starring film to rent to theatres that booked his attraction." Further, per Walker: "*The Horror* was shot at a studio in Long Island and starred the Rajah, a chimp and a dwarf... [T]he feature was never released." John Wooley, screenwriter and author of the genre study *Hot Schlock Horror!*, called our attention to Walker's 1991 book, *Ghostmasters*, which is a gem of show-biz esoterica.

The Shadow Laughs (Trojan Pictures, Inc.) — A skulking killer's doomed accomplice lifts $100,000 from a bank vault in this severely conventional exercise in weird mystery from director Arthur Hoerl, who gravitates to a run-of-the-mill racket-buster plot but applies the creepier business as a welcome *lagniappe*. Hal Skelly stars, with Rose Hobart as a menaced secretary and Walter Fenner as the bigshot banker who proves to be the menace. A battered surviving print was cleaned up nicely by Sinister Cinema for a 1999 video release.

A Jungle Gigolo (Prosperity Pictures Corp./Principal Distributing Corp.) — Bigoted, tongue-in-cheek piece, presented as a documentary but very much a mocking comedy. A Sumatran native is assigned the demeaning name of "Clarence." The yarn follows and exaggerates his misadventures as a wandering laborer, gun bearer on a crocodile hunt and rescuer of a village from a rampaging elephant.

Matto-Grosso (Principal Distributing Corp.)—Routine expeditionary piece, distinguished by the elaborate rituals heralding a hunt for jaguars.

Jungle Bride (Monogram Pictures Corp.)—Murder yarn with musical interludes. Shipwreck survivors Anita Page, Charles Starrett and Eddie Stevens wash ashore on an African beach, where personal antagonisms overshadow the threat of marauding wildlife.

What Price Decency? (Equitable Pictures/Majestic Pictures)—Jungle melodrama, with Dorothy Burgess as the abused wife of trading-post operator Alan Hale. She finally turns the tables on Hale, blinding him with a brutal whip-lashing, and the local natives spear him to death.

Charles Starrett and Anita Page in the *Jungle Bride* (Photofest)

Sing Sinner Sing (Majestic Pictures)—Lurid soaper, based on a 1932 police case in which tobacco heir Zachary Smith Reynolds was shot to death—likely a suicide—and his wife and a family friend were charged with murder. Donald Dillaway plays the Reynolds surrogate, a drunken, self-pitying brute of a millionaire, for reasonably loathsome impact.

Mr. Broadway (Broadway-Hollywood Productions/Malcomar Productions/Arthur Greenblatt, Inc.)—Show-biz columnist Ed Sullivan conducts a travelogue of his turf—a musical-comedy excursion that takes a jarring turn into murder and suicide.

The Emperor Jones (Krimsky & Cochran, Inc./United Artists Corp.)—Correction, please: Film historian Scott MacQueen notes that the out-of-doors shooting location lies in Westchester County, New York—not Westchester, New York. See *Forgotten Horrors: The Definitive Edition*.

Curtain at Eight (Majestic Pictures Corp.)—Serial murder case, involving a cold-hearted matinee idol (Paul Cavanaugh) and a man-killing chimpanzee. The distinguished C. Aubrey Smith plays a genial detective who makes a questionable but highly satisfying moral judgment.

Eat 'Em Alive (Harold Austin/Real Life Pictures)—Wildlife documentary, shot in Texas, Nevada and Arizona, indicts man as the deadliest of the desert's inhabitants. Various creatures are shown in kill-or-be-killed situations: Standouts are bat-tles between a black widow spider and a centipede, and a gila monster and a diamondback rattlesnake. For the climax, a bull terrier rescues a human infant from a rattler.

Beyond the Horror Ban

The Sin of Nora Moran (Majestic Pictures)—Withering, soap-operatic pageant of drug addiction, rape, madness, murder, political scandal and suicide. *The Mummy*'s Zita Johann stars as Death Row denizen Nora Moran, whose tormented life ends in the electric chair. Paul Cavanaugh plays the big-shot politico who receives an unnerving visit from Nora's ghost.

1934

Sixteen Fathoms Deep (Monogram Pictures Corp.)—Lon Chaney, Jr., under his christened name of Creighton, plays a sponge fisherman who runs afoul of sabotage. An undercurrent of Third World superstition blames Chaney's problems on a supernatural jinx—but it's just plain old human villainy at work here.

The Cactus Kid (Reliable Pictures/William Steiner)—In this starring picture for Western champ Jack Perrin, supporting player Jayne Regan shocks a confession out of murderer Jo de la Cruz by masquerading as the ghost of a murdered man.

Found Alive (Ideal Pictures/Excelsior Pictures)—Estranged-family soaper in an exotic jungle setting, with Barbara Bedford and Robert Frazer.

Gow; a.k.a. *Gow the Killer* and *Cannibal Island* (Capt. Edward A. Salisbury)—No kin to the Borden Co.'s Elsie the Gow. Just kidding. Compilation of South Seas expeditionary footage, as superficially talkie-fied from 1928's *Gow the Head Hunter*. Chieftain Gow re-enacts an epic raid he once pulled on a neighboring tribe. Gow also shows off his collection of human skulls, presumably harvested first hand. The expeditionary filmmakers Merian C. Cooper and Ernest B. Schoedsack, whom the intrepid Capt. Edward Salisbury credited as cameramen on the silent cut, go unacknowledged in the prints we have seen of this version.

Beggars in Ermine (Monogram Pictures Corp.)—Corporate intrigues and social reforms figure in this tale of a well-loved steel manufacturer (Lionel Atwill) who loses his legs in a molten-metal spill. While treacheries mount within the factory and within Atwill's estranged family, he becomes instrumental in a campaign to better the lot of handicapped citizens.

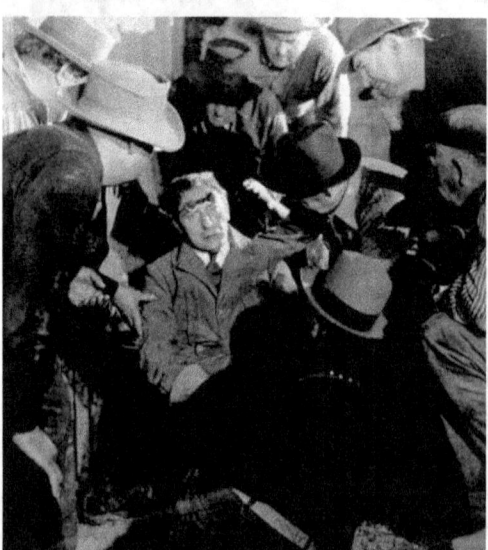

Corporate intrigues and social reform concern the *Beggars in Ermine*. (Photofest)

Dorothy Appleby, Dorothy Lee, Lona Andre, Toby Wing, Kathleen Burke in *School for Girls*. (Photofest)

Playthings of Desire (Pinnacle Productions, Inc.) — In which homicidal gambler Jack Chapin goes gunning for playboy James Kirkwood in Florida — only to wind up eaten alive by alligators.

Kidnapping Gorillas*, a.k.a. *Life in the Congo (Kinematrade, Inc.) — Not just another *Ingagi* knockoff, but rather a respectably informative documentary about an expedition into Africa to capture gorillas for U.S. zoological gardens. No kin to a like-titled picture from 1941.

Sing Sing Nights (Monogram Pictures Corp.) — Three men confess to a murder that only one of them can have committed, and all three are sentenced to die. Investigator Ferdinand Gottschalk determines that the victim was already dead before two of the shooters entered — and that the real killer had caused the corpse to move in a threatening manner.

1935

Circus Shadows (Peerless Pictures Corp.) — Crooked dealings on the carnival midway, with William Ruhl as a spiritualistic racketeer.

The Lone Bandit (H&H Productions, Inc.) — Lane Chandler and Ray Gallagher are suspected by turns of being the "Phantom Bandit," who turns out to be somebody else altogether.

School for Girls (Liberty Pictures Corp.) — In which an abusive matron (Lucille LaVerne) at a girls' reformatory is murdered with a pistol rigged to a radio dial.

Hei Tiki (Principal Productions, Inc.) — New Zealand's Isle of Ghosts is the setting for this life-among-the-Maoris romantic fantasy. A tribal chief's daughter is off-limits to all but the God of War. So a womanizing enemy prince impersonates the God of War. Mayhem ensues.

Great God Gold deals with the timely issue of the stock market crash and greed. (Photofest)

Mutiny Ahead (Larry Darmour Productions/Majestic Producing Corp.)—Dire natural perils and cruel humanity gang up on undersea explorers in this high-octane fusion of a high-society crime melodrama and an ocean-going treasure hunt. Neil Hamilton is aces as a playboy whose gambling debts drive him to commit a heist. The segue from landlubber thrills to shipboard excitement is simply a matter of Hamilton's encounter with a mob of crooked sailors. By a similar token, débutante Kathleen Burke has a perfectly valid reason for moving from scene-of-the-crime to scene-of-the-mutiny. Reginald Barlow stands out as a heroic skipper.

Great God Gold (Monogram Pictures Corp.)—Superstitious financier Sidney Blackmer is saved from the Crash of 1929 by a lucky coin-toss that counsels him to sell out. But then, he fails to heed another toss and falls into disastrously bad company.

The Mystery Man (Monogram Pictures Corp.)—LeRoy Mason plays a murderous bandit known as the Eel in this journalistic mystery, starring *King Kong*'s Robert Armstrong as a crackerjack reporter.

The Last Wilderness (DuWorld Pictures, Inc.)—Championship archer Harold Hill leads this documentary trek into Wyoming, felling a rattlesnake, a buffalo and a mountain goat along the way. A glacier yields the remains of prehistoric insects. Climax is a harrowing fight between bears. Hill adopts the surviving cubs, then takes revenge on their behalf by slaughtering the bear that had killed their mother.

Vanishing Riders (Spectrum Pictures Corp./Ray Kirkwood Productions)—Bill Cody and Bill Cody, Jr., star as vigilantes who rout a rustling mob by disguising themselves—and their horses—as skeletons. Laughable in the extreme, but the gimmick seems to scare the bad guys.

Let 'Em Have It! (Reliance Pictures, Inc.)—This Bruce Cabot starrer was originally part of the *Forgotten Horrors* package—until we transplanted it to our subsequent collection, *Human Monsters: The Bizarre Psychology of Movie Villains*. That volume has been out of print since 1997, but a revised and expanded edition is in preparation as of 2001. Cabot plays a murderous hoodlum whose face undergoes a hideous transformation via plastic surgery. Reliance was a bigger outfit than the typical Poverty Row studio, but hardly on the same social or economic keel with the major-leaguers.

Lem Hawkins' Confession (Micheaux Pictures Corp.)—Strangler-at-large thriller with sociological overtones, from black independent filmmaker Oscar Micheaux.

The Spanish Cape Mystery (Liberty Pictures Corp./M.H. Hoffman/Republic Pictures Corp.)—Ellery Queen mystery, in which a vanished Huntly Gordon hides on an island off Spanish Cape, California, coming ashore at high tide to murder his relatives. An inheritance is at stake. Donald Cook plays Ellery Queen in this series-opener.

Virginia Bruce and Bruce Cabot star in *Let 'Em Have It!* (Photofest)

Alias John Law (Supreme Pictures Corp.)—Bob Steele stars as a wrongly accused fugitive-turned-lawman who must capture frontier killer Earl Dwire.

Lelong (Dance of the Virgins): A Story of the South Seas (Bennett Pictures Corp.)—Balinese documentary, encompassing a tragic romance that ends in suicide. Originally in two-color Technicolor. See *Kliou (The Tiger)*, in our 1936-37 section.

Phantom Patrol (Ambassador Pictures, Inc.)—Harry Worth, the tormented revenge killer of 1936's *Lightnin' Bill Carson*, scores in a dual role as a notorious assassin and the vacationing author whom he captures and impersonates. The bad Worth is revealed as a fake when his purported writings are recognized as a swipe from Guy de Maupassant.

Rescue Squad (Mayfair Productions, Inc./Empire Film Distributors, Inc.)—An accursed effigy of Buddha and a poisoning plot figure in this otherwise lighthearted romance starring Ralph Forbes and Verna Hillie.

The Phantom Cowboy (Aywon Film Corp.)—The nefarious title character motivates the mayhem in this long-mislaid film from a poor-but-proud company that delivered only four Westerns during 1934-35. As studio identities go, *Aywon* sounds like a great name for a brand of steak sauce—and in fact it is precisely that: *A-1*, phoneticized. Ted Wells plays both the Phantom and a rip-snorting cowboy named Bill Collins, who also pretends to be the Phantom at one point.

Kathleen Burke and Charles Locher in *The Lion Man*, based on a story by Edgar Rice Burroughs. (Photofest)

1936-37

THE LION MAN
(Normandy Pictures Corp.)

Little known even among the *Tarzan* enthusiasts, this reasonably loyal adaptation of an Edgar Rice Burroughs yarn is the final production of Normandy Pictures Corp., whose output of six titles is otherwise confined to Westerns. *The Lion Man*'s Ronald Chatham (played by Charles Locher) is a desert-bound counterpart to Burroughs' jungle-dwelling Lord Greystoke. The story has to do with a caravan massacre of which Ronald (as a child) is the lone survivor. He grows up in the care of an Arabian holy man, who teaches the boy to commune with the lions of the desert. Finally, the adult Ronald takes revenge on the marauding sheik who had murdered his father.

Charles Locher was en route to a crucial name-change: He tried Lloyd Crane briefly, but then as Jon Hall he would play the lead in John Ford's *The Hurricane* (1937) and as a consequence would become one of the more important action-adventure stars of the next decade, with such crackerjack entries as *Arabian Nights* (1942), *Invisible Agent* and *Invisible Man's Revenge* (1943-44), and *Last of the Redmen* (1947). Hall later became a television star, with *Ramar of the Jungle* in the 1950s. Perhaps the misspelling of his name (as Loucher) on *The Lion Man*'s screen credits helped settle him on a rechristening. Locher/Hall's leading lady here is the beauteous Kathleen Burke, still struggling to no avail to shake the exotic typecasting that *Island of Lost Souls* (1932) had imposed upon her.

A silent-screen filming of the same story is *The Lad and the Lion*, from 1917.

CREDITS: Producer: Arthur Alexander; Supervisor: Max Alexander; Director: John McCarthy; Adaptation: Richard Gordon and John Williams; Based upon: Edgar Rice Burroughs' *The Lad and the Lion*, as Serialized in *All-Story Weekly* Magazine during 1917; Photographed by: Robert Cline; Assistant Director: Myron Marsh; Editor: Tony Martinelli; Recording Engineer: Hans Weeren; Technical Director: Fred Preble; Running Time: Approx. 70 Minutes; Released: Beginning in Early 1936 on a State-by-State Basis

CAST: Kathleen Burke (Ulayla); Charles Locher (Ronald Chatham); and Richard Adams, Richard Carle, Finis Barton, Eric Snowden, James Aubrey, Lal Chand Mehra, Bobby Fairy

THUNDERBOLT
(Regal Productions)

A heroic dog is the title character of this crudely exhilarating study in violence and retribution. In a holdup gone haywire, two corrupt frontier lawmen kill an express office clerk, the local sheriff and a dog belonging to the clerk's son. A miner (Kane Richmond) is accused. The miner's police dog, Thunderbolt (played by Lobo the Marvel Dog), and the clerk's son (Bobby Nelson) track a stolen cargo of gold to a barn. One of the outlaws chokes the boy into unconsciousness. Thunderbolt rescues the youngster and lets the killer roast.

Variety, in turn, roasted *Thunderbolt*, bemoaning its brutality for the sake of throwing a sop to the anti-violence stance of the industry's Hays Office, which was supposed to put a halt to such irresponsible thrills. In point of fact, the violence is the saving grace of the picture, which otherwise might just sit there looking shabby. Roland C. Price's camera is more a passive observer than a propulsive storytelling device, and the acting is less than convincing, however ferocious. Lobo is no Rin Tin Tin, but at least he knows how to strike an intimidating pose. Sherman S. Krellberg's short-lived Regal Productions, Inc., a spin-off of Regal Distributing Corp., made only four pictures, all during 1936.

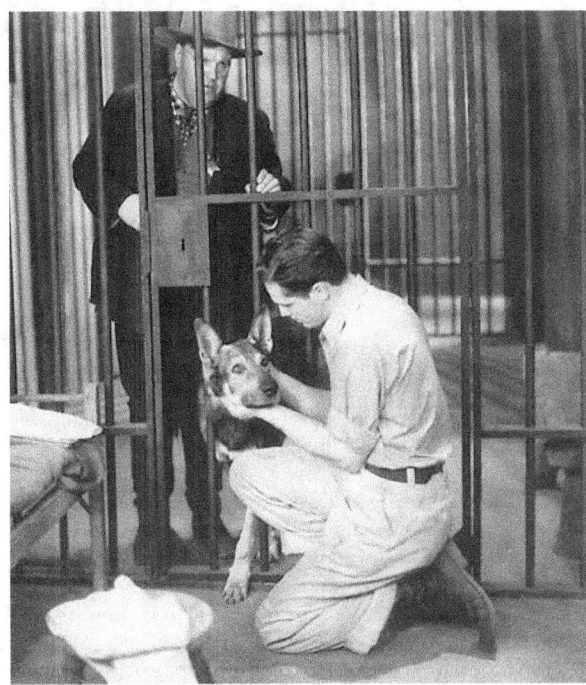

Bob McKenzie, Lobo the Marvel Dog and Kane Richmond in *Thunderbolt*. (Photofest)

CREDITS: Presented by: Sherman S. Krellberg; Director: Stuart Paton; Story and Screenplay: Jack Jevne; Photographed by: Roland C. Price; Assistant Director: Eddy Graneman; Editor: Charles Craft; Running Time: 55 Minutes; Released: January 2, 1936

CAST: Kane Richmond (Miner); Lobo the Marvel Dog (Thunderbolt); Bobby Nelson (Boy); and Fay McKenzie, Hank Bell, Frank Hagney, Barney Furey, Lafe McKee, Frank Ellis, George Morell, Wally West, Jack Kirk, Blackie Whiteford, Bob Burns

Jean Rouverol, Norman Foster, Maude Eburne and Clay Clement in *The Leavenworth Case* (Photofest)

THE LEAVENWORTH CASE
(Republic Pictures Corp.)

And no, it's not a prison picture. Leavenworth is the name of an aged Wall Street predator who proposes to make costly amends for his crooked stock-market dealings. The film works well enough as conventional mystery-farces go, with the interesting gimmick of having a trained monkey commit murder. But it is more significant as a benchmark pointing toward the British-European horror ban that left the genre high and dry in Hollywood.

No single picture could have provoked the embargo, of course, but Republic Pictures performed some interesting bending-over-backwards (establishing an ill-advised precedent) to placate the English bluenoses, who initially voiced misgivings over *The Leavenworth Case* for its suggestion that an upstanding physician might be capable of committing murder. The British Board of Censors had practically herniated itself over Universal's *Frankenstein* in 1931 and Paramount's *Island of Lost Souls* in 1932—both boasting fundamental contributions from assorted respectably English talents—on account of those films' shared Promethean conceit, and had banned *Life Returns* (1934-38) outright in view of its claim to documentary fact. On into the 1940s, the British censors would reserve a singular revulsion, not for the floodtide of increasingly outlandish mad-doctor fantasies but rather such truer-to-life *bad*-doctor melodramas as Paramount's ironically titled *The Mad Doctor* and Fox's *Shock*, respectively starring Basil Rathbone and Vincent Price as menacing psychiatrists. All this reactionary reverence for the healing profession, from a society whose own Jack-the-Ripper was likely as not an influential physician.

Great Britain, being a lucrative market for American studios large and small, also wielded a tremendous influence as to the pictures' very content. So when the British censors told Republic—in advance of production—that they would not permit a picture depicting a healer as a heel, Republic foolishly backtracked and created an alternate framing scenario-and-finale for export. *The Leavenworth Case* and its alternate-reality fill-ins were shot between the end of November and mid-December of

1936. This remarkable indulgence could not have been allowed to become a habit—fancy a polite version of every American horror picture for our sensitive English cousins!

In the version that America saw, Dr. Truman Hartwell (Donald Cook) assures wealthy patient Silas Leavenworth (Frank Sheridan) that he has plenty of life left in him. Hartwell is in love with Silas' glamorous young wife, Gloria (Erin O'Brien-Moore). Silas, sensing the approach of death, wants to make up for his life of fountain-pen banditry by leaving his estate to charity. The family is predictably appalled. Niece Eleanor (Jean Rouverol) declares that she will thwart Silas' plan. Silas is found dead—apparently a suicide, but then again maybe not. Henry Clavering (Gavin Gordon), Silas' business partner and Eleanor's fiancé, is found to have embezzled a fortune. Gloria accuses Hartwell, who accuses Eleanor. Silas' old-maid sister, Phoebe Leavenworth (a cranky Maude Eburne), proves to have been slowly poisoning Silas while waiting to dispose of other members of the family. Finally, the agent of murder proves to have been Hartwell's pet monkey, which had been trained to open the gas jet in Silas' bedroom.

In the cop-out version for U.K. consumption, Dr. Hartwell simply reveals that he had suspected Phoebe and trained his monkey to replace Silas' nightly raw-egg-in-milk with an uncontaminated serving—but the damage had already been done. And so was damage done in the Real World to the film itself.

Originally planned as a Monogram project, *The Leavenworth Case* suffered other, more internalized, frustrations en route to completion. Once the property had lapsed to Republic, Warners loaned William Gargan for the key detective role, but at the last moment Norman Foster was installed instead. Director Arthur Lubin had been attached, but Lewis D. Collins stepped in. For all its difficulties, *The Leavenworth Case* holds together as a sprightly mystery-thriller, with Frank Sheridan in fine curmudgeonly form as the late-to-repent market-manipulator, Maude Eburne as a matronly menace with the good intention of killing bad people, and Warren Hymer at the top of his game as a thickheaded investigator.

Anna Katherine Green's novel, *The Leavenworth Case*, is a historically important piece of American detective fiction, dating from 1878. It was also filmed in 1923, under director Charles Giblyn.

CREDITS: Producer: M.H. Hoffman; Supervisor: Ken Goldsmith; Director: Lewis D. Collins; Screenplay: Albert Demond and Sidney Sutherland; Based upon: Anna Katherine Green's 1878 Novel, *The Leavenworth Case*; Photographed by: Ernest Miller and Jack Marta; Editor: Dan Milner; Supervising Editor: Joseph H. Lewis; Sound Engineer: Terry Kellum; Sound Effects: Roy Granville; Running Time: 68 Minutes; Released: January 20, 1936

CAST: Donald Cook (Dr. Truman Hartwell); Jean Rouverol (Eleanor Leavenworth); Norman Foster (Bob Gryce); Erin O'Brien-Moore (Gloria Leavenworth); Maude Eburne (Phoebe Leavenworth); Warren Hymer (O'Malley); Jocko (Monkey); Frank Sheridan (Silas Leavenworth); Gavin Gordon (Henry Clavering); Clay Clement (Inspector Holmes); Ian Wolfe (Hudson); Peggy Stratford (Miss Owens); Archie Robbins (Duke); Bess Stafford and Lucille Ward (Women with Dogs); Belle Mitchell (Woman with Cat); Marie Rice (Sarah); Carl Stockdale (Bookkeeper); Dagmar Oakland (Miss Hill); Lee Prather (Forensics Investigator)

I CONQUER THE SEA!
(Halperin Pictures/
Academy Pictures Distributing Corp.)

Edward and Victor Hugo Halperin, the highly methodical artists behind *White Zombie* (1932), spent much of a year filming a Newfoundland whaling crew in action. Their point was to bring authenticity to a romantic-triangle tragedy in a craggy naturalistic setting. The result is highly unsatisfactory in dramatic terms, but the location work lends a helpful realism.

What *I Conquer the Sea!*, with its protracted agonizing over emotional disloyalties and physical disabilities, is doing in a book of this nature—now, there lies a question we had asked ourselves. It

I Conquer The Sea!
with
Steffi Duna, Dennis Morgan.

all boils down to the Halperin brothers, whose more generalized body of work is of interest here in light of *White Zombie* (1932), *Supernatural* (1933) and *Revolt of the Zombies* (1936). Not to mention the ghost that crops up at the end of *I Conquer the Sea!*

Stanley Morner plays Tommy, a master harpoonist, who loves Rosita Gonzales (Steffi Duna), a Portuguese immigrant. Rosita's brother, Pedro (Johnnie Pirrone, Jr.), cannot walk. When Tommy's brother, Leonard (Douglas Walton), a surgeon, corrects Pedro's disability, Rosita falls for Leonard. Then, Tommy loses an arm during a whaling expedition but hasn't any better sense than to head out with Leonard on another ill-starred voyage. The brothers find themselves stranded on an outcropping of rock. Leonard swims to summon assistance. Tommy chooses to drown. At length, his spirit drops in on his own memorial ceremony at the village church.

Apart from a behind-the-scenes copyright-control complaint that dragged on into the 1950s, the most interesting thing about this syrupy tear-jerker is the early starring role for Stanley Morner, as the doomed brother. The Wisconsin-born actor was handling lesser roles at MGM when the big studio loaned him out to the Halperins. Morner changed his performing name in 1938 to Richard Stanley, then finally settled on Dennis Morgan—an identity that would see him through such gems as *Waterfront* and *The Return of Dr. X* (both from 1939) into a lasting stardom in musical comedies and action pictures. Morgan also toplined the late '50s teleseries *21 Beacon Street*.

The credited screenwriter, Richard Carroll, somehow got it into his head that *I Conquer the Sea!* must owe more to his brilliance than to any artistry on the part of the Halperins. As late as 1951, Carroll was haranguing the tradepapers about some crackpot scheme to sue for distribution rights—even as he declared that all rights were contracted to revert to him, in any event. One can only wonder whether Carroll had actually bothered to watch the picture, which is hardly something to make an author proud.

CREDITS: Producer: Edward Halperin; Director: Victor Halperin; Dialogue Director: George Cleveland; Assistant Director: Leander de Cordova; Production Director: John Hicks; Story, "Storm in Their Hearts," and Adaptation: Richard Carroll; Dialogue: Rollo Lloyd and Howard Higgin; Photographed by: Arthur Martinelli; Art Director: F. Paul Sylos; Editor: Douglas Briggs; Musical Director: Arthur Kay; Musical Supervisor: Abe Meyer; Sound Engineer: G.P. Costello; Technical Director: Leigh Smith; Running Time: 70 Minutes; Released: January 24, 1936

CAST: Steffi Duna (Rosita Gonzales); Stanley Morner (Tommy); Douglas Walton (Leonard); George Cleveland (Caleb); Johnny Pirrone, Jr. (Pedro Gonzales); Fred Warren (Sebastian); Anna De Linsky (Mrs. Gonzales); Charles McMurphy (Zack); Frederick Peters (Stubby); Tiny Skelton (Flukes); Olin Francis (Gabe); Albert Russell (Josh); Dorothy Kildaire (Mrs. Gabe); Renee Daniels (Mrs. Stubby); James Hertz (Tiny); Margaret Woodburn (Widow); and Elaine Deane, John Deane

PRISON SHADOWS
(Mercury Pictures Corp./Puritan Pictures Corp./Victory Pictures Corp.)

Prizefighter Gene Harris (Eddie Nugent), sentenced to prison after an opponent had died in the ring, is paroled. Gene is reunited with his pet dog, Babe, through the affectionate courtesy of Mary Grant (Joan Barclay), an employee of Gene's manager, George Miller (Forrest Taylor). Miller's sweetheart, Claire Thomas (Lucille Lund), feigns a fondness for Gene. Gene had been framed in the first fatality, and now Claire and crooked gambler Bert McNamee (Monte Blue) are conspiring to let him take the rap in another fatal bout. McNamee acts as the rival's second during the fight, rubbing him down with a towel saturated in an exotic poison.

Gene is arrested in this new case, but he convinces the police that his punches were too light to kill anybody. Mary and Dave Moran (Sid Saylor), Gene's trainer, find Babe writhing in agony. The dog, which has been playing with the corrupted towel, dies in a veterinarian's office. Gene retrieves the towel. The coroner recognizes the deadly substance. Developing a plot to catch the killers, Gene agrees to play dead after another match. After hearing Claire and Bert gloat, Gene drops the charade and reveals that Dave had switched towels on the culprits.

This gem-in-the-rough from Sam Katzman's stock production unit is a companion piece to the slightly earlier *The Rogues Tavern* (see *Forgotten Horrors: The Definitive Edition*). Again, Katzman takes a low profile—but the presence of director Bob Hill, screenwriter Al Martin, cinematographer Bill Hyer *et al.* trumpets the Katzman identity. *Prison Shadows'* mystery is not so much a matter of "who?" as it is the suspenseful matter of whether the arrogant perpetrators will get away with another gambling-racket slaying. Eddie Nugent is fine as the wrongly accused boxer who comes up with a risky solution, and Joan Barclay makes a patient romantic interest. The poisoning of the dog is a jarring touch that proves crucial. Comic relief specialist Syd Saylor gets in the last word, with an uncharacteristically philosophical monologue.

Eddie Nugent starred as Gene Harris in *Prison Shadows*.

CREDITS: Producer: Sam Katzman; Director: Bob Hill; Screenplay: Al Martin; Photographed by: Bill Hyer; Settings: Fred Preble; Editor: Dan Milner; Production Manager: Ed W. Rote; Running Time: 70 Minutes; Released: June 15, 1936

CAST: Eddie Nugent (Gene Harris); Lucille Lund (Claire Thomas); Joan Barclay (Mary Grant); Forrest Taylor (George Miller); Syd Saylor (Dave Moran); Monte Blue (Bert McNamee); John Elliott (Police Captain); Jack Cowell (Graham); Willard Kent (Veterinarian); Walter O'Keefe (Referee)

IT COULDN'T HAVE HAPPENED (BUT IT DID)
(Invincible Pictures Corp./Chesterfield Motion Pictures Corp.)

Not to be confused with *It Could Happen to You* or *It Happened Out West* or *It Happened in Chicago* or *It's All in Your Mind*, this comedy-romance-thriller is a perplexing delight, complete with an all-but-impossible murder, a likably temperamental gangster with show-biz aspirations and enough backstage hanky-panky to ground the fanciful plot in a recognizable reality. *It Couldn't Have Happened (But It Did)* is a Broadway counterpart to the 1932 Hollywood-studio murder yarn *The Death Kiss*, right down to the playwright who beats the law to a solution.

Dapper Reginald Denny plays Greg Stone, author of a murder mystery in production by New York impresarios Ellis Holden (Claude King) and Norman Carter (Bryant Washburn). The backer is Smiley Clark (career tough guy Jack La Rue), a glad-handing racketeer who turns menacing when the producers nix his idea of installing a not-so-promising young actress named Louise (Diane Manners) in the cast. The leading lady, Beverly Blake (Evelyn Brent), is producer Holden's wife—and a demanding shrew who orders the firing of actor Bob Bennett (Crauford Kent). Beverly is also involved in an illicit affair with Carter, and as though that weren't enough, her naive leading man, Edward Forrest (John Marlowe), is infatuated with her.

Inez Courtney and Reginald Denny in *It Couldn't Have Happened (But it Did)* (Photofest)

For the staging of a murder scene, Smiley suggests a means of making homicide resemble suicide; he should know. Later, Carter is shot to death, but no bullet can be found. Holden, the likeliest suspect, turns up dead elsewhere. The producers' secretary, Linda Sands (Inez Courtney), who has a crush on Greg, interferes to an infuriating extent. Smiley has the right alibi: He was attending a Shirley Temple movie.

Following a hunch, Greg finds a published report of a remarkable suicide case. He survives an attempt on his life and concludes he is on the right track. Finally, in a re-enactment of the Carter murder, Greg dramatizes his theory that the weapon was a gun loaded with compressed water—an untraceable missile. Greg identifies the killer as a man who had loved Beverly, and whom Beverly manipulated into committing murder. Beverly impulsively names Bennett as the brains behind the crime. Bennett, hiding in plain sight, is captured after a wild struggle, and Smiley promises to underwrite Greg's next show.

With its hair-raising qualities sturdily underpinned by droll wit, *It Couldn't Have Happened (But It Did)* benefits from the sharp contrast of suave Reginald Denny with rock-jawed Jack La Rue, the latter in a role that serves as both red herring and comic relief. Inez Courtney is just right as the impetuous secretary, and Crauford Kent makes an effectively jolting late re-entrance as the murderer. Pioneering cinematographer-turned-director Phil Rosen juggles the contrasting elements gracefully, allowing for a fair deployment of clues along the way.

CREDITS: Producer: Maury M. Cohen; Supervisor: Herbert S. Cohen; Director: Phil Rosen; Story and Screenplay: Arthur T. Horman; Photographed by: M.A. Anderson; Art Director: Edward C. Jewell; Assistant Director: Melville Shyer; Editor: Roland D. Reed; Sound Engineer: Richard Tyler; Running Time: 70 Minutes; Released: August 1, 1936

CAST: Reginald Denny (Greg Stone); Evelyn Brent (Beverly Blake); Jack La Rue (Smiley Clark); Inez Courtney (Linda Sands); John Marlowe (Edward Forrest); Claude King (Ellis Holden); Bryant

Washburn (Norman Carter); Robert Homans (Lt. O'Neill); Crauford Kent (Bob Bennett); Robert Frazer (Lloyd Schaefer); Miki Morita (Hashi); Emily La Rue (Ingenue); Henry Herbert (Sherwood); Lynton Brent (Lansdale); Broderick O'Farrell (Johnson); Diane Manners (Louise)

KLIOU (THE TIGER)
a.k.a.: KLIOU
a.k.a.: KLIOU, THE KILLER
(Bennett Pictures Corp./DuWorld Pictures)

For his second stab at the independent production racket—after the 1935 release *Lelong (Dance of the Virgins)*—Henri de la Falaise shot 30,000 feet of Technicolor stock in the Southeast Asian wilds. *Variety* reported in 1934 that this first all-Technicolor jungle-location feature received the support of not only the French colonial government but also the local rulers. De la Falaise, whose wife at the time was actress Constance Bennett, suffered during the shoot from a tropical virus and was later hospitalized in Paris. He edited *Kliou* during late 1934 and early 1935 at General Service Studios.

For all the appeal of its vivid camerawork, *Kliou* also suffered in its day from a purely silent presentation. The music-only soundtrack and use of insert cards for narration seem quaintly charming today, but the film struck its mid-'30s audiences as an unwelcome throwback to the supposedly antiquated silent screen of less than a decade earlier.

De la Falaise and French Army Lt. Charles Carney introduce Bhat, an Indo-Chinese village boy, who is rejected as a suitor for Dhi because her father, Khan, finds Bhat lacking in courage. Kliou, a tiger, is on a rampage, and Khan suffers a mauling. Bhat and Dhi's brother, Nyan, pursue the beast. After surviving any number of dangerous encounters with other wildlife, the friends kill the tiger. Bhat returns a hero, and he and Dhi receive Khan's blessing.

Release dates and distribution credits vary for the film, and *Daily Variety*'s identification of RKO-Radio as the releasing company is patently a mistake. The *Motion Picture Herald* shows a 1937 release, but DuWorld clearly had *Kliou* in circulation during 1936. The alternate titles may have been misreadings by the various publications that reviewed the picture—although a newspaper advertisement from a late-'30s playdate touts the film as *Kliou, the Killer*. This curious advert is a patchwork job, cannibalizing promotional art that Paramount Pictures had prepared for Ernest B. Schoedsack's documentary-styled Natural Drama from 1931, *Rango*.

CREDITS: Producer and Director: Henri de la Falaise; Titles: Paul Perez and Ray Doyle; Photographed by: William Gordon Greene; Editor: Ralph Dietrich; Music: Heinz Roemheld; Orchestra Director: S.K. Wineland; Music Supervised by: Abe Meyer; Running Time: 55 Minutes; Released: October 1, 1936

CAST: Dhi (Herself); Bhat (Himself); Nyan (Himself); Khan (Himself); and Henri de la Falaise, Lt. Charles Carney

ROBINSON CRUSOE OF CLIPPER ISLAND
(Republic Pictures Corp.)

Ray Mala, who was often conveniently mistaken for a tropical sort, actually was Ray Wise, the Alaskan-born son of a white-guy American trader and an Eskimo Indian woman. Mala lived as a hunter and fisherman under a tribal name, Chee-Ak, until a featured appearance in the 1932 expeditionary film *Igloo*—a late-in-the-game silent, issued with a sound-effects track by Universal—went over well enough to encourage his prospects as a Hollywood player. Mala's fourth film, *Robinson Crusoe on Clipper Island*, is an all-out star vehicle for the matinee crowd, with Mala handling the title role—a Polynesian agent of U.S. Intelligence—in an athletic and likable if dramatically stodgy style. Neither the spirit nor the letter of Daniel Defoe particularly figures here, but the *Crusoe* angle is a clever conceit.

Sabotage has wrecked a mighty dirigible, and Mala is sent to the evident source of the tragedy, Clipper Island, where he becomes a modern-day Crusoe. Mala's radio signals provoke an international spy ring to trigger a volcanic eruption. The superstitious islanders, believing Mala responsible, sentence him to death, but Mala and his cohorts are too clever for the natives.

At length, Mala unites with the tribe's Princess Melani (Mamo Clark) to put down a rebellion by High Priest Porotu (John Picorri)—all the while accumulating evidence against the saboteurs and dodging their science-fictional death-traps. Porotu, believing Melani and Mala have died in a second volcanic blast, proclaims himself king. Mala recovers Melani's sacred headdress from the would-be dictator and heads back to the States for assistance. He puts down both the spies and the islanders' rebellion in short order.

Fourteen weekly chapters is a peculiar measure for the serial form, whose installments usually ran to 12 or 15 over the long haul, with the occasional 13-chapter entry. In the case of *Robinson Crusoe of Clipper Island*, the count proves to have been an afterthought, with altogether too much repetitive padding in evidence for the streamlined narrative manner that was fast becoming the hallmark of Republic. *Crusoe* was only the fourth such production for the ambitious new company: Republic was carrying on and refining the style of its rough-and-ready ancestor, Mascot Pictures, while establishing an original manner that could not be confused with the serials of Universal or Columbia.

Mala makes a stalwart hero, despite his uneasy handling of even the most simplistic dialogue, and Mamo Clark is an effective secondary presence, presaging the *femme* leads whom Republic would later exploit. John Picorri, in a warm-up for his more flamboyant bad-guy part in the next Republic serial, *Dick Tracy*, makes a suitably loathsome Third World dictator-in-waiting. Ray Mala continued as an action star and exotic supporting player until his death of a heart attack at age 46 in 1952.

CREDITS: Associate Producer: Sol C. Siegel; Directors: Mack V. Wright and Ray Taylor; Supervised by: J. Lawrence Wickland; Screenplay: Maurice Geraghty, Barry Shipman and John Rathmell; Original Story: Morgan Cox, Winston Miller and Leslie Swebacker; Supervising Editor: Murray Seldeen; Photographed by: William Nobles; Film Editors: Helene Turner and William Witney; Sound Engineer: Harry Jones; a Serial in 14 Chapters, Running Time: 253 Minutes; Later Issued to Television in Six Chapters, 26 Minutes each; and in a Feature Version, *Robinson Crusoe of Mystery Island*, Running Time: 100 Minutes; Released: November 14, 1936

CAST: Ray Mala (Mala); Mamo Clark (Melani); Herbert Rawlinson (Jackson); William Newell (Hank); John Ward (Tupper); Selmer Jackson (Canfield); John Dilson (Ellsworth); John Picorri (Porotu); George Chesebro (Draker); Robert Kortman (Wilson); George Cleveland (Goebel); Lloyd Whitlock (Lamar); Tiny Roebuck (Eppa); Tracy Layne (Larkin)

AFRICAN HOLIDAY
(Harry C. Pearson)

Gawking white explorers blithely treat themselves to a pageant of Dark Continent horrors in this condescending entry, assembled from two years' worth of safari footage. Mr. and Mrs. Harry C. Pearson announce their travel plans to a friend, then load out for what they clearly consider to be a natural sideshow staged for their private amusement. Courageous Mrs. Pearson kills an elephant in purported self-defense, supplying steaks for a village and saving the legs to manufacture keepsakes for wealthy friends back home. Apart from the spectacle of these dilettante mock-anthropologists, the most shocking incident is a ritual where tribesmen present themselves as willing victims of snakebite.

CREDITS: Presented by: Harry C. Pearson; Photographed by: Mr. and Mrs. Harry C. Pearson; Editor: Hal Hall; Film Cutter: Ed Taylor; Music: Dr. Edward Kilenyi; Sound: RCA High Fidelity; Running Time: 60 Minutes; Released: During 1937 on a State-by-State Basis

CAST: Mr. and Mrs. Harry C. Pearson

BLAKE OF SCOTLAND YARD
(Victory Pictures Corp.)

As Republic matured into what would today be called a mini-major studio—hovering between Poverty Row independence and larger corporate pretensions—that resourceful maverick, Sam Katzman, gave Republic's cliffhanger machine a stiff shot of old-fashioned competition with *Blake of Scotland Yard*, the last of the true Poverty Row serials. *Blake* excited much interest among the chapter-play enthusiasts with its colorful masked menace: The Scorpion is fascinatingly monstrous, although such a vigorous master criminal must have found the prosthetic deformities of his claw-wielding hunchback disguise more a liability than an asset. *Blake* took its cue, its title and its very director, Robert S. Hill, from a successful Universal serial of 1927.

An important writer-director of the silent era, Bob Hill found himself plagued with failing health during the 1930s and spent most of his talkie career with the small companies. At Victory, Katzman's Culver City studio, Hill made seven features and two serials during 1937-38. He also wrote under the pseudonym of Rock Hawkey and filled in as a bit player.

Sir James Blake (Herbert Rawlinson), retired from Scotland Yard, finances a death ray invented by Jerry Sheehan (Ralph Byrd) and Blake's niece, Hope Mason (Joan Barclay). Count Basil Zegaloff (William Farrell) hires the mysterious Scorpion to nab the machine. Creating a hostage situation, the Scorpion gang forces Blake to surrender the gizmo. Blake and his cohorts, including a friend named Dr. Marshall (Lloyd Hughes), track the Scorpion to Paris, where Blake is captured and threatened with the ray. Back in London, Marshall is unmasked as the Scorpion and captured in an electrical field created by Blake. Blake entrusts the invention to the League of Nations, the better to prevent a new war.

The slight and politically naive plotline comes ill equipped to sustain 15 episodes; the 73-minute feature version, released almost simultaneously, plays a great deal better. Hill rescues the serial presentation, however, with a brisk pace and savvy use of the manufactured London and Parisian settings. Top-notch stunt artist George de Normand makes the numerous altercations extraordinarily thrilling. The secret of the Scorpion's identity is not as well kept as that of the usual serial villain because there is a scarcity of suspects—and because the helpful Dr. Marshall seems just too blasted helpful. The welcome comedy relief includes a slapstick battle where Ralph Byrd and Joan Barclay escape from an ambush in a restaurant by pelting their attackers with tableware.

Byrd, newly situated at Republic as the star of *Dick Tracy*, is fine as *Blake*'s youthful hero. Silent-era serial champ Herbert Rawlinson plays Blake with an energetic dignity. There is a good assortment of players representing thugs, secret agents, streetwalkers, grotesque beggars, Cockneys, French Apaches, a giant homicidal idiot and a terrifying hag who blows her nose on her shawl. The extensive fog-filtered photography helps to mask the low budget—but also enhances the mood while suggesting the right mock-foreign look. The sound recording is tinny by comparison with major-studio work of the period.

The economic realities of Poverty Row are strikingly evident in the uncredited appearance of a heavily disguised Herman Brix: He's the bad guy with the mustache and the eye-patch. Brix (later known as Bruce Bennett) was officially Katzman's biggest feature-film star at the time (see *Sky Racket*, later on in this section).

Victory Pictures' studio was wiped out in a fire, but Katzman rose from the ashes with production/distribution deals at Monogram and, later, Columbia. His pictures were anything but prestigious, but they were almost invariably profitable and remain robustly entertaining.

CREDITS: Producer: Sam Katzman; Supervisor: Robert Stillman; Director: Bob Hill; Screenplay: Basil Dickey and William Buchanan; Story: Rock Hawkey [Bob Hill]; Photographed by: Bill Hyer; Sets: Fred Preble; Film Editors: Holbrook Todd and Fred Bain; Sound: Hans Weeren: Production Manager: Ed W. Rote; a Serial in 15 Chapters, 30 Reels; Released: During 1937 on a States'-Rights Basis; Feature Version: Also Released during 1937; Running Time: 73 Minutes

CAST: Ralph Byrd (Jerry Sheehan); Herbert Rawlinson (Sir James Blake); Joan Barclay (Hope Mason); Lloyd Hughes (Dr. Marshall); Dickie Jones (Bobby Mason); Lucille Lund (Duchess); Nick Stuart (Julot); Sam Flint (Inspector Henderson); Gail Newbury (Mimi); Jimmy Aubrey (Baron Polinka); Ted Lorch (Daggett); George de Normand (Pedro); Bob Terry (Peyton); William Farrell (Count Basil Zegaloff); Frank Wayne (Charles); Dick Curtis (Nicky);

THE FIGHTING DEPUTY
(Spectrum Pictures Corp.)

Veteran heavy Charles King dominates the proceedings as a scarred menace named—what else?—Scar Adams in this otherwise slight, part-musical horse opera from the classically inept producer Jed Buell. Sam Newfield, whose indiscriminate choices of assignment often neutralized his gifts as a director, helms *The Fighting Deputy* with a jarring split-personality type of approach: Here, he seems right on the money with the Cowboy Gothic attitude; there, he indulges the emerging market for romantic Westerns.

King surfaces early as a suspect whom the law tips off about a stagecoach payload in an attempt at entrapment. The resulting robbery goes just fine for Scar, but Sheriff Bentley (Frank LaRue) is wounded. Scar, who is in fact an estranged ranch heir, had been maimed years ago in a struggle with his father.

Deputy Tom Bentley (Fred Scott) fills in for his wounded father as sheriff. Tom's sweetheart (Phoebe Logan) refuses to go through with their wedding unless he resigns. Which he does, enraging his father. Sheriff Bentley takes out after Scar, who kills the lawman. Tom and his pal Fuzzy (Al St.

John) dispatch a posse, and Fuzzy is wounded. Scar's father (Lafe McKee) draws on the homicidal prodigal but is gunned down. Tom arrives and tears into Scar, who is slain by his dying father.

The ferocity of the central story, including the proto-*High Noon* element of a bridegroom sheriff's marital conflicts, is only watered down by the drugstore-cowboy music, which includes a cringe-inducing song called "Yellow Mellow Moon." Phoebe Logan makes a shrill nag of a love interest. Fred Scott is an indifferent hero, but at least he rises to the occasion for violence. Sidekick Fuzzy St. John is a welcome presence, surprisingly serving as cannon fodder. King gives a brilliant reading of the irrepressible bad guy, who at one point not only kills the hero's father—but also has the corpse delivered to the chapel where Scott and Miss Logan intend to get themselves hitched.

CREDITS: Producer: Jed Buell; Associate Producer: George H. Callaghan; Director: Sam Newfield; Story: Bennett Cohen; Adaptation: William Lively; Story Editor: Helen Gurley; Editor: William Hess; Supervising Editor: Arthur A. Brooks; Music Supervisor: Abe Meyer; Sound Engineer: Hans Weeren; Production Manager: Bert Sternbach; Running Time: 60 Minutes; Released: During 1937 on a States'-Rights Basis

CAST: Fred Scott (Tom Bentley); Phoebe Logan (Alice Denton); Al St. John (Fuzzy); Marjorie Beebe (Peaches); Charles King (Scar Adams); Frank LaRue (Sheriff Bentley); Eddie Holden (Axel); Lafe McKee (Frank Denton); Jack Smith (Jed); Jack Evans (Shorty); Sherry Tansey (Buck)

LARCENY ON THE AIR
(Republic Pictures Corp.)

Radium and radiation poisoning had taken hold of the popular imagination during the waning 1930s, when the fascination surfaced in such wildly disparate entertainments as Herb Jeffries' black-ensemble cowboy movies; William Wellman's classic antagonistic-romantic comedy *Nothing Sacred*; and this quack-medicine thriller from old-time Poverty Row producer Nat Levine and up-and-coming actor-turned-director Irving Pichel.

The menace makes an ominous plot device in *Larceny on the Air*, which concerns a campaign by radio-personality physician Robert Livingston to put a manufacturer of radium-based cure-all products out of business. Distinguished Pierre Watkin plays the bad-medicine man as far more than just a charlatan: As his customers begin turning up poisoned—including a heart-rending portrayal by Byron Foulger—Watkin retrenches deeper and deeper into extortion, kidnapping and attempted murder, at length forcing a captive Livingston to help develop a radioactive treatment for the common cold. Pichel paces the ordeal briskly, and the safe-and-sound ending even includes a promise of reform for one of Watkin's mock-respectable cohorts (Granville Bates).

CREDITS: Producer: Nat Levine; Associate Producer: Sol C. Siegel; Director: Irving Pichel; Screenplay: Endre Bohem and Richard English; Story: Richard English; Photographed by: Jack Marta; Assistant Directors: Sergei Petschnikoff and Ed Tyler; Editor: Edward Man; Supervising Editor: Murray Seldeen; Costumes: Eloise; Sound: Terry Kellum and Harry Jones; Running Time: 67 Minutes; Released: January 11, 1937

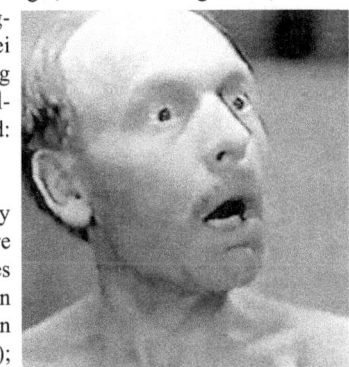

Byron Foulger: victim of the radium quacks in *Larceny on the Air*.

CAST: Robert Livingston (Dr. Lawrence Baxter); Grace Bradley (Jean Sterling); Willard Robertson (Mac McDonald); Pierre Watkin (Kennedy); Smiley Burnette (Jimmy); Granville Bates (Prof. Rexford Sterling); William Newell (Andrews); Byron Foulger (Pete Andorca); Wilbur Mack (Thompson); Matty Fain (Burke); Josephine Whittell (Nurse); Charles Timblin (Swain); William Griffith (Kellogg); De Wolf Hopper (Radio Announcer); Frank du Frane (Golden); Florence Gill (Spencer)

THE DEVIL DIAMOND
(Conn Pictures Corp.)

The curse that propels *The Devil Diamond* has more to do with human greed than with any supernatural perils, but the terrors stack up nicely, in any event. The title treasure is a fabulous gem that detective Kane Richmond means to protect at any cost, and never mind a racketeers' campaign to steal the jewel once it has been cut into untraceable finished stones. Murders committed en route to the big theft are, of course, chalked up to the legendary curse. Kane Richmond is a dashingly old-fashioned hero, and Frankie Darro earns plenty of laughs as a messenger boy who wants desperately to become a hot-stuff prizefighter. June Gale makes an intolerably hysterical/sentimental love interest. The villainy is, unfortunately, too generic for such high stakes, and the slight production values test one's tolerance for the shortcomings of the Poverty Row studios.

CREDITS: Producer: Maurice Conn; Director: Les Goodwins; Screenplay: Sherman S. Lowe and Charles Condon; Story: Peter B. Kyne; Photographed by: Jack Greenhalgh; Sound: Hans Weeren; Running Time: Approx. 55-60 Minutes; Released: January 15, 1937

CAST: Kane Richmond (Jerry Carter); June Gale (Dorothy Lannings); Frankie Darro (Lee); and Rosita Butler, Burr Caruth, Edward Earle, George Cleveland, Jack Ingram, Robert Fiske, Byron Foulger, Fern Emmett

HIT THE SADDLE
(Republic Pictures Corp.)

William Colt MacDonald's *Three Mesquiteers* yarns turned promptly into a hit property for Republic, which made the series not only a model for rival teamings at Monogram and PRC, but also a springboard for some impressive careers—including, at length, that of John Wayne.

This showcase for the original Mesquiteers—Bob Livingston as Stony Brooke, Ray Corrigan as Tucson Smith and comical Max Terhune as Lullaby Joslin—is predicated on the terrifying notion of a stallion that has been conditioned to kill on a whistled command. Not only does the horse, known as Volcano, lead bad guy J.P. McGowan's herd on destructive raids, but it also endangers a campaign to uphold a law preventing the slaughter of wild horses. As though that were not bad enough, a friendly wild pinto is framed for Volcano's depredations.

Stony and Tucson have a cruel falling-out over romance, money and the horse-protection issue. Stony is about to be trampled to death when the pinto charges in and attacks Volcano. As the Mesquiteers are reunited in a crisis, McGowan tries to ride away on Volcano, but Stony has learned the death-command—and don't go thinking he doesn't use it.

The plot also involves a troubled romantic entanglement for Livingston and 18-year-old Rita Hayworth, still working under her Spanish ancestral name of Cansino but oozing with the promise of star quality. It was in 1937 that she married the well-heeled automobile salesman Edward Judson, who was a generation her senior, and found herself transformed under his influence from a darkly exotic type to a redheaded figure of worldly glamour, under contract to Columbia. Miss Hayworth's breakthrough to leading roles came only gradually, all the same.

Forgotten Horrors 2

Hit the Saddle ends with an ahead-of-its-time animal-rights argument that the wild horses of the Plains must be safe to run free. Terhune commandeers the closing gag, when the hog calls he has been practicing prove quite effective—at summoning a skunk.

Republic remade *Hit the Saddle* in 1944 as *Pride of the Plains*, an entry in the *John Paul Revere* series starring Bob Livingston and Smiley Burnette. *Pride* is less ferocious than *Saddle*, but it gives Burnette the progressive role of a natural-born "horse whisperer," a folkloric concept that would account for a hit movie of 1998 starring Robert Redford.

CREDITS: Producer: Nat Levine; Associate Producer: Sol C. Siegel; Director: Mack V. Wright; Screenplay: Oliver Drake; Story: Oliver Drake and Maurice Geraghty; Based upon: Characters Created by Wallace Colt MacDonald; Photographed by: Jack Marta; Assistant Director: George Blair; Editor: Tony Martinelli; Supervising Editor: Murray Seldeen; Music Supervisor: Harry Grey; Songs by: Oliver Drake and Sam H. Stept; Sound Engineer: Terry Kellum; Running Time: 61 Minutes; Released: March 3, 1937.

CAST: Robert Livingston (Stony Brooke); Ray Corrigan (Tucson Smith); Max Terhune (Lullaby Joslin); Rita Cansino (Rita); J.P. McGowan (Rance McGowan); Edward Cassidy (Sheriff Miller); Sammy McKim (Tim Miller); Yakima Canutt (Buck); Harry Tenbrook (Joe Harvey); Robert Smith (Hank); Ed Boland (Pete); George Plues and Jack Kirk (Henchmen); and Bob Burns, Russ Powell, Alan Cavan, George Morrell, Budd Buster, Kernan Cripps, Wally Wales

THE GIRL FROM SCOTLAND YARD
(Major Pictures Corp./Paramount Pictures, Inc.)

Emmanuel Cohen's Major Pictures was anything *but* major—although it delivered an every-dollar-on-screen product and enjoyed a stepchild relationship with big-time Paramount Pictures. During its last year, 1938, Major became a convenient harbor where Bing Crosby and Mae West could develop their own starring pictures—*Dr. Rhythm* for Crosby and the deliberately but inappropriately wholesome *Every Day's a Holiday* for Miss West—with comparative autonomy.

Corporate ties notwithstanding, the prestige of a Paramount release sits somewhat awkwardly on this little science-fictional action-mystery. Paramount had planned seven years earlier to base a picture called *Uncertain Woman* on Edgar Wallace's novel, *The Girl from Scotland Yard*. That project was scuttled, however—and as tempting as it is to read this *Girl from Scotland Yard* as a renewed attempt at a Wallace takeoff, the prolific mystery-thriller author has no bearing here.

Coningsby Dawson's original yarn, as adapted to the screen by Doris Anderson and Dore Schary, has to do with the disappearance, rediscovery (in an ominous wax-museum setting) and murder of the husband of one Mary Smith (Lynn Anders), a friend of news reporter Derrick

The Girl from Scotland Yard tries to stop a aerial death ray during the coronation of King George VI. (Photofest)

Holt (Robert Baldwin). Holt is accused in the slaying. The victim proves to have been connected with Linda Beech (Karen Morley), a Scotland Yard undercover operative assigned to investigate a series of military aircraft explosions. A political exile named Franz Jorg (Eduardo Cianelli) is the menace at large, who plans to deploy a death ray during the coronation of King George VI to destroy the Royal Air Force. Holt and Miss Beech take to the air in search of Jorg, who takes out a number of planes before he can be shot down.

Beyond the Horror Ban

Karen Morley's title-role portrayal is squarely in the no-nonsense assertive vein in *The Girl from Scotland Yard*. (Photofest)

Vivid character portrayals compensate for the comparative lack of spectacle, and Robert Baldwin is especially fine as a determined but bumbling hero-in-spite-of-himself—with a deep-seated fear of flying—who thinks fast in one emergency after another. Especially pleasing is a suspenseful/comical sequence where Baldwin eludes the police by hiding within an orchestra during a party, only to give himself away with his inept musicianship. Eduardo Cianelli makes a suitably hateful enemy of the state. Karen Morley's title-role portrayal is squarely in the no-nonsense assertive vein.

Co-screenwriter Dore Schary (1905-1980) is remembered today as a big-leaguer, a producer for David O. Selznick and later chief of production for RKO-Radio Pictures and MGM, as well as a Tony-winning playwright/producer, outspoken opponent of Congress' anti-Communist witch-hunts and Commissioner of Cultural Affairs for the City of New York. But before he hit the big time as a co-author of MGM's *Boys Town* in 1938, Schary was a struggling scenarist who took what work he could get and delivered the goods. *The Girl from Scotland Yard* is hardly a benchmark, but it displays emphatically the larger political concerns that would come to distinguish Schary's career among the high rollers.

CREDITS: Presented by: Adolph Zukor; Executive Producer: Emmanuel Cohen; Director: Robert Vignola; Screenplay: Doris Anderson and Dore Schary; Story: Coningsby Dawson; Photographed by: Robert Pittack; Art Director: Wiard "Bill" Ihnen; Editor: George McGuire; Wardrobe: Basia Bassett; Musical Director: George Stoll; Song: "We Haven't a Moment To Lose," by John Burke & Arthur Johnston; Sound: Hugo Greenbach; Production Manager: Joe Nadel; Assistant Production Manager: David Sussman; Running Time: 62 Minutes; Released: April 9, 1937

CAST: Karen Morley (Linda Beech); Robert Baldwin (Derrick Holt); Eduardo Cianelli (Franz Jorg); Katharine Alexander (Lady Helen Lovering); Lloyd Crane (Bertie); Bud Flanagan (John); Lynn Anders (Mary Smith); Richard Ted Adams (Valet); Odette Myrtil (Mme. Dupré); Claude King (Sir Eric Ledyard); Leonid Kinsky (Mischa); Milli Monti (Herself); Phil Sluman and Alphonse Martel (Valets); Don Brodie (Joe); and Major Fred Farrell (Porter)

IT HAPPENED OUT WEST
(Principal Productions, Inc./Twentieth Century-Fox Film Corp.)

Sol Lesser's indie production of *The Mine with the Iron Door* (1936) is a linchpin of the *Forgotten Horrors* collections. Based upon a long-in-demand novel by Harold Bell Wright and boasting a powerfully menacing late-in-life performance from the first-generation movie star H.B. Walthall, *The Mine with the Iron Door* also has a more thoroughly forgotten companion film that we herewith drag back into the light. *It Happened Out West*, from another Wright yarn, is a more romantically bright adventure than *The Mine with the Iron Door*, and less concerned with obsessive madness than with plain homicidal treachery. Former theatre owner Lesser is the producer here, too, and his strategic releasing deal with Twentieth Century-Fox bespeaks the ambition that would distinguish his career over the long haul, alternating between big-studio executive stints and an overriding ferocious independence.

It Happened Out West happens to take place on a benighted ranch in Arizona. Heiress Anne Martin (Judith Allen) is losing money by trying to run the place as a dairy farm, and Gibraltar Trust agent Richard Howe (Paul Kelly) is assigned to convince her to sell. Howe and timid Thaddeus Cruikshank (Johnny Arthur), a dairy economist, stumble into a plot by Anne's murderous foreman, Travis (Leroy Mason), and a businessman named Middleton (Reginald Barlow) to sabotage the dairy and force a sale before Anne can discover a vein of silver. It would seem that Howe's assignment might inadvertently help the crooks, but then Thaddeus finds that Anne's dairy operation is a potential moneymaker—just the ticket to carry on the family business. Thad is wounded when he stumbles onto the silver lode. Howe and Anne fall in love. Travis' slaying of a trusted ranchhand comes to light, and the plot is foiled. Thaddeus attempts to tell Anne about the silver strike, but she is too busy smooching on Howe to care about much else.

Leroy Mason makes an ominous heavy, a man who would sooner commit sabotage than murder, but is nonetheless possessed of the killing urge. Johnny Arthur, best remembered as a whiny father-figure in Hal Roach's *Our Gang* comedies, lends a welcome mixture of courage and comedy as a mild-mannered egghead who beats blustery hero Paul Kelly to the solution. Kelly and Judith Allen make an appealing romantic match, especially when bickering.

CREDITS: Presented by: Sol Lesser; Producers: Sol Lesser and Edward Gross; Director: Howard Bretherton; Screenplay: Earle Snell and John Roberts; Story: Harold Bell Wright; Photographed by: Harry Neumann; Art Director: Lewis J. Rachmil; Assistant Director: W.B. Eason; Film Editors: Arthur Hinton and Olive Hoffman; Sound Engineer: Richard Tyler; Running Time: 56 Minutes; Released: May 7, 1937

CAST: Paul Kelly (Richard P. Howe); Judith Allen (Anne Martin); Johnny Arthur (Thaddeus Cruikshank); Leroy Mason (Burt Travis); Lew Kelly (Gus); Russell Hicks (Cooley); Reginald Barlow (Middleton); Esteban "Steve" Clemento [a.k.a. Clemente] (Pedro); Nina Compaña (Maria); Frank LaRue and Edwin J. Brady (Sheriffs); Evelyn Zelle (Miss Franklin); Ben Corbett (Dizzy); Tom Forman (Cal); Slim Lucas (Smokey); Archie Ricks (Red); Jack Shannon (Pete); Charles Treadwell (Slim); and Henry Otho, Richard Adams

KILLERS OF THE SEA
(Grand National Films, Inc./Raymond Friedgen Productions)

This vanity documentary tracks Florida-based Capt. Wallace Caswell's fool's-errand campaign to destroy single-handedly what he calls "the killers of the sea." Caswell had made himself something of a provincial celebrity by ranting about how predatory fish were wrecking the South-Southeastern fishing economy, and never mind any balance of nature.

Caswell proves to be a shameless grandstander as well as a reckless fighter. On a cruise in the Gulf of Mexico, Caswell signifies that he is ready to do battle by removing his trousers. He dives in to attack a bottlenose whale, which escapes despite the schooner's ropes and harpoons. A hammerhead shark is slaughtered. The ship's black, peg-legged cook, Evolution Henderson, alerts Caswell to a tiger shark, which is knifed to death. A diver finds a sunken chest amid the remains of a ship, attended by a skeleton—doubtless a bit of staged hokum. A sea turtle disables the diver's air supply, and an octopus attacks him. Caswell kills the octopus and rescues the diver. Finally, Caswell is hospitalized after a struggle with a sawfish. He recovers to resume his crusade. The popular news commentator Lowell Thomas supplies a fatuous blowhard narration, ascribing to Caswell almost an epic-calibre heroism. Uneasy thrills abound, whether because of or despite the film's destructive attitude.

CREDITS: Presented by: Edward L. Alperson; Producer and Director: Raymond Fridgen; Screenplay: Frederick H. Wagner (from His Story) and Adrian Johnson; Dialogue: Lowell Thomas and John P. Medbury; Photographed by: Herman Schopp; Assistant Director: Fred Turner; Editor: Helene Turner; Running Time: 49 Minutes; Released: May 8, 1937

CAST: Lowell Thomas (Narrator); and Capt. Wallace Caswell, Spot Hayes, Bruce Stillwell, Steve Peaden, Hubert Dykes, Evolution Henderson, Bryant Lee, Julius Randy

ANGKOR, OR FORBIDDEN ADVENTURE (IN ANGKOR)
a.k.a.: FORBIDDEN ADVENTURE; FORBIDDEN ADVENTURE IN ANGKOR; THE GO-RILLA WOMAN; JUNGLE GORILLAS; THE PRIVATE LIFE OF INGAGI
(Warner & Purdon/Esper Road Show Attractions/Mapel Attractions/Sonney Amusements

A trove of long-hidden motion-picture film yields a startling discovery: In 1912, two explorers had photographed their own expedition to Southeast Asia, where they sought out not only the ruined city of Angkor, in Cambodia, but also the descendants of a ruling society of apes. The native bearers—all women, in a state of toplessness, seeing as how the local menfolk prefer to give the apes a wide right-of-way—seem rather unwholesomely attracted to the scene, and they threaten to mutiny if the chief ape should be harmed. A "mad" "Buddhist" "priest" menaces the safari. One of the explorers dreams of an ape-worship ceremony and a violent rebellion in ancient Angkor. And never mind how the cameraman managed to work a dream-state fantasy into this muddle of "authentic" "documentary" footage.

So goes just one of several versions of *Angkor, or Forbidden Adventure (in Angkor)*, to use the film's mouthful of a formally copyrighted title. A more coherent and presumably complete cut, rediscovered in recent years, frames all the phonus-balonus hokum in a vaguely respectable context: The pioneering filmmaker and actor Wilfred Lucas introduces the spectacle that we are about to see, lying through his teeth about some long-ago expedition in search of clues that would explain the collapse of the once-mighty city of Angkor, 10 centuries past. Lucas also explains that the mock-expeditionary footage has been augmented with newly filmed dramatizations. Which would account for the nightmare sequences.

Ersatz-*Ingagi* hijinks in *Angkor*.

One of the elaborate theatre-front displays for Angkor, under its most notorious proxy title.

Thus purported to be a documentary within a documentary within a documentary, *Angkor* resembles nothing quite so much as an ancestor of Peter Jackson's playful telefeature, *Forgotten Silver* (New Zealand; 1993)—but without Jackson's redeeming audacious humor or his epic sense of the absurd.

Angkor, which takes itself a bit too seriously, yielded impressive box-office results for several distributors—no small accomplishment, given the picture's origins as a blatant knockoff of 1930's *Ingagi* (see *Forgotten Horrors: The Definitive Edition*). Certainly, it fared better with the paying customers than with the Production Code Administration, which at one point actually granted its elusive Purity Seal to distributor Dwain Esper. (For an account of Esper's earlier dealings with PCA chief Joseph I. Breen, see our chapter on *Maniac* in *Forgotten Horrors: The Definitive Edition*.)

As offended as Breen was with the abundant nudity, he reserved his greater indignation for "dialogue which in any way brings up the idea of possible sexual intimacy between women and monkeys." If Breen, Hollywood's High Sheriff of Morality in those repressed days, could not tell a mobilized gorilla suit apart from a monkey, then perhaps it is not unfair to suggest that he did not know his arse from his elbow. In fairness, however, the film's own narration neglects to distinguish between the great apes and the lesser primates.

But we digress. As usual. At any rate, Esper replied to Breen that the suggested trims would be made, and on March 17, 1937, the cherished certificate of wholesomeness was granted. A year later, after an alert PCA member had viewed a release print under the title *Forbidden Adventure*, the Purity Seal was revoked. Esper had no doubt made cuts in *one* version, but the early-talkie cinema's greatest confidence artist was taking no chances at losing his primary audience of oglers. Esper put plenty of oscamazoola into the film's promotion, providing such theatre-lobby props as larger-than-life gorillas and snakes.

Nowhere did Breen register an objection to *Angkor*'s conspicuous fakery, which is what a critic from *Variety* noticed most: "Phoney stuff is plentiful," declared the tradepaper in 1937, noting that the big ticket-selling element is "that the colored [Asian, actually] girls wear a ragged towel around their waists and nothing else."

Angkor is among the last several films to feature an appearance by Wilfred Lucas, who proceeded through such more honorable assignments as *Criminal Lawyer* (1937), *The Baroness and the Butler* (1938), *Zenobia* (1939), and *A Chump at Oxford* and *Brother Orchid* and *The Sea Wolf* in 1940, the year of his death. The Canadian-born Lucas had started out with Biograph in 1907, becoming a favored leading man of D.W. Griffith and Mack Sennett while directing and writing as a sideline. His filmography includes the 1925 *Riders of the Purple Sage* and such fine early talkers as *I Cover the Waterfront* and *Fra Diavolo* (both 1933), which make for rather an intriguing contrast with the shabby mockery of natural history that is *Angkor*. The film, incidentally, is often confused with *Love Life of a Gorilla*, a later production of the same sort. Confusion, if not outright obfuscation, also arises from there being two other *Forbidden Adventure*s: One is a cute-kid comedy from Paramount, vintage 1931, starring Mitzi Green and Edna May Oliver; the other, a goona-goona exploitationer whose copyright dates from 1934 but whose release appears not to have occurred until 1938.

A curious sidelight comes from the veteran pulp-fiction agent and comic-book pioneer Julius Schwartz, who told us in 1993 that it was *Angkor* and its mock-African ancestor, *Ingagi*, that inspired him and the writer Gardner Fox to create the "Gorilla City" subplot that runs through their *Flash* comics series of the 1960s. "We just took out the 'women-love-apes' business..." Schwartz said. "If the Comics Code Authority had known where we were coming from with that idea, we'd never have gotten away with it!"

CREDITS: Producers and Screenwriters: Henry Warner and Roy Purdon; Director: George M. Merrick; Adaptation: Armine von Tempski and Minnie F. Shrope; Effects: Ray Smallwood; Editor: Grace McKee; Musical Score: Dominic McBride; Research: Gladys McConnell; Running Time: Varies According to Version, 61 Minutes to 80 Minutes; Color-Tinted Dream Sequence; Released: Following Opening in Lincoln, Nebraska, in June of 1937; Copyrighted in a Cut of 8 Reels, 80 Minutes, on: October 23, 1937

CAST: Wilfred Lucas (Himself); J.S. Horne (President, Los Angeles Adventurers' Club)

DR. JEKYLL & MR. HYDE
(Pixilated Pictures)

While the U.S. motion-picture industry waited out a British-European censors' ban on horror films and the fans made do with what hair-raising delights they could find in other genres, a few enterprising souls knuckled down and rolled their own. Most amateur films seldom make it past the raw-footage stage, but Texan Glenn Alvey, Jr., entertained larger ambitions.

With several neighborhood pals, Alvey organized a production company while a junior-high student in San Antonio, starting out on a neighborhood-playhouse scale but shooting throughout in 16-millimeter semiprofessional format. Eventually, the ensemble established helpful, however limited, connections with the Dallas-based Interstate Theatres Circuit. And the youngsters delivered five featurettes—including this *Jekyll & Hyde*, and then, in 1940, a *Frankenstein*—that merited modest commercial play.

Mr. Stevenson's familiar tale of the benevolent scientist who wakes a primordial evil in himself fared impressively under Alvey, according to an account of the film from Mike Price's theatreman uncle Grady L. Wilson, who operated many of Interstate's West Texas showplaces from the 1930s until his death in 1968.

"Came off pretty good for a bunch of kids," Grady recalled during the 1960s. "Glenn followed the 1932 Paramount version fairly closely, patterned his makeup—he played the Jekyll-and-Hyde role—after [Fredric] March's appearance, and came up with a slick little job of work. The novelty, of course, was that it was kids, the oldest of 'em in their early-middle teens at the time. We had to make special arrangements to throw the 16-millimeter film and play its soundtrack discs in synch, 'cause our big houses were set up for 35mm sound-on-film. Truthfully, I suspect the pictures played better in the school auditoriums and recreation halls where Glenn mainly was showing 'em, in his hometown.

A 1940 editing session with Glenn Alvey, Jr., and Babe Price, for the double-feature presentation of their *Jekyll & Hyde* and *Frankenstein*.

"With the *Frankenstein*, now, Glenn was somewhat older and the production was more polished—I mean, even though there was no question this was kid stuff. That was mostly the charm of it, this kind of 'home-grown Orson Welles' mystique. Glenn made personal appearances in a few of the cities where we played his pictures.

"There was some talk among the Interstate brass of blowing his *Jekyll & Hyde* and *Frankenstein* up to 35mm, but I don't believe anything ever came of that," Grady added.

The Alvey productions caused a popular sensation in San Antonio and even received national press coverage in *The American Cinematographer* and the Bell & Howell house organ, *Filmo Topics*. These early accomplishments notwithstanding, Alvey seems not to have pursued a career in filmmaking. A more detailed account of Alvey's ambitious communal hobby appears under *Frankenstein* in our 1940 section.

CREDITS: Producer, Director and Screenwriter: Glenn Alvey, Jr.; Photographed by: Jack Locke; Script Supervisor: Babe Price; President of Pixilated Pictures: Howard Hudson; Silent, with Disc-Recorded Sound Effects and Dialogue Added in 1940; Running Time: Approx. 20-30 Minutes; Publicly Shown: Beginning in June of 1937 at Community Functions in San Antonio

CAST: Glenn Alvey, Jr. (Henry Jekyll and Edward Hyde); and Edith Jarrell and Tish Walker

THE 13TH MAN
(Monogram Pictures Corp.)

Hollywood has lunched out for generations on superstitions surrounding the number 13, and Monogram was no exception—with such entries as *The Thirteenth Guest* and its remake, and of course this eerie mystery involving a rackets crackdown and a murder-by-poison gimmick borrowed from Malaysian headhunters.

District Attorney Robert E. Sutherland (William Gould) has predicated his re-election campaign upon a dozen gangland arrests. To cap the purge, Sutherland announces the imminent capture of a 13th man and takes a dig at the local newspaper, which he insists has compromised his investigation. Newspaperman and radio announcer Swifty Taylor (Weldon Heyburn) attends a prizefight, where he notices Sutherland and the three likeliest "13th man" suspects. At the moment of a kayo in the ring, Sutherland drops dead—from heart failure, according to an attending physician who is known to hold a grudge against the D.A.

Reporter Jimmy Moran (Milburn Stone) soon learns that Sutherland was shot with a dart coated with the drug curare. As complications mount, Swifty gathers all suspects in a radio studio, intending to name the killer over the air. He dodges an assailant, who is gunned down by a police officer (Robert Homans). The killer and underworld kingpin turns out to be the newspaper's publisher (Selmer Jackson)—who was not among Sutherland's likeliest suspects.

Director William Nigh was warming up for the following year's launch of the *Mr. Wong* series, which started off well but soon deteriorated into a state of business-as-usual competence. The *Mr. Wong*s could have used *The 13th Man*'s screenwriter, John Krafft, who crams enough dirty deeds into these 71 minutes to fill twice the running time. Weldon Heyburn and Milburn Stone make an efficiently relentless journalists-turned-vigilantes team. The principal villain stays well hidden behind a facade of good citizenship, and the suspects and their accomplices are crooked enough to keep the audience guessing. It helps the suspense along that key victim William Gould seems certain that he has narrowed the field of suspects to only three. Inez Courtney is just right as the newsroom secretary who helps Heyburn for the sake of sheer affection, and Eadie Adams makes a splendid *femme fatale*.

CREDITS: Associate Producer: Lon Young; Director: William Nigh; Screenplay: John Krafft; Photographed by: Paul Ivano; Assistant Director: Herman Weber; Editor: Russell Schoengarth; Musical Director: Abe Meyer; Song: "My Topic of Conversation," by: Joseph Myrow & Milton Royce; Sound Engineer: Glen Rominger; Running Time: 71 Minutes; Released: June 30, 1937

CAST: Weldon Heyburn (Swifty Taylor); Inez Courtney (Julie Walters); Selmer Jackson (Andrew Baldwin); Marry Fain (Louie Cristy); Milburn Stone (Jimmy Moran); Grace Durkin (Alice Bryant); Robert Homans (Lt. Tom O'Hara); Eadie Adams (Stella Leroy); Sydney Payne (Suspect); Dewey Robinson (Romeo Casanova); Wiliam Gould (Robert Sutherland); Warner Richmond (George Crandall); Eddie Gribbon (Ironman); Sidney D'Allbrook (Legs Henderson)

ROD LA ROQUE'S "SHADOW" PICTURES
(Colony Pictures, Inc./Grand National Films, Inc.)

The Shadow, that mystifying hero of the pulp magazines and radio, has long proved too complex a character for any one movie to contain. Universal Pictures had attempted to do the Shadow justice in a string of short subjects dating from 1931's *A Burglar to the Rescue*. Then in 1937, Max Alexander and Arthur Alexander—nephews of Universal honcho Carl Laemmle—announced a series of four *Shadow* features for Colony Pictures, starring former silent-screen matinee idol Rod La Rocque. Only two got made, and here we have them:

THE SHADOW STRIKES (1937)—In his civilian identity of Lamont Cranston, the Shadow passes himself off as a lawyer whose client, wealthy Caleb Delthern (John St. Polis), is shot dead just after ordering a niece disinherited. An estate-takeover scam is revealed, and the Shadow foils it. La Rocque, who had become entrenched in character roles by this time, spends much of the picture impersonating other personages, to such an extent that the masked Shadow's rare appearances come as welcome surprises, though hardly as mystifying as the pulp-Shadow's fans might hope. Director Lynn Shores keeps the tone breezier than one would expect—or desire—and the revelation and dispatching of the murderer, the prospective father-in-law of the rejected niece, seem slight in view of the intrigues that have gone beforehand. The finale is almost a gag situation: The lawyer whom Cranston has impersonated seems grateful that the deception has cracked a case.

CREDITS: Presented by: Edward L. Alperson; Producers: Max Alexander and Arthur Alexander; Director: Lynn Shores; Screenplay: Al Martin; Based upon: "The Ghost of the Manor," in *The Shadow Magazine*, 1933, by Maxwell Grant (a.k.a. Walter S. Gibson); Adaptation: Al Martin, Rex Taylor and George Harmon Coxe; Contributor to Screenplay: John Krafft; Photographed by: Marcel Le Picard [Given Here as Marcel Pickard]; Assistant Director: Henry Spitz; Art Director: Fred Preble; Editor:

Charles Henkel; Gowns: Jahnke; Sound Engineer: Richard Tyler; Running Time: 63 Minutes; Released: July 9, 1937

CAST: Rod La Rocque (the Shadow); Lynn Anders (Marcia Delthern); James Blakely (Jasper Delthern); Walter McGrail (Winstead Comstock); Bill Kellogg (Humphrey Comstock); Cy Kendall (Brossett); Kenneth Harlan (Capt. Breen); Norman Ainsley (Hendricks); John St. Polis (Caleb Delthern); Wilson Benge (Wellington); John Carnivale (Warren Berranger); James Morton (Kelly); and John Dilson, John Elliott

INTERNATIONAL CRIME (1938)—Lamont Cranston has somehow found the time to become a crimebusting newspaper columnist as well as a radio star, broadcasting as the Shadow over his newspaper's own radio station. Sounds like a conflict of interest to us—to say nothing of a risky proposition for one's secret identity. But then, the movies have consistently played it fast and loose with the complicated mythologies of the *Shadow* magazines and radio serial. This time, a financier's murder casts suspicion on a gentlemanly safecracker (William Pawley), whom the Shadow believes innocent. The Shadow himself is thrown into the hoosegow and finds himself humiliated into writing conciliatory letters to the police—an indignity for which the pulps' Shadow would never have stood. The Shadow solves the mystery just in time to get back to the studio for his nightly broadcast. Rod La Rocque bears up amiably, and it's difficult not to like a picture where garrulous Lew Hearn plays a taxi driver named Moe. La Rocque would retire early during the 1940s to become a wealthy real estate broker.

Rod La Rocque is the crime fighting Shadow in *The Shadow Strikes*. (Photofest)

After the series-in-miniature at Colony, Victor Jory toplined a 15-chapter serial, *The Shadow* (1940), at Columbia Pictures. Monogram Pictures took a stab at the franchise in 1946 with *The Shadow Returns*, *Behind the Mask* and *The Missing Lady*—which add up to fodder for a third volume of *Forgotten Horrors*. A dozen years later, Republic would attempt to do the character justice with *Invisible Avenger* (1958). In 1994, Russell Mulcahy directed a big-budget *The Shadow*, starring Alec Baldwin.

CREDITS: Presented by: Edward L. Alperson; Producers: Max Alexander and Arthur Alexander; Associate Producer: Alfred Stern; Director: Charles Lamont; Screenplay. Jack Natteford; Dialogue: John Krafft; Based upon: "The Fox Hound," by Maxwell Grant (Walter S. Gibson); Photographed by: Marcel Le Picard; Art Director: Ralph Berger; Assistant Director: Henry Spitz; Editor: Charles Henkel, Jr.; Musical Director: Dr. Edward Kilenyi; Sound Supervisor: A.E. Kaye; Sound Engineer: Glen Rominger; Production Manager: Harold Lewis; Running Time: 65 Minutes; Released: April 2, 1938

CAST: Rod La Rocque (the Shadow); Astrid Allwyn (Phoebe Lane); Thomas Jackson (Commissioner Weston); Oscar O'Shea (Heath); Lew Hearn (Moe); William von Brinken (Flotow); Tenen Holtz (Storkhov); William Pawley (Honest John); William Moore (Burke); John St. Polis (Roger Morton); Jack Baxley (Matthews); Walter Bonn (Steffan); Harry Bradley (Burrows); Will Stanton (Drunkard); Lloyd Whitlock (Lawyer)

Movita Castañeda and the largely Polynesian backup cast lends a helpful push toward the illusion of authenticity in *Paradise Isle*. (Photofest)

PARADISE ISLE: A ROMANCE OF THE SOUTH SEAS
a.k.a.: SIREN OF THE SOUTH SEAS
(Monogram Pictures Corp.)

An earnest if over-emotional polemic with the ruinous myth of race distinguishes this ostensibly routine action/romance melodrama. The more obvious entertainment value lies in a tangle of homicidal greed and erotic tensions surrounding a shark-infested, supposedly accursed patch of pearl-rich undersea real estate.

Warren Hull gives a seething performance as blind painter Richard Kennedy, who becomes a castaway on a South Seas island while traveling to meet a surgeon who can restore his vision. Ila (Movita Castañeda), a native beauty, nurses Kennedy back to health. A trader (William Davidson) refuses to help Kennedy continue on his way unless the artist can pay up front. The local economy has gone bust because of a curse surrounding the pearl-diving grounds. Ila defies the taboo to help Kennedy; she finds a huge pearl but is attacked by a shark. Tono (George Piltz), a lovestruck native, rescues her. The trader persuades a beach bum (John St. Polis) to pose as the doctor so that they can get hold of the pearl, but the crooks wind up killing each other.

Tono fetches the surgeon, certain that Kennedy will abandon Ila when he can see that she is not of his color. The doctor (Pierre Watkin) consents to operate on condition that Kennedy abandon the girl. Kennedy agrees. Once his eyesight returns, however, Kennedy understands the truth: He's too crazy about Ila to let anything stand between them.

Dorothy Reid—a key figure among the talents represented in *Forgotten Horrors: The Definitive Edition*—took a direct hand in the shooting of this rambunctious delight, supervising second-unit location work in Samoa. The largely Polynesian backup cast lends a helpful push toward the illusion of authenticity, and so does an especially commissioned score of ethnic music. Hull and the Mexican cinema's Movita Castañeda make an appealing match. And was there ever a keener name than *Movita* for a movie star?

CREDITS: Associate Producer: Dorothy (Mrs. Wallace) Reid; Director: Arthur Greville Collins; Based upon: "The Belled Palm," by Allan Vaughan Elston; Adapted by: Marion Orth; Photographed by: Gilbert Warrenton; Special Effects: Fred Jackman; Assistant Director: Harry Knight; Editor: Russell Schoengarth; Musicians: Sam Koki, Napo Tuiteleleapaga and Lani McIntyre & His Hawaiians; Sound: William Wilmarth; Technical Director: E.R. Hickson; Running Time: 73 Minutes; Released: July 21, 1937

CAST: Movita Castañeda (Ila); Warren Hull (Kennedy); William Davidson (Hoener); John St. Polis (Coxon); George Piltz (Tono); Pierre Watkin (Dr. Otto Steinmeyer); Kenneth Harlan (Johnson); Russell Simpson (Baxter); and Tau Mana, Malia Makua

SHADOWS OF THE ORIENT
(Larry Darmour Productions/Monogram Pictures Corp./Empire Film Distributors)

Shadows of the Orient and *Outlaws of the Orient* (immediately below) add up to what we might call a separated-at-birth combo. Both issue from a single low-rent production outfit, but *Outlaws* merited the prestige of a Columbia release where *Shadows* stayed within its Poverty Row province as a Monogram title.

Shadows' embellishment upon a Yellow Peril theme involves a campaign to halt a Chinese-smuggling racket in cahoots with Flash Dawson (Eddie Featherstone), a renegade aviation hero. Dawson gets crosswise with chief smuggler Chin Chu (James B. Leong) and rats on the gang—only to find himself ambushed and slain. Rookie cop Baxter (Regis Toomey) finds himself attracted to a mysterious woman named Viola Avery (Esther Ralston). The Chinese mobsters at length take Viola hostage, but she escapes by stealing a plane crammed with illegal immigrants, rendering herself a suspect when Baxter forces her to land. All ends romantically for Baxter and Viola.

The resolution is lacking in excitement, with case-breaker Regis Toomey evidently content to have accumulated evidence that will lead to the appropriate arrests. James B. Leong is a properly menacing gang boss, and Sidney Blackmer is up to his usual suave-and-sinister tricks as the Occidental backer of the racket. Old-timer J. Farrell MacDonald is a level-headed, however befuddled, backup investigator.

CREDITS: Producer: Larry Darmour; Director: Burt Lynwood; Story: L.E. Heifetz; Screenplay: Charles Francis Royal; Photographed by: James S. Brown, Jr.; Assistant Director: Harry Knight; Sets: Paul Palmentola; Editor: Dwight Caldwell; Musical Director: Lee Zahler; Sound: Tom Lambert; Running Time: 70 Minutes; Released: August 18, 1937

CAST: Esther Ralston (Viola Avery); Regis Toomey (Baxter); J. Farrell MacDonald (Sullivan); Oscar Apfel (Judge Avery); Sidney Blackmer (King Moss); Eddie Featherstone (Flash Dawson); Matty Fain (Gangster); Kit Guard (Spud Nolan); James B. Leong (Chin Chu)

OUTLAWS OF THE ORIENT
(Larry Darmour Productions/Columbia Pictures Corp.)

A slumming Ernest B. Schoedsack—best known as the co-producer/co-director of 1933's *King Kong*—helmed this more polished companion-piece to *Shadows of the Orient* during a dry spell between his first span at RKO-Radio and a resurgence with Paramount's bombastic science-fiction thriller *Dr. Cyclops* (1940). Schoedsack also directed Darmour-Columbia's *Trouble in Morocco* in 1937.

Outlaws of the Orient milks the Yellow Peril angle for all its diminished relevance. Rugged Jack Holt, a popular player since the middle 1910s, stars as Chet Eaton, an American oilman on assignment in China, who runs afoul of not only his drunken brother (James Bush) but also a sabotage mob led by the warlord Ho Fang (Harold Huber). A vindictive accountant (Mae Clarke, well past that better

Ho Fang is the name, and Yellow Peril is the game: Jack Holt confronts and unconcerned Harold Huber in the less-than-P.C. *Outlaws of the Orient*. (Photofest)

day of *Frankenstein* and *The Public Enemy*), complicates Chet's attempt to bribe Ho Fang into a truce. Finally, Chet settles the matter by bombarding the troublemakers from the air.

Outlaws of the Orient plays okay today, with a particularly exciting wrap-up, although the film is scarcely a patch on Schoedsack's work at the bigger studios. There are also problems of semantics afflicting the picture's rediscovery, starting with the simple fact that *Orient* is no longer a Politically Correct term. Harold Huber, if one can get past his equally anti-P.C. yellowface portrayal, makes a grimly intimidating Ho Fang. He would be even more intimidating without the unwholesome laughter that the name *Ho Fang* inspires among present-day viewers.

Larry Darmour became more solidly ensconced at Columbia as the 1930s wore on into the 1940s, with such mystery franchises as *Ellery Queen*, *The Crime Doctor* and *The Whistler* to his credit.

CREDITS: Producer: Larry Darmour; Director: Ernest B. Schoedsack; Screenplay: Charles Francis Royal and Paul Franklin; Story: Ralph Graves; Photographed by: James S. Brown, Jr.; Assistant Director: Paoul Pagel; Editor: Dwight Caldwell; Sound: Tom Lambert; Technical Director: Frank Tang; Aeronautical Advisor: Marion McKeen; Running Time: 61 Minutes; Released: August 27, 1937

CAST: Jack Holt (Chet Eaton); Mae Clarke (Joan Manning); Harold Huber (Ho Fang); Ray Walker (Lucky Phelps); James Bush (Johnny Eaton); Joseph Crehan (Snyder); Bernice Roberts (Alice); Harry Worth (Sheldon)

S O S COAST GUARD
(Republic Pictures Corp.)

Bela Lugosi had been set to star in Republic's espionage thriller *The House of a Thousand Candles* (1936; see *Forgotten Horrors: the Definitive Edition*) but relinquished the spymaster role to Irving Pichel when sidelined by illness. Hard times followed in short order for Lugosi, what with the international horror ban calling for a strategic resourcefulness that the actor scarcely possessed. Although Lugosi had long since established himself as a rounded talent, as adept at comedy and straightforward dramatic assignments as at grand-manner villainy, he cratered under the pressures of typecasting at this crucial remove and suffered for want of work as a consequence. Lugosi was largely idled until Universal stepped in to challenge and collapse the embargo with *Son of Frankenstein* during 1938-'39. Lugosi's stopgap film, Republic's epic-scale *S O S Coast Guard*, is a horror picture in the truest sense, but it proved subversive enough to get past the censors: The clue-deficient Brain Police who enforced the ban considered serials to be harmless diversions for children.

And so perhaps they were—and still are—but no cinematic form ever faced a more discriminating, loyal or adventurous audience than the serials. Beyond the generally simplistic storylines, frequent narrative padding and uneven quality of ensemble acting, the chapter-a-week cliffhangers excelled at treating their followers to a sustained quality of suspense that is beyond the scope of a self-contained feature film; schoolkids had an entire week to worry about what was going to happen next. The serials delivered stunt action far more lifelike than that of many top-dollar productions. And the serials boasted special-effects extravaganzas that, in their hand-wrought craftsmanship, remain impressive today. The kids who made up the majority of the serials' audience were no fools: They might tolerate a cheating segué from one installment to the next, where certain doom for the hero turns to triumph as the following chapter opens, but an obviously faked stunt fall would provoke an outcry that might cost the offending studio plenty of traffic over the long haul.

The youth market was also the audience frustrated most by the horror ban. When the Hollywood establishment called an official halt to such movies in 1937, in response to the British and European censors' refusal to accept overtly hair-raising subject matter, the effect on the customers who loved a good scare was rather like that of Prohibition on the tippling populace. But there were no horror-movie speakeasies, to speak of, and the resort of seeing a beloved bogeyman like Boris Karloff hold forth in the *Mr. Wong* detective pictures was just a matter of marking time until saner heads could prevail.

Lugosi may not have shown the gumption of Karloff, who kept working steadily no matter what, but at least Lugosi kept the faith with the thriller fans. His limited work during this period provided an oasis of horrific treats—if one knew that the serials were the place to look—right there in the generous shade of the censors' big blue noses.

In *S O S Coast Guard*, seventh of Republic's 66 serials, U.S. Coast Guardsman Terry Kent (Ralph Byrd) learns that Boroff (Lugosi), a crazed inventor and munitions magnate, has arranged to supply a disintegrating gas to a hostile foreign power. In a standoff, Boroff kills Kent's brother, Jim (played by future director Thomas Carr). Kent swears revenge and begins setting an elaborate trap.

Kent's sweetheart, journalist Jean Norman (Maxine Doyle), and Jean's photographer, Snapper McGee (Lee Ford), narrowly escape Thorg (Richard Alexander), Boroff's monstrous and ill-treated slave. Kent steals a sample of the gas and puts chemist Dick Norman (Allen Connor), Jean's brother, to work on an antidote. Captured by Boroff at a coastal hideout, Kent breaks free and summons the Coast Guard. Boroff intends to kill the raiding party with a chemical barrage, but Jean arrives just in time with an airborne payload of the neutralizing gas.

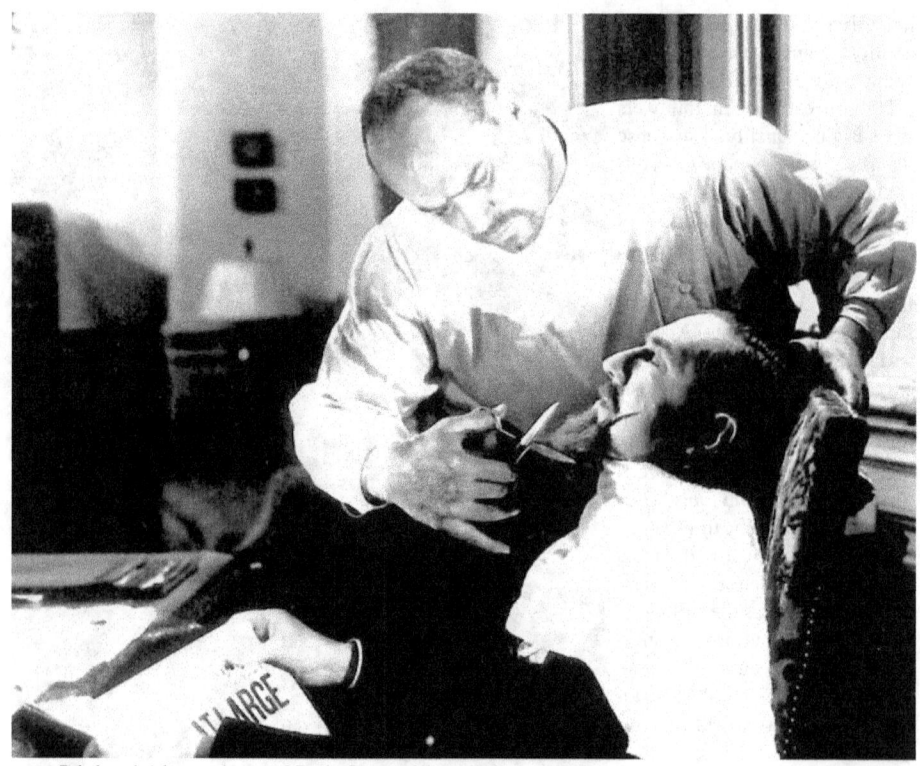

Richard Alexander and Bela Lugosi in a hairy moment from *S O S Coast Guard*

Boroff speeds away in a motorboat, only to find Thorg lurking. The giant has suffered enough at Boroff's hands, and now he wants revenge. Boroff fires on Thorg, but the servant kills the traitor with a gas bomb.

In what may be his most unremittingly evil role since 1932's *White Zombie*, Lugosi creates a turncoat who revels in sadomasochistic misconduct. Boroff—a name that sounds suspiciously like an elision of *Boris* and *Karloff*—entrusts his daily barbering to his servant even as he taunts the pathetic monster: "Thorg would like to cut my throat—*would*n't you, Thorg?" A henchman (Lawrence Grant) kibitzes right along: "Why shouldn't he? He has never forgiven you for mutilating his mind." As Thorg, Richard Alexander takes the cue to develop a cringe-inducing nervous spasm. The effect is not unlike that of watching W.C. Fields wield a straight-razor at deadly close range in the 1933 Mack Sennett short subject "The Barbershop," but the stakes here are immeasurably higher. Thorg *would* love to slit the boss's throat, but there is about the giant a simian dutifulness that stays his hand. Grant is unnerved: "I have never seen such fear and love—dumb loyalty and consuming hatred in such violent opposition..." Boroff replies: "Thorg isn't human—but he can be *very* useful."

Elsewhere, Boroff plots to test a fresh batch of disintegrating gas on a tethered dog. "*Nice* puppy," he says, patting the animal. "*Don't* be afraid." He changes his mind only when reminded of a human captive, the rather dimwitted newspaper photographer Snapper McGee. As energetically played by Lee Ford, McGee lapses here from comic relief to honest terror. It is hardly giving away too much to note the timely arrival of the hero-of-record, Ralph Byrd—Republic's once-and-future Dick Tracy—and a scary cliffhanger in the literal melting of the laboratory set.

All of which is pretty heady fare for a kid-stuff entertainment, although of course the psychological torments are leavened throughout by the bravura spirit of adventure that would characterize all of Republic's serials. Ralph Byrd lends gravity, too, as the hero whose patriotic duty runs a distant second to good old-fashioned blood vengeance. The film's sense of justice cuts even deeper than the hero's grudge, however, and finally the tensions between Lugosi's Boroff and Alexander's Thorg come violently to a head. Byrd makes an able self-appointed Nemesis for Lugosi, and Maxine Doyle renders her gal-reporter character more heroic than decorative—but it is in the psychological realm, in old hatreds shared between monsters, that *S O S Coast Guard* excels.

Excellence figures, too, in the special effects, which include a refined version of the illusion of melting that had been invented for *The Phantom Empire* (1935), a late-in-the-game Mascot serial that is among *S O S Coast Guard*'s most direct and influential ancestors.

Less obviously within the realm of special effects is the utterly convincing work of Ellis "Bud" Thackery, master photographer, and the up-and-coming sculptors and prop builders, Howard "Babe" Lydecker and Theodore Lydecker. During many years as chief of special-effects cinematography for Republic, Thackery provided full-scale and miniature projections, matte and glass shots and hundreds of superb miniature shots. The miniatures were made in collaboration with the Lydecker brothers, whose most striking contribution to *S O S Coast Guard* is an early-in-the-game sequence where Lugosi's smuggling ship runs aground.

Although Thackery preferred to photograph the Lydeckers' detailed miniatures outdoors in natural light, the shipwreck sequence required a night sky with lights just beyond a distant horizon. First, the ship is shown crashing, and later it slides off a reef and is visited undersea by miniature divers. The illusion of reality is perfect.

Republic had hit its stride with *S O S Coast Guard*, whose stirring original music, unflagging attitude of desperate excitement and wealth of custom-crafted visual delights put Universal's Lugosi starrer *The Phantom Creeps* (1939), with its recycled music and recycled footage (from 1936's *The Invisible Ray*, among others), decidedly in the shade. Both serials are entertainments to cherish, however—especially *S O S Coast Guard*, if only because it allowed Bela Lugosi the chance to strut some formidable stuff during those dark days when his greatest talent had become his worst professional liability.

CREDITS: Associate Producer: Sol C. Siegel; Directors: William Witney and Alan James; Supervised by: Robert Beche; Screenplay: Barry Shipman and Franklyn Adreon; Story: Morgan Cox and Ronald Davidson; Photographed by: William Nobles; Special Effects Photography: Ellis "Bud" Thackery; Special Effects Artisans: Howard and Theodore Lydecker; Supervising Editor: Murray Seldeen; Film Editors: Helene Turner and Edward Todd; Sound Engineer: Terry Kellum; Musical Director: Raoul Kraushaar; Sound System: RCA Victor High Fidelity; a Serial in 12 Chapters; Released: August 28, 1937; Feature Version, 71 Minutes in Length, Released April 17, 1942

CAST: Ralph Byrd (Terry Kent); Bela Lugosi (Boroff); Maxine Doyle (Jean Norman); Herbert Rawlinson (Commander Boyle); Richard Alexander (Thorg); Lee Ford (Snapper McGee); John Picorri (Rackerby); Lawrence Grant (Rubinisi); Thomas Carr (Jim Kent); Carleton Young (Dodds); Allen Connor (Dick Norman); George Chesebro (Delgado); Ranny Weeks (Weiss); Roy Barcroft (Goebels and Black)

SKY RACKET
(Victory Pictures Corp.)

Anyone who might believe Julia Roberts holds prior claim on the runaway-bride franchise will do well to look back to this science-fictional/romantical/criminological oddity from the heyday of "Jungle Sam" Katzman. He hadn't become "Jungle Sam," not quite yet—that moniker would have to wait until Katzman hooked up with Johnny Weissmuller for the *Jungle Jim* features of the postwar years—but his heyday was a long one, reaching from the Great Depression on into the Vietnam era. Katzman had an exploitation for every occasion, and with *Sky Racket* he not only cashed in on a popular fascination with airborne piracy and fantastic gadgetry but also weighed in with an entry for the emerging screwball school of romantic comedy. Katzman was known as an ultra-frugal, ultra-efficient moneymaking producer, but he also possessed a rudimentary talent (rarely indulged) for directing. Here we have one of those rare indulgences.

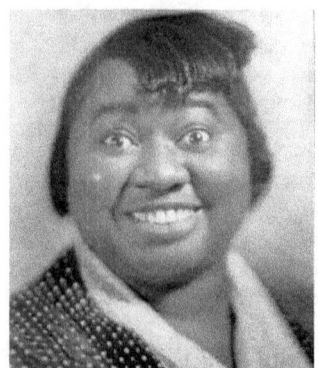

Hattie McDaniel portrayed a maid in *Sky Racket*.

In the screwball respect, *Sky Racket* is nothing to mention in the same breath with Frank Capra's *It Happened One Night* (1934) or William Wellman's *Nothing Sacred* (1937), but it does anticipate William Keighley's *The Bride Came C.O.D.* (1941) in its tale of aviational antagonisms leading to a sweetheart situation. Too, the little film boasts an exaggerated comical tone that compares favorably with those three acknowledged classics from the major-leaguers. Herman Brix and Joan Barclay are no Cagney-and-Davis, but the teaming meant pure star power within its Poverty Row context. That *Sky Racket* mixes its romantic shenanigans and laugh-provoking indignities with a menacing mail-robbery racket and a strange means of tracking the doomed planes, sets it quite apart.

Marion Bronson (Miss Barclay), a stubborn high-society brat, balks at an arranged marriage and runs away at the very moment of her wedding. Reaching an airfield, Marion sneaks onto an airplane that happens to be piloted by Eric Lane (Herman Brix), a federal operative on the trail of a mail-bandit gang. The crooks track and disable the craft with a radical new radio-beam device. Eric had intended to use this flight to bait the robbers, but Marion's presence requires a parachute leap. Before Eric can arrest her for her interference, they are captured by mobsters in the service of the ringleader, Arnold (Monte Blue). Marion, thinking fast, claims that Eric had kidnapped her—leading Arnold to consider Eric a prospect for gang membership. The masquerade does not work for long, but Eric manages to send up a decoy plane that smokes out the mob. Eric and Marion elope.

Sky Racket starts off as pure slapstick, with the members of the upper-crust household laying it on thick with the pre-nuptial jitters and Hattie McDaniel—just two years away from her *Gone with the Wind* breakthrough—exaggerating every syllable and every move as Miss Barclay's anxious maid. Katzman sustains this tone until Miss Barclay and Brix find themselves airborne, just as Monte Blue's mob makes with the remote-control sabotage. The hostage situation is played for wisecracking wit and considerable suspense, and the romance that develops as a consequence is surprisingly convincing despite its abruptness. More abrupt romances have happened.

CREDITS: Producer and Director: Sam Katzman; Story and Screenplay: Basil Dickey; Photographed by: Bill Hyer; Editor: Holbrook Todd; Sound: Hans Weeren [as Weerin]; Settings: Fred Preble; Production Supervisor: Bob Stillman; Running Time: 63 Minutes; Released: September 1, 1937

CAST: Herman Brix (Eric Lane); Joan Barclay (Marion Bronson); Hattie McDaniel [as McDaniels] (Jennie); Monte Blue (Arnold); Henry Roquemore (Roger Bronson); and Jack Mulhall, Edward Earle, Duncan Rinaldo, Earl Hodgins, Roger Williams, Frank Wayne, Ed Cassidy

SPECIAL AGENT K-7
a.k.a.: SECRET AGENT K-7
(C.C. Burr Productions, Inc.)

Presumably based on a broadcast serial "familiar to a large radio audience," according to a credulous report in *Daily Variety*, this launcher of an intended string of half a dozen *Special Agent K-7* thrillers proved to be the only one of its kind. Walter McGrail has the title role, an F.B.I. man who intends to retire as soon as he has completed a crackdown on the rackets. The *real* star of the show is Irving Pichel, who plays a spellbinding defense lawyer at the center of a serial-murder case. After Pichel breaks stride in the courtroom and bungles his defense of a clearly innocent accused killer (Donald Reed), Agent K-7 concludes that the incriminating fingerprints are forgeries. Pichel is unmasked as not only the killer—but also a master engraver who has perfected the art of creating bogus fingerprints. Pichel is better than the material, which is more than we can say for anyone else on duty here.

CREDITS: Director: Raymond K. Johnson; Screenplay: Phil Dunham; Story: George F. Zimmer; Photographed by: Elmer Dyer; Editor: Charles Henkel; Song: "Action Speaks Louder than Words," by Russ Magnus & Billy Rice; Running Time: 66 Minutes; Released: Following New York Opening on September 2, 1937

CAST: Walter McGrail (Vince Landers, Special Agent K-7); Queenie Smith (Olive O'Day); Irving Pichel (Lester Owens); Donald Reed (Billy Westrop); Willy Castello (Eddie Geller); Duncan Renaldo (Tony Black); Joy Hodges (Peppy); Richard Tucker (Adams); Malcolm McGregor (Silky Samuels); Captain John (Schmidt); George Eldredge (Prosecutor); Henry Menjou (Smaltz); David MacDonald (Goodwin); William Royle (Capt. Hall); Harry Harvey (Speedy); James Guilfoyle (Kennedy); Snub Pollard (Waiter); and Harrison Greene, John Peters

SAFARI ON WHEELS
(Esso, Inc.)

The corporate name of Esso, Inc., is all but forgotten today; it is the ancestor of Exxon. In its early years, the company unwittingly contributed to the development of an important Afro-Caribbean musical form: Native musicians would transform discarded Esso petroleum barrels into melodic drums by hammering and welding the steel vessels to register varying pitches. The artists took care, first, to purge the barrels of ferocious tropical bees, which found the empties convenient for building hives. Hence the wise old tribal saying, "Watch out for those Esso bees!"

The Esso-produced oddity *Safari on Wheels* is a featurette designed for in-house and classroom use, the better to tout the company's products in an adventurous context. Safari members journey by truck convoy through the Atlas Mountains, tour French fortresses in the desert and reach the Equatorial jungles in time to celebrate Christmas with a festooned tropical plant in lieu of the traditional evergreen. Nothing particularly menacing here, although there is a generous measure of the grotesque—including the Ubangi tradition of slitting women's lips and stretching them around platter-sized wooden discs. Pygmy tribesmen, diminutive by definition, are placed alongside Esso lubricant tanks as a measure of height. The 11,000-mile trek ends with an impeccable performance record for Esso gasoline and crankcase oil.

CREDITS: Written by: Emma-Lindsay Squire Brand; Running Time: Approx. 40 Minutes; Copyrighted: September 15, 1937

CAST: Natives and Colonial Residents of Africa

WALLABY JIM OF THE ISLANDS
(Grand National Films, Inc.)

Produced back-to-back with Grand National's first *Renfrew of the Royal Mounted* manhunt (look under 1940's *Sky Bandits*) during the summer of '37, this seafaring adventure made an ambitious launching for a series that never quite managed to set sail. Four *Wallaby Jim* pictures were announced, all drawn from Albert Richard Wetjen's *Collier's* magazine yarns. The one that made it into production was little seen in America, but it became a hit over the long haul Down Under—this, according to Aussie teevee-and-film personality Paul Hogan, who has recalled *Wallaby Jim* fondly and acknowledged the little picture as an ancestor of his own *Crocodile Dundee* action-thriller comedies of times more recent.

George Houston is Wallaby Jim, a good-natured brawler who is detoured from a voyage to claim a pearl bed when a stowaway named Allison (Ruth Coleman) proves to be the fiancée of Jim's long-absent pal, Norman (Douglas Walton). Allison is appalled by Jim's proclivity for violence, which erupts when a greenhorn crewman (Juan Toreña) is caught stealing. At the port where they had expected

to meet Norman, Allison finds a rival of Jim's, the suave and arrogant Adolph Rickter (William von Brincken), to be a worse brute by far, a sadist who disciplines his divers with murder. Norman has gambled away a grubstake entrusted to him by Jim. Rickter learns of Jim's pearl strike and hastens to get there first. A native girl named Lana (Mamo Clark) seduces Jim. In a desperate fight at the pearl bed, Norman squares himself with Jim by stopping a bullet from Rickert's gun. Jim soon finds himself in search of the next barroom brawl, and the next adventures—which were never to transpire. George Houston, better known as a lead in low-budget musicals and a supporting player in larger films, went on to star in Sig Neufeld's *Lone Rider* Westerns. Houston died of a heart attack at age 46 in 1944.

Wallaby Jim's convincing scenic representations of a South Seas setting were found at Sunland, California's Lancaster Lake, and at Catalina, where Fox had shot much of its abolitionist epic *Slave Ship* (1937) during 1936-1937. The make-believe native ranks were peopled with extras of Tahitian, Hawaiian and Polynesian descent. The latter-day Poverty Row producer Sidney Pink (of *Reptilicus* and *Angry Red Planet*) has identified himself 'way after-the-fact as a honcho of the *Wallaby Jim* production crew and cited additional pictures in such a series; the claim stands at odds with the historical record as kept by the American Film Institute.

CREDITS: Presented by: Edward L. Alperson; Producer: Bud Barsky; Director: Charles Lamont; Screenplay and Adaptation: Bennett Cohn and Houston Branch; Based upon: the *Collier's* Magazine Stories by Albert Richard Wetjen; Photographed by: Ira Morgan; Art Director: Paul Palmentola; Assistant Director: Joe Boyle; Editor: Guy V. Thayer, Jr.; Musical Director: Arthur Kay; Songs: "Hi-Ho-Hum," "Moon over the Islands," "The Lady with the Two Left Feet" and "Ia-Ora-Na," by Felix Bernard & Irving Bibo; Sound: William Wilmarth: Sound Technician: A.E. Kaye; Technical Adviser: Jim Spencer; Unit Manager: Sidney Algier; Production Supervisor: Harold Lewis; Running Time: 73 Minutes; Released: October 15, 1937

CAST: George Houston (Wallaby Jim); Ruth Coleman (Allison); Douglas Walton (Norman); Mamo Clark (Lana); Juan Toreña (Pascal); William von Brincken (Adolph Rickter); Syd Saylor (Jake); Colin Campbell (Limey); Warner Richmond (Karl Haage); Nick Thompson (Michael Corell); Edward Gargan (Morgan); Wilson Benge (Macklin); Chris Martin (Mike)

LOVE LIFE OF A GORILLA
a.k.a.: KIDNAPPING GORILLAS; LIFE OF A GORILLA
(Jewel Productions, Inc.)

A late boarder—like *Angkor*—of the bogus-documentary bandwagon that *Ingagi* had launched in 1930, *Love Life of a Gorilla* is a sloppily assembled collection of stagings and expeditionary footage. A "Col. Hubert Winstead" is listed among the expeditioners, and might even be the same Hubert Winstead (if not an inside-joke reference) who is credited along with one Daniel Swayne as being responsible for *Ingagi*'s brummagem of a safari. Even if the Winstead personage should prove genuine, the military rank can reliably be held fraudulent. And truth be known, the Turner & Price Expedition into the Nether Reaches of Old Hollywood has frankly grown annoyed with sorting through this morass of spurious ape-rampage pictures, what with their amateurish photography, patent fakery and overabundance of misleading proxy titles.

The pageantry of *Love Life of a Gorilla* includes all-but-nude native women, some authentically native and all authentically bare; an attack by lions on a jungle village; hunting excursions in search of monkeys, elephants, rhinos, gazelles, big cats and undersea denizens; and a struggle-unto-death between snakes. Ubangis, their lower lips distended by primitive cosmetic surgery, and assorted Kavirondus and Pygmies are gawked at with bigoted curiosity. The payoff finale—heavily scissored in many regions—involves the standard "sacrifice" of a "native" "girl" to a gorilla-suited stuntman. The bold mock-expeditioners fell the creature with gunfire. The *Variety* reviewer in New York remarked: "Narrator becomes more excited than the audience, which hardly stir[s] at the inane series of events." We have found four distinct cuts of *Love Life of a Gorilla*; two, under the proxy reissue title of *Kidnapping Gorillas*, contain scraps from *Ingagi* and *Angkor*, probably inserted by unauthorized roadshow distributors. There is yet an entirely different picture called *Kidnapping Gorillas*, from 1934, which receives its due in the present book's "Annotations, Marginalia & Addenda" section.

CREDITS: Assembled and Edited by: Samuel Cummins; Assistant Editor: Raymond Lewis; "Based upon Major Frederick Brown's Expedition into Africa"; Running Time: 77 Minutes; Copyrighted as *Love Life of a Gorilla* on: October 29, 1937; Running Time in 1941 as *Kidnapping Gorillas*: 69 Minutes.

CAST: Sir Cecil Deberrie, Col. Hubert Winstead, Maj. Frederick Brown

VU IZ MAYN KIND?
(WHERE IS MY CHILD?)
(Menorah Productions)

Based upon a Yiddish stage play called *Forgotten Mothers*, this agonized study of estrangement and inflicted mental illness pivots on an intense portrayal by Celia Adler—evidently her only screen performance—of a widowed new mother whose child is placed with adoptive parents by a deceitful physician, Dr. Adolf Reisner (Morris Strassberg).

Realizing too late that she has signed away her maternal rights, Esther Leibmann (Miss Adler) spends the next several years searching for a way back into the child's orbit. Reisner hovers perilously close to these intrigues, finally intervening when Esther is arrested on charges of stalking the youngster, Victor (Leo Schectman). Promising assistance, Reisner instead arranges to imprison Esther in an asylum. The horrors she endures in this healing environment finally render her withdrawn, and 20 years later—when Victor (played now by Mischa Stuchkof) begins working at the institution as a benevolent doctor—Esther cannot recognize her own son. Victor takes an especial interest in Esther, vowing to punish whoever the rotter was who had stranded such a nice lady in this snake pit. Victor is now engaged to marry Reisner's daughter (Ceril Arnon). Dr. Reisner agrees to examine Esther, who struggles to remember his face. As Reisner, nervously denying recognition, declares Esther insane, she transfixes him with a withering stare and demands: "Where is my child?" Victor's adoptive mother (Anna Lillian) finally comprehends who this madwoman must be, and Victor threatens Reisner with disgrace if not a hitch in prison. Esther regains her son and her presence of mind, and she is welcomed into Victor's adoptive family.

Powerfully moving in ways beyond the grasp of conventional Hollywood, *Where Is My Child?* has remained largely unknown outside the realm of Jewish film scholarship. The film does not intend itself to shock or thrill—and the ultimate message amid all the contrived ironies is one of piety and reconciliation. Morris Strassberg's evil Dr. Reisner bears mentioning in the same breath with all those magnificent figures of abusive authority defined over the long haul by the likes of Erich von Stroheim, Basil Rathbone, Lionel Atwill, Bela Lugosi, Boris Karloff, Vincent Price and George Zucco. *Where Is My Child?* is enacted in Yiddish, with English subtitles.

CREDITS: Presented by: Abraham Leff; Directors: Abraham Leff and Henry Lynn; Screenplay: Henry Lynn; Based upon: the Play *Forgotten Mothers* by Sam Steinberg and William Siegal; Photographed by: J. Burgi Contner; Editor: George Roland; Musical Director: Jack Stillman; "The Lullaby Song" Composed for Miss Adler by: Ludwig Satz; Recording Engineer: Edwin Schabbehar; Running Time: 95 Minutes; Released: Following New York Opening on November 23, 1937

Judith Allen, Grant Withers and Warren Hymer try to save the town in *Telephone Operator*. (Photofest)

CAST: Celia Adler (Esther Liebmann); Anna Lillian (Alice Gross); Morris Strassberg (Dr. Adolf Reisner); Ruben Wendorf (Elick); Morris Silberklasten (Morris Gross); Blanche Bernstein (Molka); Mischa Stuchkof (Victor); Ceril Arnon (Julia Reisner); Solomon Steinberg (Anderson); Esther Gerber (Nurse); Leo Schectman (Victor as a Child)

TELEPHONE OPERATOR
(Monogram Pictures)

Monogram is often accused of making disastrous movies, but the prolific little studio made only one prototypical Disaster Movie. *Telephone Operator* is, of course, a disastrous Disaster Movie if measured against such bravura works as 1933's *Deluge* or 1935's *The Last Days of Pompeii*, but it works reasonably well on a purely human scale of boisterous horseplay and blue-collar heroism.

Red (Grant Withers) and Shorty (Warren Hymer) are Bell System linemen newly arrived in town to connect telephone service to a damsite. Only logical that they should meet up with switchboard operators Helen (Judith Allen) and Dottie (Alice White). Dottie and Shorty find love at first sight; not so with Helen and Red, despite Red's best efforts.

Red finds a way to impress Helen when she needs help during a worsening rainstorm. The task is to pick up her friend, Sylvia Sommers (Greta Grandstedt), from a cabin owned by Sylvia's adulterous sweetheart (Cornelius Keefe). Sylvia's husband, Tom, is the operators' boss. Tom (Pat Flaherty) arrives in search of Sylvia, who escapes with Red, leaving Helen behind. Tom gets the wrong idea about Helen and fires her. Red gets canned for slugging his boss (William Haade), who is spreading gossip about Helen.

Then the dam breaks. Helen, moved by a sense of duty, commandeers the switchboard to transmit evacuation notices. Red, Shorty and Dottie pitch in despite the mounting floodwaters. Finally, Helen and Red float away on a telephone pole. The desperate adventure ends on a romantic note, as Helen and Red decide to get married as soon as they can find a justice of the peace who can swim. The closing gag is their decision to take their honeymoon in Niagara Falls.

Rambunctious character portrayals abound, rendering the urgency of the situation fairly lighthearted, even corny, throughout. The four principals pull together at the climax to register a desperation that the limited action scenes come ill-prepared to support: One grows to believe that Judith Allen's switchboard has become the nerve center of a life-saving campaign. The special-effects quotient is covered largely by stock footage of actual storms and floods, although some adequate miniature work figures into the mixture. *Telephone Operator* is more fun than most of the self-serious mock-epic flood-fire-earthquake-meteor mayhem that would proliferate on the big screen during the 1970s and again during the '90s.

CREDITS: In Charge of Production: Scott R. Dunlap; Associate Producer: Lon Young; Director: Scott Pembroke; Screenplay: Scott Darling; Story: John Krafft; Photographed by: Gilbert Warrenton; Assistant Director: W.B. Eason; Editor: Russell Schoengarth; Musical Director: Abe Meyer; Recording Engineer: W.C. Smith; Technical Director: E.R. Hickson; Production Manager: George E. Kahn; Running Time: 62 Minutes; Released: December 7, 1937

CAST: Judith Allen (Helen Molloy); Grant Withers (Red); Warren Hymer (Shorty); Alice White (Dottie Stengal); Ronnie Cosbey (Ted Molloy); Pat Flaherty (Tom Sommers); Greta Grandstedt (Sylvia Sommers); William Haade (Heaver); Cornelius Keefe (Pat Campbell); Dorothy Vaughn (Mrs. Molloy); and Walter McGrail, Ethel Jackson, Michael Gover

ORPHAN OF THE PECOS
(Victory Pictures Corp.)

The art of ventriloquism is supposed not to work outside the realm of in-person presentation, for the illusion is lost without the misdirection that results from deflected eye contact between an in-the-flesh performer and the audience. Try telling that to the movies and radio, which worked wonders for the careers of Edgar Bergen and his "talking" mannequins, Charlie McCarthy and Mortimer Snerd, and for *Three Mesquiteers* and *Range Busters* series regular Max Terhune and his dummy, Elmer.

The ventriloquy gimmick is used to grimmer effect in Sam Katzman's *Orphan of the Pecos*, where Tom Tyler uses voice-thrower Ted Lorch to pipe ghostly words into the air, the better to spook a confession out of a murderer. The culprit is that master of snarling intimidation, Forrest Taylor, an outwardly respectable ranch foreman who does away with his boss—kindly old Lafe McKee—and escapes with a small fortune, framing Tyler for the crime. Tyler, who had been summoned by McKee to set things right at the ranch, will have none of this crooked scam and begins compiling a list of the likelier suspects. The ventriloquist ploy works like nobody's business, unnerving Taylor to a point near madness. The matter is settled with a good old-fashioned fistfight, one of several that punctuate the picture.

The title would suggest the presence of a child star, but the orphan in question is actually Tyler's wife, Jeanne Martel, who plays McKee's embittered daughter and Tyler's eventual romantic interest. Lorch accounts for some lighter moments in addition to his crucial role in cracking the case, but the greater comical burden falls to sidekick Howard Bryant and to Marjorie Beebe, a google-eyed player with years of experience in the two-reeler comedies, as Miss Martel's scared-silly pal.

Sam Katzman was a producer by choice and a director on occasion, "mostly by default," as he told us during the 1960s. "I kept a hand in as needed, but I'd rather be the guy who rides herd on the bank book." Katzman produced and directed *Orphan of the Pecos* back-to-back with *Lost Ranch* (1938), in which Tyler, Bryant, Miss Martel and Miss Beebe set out to rescue McKee from kidnapper Taylor.

CREDITS: Producer and Director: Sam Katzman; Story and Screenplay: Basil Dickey; Photographed by: Bill Hyer; Settings: Fred Preble; Editor: Holbrook Todd; Recording Engineer: Hans Weeren; Production Manager: Ed W. Rote; Running Time: 57 Minutes; Released: December 30, 1937

CAST: Tom Tyler (Tom Rayburn); Jeanne Martel (Ann Gelbert); Howard Bryant (Pete); Slim Whittaker (Sheriff); Theodore Lorch (Jeremiah Mathews); Forrest Taylor (Jess Brand); Marjorie Beebe (Mrs. Barnes); Lafe McKee (Hank Gelbert); Roger Williams (Slim)

1938

WOLVES OF THE SEA
(Guaranteed Pictures/J.D. Kendis)

An heiress and a cargo of exotic animals are the survivors of a tropical shipwreck in this stock-footage jungle epic from the notoriously cheap J.D. Kendis. Jeanne Carmen, as the lovely castaway, has little more to occupy her time than to protect the gentler creatures from the carnivores until a shipload of treasure hunters shows up. These opportunists are led by crusty old Hobart Bosworth as a captain driven by greed, with Warner Richmond lurking about as a snarling mutineer. Miss Carmen's acting is shrill enough to counteract her good looks, but at least she is evenly matched with romantic lead Dirk Thane, a dreadful actor in his own right. To no one's surprise, the sunken diamonds that Bosworth seeks prove to belong to Miss Carmen; she does not object to his claiming the jewels, presumably because she has more where those came from.

True love prevails, even though Thane puts up a remarkably thickheaded resistance to Miss Carmen's aggressive pursuit. The film is as short on thrills as it is on running time, and the clunky editing of patchwork footage is evident throughout.
CREDITS: Producer: J.D. Kendis; Scenarist and Director: Elmer Clifton; Photographed by: Eddie Linden; Art Director: Fred Preble; Editor: Duke Goldstone; Running Time: 65 Minutes; Released: Following New York Opening on January 28, 1938

CAST: Hobart Bosworth (Capt. Wolf Hansen); Jeanne Carmen (Nadine Miller); Dirk Thane (William Rand); Pat West (Jim Lane); Warner Richmond (Snoden); John Merton (Mitchell); Edward Kaye (Frankie).

THE BLACK DOLL
(Walter A. Futter/Crime Club Productions/Universal Pictures Co.)

Poverty Row's occasional infiltration of the major leagues had seen its highest accomplishment in the United Artists release of the Halperin Bros.' *White Zombie* in 1932. The distinct sectors were constantly conversant with one another—witness the graduation of director Edwin L. Marin to big-time MGM from little Tiffany Studios, for example. And the majors' lucrative B-picture units took many a cue from the independent production outfits. Here, in *The Black Doll*, is another remarkable crossover: a key series entry for Universal, courtesy of the bare-bones producer Walter A. Futter.

Futter, who would not remain long in such regimented company, soon relinquished his involvement with Crime Club Productions, a franchise tied to a series of popular novels, to other, higher-minded overseers—the better to concentrate on stuff, like 1940's lurid *The Leopard Men of Africa*, that a big outfit like Universal would not remotely consider. Some sources, including George Turner's own Hollywood-based archive, have held that Futter merely acquired *The Black Doll* for independent distribution after Universal had dropped it from the active program—but the Futter name appears on the formal Universal screen billing of the first-run theatrical release prints.

The Black Doll, which is enjoyably lurid in more conventional ways, hangs on C. Henry Gordon's seething portrayal of wealthy Nelson Rood, a hateful grouch who threatens a free-spending nephew (William Lundigan); berates his sister (Doris Lloyd); drives Nick Halstead (Donald Woods), a freelance

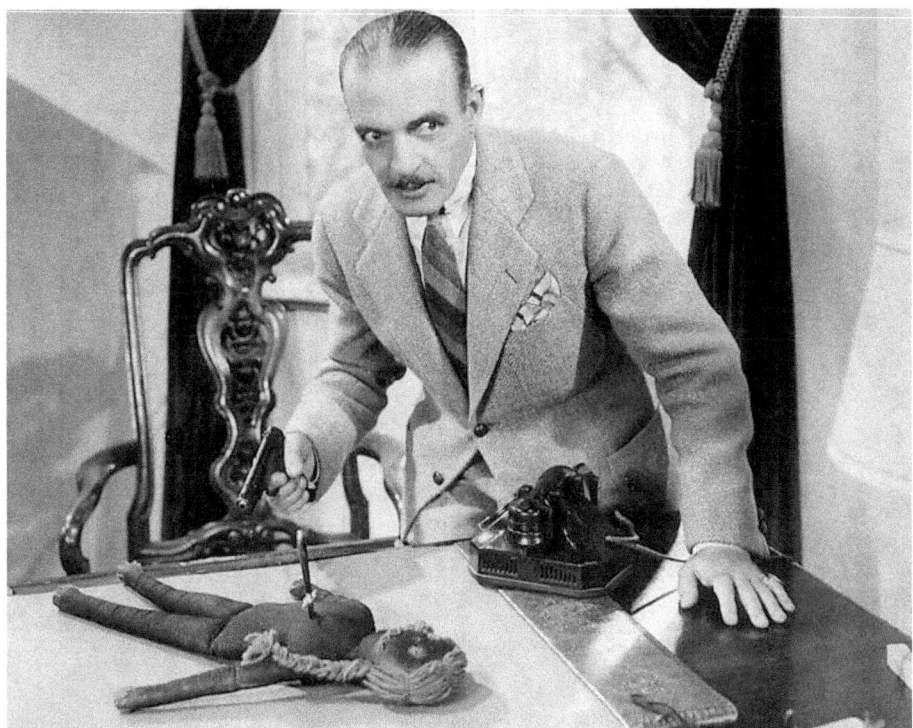

His discovery of the Black Doll makes C. Henry Gordon even grouchier than usual. A pivotal scene from—what else?—*The Black Doll*. (Photofest)

detective, off a campsite on the estate; and torments his Mexican servants, Esteban (Fred Malatesta) and Rosita (Inez Palange). The sudden appearance of *la muñeca negra*—the black doll, symbolic of a curse—in his study leads Rood to summon Walling (John Wray) and Mallison (Addison Richards), his former partners in a Mexican mining venture. They suspect the hideous token is connected with a fourth partner, Barrows, whom Rood had murdered long ago.

Rood is stabbed to death outside the rooms of his daughter Marian (Nan Grey). She dashes out to find Nick, who takes up the case alongside an incompetent sheriff (Edgar Kennedy). Esteban is killed while guarding Marian. Mallison is next to die. Nick learns that Rood had prevented his sister from marrying a family friend, Dr. Giddings (Holmes Herbert), and had claimed Marian, Barrows' daughter, as his own. Giddings is revealed as the murderer.

The accursed household yields plenty of shivers, all right, but it is veteran slow-burn comic Edgar Kennedy's performance as the hick sheriff that carries the yarn along on a crest of broad humor. Boyish Donald Woods upstages Kennedy in the detection department but plays second fiddle to Kennedy's overblown irascibility in terms of too-much-is-not-enough entertainment value. Texas-born Nan Grey, soon to become a dependable talent in such bigger Universal productions as *Tower of London* (1939) and *The Invisible Man Returns* (1941), turns in an indifferent performance as the menaced daughter. C. Henry Gordon, for all the brevity of his performance, leaves a lasting impression.

The Universal identity sits with a particular unsteadiness on *The Black Doll*, which—despite some striking work by that great cinematographer, Stanley Cortez—looks and moves more like a Monogram or a lesser Republic. The little film seemed more properly in its element during the late 1980s, when a company descended from Republic had it in television syndication. The *Crime Club* series had started out rather more auspiciously in 1937 with *The Westland Case* and would continue on bolder notes with such titles as *Danger on the Air*, *Gambling Ship*, *The Lady in the Morgue* and *The Last Express* (all 1938) and *The House of Fear*, *Inside Information*, *The Last Warning*, *Mystery of the White Room*

Hollywood Stadium Mystery **wallows to a surprising extent in relentless menace and, ultimately, madness. (Photofest)**

and *The Witness Vanishes* (all 1939). By comparison with the *Crime Club*s, however, Universal's own in-house *Inner Sanctum* series of the '40s looks positively top-of-the-line.

CREDITS: Presented by: Walter A. Futter; Producer: Irving Starr; Director: Otis Garrett; Screenplay: Harold Buckley; Based upon: William Edward Hayes' 1936 Novel *The Black Doll*; Photographed by: Stanley Cortez and Ira Morgan; Art Director: Ralph Berger; Sets: Emile Kuri; Assistant Director: Phil Karlstein; Editor: Maurice Wright; Gowns: Vera West; Musical Director: Charles Previn; Sound: Charles Carroll; Production Manager: Ben Hersh; Running Time: 66 Minutes; Released: January 30, 1938

CAST: Donald Woods (Nick Halstead); Nan Grey (Marian Rood); Edgar Kennedy (Sheriff Renick); C. Henry Gordon (Nelson Rood); Doris Lloyd (Laula Leland); John Wray (Walling); Addison Richards (Mallison); Holmes Herbert (Dr. Giddings); William Lundigan (Rex Leland); Fred Malatesta (Esteban); Inez Palange (Rosita); Syd Saylor (Red); Arthur Hoyt (Coroner)

HOLLYWOOD STADIUM MYSTERY
(Republic Pictures Corp.)

The suspense runs high, deep and wide despite an absurdly contrived script that "builds up suspicion against everybody but the [film's] producer," as *Variety* cleverly described *Hollywood Stadium Mystery*. For a picture made during the official span of an international ban on horror, *Hollywood Stadium Mystery* wallows to a surprising extent in relentless menace and, ultimately, madness.

Mystery writer Polly Ward (played by Evelyn Venable) finds herself fascinated with the peculiar slaying of a prizefighter on the verge of a championship bout. Polly must be a better storyteller than she is a detective, for she proves as much a hindrance as a help to District Attorney Bill Devons (Neil Hamilton), who himself is no great shakes at solving the crime. About all they manage to accomplish as a team is to fall in love, and ultimately it is left to the killer himself, a flamboyant sportscaster named Nick Nichols (Jimmy Wallington), to crack up and 'fess up.

Wallington steals the show admirably with a tightly wound performance that makes the character almost *too* likable until he inadvertently reveals his depraved nature in an unnerving turnabout. Director David Howard keeps the action brisk as he inventories his assorted red herrings—notably, weasly Lucien Littlefield, as a security cop, and gaunt Reed Hadley—without sufficient explanation. The finale is well played despite its abruptness. Neil Hamilton makes a more convincing romancer than an authority figure, and either of the secondary *femmes*, Barbara Pepper and Lynn Roberts, could have fared as agreeably in Miss Venable's part. Smiley Burnette, better known as Gene Autry's Popeye-voiced sidekick Frog Millhouse, contributes some welcome lowbrow humor, including a mouthy sound-effects showcase where he mimics the noises of a hot-rod race.

CREDITS: Associate Producer: Armand Schaefer; Director: David Howard; Screenplay: Stuart Palmer, Dorrell McGowan and Stuart McGowan (from His Story); Photographed by: Ernest Miller; Art Director: Victor Mackay; Assistant Director: Phil Ford; Editor: Edward Mann; Supervising Editor: Murray Seldeen; Costumes: Irene Saltern; Musical Director: Alberto Colombo; Production Manager: Al Wilson; Running Time: 66 Minutes; Released: February 21, 1938

CAST: Neil Hamilton (Bill Devons); Evelyn Venable (Polly Ward); Jimmy Wallington (Nick Nichols); Barbara Pepper (Althea Ames); Lucien Littlefield (Watchman); Lynne Roberts (Edna); Charles Williams (Jake); James Spottswood (Slate Keefe); Reed Hadley (Ralph Mortimer); Robert Homans (Capt. Filson); William Haade ("Champ" Madison); Pat Flaherty (Ace Cummings); Dan Toby (Announcer); Smiley Burnette (Himself, More or Less); Al Bayne (Max)

FORBIDDEN ADVENTURE
a.k.a.: JUNGLE VIRGIN; INYAAH THE JUNGLE GODDESS; INYAAH (JUNGLE GODDESS); THE VIRGIN OF SARAWAK; STRANGE ADVENTURES
(Ace Productions, Inc./Road Show Attractions Co./J.H. Hoffberg Co./Mapel Attractions/Hollywood Producers & Distributors/Warner-Allender Roadshow Attractions, Inc.)

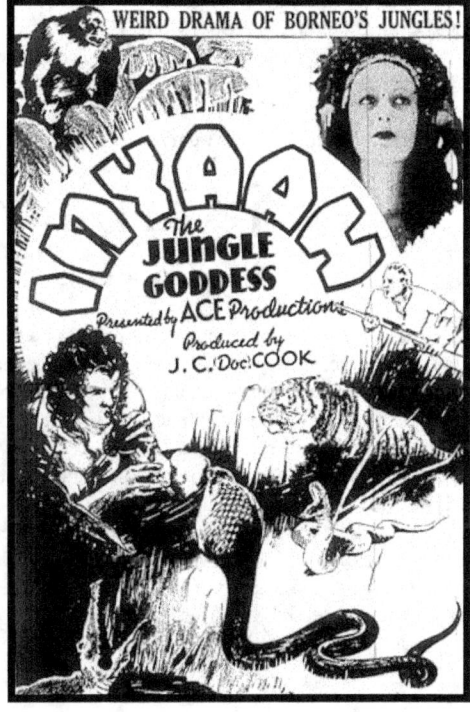

Here we go again with the *Forbidden Adventure* confusion: This wilds-of-Borneo piece bears no kinship to the 1937 *Angkor*, which *Variety* dissected as *Forbidden Adventure*, and it in fact predates that Southeast Asian women-love-apes picture by a few years. This particular *Forbidden Adventure* was produced in 1934 and may have been shown late in 1936, per the American Film Institute. But a formal announcement of release appeared in *The Film Daily* in March of 1938. A print entitled *Jungle Virgin* bears a 1942 copyright but identifies no proprietor. The 1934 copyright registration records indicate the original title had been *Inyaah the Jungle Goddess*—a name that appears, with slight variations, on 16-millimeter TV-syndicate prints dating from the 1950s. There appears, meanwhile, to have been another *Inyaah*, from 1936, that must for now remain a mystery, whether an alternate version or a different work altogether. Not that we're predisposed to go looking for one more stray piece of a puzzle that is scarcely all that fascinating in the first place. Let it come looking for us for a change.

This one involves the Dyak settlements of Borneo, where two white expeditioners become intrigued with the legend of a white-skinned goddess. Taking up the trail, they are captured by indignant natives but released and welcomed on a command from an unseen presence. Within the tribal grounds, they notice a young white woman who is venerated by the tribespeople. She and one explorer, Tom, fall in love. The purported goddess tells him how she came to this place:

The daughter of planters from Russia, the girl, Ileana, saw her happy existence shattered when a rival planter kidnapped her and her mother and murdered her father. The killer raped Ileana's mother so savagely that "the spirits took her mind away." Freed into the jungle with her daughter, the mother then learned to charm the animals of the wild into doing her bidding—which naturally included revenge on the planter and his thugs. The mother and daughter at length were granted shelter by the tribe. Tom and Sandy, his pal, plead with Ileana to leave the jungle, but she cannot take her deranged mother to civilization. A fire conveniently does away with the mother, and Ileana agrees to leave.

It all reads more rousingly than it plays. An inappropriate pipe-organ score drones throughout, underscoring some equally droning narration and emphasizing the silent-era aura. The production's stranger intrigues took place off-screen, and it comes as little surprise that Dwain Esper, that most notorious of the exploitation-picture impresarios, had a hand in matters. The Motion Picture Producers & Distributors Association's Production Code Administration rejected *Forbidden Adventure* in August of 1938 on grounds of nudity and the episode of ravishment that motivates most of the mayhem.

Esper was in charge of the film's affiliated Hollywood Producers & Distributors, a name purposefully concocted to sound like that of the industry's own watchdog agency, the Motion Picture Producers & Distributors Association. Esper finally secured a seal of approval upon agreeing to remove footage showing women's breasts and boys' genitalia. Another distribution affiliate, Warner-Allender Roadshow Attractions, Inc., objected to Esper's receipt of the approval, on grounds that neither Esper nor director J.C. "Doc" Cook had authority to represent the film. It was further claimed that Cook had stolen the negative. Records from this point onward seem no longer to exist, and the later theatrical prints bear not only proxy titles but also different distributor identities. If these 1940s prints are any indication, Esper's idea of "removing" the "offending" footage consisted of masking black strips across those frames containing the bodily parts at issue.

CREDITS: Director: J.C. "Doc" Cook; Editor: Grace McKee; Musical Score: "C. Sharpe-Minor" [the Patently Phony Name Would Indicate Stock-Library Scoring]; Running Time: 70 Minutes; Copyrighted: July 1, 1934; Released: During March of 1938 on a State-by-State Basis

CAST: Gayne Whitman (Narrator)

IT'S ALL IN YOUR MIND
a.k.a.: FOOLS OF DESIRE
(Bernard B. Ray/Continental Pictures, Inc.)

The adults-only crowd could not have known what to make of *It's All in Your Mind* when the admitted sex picture began its tedious search for a mature-of-intellect audience during 1938. "To the vulgar," cautioned a press release from the distributor, "it may have vulgar appeal. To the thoughtful observer, its appeal will be pathetic. To the psychologist, it is a representative case history of a man tortured by libidinous repressions."

At the risk of taking an anonymous publicity flack too seriously, we have grown to regard *It's All in Your Mind* as a groundbreaking work by any standard. The film proves at once lurid and tasteful, provocative by measures both intellectual and visceral, and as much a study in the cruel absurdity of lust as a portrait of a soul in torment. The movie also is as cheap and as cheesy as its advertising campaign would suggest, and its method of revealing inner thoughts and the relentless voice of conscience is patently derivative of Eugene O'Neill's experimental play of 1927, *Strange Interlude* (filmed in 1932), and the Hecht & MacArthur film *Crime Without Passion* (1934). But in its reconciliation of mental anguish with a desperate physicality—often achieved with disturbingly surreal trick photography and expressionistic audio collages—*It's All in Your Mind* bespeaks a bold détente between the cinema of ideas and the cinema of sensationalism. The picture bears mentioning in the same breath with any of the better-respected films that have confronted the erotic obsession over the long haul, from Erich von Stroheim's *Foolish Wives* (1922) to Stanley Kubrick's *Eyes Wide Shut* (1999).

Mousy Byron Foulger—whom the casting profession considered the very embodiment of cartoonist H.V. Webster's famous Timid Soul, Caspar Milquetoast—plays Wilbur Crane, a trusted bookkeeper whose bullying wife (Betty Roadman) treats him only to insults and nagging. Crane's desire for feminine companionship is stoked by the idealized portraits of womanhood that are the stock-in-trade of the advertising agency where he works. Emboldened by advice from a ladies'-man illustrator, Crane proves a flop at flirting, only to find willing companionship in a brash blonde named Dorothy (Constance Bergen). Unaware that she is a tramp who pegs him as a first-class chump, Crane wipes out his savings and finally resorts to theft, led on by Dorothy's promise of a long-awaited night of passion. Having kept the affair a secret despite all the extravagances, Crane finds his overdue satisfaction undermined by fear of arrest. Finally, Dorothy and her convict lover ridicule him—driving Crane to an unaccustomed rage, which moves Dorothy to fork over the ill-gotten money. Crane is not yet out of the woods, though, and just as he is attempting to right his wrongdoing, the threat of detection drives him to a suicidal madness. Dorothy, taking pity, rescues Crane and saves his reputation in the process. Crane returns home, where he begins to see his wife in a more sympathetic light.

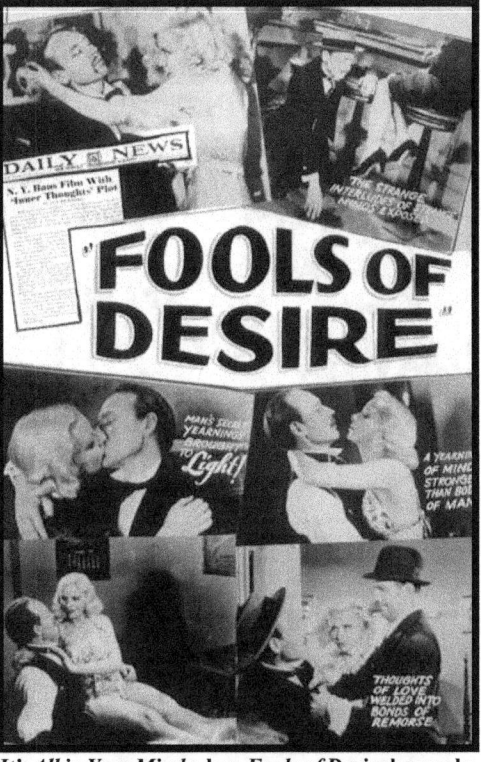

It's All in Your Mind a.k.a. *Fools of Desire* bespeaks a bold détente between the cinema of ideas and the cinema of sensationalism. (Photofest)

The moral lesson could scarcely be blunter, or the resolution more simplistic, but filmmaker Bernard B. Ray has fashioned here a study of gathering madness so complex as to obscure its rudimentary framework. Byron Foulger delivers a commanding performance that trades on his familiar screen personality—more commonly applied for comical purposes—even as it gradually reveals a self-loathing brute lurking beneath the bland surface. The naturalistic situation becomes engulfed with pure artifice as Foulger's troubled Wilbur Crane finds himself emotionally drawn and quartered: He is driven headlong by the forbidden urges of satyrism and simultaneously pulled back toward his hated state of normalcy. The voices that taunt and warn him may belong to his conscience, literalized, or they may be mere auditory hallucinations brought on by an overwhelming guilt. As Crane's self-control slips by vaguely perceptible degrees, director Ray wavers between subtlety and blatancy, augmenting the film's dense sound design with visual distortions that border on surrealism. These stylistic flourishes, coupled with Foulger's air of intensity, overshadow the supporting players. Constance Bergen seems precisely the type to drive a horny nerd to distraction, although her performance gets by on looks and attitude alone.

For a film that reeks of erotic exploitation, *It's All in Your Mind* plays out with a surprising degree of restraint and puritanical tastefulness. The flashes of nudity are as tantalizing to the viewer as they must be to Foulger's character. The unimaginative grindhouse audiences of the day must have felt cheated by Ray's having left so much to the imagination: *It's All in Your Mind* is indeed a strategic title.

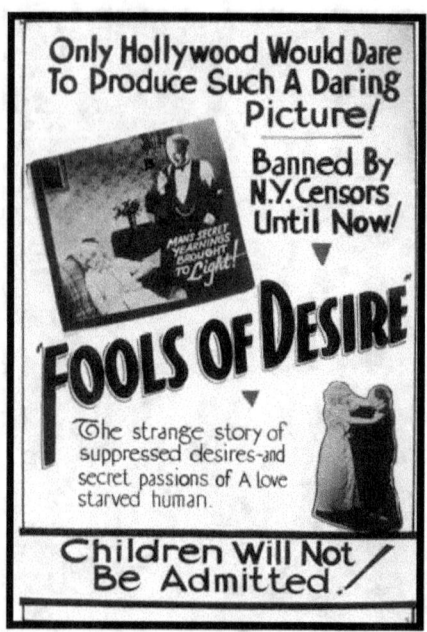

The censors' imaginations, conversely, kicked into overdrive: The Production Code Administration's Joseph I. Breen declared that he "knew" full well the meaning of the *It* in the title: "the libidinous desires of a sex-hungry, middle-aged accountant." The PCA withheld its Purity Seal, on grounds of "improper treatment of illicit sex." Breen insisted in a memo to Will H. Hays, president of the Motion Picture Producers & Distributors Association, that "the pretense of a psychological study...ought not to be taken seriously."

Whatever the connotations of *It*, the title proved of scant marquee value, and a rechristened *It's All in Your Mind* played the adults-only circuit well into the 1950s under a more titillating proxy title, *Fools of Desire*. Meanwhile, Byron Foulger—who had become a valued character man in 1937 via such films as *The Awful Truth*, *A Day at the Races* and *The Prisoner of Zenda*—became ever more popular as a specialist at portraying schemers, amusingly henpecked husbands and under-assertive nebbishes. One can only wonder how he might have regarded his star turn here, what with the mixed blessing of dramatic challenge and sleazy promotion, in the greater scheme of his career.

Bernard B. Ray (billed elsewhere as B.B. Ray) had been a busy producer/director in the realm of Depression-era Westerns and *Forgotten Horrors*-type pictures, with such credentials as *The Mystic Hour* (1934), English and Spanish-language versions of *Midnight Phantom* (1935) and Richard Talmadge's high-octane stunt opus *The Live Wire* (1935). Ray's output lessened to a picture a year during the late 1930s, and by the early '40s he had delivered two of PRC's more ambitious efforts, *Dangerous Lady* and *House of Errors*.

Its blatant exploitation only kept *It's All in Your Mind* out of the reach of those who might have taken it more seriously, the intellectuals' community and the Surrealist/Dadaist movements of the finer-arts world. The publicity strategy, ultimately self-defeating, cautioned theatre operators nearer the cultural mainstream: "Don't be afraid of the label 'sex picture'...This is a modern age, and hitherto subjects taboo for years are openly discussed in home and office. Take advantage of the modern liberalism, and let your patrons know that in this picture you have a new and novel piece of entertainment, possibly frank, but so finely handled they will have no cause to be embarrassed or ashamed...[T]o every adult, it is a picture that will linger long in one's memory, as a mere written description cannot describe [its] infinite beauty and daring entertainment."

And yes, right about here is where the publicists' hyperbole gets a tad thick—but still and all, the dark fascination of this hidden gem is undeniable. *It's All in Your Mind* is particularly noteworthy for its presaging of the quietly nightmarish style developed almost 50 years later by David Lynch. Lynch's *Blue Velvet* (1986) is a similarly puritanical, outwardly sensational fable that also concerns itself with a perfectly respectable, straight-arrow neo-Timid Soul who goes searching for forbidden kicks on the seamier side of existence.

CREDITS: Producer, Director and Screenwriter: Bernard B. Ray; Dialogue: Carl Krusada; Photographed by: Pliny Goodfriend; Special Effects: Ray Mercer; Editor: Robert Jahns; Music Composed, Arranged and Conducted by: Modést Altschuler; Sound: Glen Glenn; Production Manager: Leo Taub; Running Time: 63 Minutes; Released: Following Previews during March-April of 1938

CAST: Byron Foulger (Wilbur Crane); Constance Bergen (Dorothy); Martha Crane (Betty Roadman); Lynton Brent (Danny)

FURY BELOW
(J.E. Baum/George Mercader Productions)

Jim Cole, III (Russell Gleason) takes on the family trade of running a coal mine at just the right time to confront an underground mutiny. The nugget of horrific appeal at the core of this primitive effort is John Merton's impersonation of a driller driven mad by the dehumanizing nature of the work. Gleason is quite good as the ill-prepared youngster who rises to the occasion, but the truer heroism belongs to Rex Lease, as the supervisor who routs the bad guys. Speaking of whom, Mathew Betz is particularly memorable as a thug bent on making the takeover as violent as possible.

Fury Below was filmed late in 1936 under the title Hell Diggers, but the Production Code Administration demanded a rechristening. PCA chief Joseph I. Breen declared in a letter to producer George Mercader that the word Hell automatically disqualified the film for a Purity Seal.

CREDITS: Producer and Original Screenwriter: George R. Mercader; Director: Harry Fraser; Shooting Script: Phil Dunham; Photographed by: Paul Ivano; Editor: Arthur Brooks; Running Time: 67 Minutes; Released: Following New York Opening on March 11, 1938

CAST: Russell Gleason (Jim Cole, III); Maxine Doyle (Mary Norsen); LeRoy Mason (Fred Johnson); Sheila Terry (Claire Johnson); Matthew Betz (Dorsky); Rex Lease (Joe Norsen); John Merton (Emil); Ruth Frazer (Molly); Phil Dunham (Jim Cole, Sr.); Elliott Sullivan (Miner)

THE ADVENTURES OF CHICO
(Woodard Productions)

Though clearly intended as an educational entry and a heartwarmer for the family trade, this unusual documentary piece is also an unnervingly naturalistic examination of the lonely and perilous existence of a Central Mexican farmboy who communes with the desert's many species of wildlife. The influence of Rudyard Kipling's "Rikki-Tikki-Tavi" is patent, with a chapparal rooster and a rattlesnake subbing for Kipling's mongoose-vs.-cobra death match in a terrifying set-piece. The story finds Chico sheltering a nest of roadrunner hatchlings whose mother has been killed by a coyote. One of the flightless birds becomes devoted to the boy and at length saves him from a marauding rattlesnake. The attack and rescue are captured with a confrontational intimacy; the sequence yielded some of the most frequently used stock footage in the history of filmmaking, but of course the battle is best viewed in its original context.

Filmmakers Stacy Woodard and Horace Woodard were two-time Oscar winners (1933-1934) in the Motion Picture Academy's short-subject category. Stacy Woodard also had photographed Pare Lorentz' federally subsidized documentary feature, The River (1937), about catastrophic soil erosion in the Mississippi Basin. The now-sentimental, now-austere musical score that graces The Adventures of Chico is the work of the fine Hungarian composer, Dr. Edward Kilenyi, mentor to George Gershwin, veteran of silent-screen scoring and co-supervisor of the stirring orchestral score for the 1933 nature-amok epic, Deluge.

CREDITS: Producers, Directors, Writers, Photographers and Editors: Stacy and Horace Woodard; Musical Score: Dr. Edward Kilenyi; Running Time: 56 Minutes; Released: April 10, 1938

CAST: A native Central Mexican ensemble

Zamboanga deals with woman-hunting rivalries among the Moro Sea islanders of the Western Philippines. (Photofest)

ZAMBOANGA
(Filippine Film Productions, Inc./Grand National Films, Inc.)

Tribal nudity is conspicuously lacking in this account of woman-hunting rivalries among the Moro Sea islanders of the Western Philippines. The production outfit was Filipino-American, having been organized in Manila earlier in the decade by George F. Harris and Edward Tait. Musical scoring and the final cut were accomplished in Hollywood. The extensive use of Tagalog, the native language, required English subtitling.

The story suggests a broad template for Hal Roach's 1939-40 production of *One Million B.C.*, with the ruler of one island casting his sights on a princess of another and conspiring to abduct her—and the rest of the ladies, as long as he's about it—while the men of her clan are away on a pearl-diving expedition. The native players seem to have absorbed some silent-screen acting techniques from director Eduardo de Castro, with conspicuously Pickford-like mugging from the leading lady and a melodramatically clownish show of villainy from the abductor. Dr. Edward Kilenyi's musical score is quite prophetic, foreshadowing the tiki-lounge melodic conceits of the mid-century jazz-pop artists Martin Denny and Les Baxter.

CREDITS: Presented by: Edward L. Alperson; Producers: George F. Harris and Edward Tait; Director: Eduardo de Castro; Photographed by: William H. Jansen; Editor: Ralph Dixon; Musical Score: Dr. Edward Kilenyi; Recording Engineer: Louis R. Morse; Running Time: Originally 110 Minutes, Cut to 65 Minutes for Release; Released: April 15, 1938

CAST: Frederick Lindsey (Narrator); Hadji-Razul (Himself)

TOPA TOPA
a.k.a.: KILLERS OF THE WILD; CHILDREN OF THE WILD
(Pennant Pictures Corp./Fine Arts Pictures)

Not even the great Rin Tin Tin ever got to make such a wild wonder-dog thriller as *Topa Topa*, which stars the mighty—and mighty friendly—Silver Wolf. The camera-savvy Shepherd/wolf mix had performed a crucial supporting part as a furry red herring in the 1936 old-dark-house shocker *The Rogues Tavern*. In this more prominent role, the dog upstages all concerned as a half-wild creature wrongly branded a man-killer.

Trapper Joe Morton (Trevor Bardette) is slain by his partner, Pete Taylor (LeRoy Mason), who mutilates the corpse with the teeth of a wolf carcass. Fangs (Silver Wolf), Joe's loyal pet, escapes into the woods with a bounty on his head. Taylor knows that Fangs will return for vengeance, so he starts a fire in the underbrush to trap the wolf-dog. The inevitable forest fire distracts the villagers. Scientist Jim Turner (James Bush) finds the bloodied wolf-pelt.

It gets crazier: Pete, heedless of the havoc he has already caused, steals a nestful of eaglets, intending to train the birds as hunters. Morton's little girl, Jill (Jill L'Estrange, daughter of co-producer Dick L'Estrange), is playing nearby when the mother eagle attacks—carrying Jill away. Jim and Pete, who have been bitter rivals for the affections of Morton's niece, Margaret (Joan Valerie), unite to rescue the child. Fangs, lurking in the woods, forces Pete into a fatal fall. The dog locates the eagle's nest—drives away the mother bird—rescues the child—and then brings his born-wild pups back home with him.

Some fun—and all in just over an hour! *Less* than an hour in other versions, which trickled out at intervals into the 1940s. The *Motion Picture Herald* represented the picture as a 1939 Grand National release called *Children of the Wild*, and later as a 1940 Grand National called *Killers of the Wild*. The confusion seems less confusing when it is considered that Fine Arts Pictures had absorbed Grand National in a salvage-job merger during 1938.

By whatever title, whenever it might have happened to play *your* neck of the woods, *Topa Topa* is a raggedy winner that belongs on practically anybody's list of Great Canine Adventures—with the bonus of a co-director job by that grandmaster of the silent serials, Charles "Hurricane Hutch" Hutchison. Source-author Charles Diltz' cutting of the action sequences is dead-on-the-money exciting.

CREDITS: Producers: Dick L'Estrange, William M. Vogel and William Steiner; Director: Vin Moore and Charles Hutchison; Scenarist and Editor: Charles Diltz; Adaptation: Hilda May Young; Continuity: Arthur Hoerl; Photographed by: Robert Doran; Musical Director: Dr. Edward Kilenyi; Songs: Rudy Sooter; Sound: Corson Jowett; Running Time: 65 Minutes (as *Children of the Wild*, 58 Minutes; as *Killers of the Wild*, 57 Minutes); Released: April 16, 1938

CAST: Silver Wolf (Fangs); Joan Valerie (Margaret Weston); James Bush (Jim Turner); LeRoy Mason (Pete Taylor); Ruth Coleman (Laura Morton); Jill L'Estrange (Jill Morton); Trevor Bardette (Joe Morton); Fred Santley (Chuck Foster); Lyons Wickland (Coroner); Goldie (Eagle); and Helen Hughes, Patsy Moran

WAJAN
a.k.a.: SON OF A WITCH; SINS OF BALI
(Tomfilms, Inc.)

Some mumbo-jumbo about a Balinese conjurer's curse motivates the limited mayhem and frenzied romance of this goona-goona travelogue, which feigns a cultural authenticity for the sake of a fair amount of Third World titillation. From its lurid pun of a proxy title to its emphasis on a mock-tribalistic shimmy dance, *Wajan* is purely cynical exploitation. There is a "plot"—*skit* is more like it—involving a forbidden romance, and the rival "gods" of "good" and "evil" put in token appearances, but the greater point is ogling, plain and simple.

CREDITS: "An Account of the Expedition by Dr. Frederick Dalsheim and Victor Baron von Plessan"; Director: Curator Walter Spies "of the Bali Museum"; "Authenticated" by: Walter Spies and Gdeh Ray, Governor General; Musical Score: Wolfgang Zeller; Running Time: 70 Minutes; Released: April 16, 1938

CAST: "Native Cast Picked from Families in Government Service"—Nodonk (Witch); Wajan (Son of Witch); Sari (Son's Sweetheart); Lombos (Her Father); Borang (God of Good); Rangda (God of Evil)

LIFE RETURNS
(ScienArt Pictures/Universal Pictures)

In May of 1934, in Berkeley, California, Dr. Robert Cornish and a small team of researchers announced that they had restored life to a dog whose death Cornish had caused by clinical means. This canine *Frankenstein* episode, a supposed breakthrough that seems to have led no further, was bolstered in turn by motion-picture footage, presented as a document of the experiment.

True or false? No one seems capable of saying, beyond Cornish's obviously self-interested account. Cornish later was denied access to the bodies of executed criminals in attempts to further his research, and he seems to have abandoned the cause. In any event, the early declaration of success inspired an ambitious dilettante filmmaker, Dr. Eugen Frenke, to develop a heart-tugging science-fictional soap opera around the remarkable but rather dry clinical case.

Life Returns is a poorly made but nonetheless fascinating relic of a short-lived *cause celébre*. Though by no means a horror film, it pertains to the genre because of the very topic—to say nothing of the presence of Valerie Hobson, of 1935's *Bride of Frankenstein*, and Onslow Stevens, who only several years later would play a Frankenstein-styled physician-turned-vampire in *House of Dracula* (1945).

The dramatic set-up is a monotonous exercise in which Cornish himself, Stevens and Lois Wilson play medical students seeking to conquer death. Stevens breaks with his friends on a maverick whim and finds himself courted by a big-time research laboratory and then rejected as a crackpot. Just when it seems matters cannot grow any worse, he is confronted with the death of his wife, played by Miss Hobson.

***Life Returns* value lies in its inadvertent suggestion that all those fictional mad doctors might have something on the ball, after all. (Photofest)**

Frenke and his co-scenarists unwisely resisted the obvious temptation to have the scientist resurrect his better half. A juvenile-delinquency subplot, involving Stevens' rebellious son (George Breakston) and his pet dog, brings the radical theories back into play when the pooch runs afoul of the local dogcatcher (Stanley Fields) and is gassed. This is the melodramatic set-up for the insertion of the Cornish lab footage, which leads to a happy—or at least hopeful—ending for all concerned.

There was no happy ending for *Life Returns*, which Universal had bankrolled to the tune of approximately $40,000 in 1934 but then pronounced "not suitable for the regular Universal Program" following ill-received preview showings, according to one trade-publication account. Dr. Frenke had been announced as director of a Tolstoi adaptation, *Father Sergius*, but wound up instead helming *Life Returns*, from his own scenario, after the big studio had become apprehensive about censorship problems with *Sergius*. Strategically threatening legal action against Universal, Frenke managed by 1935 to re-mount *Life Returns* for release under the ScienArt Pictures banner. The copyright notice contains no mention of Universal—but surviving prints still bear the Universal end-scroll under the famous heading, "A Good Cast Is Worth Repeating." Nothing happened in the way of distribution until 1938, which brought a limited release.

Seldom has such fuss been made over so insignificant a picture; today, the matter would be settled cheaply and efficiently with a direct-to-video release.

Its obvious flaws aside, *Life Returns* has met unfairly, nonetheless, with a measure of wrongheaded kvetching. We've witnessed some harrowing rants from the more single-minded souls among horror-movie buffs about the film's utter (and deliberate) lack of shock value and overt megalomania—as though the cinema hadn't enough of those qualities in innumerable other pictures! Plain insipidity is the greater problem here. The picture's truer value lies in its inadvertent suggestion that all those fictional mad doctors, from Mrs. Shelley's celebrated novel to Hollywood's Poverty Row, might have something on the ball, after all.

CREDITS: Producer: Lou Ostrow; Director: Dr. Eugen Frenke; Story: Dr. Eugen Frenke and James Hogan; Screenplay: Arthur Herman and John F. Goodrich; Photographed by: Robert Planck; Art Director: Ralph Berger; Editor: Harry Marker; Musical Score: Oliver Wallace and Clifford Vaughan; Sound Engineer: Richard Tyler; Running Time: 62 Minutes; Produced: During September of 1934 for Universal, but Denied Release; Distributed by: ScienArt Pictures in Limited Release, Beginning June 10, 1938

CAST: Dr. Robert E. Cornish (Himself); Onslow Stevens (Dr. John Kendrick); Lois Wilson (Dr. Louise Stone); George Breakston (Danny); Valerie Hobson (Mrs. Kendrick); Stanley Fields (Dogcatcher); Frank Reicher (Dr. James); Richard Carle (Arnold); Dean Benton (Intern); Lois January (Nurse); Richard Quine (Mickey); Mario Margutti, William Black, Ralph Celmar, and Roderick Krida (Colleagues of Dr. Cornish)

"DICK TRACY" REDACTUS: IN APPRECIATION OF THE REPUBLIC SERIALS

Republic hit the ground running on May 28, 1938, with *The Fighting Devil Dogs*, a Marine Corps buddy picture writ large, with Lee Powell and Herman Brix all set to save the world from a villain who brandishes manufactured thunderbolts. The prompt follow-through, *Dick Tracy Returns* (August 20, 1938), recaptures well the thrall of terror of the first *Tracy* (1937), with title player Ralph Byrd pitted against a criminal family (headed by Charles Middleton) whose rampages—shown in a convincing mock-newsreel format that probably influenced the establishing moments of Orson Welles' *Citizen Kane* (1941)—pretty well define our often-invoked notion of "the true horror of the public enemy." *Dick Tracy's G-Men* followed on September 2, 1939, with Byrd on the trail of Irving Pichel, as a condemned menace who outlasts a turn in the gas chamber to wreak 15 chapters' worth of bloody mayhem. Byrd came back in fine square-jawed form for *Dick Tracy vs. Crime, Inc.* (1941) to battle an invisibility-prone evildoer called the Ghost, whose repertoire includes a tidal wave (courtesy of stock footage from 1933's *Deluge*) aimed smack at New York.

We lavished considerable microscopic attention on the earliest Republic chapter-plays in *Forgotten Horrors: The Definitive Edition*, and we have continued that tack more selectively in this overlapping sequel, singling out such championship cliffhanger horrors as *S O S Coast Guard*, *Adventures of Captain Marvel* and *Drums of Fu Manchu*, as well as those SF-laced rip-snorters *Robinson Crusoe of Clipper Island* and *Spy Smasher*. The overriding tone of the serials by the late 1930s, however, had evolved to exploit the traditional element of weird menace more as a whipping-boy for rampant heroism than as an unadulterated *raison d'etre*.

Then, too, the handiness of most of the Republic serials in slick video editions has rendered such stunt-action/special-effects epics significantly less obscure than they used to be. These handsome packages may not surface in stacks 30-deep on the hot-rental shelf at your neighborhood Schlockbuster Video Emporium, but one seldom needs to search far or wide to find them.

In addition to those that we have trotted out, here, in full-dress regalia, we offer herewith a historical context for the serial as a class—along with our short list of recommended favorites from the long haul of Republic, 1938-55.

If Erich von Stroheim had thought to mount his cumbersome masterwork, *Greed* (1923-25), as a serial, he might at once have saved himself abundant grief—finding the film ordered whittled, in painful stages, from a 42-reel, hours-at-a-sitting exercise to a manageable 10-reel cut—and even raised the grammar of the serial idiom to something nearer fine literature. But the serials were never particularly concerned with the emotional depth or the psychosexual obsessions that drove Stroheim's art.

By the 1920s, the serials were an established crowd-pleasing form, having branched off France's continuing-adventure style of filmmaking to reach the U.S. by the 1910s. A forerunner, Edison's *What Happened to Mary?* (1912) ran simultaneously on the big screen and on the printed page, as a moving picture in monthly episodes and as continued-next-issue chapters in *McClure's Ladies World* magazine. A truer serial format, with a tantalizing cliffhanger peril closing each episode, came in the Selig group's *The Adventures of Kathlyn* (1913-14). A more rigid standardization kicked in with 1914's *The Perils of Pauline*, a 20-chapter hair-raiser that brought stardom to Pearl White. The world record for chapter-play running time rests with *The Hazards of Helen*, whose 119 episodes graced the screen from late 1914 into 1917.

France, as the wellhead of the idiom, invigorated the form with the serial-like *Fantomas* adventures in 1913 and the prototypical miniseries *Les Vampires* (1915), with its memorably anagrammed name for a menacing character, Irma Vep. Germany, too, dabbled in serialized excitement. But America remained dominant, losing momentum when the talking-picture revolution of the late 1920s posed audio-control problems in outdoor shooting—and then rapidly compensating by remembering the serials' action-over-talk imperative. Universal's *Flash Gordon* (1936) approached epic-scale production values, with a three-times-average $350,000 production tab and the star-calibre presence of Buster Crabbe. Upstart Republic, however, delivered comparable polish on lesser budgets, and its serials are more vividly remembered today than those of Universal or Columbia, the major leagues' preeminent cliffhanger factories. When the industrywide serial machinery finally creaked its last in 1956, the swan-song entry from Columbia was assigned a title, *Blazing the Overland Trail*, that is bitterly evocative of the corporate slogan of that pioneering serial studio, Mascot: "Blazing the Trail."

Conventional wisdom holds that the serial held its strongest appeal for the juvenile audience, but during the 1950s and '60s we found many (then) old-timers who had reveled in the cliffhangers as young adults. In the present day, many (now) middle-agers and (now) old-timers still cling to the serials as something more than cherished totems of childhood. The discerning viewer, of whatever generation, has always found more to admire about the serials than the standard simplistic plot with its superficial complications; the frequent cheating as to the identity of the principal heavy; the hair's-breadth rescues and near-constant slugfests and chases; and the dime-a-dozen Machiavellian schemes to enslave the civilized and/or uncivilized world.

Much of the deeper charm rests, no doubt, with the technical advancements that the serials—and Republic in particular—brought to the greater scheme of cinema. That quality figures in our chapter on *S O S Coast Guard* (see 1937), and a great deal more of it has been researched in depth by our friend Jan Alan Henderson, in a survey of the work of effects wizards Howard and Theodore Lydecker for the December 1991 issue of *The American Cinematographer*. It can scarcely be reckoned a coincidence that George Turner served as editor of *Cinematographer* from the 1980s on into the '90s.

Late in 1935, as Jan Henderson tells it, after Republic was created through a leveraged merger of Mascot, the Depression-era Monogram, Majestic, Liberty and Herbert J. Yates' Consolidated Film Industries, Mascot artist Howard summoned his brother Ted from Idaho, where Ted was working as a cowboy. The final Mascot serial, *The Fighting Marines*, came out via Republic—and featured Howard's dynamic flying-wing aircraft, a convincing and prophetic miniature that would also figure in two of Republic's own serials.

"In 1936, Republic produced the first of its 66 serials, *Darkest Africa*, with Clyde Beatty," writes Henderson. "This was a showcase for the Lydeckers' special-effects mastery. Miniature jungle cities, flying bat-men, volcanoes and earthquakes, along with Clyde Beatty's world-famous lion taming, made *Darkest Africa* most satisfying Saturday-matinee fare... filled with thrills, chills, excitement, and the Lydeckers' first flying dummies, both full-scale and miniature."

The closing of Republic in 1959 sent the Lydeckers on their separate ways. Howard worked on *Voyage to the Bottom of the Sea* (1961) and its teevee spin-off, winning an Emmy; and on *It's a Mad, Mad, Mad, Mad World* (1962) and the teleseries *Lost in Space*. Ted landed briefly at Disney, then at Universal, delivering the miniature avian-menace models for Hitchcock's *The Birds* (1963) and working on *The Andromeda Strain* (1971). Ted complained that he found the new generation of stunt players

less cooperative—and less predisposed to collaboration—than their artistic ancestors at Republic. Howard Lydecker died in 1969, Ted in 1991. As Henderson tells it: "Their pioneering, larger-than-miniature models, often photographed in natural light, provided the blueprint for the Lucas-Spielberg school of special effects."

The Lydeckers do not consistently receive screen credit for their work, which is nonetheless ever-present in the Republic serials. Speaking of which, these additional titles stand out as holding particular interest for the science-fantasy/horror-movie audience:
- **1938:** *Hawk of the Wilderness*
- **1939:** *Daredevils of the Red Circle* and *Zorro's Fighting Legion*
- **1940:** *King of the Royal Mounties* and *Mysterious Dr. Satan*
- **1941:** *Jungle Girl*
- **1942:** *Perils of Nyoka* and *King of the Mounties*
- **1943:** *G-Men vs. The Black Dragon*, *Secret Service in Darkest Africa* and *The Masked Marvel*
- **1944:** *Captain America*, *The Tiger Woman* and *Haunted Harbor*
- **1945:** *Manhunt of Mystery Island*, *Federal Operator 99* and *The Purple Monster Strikes*
- **1946:** *King of the Forest Rangers*, *Daughter of Don Q* and *The Crimson Ghost*
- **1947:** *The Black Widow*
- **1949:** *Federal Agents vs. Underworld, Inc.*, *Ghost of Zorro* and *King of the Rocket Men*
- **1950:** *Radar Patrol vs. Spy King* and *The Invisible Monster*
- **1951:** *Flying Disc Man from Mars* and *Government Agents vs. Phantom Legion*
- **1952:** *Radar Men from the Moon* and *Zombies of the Stratosphere*
- **1953:** *Jungle Drums of Africa* and *Canadian Mounties vs. Atomic Invaders*
- **1955:** *Panther Girl of the Kongo*

DURANGO VALLEY RAIDERS
(Supreme Pictures Corp./Republic Pictures Corp.)

Masked marauder time again, back at the old corral. This relic, old-fashioned even for its time, was cranked out by Sam Newfield for A.W. Hackel's Supreme Pictures, which sold it to product-hungry Republic Pictures. The yarn turns on a villain known as the Shadow, who is not only a brigand but also a polyvictim perpetrator of some ungodly ferocity. Bob Steele is right at home as a wanderer with the unlikely name of Keene Cordner, whose father, Boone (Steve Clark), had been a *compadre* of rancher Mac McKay (Karl Hackett). Mac hires Keene as foreman. In a serious turn of events, Keene is not only accused of being the Shadow—but also *becomes* the Shadow, for the sake of ferreting out the real Shadow, who years ago had sundered the partnership of Mac and Boone. The Shadow, meanwhile, is plotting to massacre his own gang, every last one of 'em. Unmasked as the local sheriff (Forrest Taylor), the Shadow is killed by Lobo (Ted Adams), his second-in-command.

Cram-packed with action and played through clenched teeth by Steele and villains Ted Adams and Forrest Taylor, *Durango Valley Raiders* is a slight but welcome reminder of the earlier 1930s' more ferocious Westerns, including *Under Texas Skies* and the Ken Maynard classic *Tombstone Canyon*.

CREDITS: Producer: A.W. Hackel; Director: Sam Newfield; Screenplay: George H. Plympton; Story: Harry F. Olmstead; Photographed by: Robert Cline; Sound Technician: Clifford Ruberg; Production Manager: Jerome S. Bresler; Running Time: 56 Minutes; Released: August 22, 1938

CAST: Bob Steele (Keene Cordner); Louise Stanley (Betty McKay); Karl Hackett (John "Mac" McKay); Ted Adams (Lobo); Forrest Taylor (Sheriff Devlin); Steve Clark (Boone Cordner); Horace Murphy (Matt Tanner); Jack Ingram (Slade)

IT HAPPENED IN CHICAGO
(General Film Laboratory of Chicago/The Chicago *Daily Times*)

This borderline mad-doctor yarn is worth noting for its (hardly sensationalistic) presaging of the role that Boris Karloff would play only two years later in Monogram Pictures' production of *The Ape* (see our 1940 section). The featurette is strictly a homegrown semiprofessional effort, featuring unknown talents in the tale of a banished physician (Charles Hughes) who retreats to the basement of his household to continue a maverick quest to cure polio. (The notion was, of course, science fiction at the time.) The doctor's son (Lawrence Ulrich) becomes infected via a laboratory monkey, and the doctor is forced to call upon the medical community that had abandoned him. Everything's going to be all right now, or so the film assures us. Local notices were charitable, and the film surprisingly attracted the Hollywood tradepapers' attention—but *It Happened in Chicago* seems never to have happened to find much of an audience anywhere else.

CREDITS: Sponsor: The Chicago *Daily Times*; Producer: Irving Yates; Director: Clark Willis; Running Time: 22 Minutes; Released: Aug. 26, 1938, in an Exclusive Chicago Run

CAST: Donna Lacher (Hope Martin); Walter Schumacher (Tom Carleigh); Charles Hughes (Dr. Martin); Lawrence Ulrich (Freddy Martin); Mary Tappendorf (Mrs. Martin); Vincent Gottschalk (J. Winn Carleigh); Charles Wilson (Gramps); William Joy (Dr. Carlsen); Lewis Prentiss (Dr. Prentiss); Dorothy Stevens (Switchboard Operator); Lewis Myers, Jr. (Intern); Roemar Feeley (State's Attorney); Jerome Greenberg (Detective); Otto Ackerman (Butler); Patsy Wright (Girl); Minta MacDonald (Guest)

THE NIGHT HAWK
(Republic Pictures Corp.)

Tough-guy sentimentality mingles uneasily with a queasy conspiracy to hijack an iron lung in this newspaperman-vs.-gangsters yarn. There is an oasis of horrific impact, amid that long dry spell for out-and-out horror movies, in a sadistic attempt to kill the hero, Robert Livingston, with blasts of steam while he is trapped in the cargo hold of a ship.

Livingston, relieved from *Three Mesquiteers* series duty by the arrival of John Wayne, is as dynamic as ever as a reporter who leads an adventurous life outside the newsroom while romancing June Travis on the side.

The big crime is a sick one, indeed: Mobsters with a grudge against Robert Armstrong—playing a tender-hearted tough guy who runs a seamy nightspot—steal an iron lung destined for Armstrong's dying younger brother (Billy Burrud), then demand a hefty sum for the return of the breathing tank. Livingston foils the plot by sneaking inside the life-saving machine; steals the gang's hauler in a hail of lead; incidentally cracks a confounding murder case and a booze-smuggling racket while he's at it; scoops the competing news-hacks; and gets himself trapped like a steamed lobster in the whiskey ship. It's rather a bit much for only an hour-and-change, but all turns out well for all who deserve it.

Livingston is as able a romancer as he is a battler, and Miss Travis makes plenty of her too little time on screen. Armstrong, in a welcome return to the screen following a year's absence, does well by his character's conflicting traits of kindliness and sleaziness. Joseph Downing is the meanest of an evil lot of hoodlums. Billy Burrud is a bit too plucky as the disabled youth. Dwight Frye has a surprisingly small background role.

CREDITS: Associate Producer: Herman Schlom; Director: Sidney Salkow; Screenplay: Earl Felton; Photographed by: Jack Marta; Art Director: John Victor Mackay; Assistant Director: Phil Ford; Editor: Ernest Nims; Supervising Editor: Murray Seldeen; Costumes: Irene Saltern; Musical Director: Cy Feuer; Song: "Never a Dream Goes By," by Walter Kent, Manny Kurtz & Al Sherman; Production Manager: Al Wilson; Running Time: 63 Minutes; Released: October 1, 1938

CAST: Robert "Bob" Livingston (Slim Torrence); June Travis (Della Parrish); Robert Armstrong (Charlie McCormick); Ben Welden (Otto Miller); Lucien Littlefield (Parrish); Joseph Downing (Lefty); Roland L. Got (Willie Sing); Cy Kendall (Capt. Teague); Paul Fix (Spider); Billy Burrud (Bobby McCormick); Charles Wilson (Lonigan); Dwight Frye (John Colley); Paul McVey (Larsen); Robert Homans (Mulrooney)

THE KARLOFF "MR. WONG" PICTURES
(Monogram Pictures Corp.)

With his meat-and-potatoes genre, the unapologetic horror film, on official hiatus with the studios, Boris Karloff retrenched to more generalized character roles, such as had been his lot as a working actor during the years before *Frankenstein*. "Any old port in the proverbial storm," Karloff told us in 1968. "The tactic was to keep one's *name* in the view of the public and the studios, even if it meant diminished circumstances. Now, Monogram was hardly as bad as all that—even though they *weren't* Universal, of course—and I took Monogram's *Mr. Wong* series gratefully."

"*Mr. Wong* meant a holiday from bogeyman typecasting—and you should know, I've always been severely *mixed* about that typecasting, appreciative and yet rather painfully aware of its limitations—but it also promised me a short enough holding pattern until such time as the public's thwarted desire for some spanking-new, good old-fashioned scares would once again be honored. I rather enjoyed being Mr. Wong, but I was also glad to be reprieved, to be allowed to wrap up my little pact with Monogram with one of those good old-fashioned chillers."

Karloff hardly took the assignment cavalierly, however eager he might eventually have become to be done with the series. Upon his signing with Monogram, Karloff wrote to his brother Sir John Thomas Pratt, a diplomat with the British Foreign Office, requesting photographs of cultured Chinese citizens. These—particularly, the face of one of Sir John's servants, who had become a casualty of combat during the Sino-Japanese War—provided Karloff and makeup artist Gordon Bau with suggestions for the countenance and bearing of Mr. Wong. The makeup required two hours to apply.

A rundown on the Karloff entries follows herewith. For the series' distinctive exit, and for Karloff's welcome escape hatch from the Monogram deal, see *Phantom of Chinatown* and *The Ape* in our 1940 section.

MR. WONG, DETECTIVE (1938):
In an auspicious beginning for a modest and uneven series, celebrated detective James Lee Wong (Karloff) is summoned too late to prevent the murder of San Francisco industrialist Simon Dayton (John Hamilton). The likeliest culprit is a surly inventor named Roemer (John St. Polis). Wong, unconvinced in view of reports that Roemer had threatened Dayton with a gun, finds shards of a glass vessel. An autopsy establishes that

Dayton was killed by poisonous gas. Suspects and slayings multiply, and finally Wong traps Roemer into betraying himself as a foreign agent by confronting him with one of the fragile spheres.

Director William Nigh strikes an uncharacteristically suspenseful tone and pace here, and Karloff lends Mr. Wong the right measures of Asian patience, British demeanor and relentless-cop severity—far more inventive a presence than the imitation-*Charlie Chan* franchise that Monogram had anticipated in securing the rights to Hugh Wiley's *Collier's* magazine series. Grant Withers is a winner as a slow-on-the-uptake police officer, whose rank and christened name vary from adventure to adventure. Monogram would eventually pick up the *Charlie Chan* series from 20th Century-Fox, and indeed the 1947 *Docks of New Orleans*, starring Roland Winters as Chan, is a desultory remake of *Mr. Wong, Detective.*

CREDITS: In Charge of Production: Scott R. Dunlap; Associate Producer: William Lackey; Director: William Nigh; Screenplay: Houston Branch; Based upon: Characters Created by Hugh Wiley; Photographed by: Harry Neumann; Assistant Director: W.B. Eason; Editor: Russell Schoengarth; Musical Director: Abe Meyer; Recording Engineer: Karl Zint; Technical Director: E.R. Hickson; Production Manager: C.J. Bigelow; Running Time: 70 Minutes; Released: Following Copyright Date of October 5, 1938

CAST: Boris Karloff (James Lee Wong); Grant Withers (Capt. Sam Street); Maxine Jennings (Myra Ross); Evelyn Brent (Olga); George Lloyd (Devlin); Lucien Prival (Anton Mohl); John St. Polis (Carl Roemer); William Gould (Theodore Meisle); Hooper Atchley (Christian Wilk); John Hamilton (Simon Dayton); Wilbur Mack (Russell); Lee Tong Foo [Elsewhere: Lee Tung Foo] (Tchin); and Lynton Brent, Grace Wood, Frank Bruno

THE MYSTERY OF MR. WONG (1939): *Mr. Wong, Detective* had turned out so surprisingly well that expectations ran unreasonably high for this second entry. The plot—somewhat derivative of 1932's *Murder at Midnight*—turns on the theft of an accursed, priceless jewel from China. The thief, an unscrupulous collector (Morgan Wallace), is the first to get croaked. Mr. Wong investigates, along with his San Francisco policeman colleague, Detective Sgt. Street (Withers). Wong has a beef with Stroganoff (Ivan Lebedeff), a sinister Russian, but other suspects and other slayings abound. In a ceremonial gathering of suspects, the master detective methodically clears all but one: the vengeful former brother-in-law (Holmes Herbert) of the first victim. The historic gem, whose accursed condition has been the reddest of red herrings, is returned to the Chinese people.

Director Nigh holds down the fort but only just, leaving it to Karloff and Grant Withers—whose witty character has one of the more uneven careers in the annals of law enforcement—to carry the story through some unnecessarily vague detours and *cul-de-sacs*. Holmes Herbert makes a sympathetic wrongdoer, and Ivan Lebedeff is eminently suspicious as a character meant to keep the audience distracted. The lovely Lotus Long weighs in as a recurring victim within the series, an accusing voice silenced by a poisoned cigarette.

Karloff and Bela Lugosi had by now completed Universal's *Son of Frankenstein*, which went into release barely two months before this second series entry. Even so, a contract was a contract, and Karloff had a Wong way yet to go.

CREDITS: In Charge of Production: Scott R. Dunlap; Associate Producer: William Lackey; Director: William Nigh; Screenplay: Scott Darling; Based upon: Characters Created by Hugh Wiley; Photographed by: Harry Neumann; Assistant Director: W.B. Eason; Editor: Russell Schoengarth; Wardrobe: Louis Brown; Musical Director: Edward Kay; Recording Engineer: Karl Zint; Technical Director: E.R. Hickson; Production Manager: Charles J. Bigelow; Running Time: 67 Minutes; Released: March 8, 1939

CAST: Boris Karloff (James Lee Wong); Grant Withers (Detective Sgt. Street); Dorothy Tree (Valerie Edwards); Craig Reynolds (Peter Harrison); Ivan Lebedeff (Stroganoff); Holmes Herbert (Prof. Ed Janney); Morgan Wallace (Brandon Edwards); Lotus Long (Drina); Chester Gan (Sing); Lee Tong Foo (Willie); Hooper Atchley (Carslake); and Bruce Wong, Jack Kennedy, Joe Devlin, Wilbur Mack, Dick Morehead

MR. WONG IN CHINATOWN (1939): Mr. Wong is appalled to learn that Lin Hwa (Lotus Long), a Chinese princess, has been murdered while a guest in his home. Wong determines that the princess was on a mission to buy armaments for China. Her bank credit has been drained through forgery. The princess' attendants are slain in turn, and Wong and banker Davidson (Huntly Gordon) are captured by two of the likelier suspects (Peter George Lynn and William Royle). Wong's police-force comrade, Inspector Street (Grant Withers), comes to the rescue—and Wong unmasks Davidson as the forger *and* the slayer.

William Nigh is fast running out of steam here, and despite a generous deployment of culprits and crimes, the picture mostly just sits there waiting for Karloff to turn up the next lead. Grant Withers helps, of course, with a portrayal that is by turns indecisive and determined. Marjorie Reynolds' portrayal of a news reporter is energetic, and accurate to the profession. The yarn would be recycled as a *Charlie Chan* entry, *The Chinese Ring* (1947).

CREDITS: In Charge of Production: Scott R. Dunlap; Associate Producer: William T. Lackey; Director: William Nigh; Screenplay: Scott Darling; Based upon: Hugh Wiley's Characters; Photographed by: Harry Neumann; Assistant Director: W.B. Eason; Editor: Russell Schoengarth; Wardrobe: Louis Brown; Musical Director: Edward Kay; Sound Engineer: Karl Zint; Technical Director: E.R. Hickson; Production Manager: Charles Bigelow; Running Time: 70 Minutes; Released: August 1, 1939

CAST: Boris Karloff (James Lee Wong); Grant Withers (Inspector Street); Marjorie Reynolds (Bobby Logan); Peter George Lynn (Capt. Guy Jackson); William Royle (Capt. Jalme); Huntly Gordon (Davidson); James Flavin (Sgt. Jerry); Lotus Long (Princess Lin Hwa); Richard Loo (Elderly Chinese); Bessie Loo (Lilly May); Lee Tong Foo (Willie); "Little Angelo" [Rossitto] (Dwarf); Guy Usher (Commissioner); and Ernie Stanton

THE FATAL HOUR (1940): For the continuity hounds in the audience, the bigger mystery here might involve how Grant Withers' Capt. Sam Street of the opening picture had changed to Inspector, to Detective Sergeant, and now to Capt. Bill Street. Which can only fall under the category of Never You Mind. A Street by any other name or rank would be just as honked off to learn that a brother officer has been slain in the line of duty.

Street and Mr. Wong tear into the case, finding a rare Oriental carving that can only be a clue and obtaining help from Marjorie Reynolds' regular character, reporter Bobbie Logan. Everything points to a crooked gambler (Frank Puglia), a smuggler (Craig Reynolds) and a small epidemic of murders—all committed with a single gun. Finally, a perfectly respectable financier (Charles Trowbridge) with ties to all concerned is unmasked when he throws down on Mr. Wong. Bobbie rescues the "Chinese copper," and Street captures the murderer. A trifle except for the sake of completeness, this one does feature a fair share of mysterious skulking and a rare show of impatience from Karloff, who seems ready to break character and walk at any moment. Or maybe that's just our perception.

CREDITS: Vice President in Charge of Production: Scott R. Dunlap; Producer: William T. Lackey; Director: William Nigh; Screenplay: Scott Darling; Story: Joseph West; Based upon: the *James Lee Wong* Stories in *Collier's* Magazine, as Created by Hugh Wiley; Photographed by: Harry Neumann; Editor: R.F. Schoengarth; Wardrobe: Louis Brown; Musical Director: Edward Kay; Sound Recording: Karl Zint, Western Electric; Technical Director: E.R. Hickson; Production Manager: Charles L. Bigelow; Running Time: 67 Minutes; Released: January 15, 1940

A classic bit of Karloffian body language brightens the actor's sustained impersonation of Mr. Wong in *Mr. Wong Detective.*

CAST: Boris Karloff (James Lee Wong); Marjorie Reynolds (Bobby Logan); Grant Withers (Capt. Bill Street); Charles Trowbridge (Forbes); John Hamilton (Belden, Sr.); Craig Reynolds (Belden, Jr.); Jack Kennedy (Mike); Lita Cheveret (Tanya); Frank Puglia (Hardway); I. Stanford Jolley (Soapy); Jason Robards (Griswold); Pauline Drake (Bessie)

DOOMED TO DIE (1940): The adventures of James Lee Wong were nearing their end as a movie commodity when Karloff puttered through this aimless effort. The time was nigh to put aside the sleuthing. With his Monogram contract yet to play out, however, Karloff found that some adjustments were in order—about which, more in our entries on *The Ape* and *Phantom of Chinatown*.

Doomed To Die is a nonetheless likable mess about the slaying of a cargo-ship tycoon and a stolen fortune in bogus securities. Everyone is under suspicion, as usual, and only Karloff's Mr. Wong can sort things out. He must resort, of course, to clues that Ralph Bettison's screenplay has scarcely bothered to show the audience.

No sooner has magnate Cyrus Wentworth's mansion been destroyed by fire—some nicely deployed stock footage of the headline-making Morro Castle conflagration—than Wentworth (Melvyn Lang) finds himself in a bitter argument with his chief competitor, Fleming (Guy Usher), over a plan to merge their companies via marriage. Wentworth's murder is a foregone conclusion, and Mr. Wong and his muddled colleague, San Francisco Police Capt. Bill Street (Grant Withers), swing into action. Karloff's air of natural-born class is a joy to watch, even under these circumstances. *Doomed To Die* is chiefly of interest as a fragment of a career strategy that had, by now, served its purpose. Withers is delightful in his recurring role, and Marjorie Reynolds is, as usual, a resourceful charmer.

CREDITS: Executive Producer: Scott R. Dunlap; Director: William Nigh; Associate Producer: Paul Malvern; Adaptation: Michael Jacoby; Screenplay: Ralph G. Bettinson; Original Story: Hugh Wiley, as Published in *Collier's* Magazine; Photographed by: Harry Neumann; Musical Director: Edward J. Kay; Editor: Robert Golden; Technical Director: E.R. Hickson; Sound Engineer: Karl Zint, Western Electric; Production Manager: Charles L. Bigelow; Assistant Director: Glenn Cook; Running Time: 67 Minutes; Released: August 12, 1940

CAST: Boris Karloff (James Lee Wong); Marjorie Reynolds (Bobby Logan); Grant Withers (Capt. Bill Street); Catherine Craig (Cynthia); Henry Brandon (Victor Martin); William Sterling (Dick Martin); Melvyn Lang (Cyrus Wentworth); Kenneth Harlan (Chauffeur); Wing [Richard] Loo (Tong Leader); Guy Usher (Paul Fleming); Gibson Gowland (Doctor); Wilbur Mack (Mathews); Jack Kennedy (Cop); and Tristram Coffin, Maxine Leslie, Mike Donovan and William Wilmering

SHADOWS OVER SHANGHAI
(Fine Arts Pictures/Grand National Pictures, Inc.)

A timely exploitation of prevailing tensions between Japan and China, this variant on a Yellow Peril theme concerns a precious amulet that is the key to a $5 million dollar munitions purchase. Too much of the tale is wasted on a soap-operatic marriage-of-convenience romance between adventuress Linda Gray and journalist James Dunn, but there is an overriding suspense—and one shattering shock-value payoff: An incense burner, sent as a wedding gift, is secretly crammed with dynamite by a Japanese agent (Paul Sutton). A treacherous Russian (Robert Barrat) lights the device and is impressively removed from the equation.

Camera chief Arthur Martinelli cannily saves the set-bound production from looking too cramped, using matte-painting seascapes and airy scenic compositions to striking effect. He gives away the game—with an inadvertent and uncharacteristic carelessness—by dwelling just a bit too long on static backdrops whose distant objects are supposed to be in motion.

CREDITS: Producer: Franklyn Warner; Associate Producer: Charles Lamont; Screenplay: Joseph Hoffman; Story: Richard B. Sale; Photographed by: Arthur Martinelli; Assistant Director: Ralph Slosser; Art Director: Ralph Berger; Editor: Bernard Loftus; Costumes: W.H. McCrary; Musical Score Arranged and Conducted by: Sam Berkowitz, Screen Music, Inc.; Running Time: 65 Minutes; Released: October 14, 1938

CAST: James Dunn (Johnny McGinty); Ralph Morgan (Howard Barclay); Linda Gray (Irene Roma); Robert Barrat (Igor Sargoza); Paul Sutton (Fuki Yokahama); Edward Woods (Peter Roma); Edwin Mordant (Dr. Adams); Chester Gan (Lun Sat Lui); Victor Wong (Wu Chang); Edward Keane (Consul); Billy Bevan (Gallicuddy); William Haade (Capt. Murphy); Richard Loo (Fong); Victor Young (Wang)

TITANS OF THE DEEP
(E.W. Hammons/Grand National Pictures, Inc.)

The *Jaws* of its day was *Titans of the Deep*, a naturally sensational featurette boasting authentic shark-attack footage and a rampant barracuda in the bargain. The film proved phenomenally popular despite the difficulties its awkward running time posed to conventional theatres, finding its truer niche—and many years of captive-audience exposure—as a perennial rental for school programs.

Dr. William Beebe and bathysphere developer Otis Barton plan an undersea expedition. All goes well on a purely observational level until one of the scientists finds himself hemmed in by a barracuda. Explorer Joan Igou must kill the marauding fish with a rifle. Later on, Barton has a harrowing encounter with a shark and is forced to throw his camera rig into the monster's mouth. The shark disables itself by swallowing the camera, and the crew members hoist the creature onto the deck and cut it open to retrieve the equipment.

Barton and Beebe, best known for their Bermuda expeditions, made numerous such moving-picture accounts, all expertly photographed and often edited into such concise entertainments as this one. Dr. Beebe's journeys had also figured in the prehistory of the breakthrough special-effects picture *King Kong* (1933), by providing a meeting-ground for the expeditionary cameraman Ernest B. Schoedsack and the writer Ruth Rose.

C REDITS: Executive Producer: E.W. Hammons; Producer and Director: Otis Barton; Continuity: Lowell Thomas; Photographed by: Frank Dalyrymple and Edward Ewer; Editor: Sam Citron; Running Time: 48 Minutes; Released: October 28, 1938

CAST: Lowell Thomas (Narrator); and Dr. William Beebe, Otis Barton, John Tee Van, Gloria Hollister, Joan Igou, Jocelyn Crane

GUN PACKER
(Monogram Pictures Corp.)

Jack Randall, kid brother of the all-'round Western-matinee champ, Bob Livingston, fared impressively as a shoot-'em-up star in his own right, segueing gradually into villainous roles during the 1940s right on up to his sudden death-in-harness in 1945. *Gun Packer* finds Randall all set to undermine a fantastic scheme to smuggle stolen gold without risk of detection.

Special deputy Jack Denton (Randall) finagles his way into gang membership and right away spots Prof. Angel (Barlowe Borland), a disappointed renegade genius who has perfected a secret process to transform the precious metal. Learning that Jack is an undercover agent, the professor switches over to the side of good, and he and Jack are maneuvered into a showdown with ringleader Chance Moore (reliable Charles King). Angel turns the tide by blowing up a mine—and himself with it. Jack and his sidekick, Pinky (the expressive black actor Ray Turner), escape, only to be pursued by Moore, whom Jack beats to a frazzle. Leading lady Louise Stanley was Randall's fiancée; their short-lived marriage occurred after the film's completion. The extremely brief film is long on doomy attitude.

CREDITS: Producer: Scott R. Dunlap; Supervisor: Robert Tansey; Director: Wallace W. Fox; Screenplay: Robert Emmett; Photographed by: Bert Longenecker; Running Time: 51 Minutes; Released: November 9, 1938

CAST: Addison "Jack" Randall (Jack Denton); Louise Stanley (Ruth Adams); Charles King (Chance Moore); Barlowe Borland (Prof. Angel); Glenn Strange (Sheriff); Raymond Turner (Pinky); Lloyd Ingraham (Chief Holmes); Lowell Drew (Dad Adams); Ernie Adams (Stagecoach Driver); Forrest Taylor (Express Boss); and Rusty, the Wonder Horse

MARUSIA
(Ukrafilm Corp.)

Staritsky's folkloric play, *Marusia*, dates from 1872 and once was a staple of the Ukrainian theatre. This little-seen film version, the lone production of Ukrafilm Corp., is American but hardly Americanized, having been shot in a capsule of ethnicity on quaint and forbidding natural locations in New York State, New Jersey and Long Island. The surviving fragments that we have seen bespeak a great care in the making—*The Hollywood Reporter* pegged the budget at a generous-for-the-circumstances $45,000—but only hint maddeningly at the dire epic of legend-come-to-life that *Marusia* must have been when intact. The dialogue is Ukrainian, without English subtitling.

An innocent romance nearly bites the dust when Khoma (played with a snarling intensity by Peter Chorniuk), a wealthy and cruel hunchback, horns in on sweethearts Marusia (Stephania Melnik) and Hyrtz (Nicholas Stehnitzky). Khoma provokes Hyrtz into hostile confrontations with a friend, Potap (Mykola Novak), and with Marusia, and Hyrtz leaves the village in disgrace. Khoma places Marusia's parents in his debt and begins to court the girl. Although she pines for Hyrtz, Marusia finally consents to marry Khoma. Hyrtz returns in time to reclaim his beloved, whereupon Khoma conspires to poison the lovers. Exposed as a menace to society, Khoma flees the angry villagers. Potap captures Khoma and throws the madman to his death from a clifftop.

CREDITS: Director: Leo Bulgakov; Screenplay: Vladimir Kedrowsky and Andrei Kist; After the Play by: M. Staritsky; Photographed by: George Hinners and Edward Hiland; Editor: Leon Levy; Musical Score: Prof. Roman Prydatekych; Choral Music: Dr. Alexander Koshetz; Dance Director: Andrei Kist; Running Time: Given Variously as 95 Minutes and 105 Minutes; Released: December 8, 1938

CAST: Stephania Melnyk (Marusia); Nicholas Stehnitzky (Hyrtz); Peter Chorniuk (Khoma); Donia Stephania Werbowetzka (Daryna); Halia Troitzka (Halyna); Mykola Novak (Potap); Michael Skorobohach (Dmytro); and Fedor Braznyk, Anton Kulyk, Halia Troyan, K. Hupalowa, Maria Skubowa, Teklia Kobzar, S. Besruchko, F. Kotowych

1939

MYSTERY PLANE
(Monogram Pictures Corp.)

The Hal Forrest–Glenn Chaffin comic strip, *Tailspin Tommy*, had inspired two serials at Universal during 1934-35—*Tailspin Tommy* and *Tailspin Tommy in the Great Air Mystery*—starring Maurice Murphy and Clark Williams, respectively, as the title aviator and featuring Noah Beery, Jr., in a recurring sidekick role. It was quite a comedown, to say the least, that the property should lapse from Universal's bravura chapter-play style to a picayunish batch of hour-long adventures at Monogram. These four entries are briskly done for the most part, however, under George Waggner's direction. The no-nonsense heroism is often played out with an undercurrent of science fiction or mad treachery in addition to the airborne hair-raisers.

Mystery Plane finds John Trent and Milburn Stone portraying flyboys Tommy and Skeeter, whose revolutionary invention—a bombing device designed for pinpoint accuracy from fantastic altitudes—attracts a mob of international spies headed by a slimy Lucien Littlefield. The test-bombing scenes are abundantly exciting, and likewise for a crisply edited final battle in which Tommy's childhood hero, a since-disgraced WWI ace (played by Peter George Lynn), saves the day in tragic fashion.

The series sequelized itself promptly with *Stunt Pilot* (1939), which follows through rather bitterly on *Mystery Plane*'s curtain-closing notion of imminent Hollywood stardom for Tailspin Tommy Tomkins. In a development that might have been borrowed from 1932's murder-in-movieland thriller *The Death Kiss*, Tommy finds himself framed for the slaying of an egotistical stunt pilot (George Meeker); a dogfight gun proves to have been loaded with live ammo. The culprit is a vengeful movie director (Pat O'Malley), who boneheadedly allows himself to be photographed while tampering with Tommy's artillery. The 1930 *Hell's Angels* is a source of much stock footage.

The short-order third *Tommy*, 1939's *Sky Patrol*, puts the Tailspinner in charge of a pilots' academy, where greenhorn Jackie Coogan manifests a paralyzing fear of guns and badman Bryant Washburn lurks about to keep protective wraps on a smuggling racket. The coda, *Danger Flight* (likewise from 1939), breaks the faith with the tone of desperate adventure, settling instead for a children's entertainment—albeit a perfectly okay one—about good citizenship through model-aircraft building.

CREDITS: In Charge of Production: Scott R. Dunlap; Producer: Paul Malvern; Director: George Waggner; Screenplay: Paul Schofield and Joseph West; Story: Hal Forrest; Based upon: the Comic Strip by Hal Forrest & Glenn Chaffin; Photographed by: Archie Stout; Special Effects: Fred Jackman; Art Director: E.R. Hickson; Editor: Carl Pierson; Interior Décor: Albert Greenwood; Musical Score: Frank Sanucci; Sound Director: William R. Fox; Production Manager: Glenn Cook; Running Time: 60 Minutes; Released: March 24, 1939

CAST: John Trent (Tailspin Tommy Tomkins); Marjorie Reynolds (Betty Lou); Milburn Stone (Skeeter); Jason Robards (Paul Smith); Peter George Lynn (Brandy Rand); Lucien Littlefield (Winslow); Polly Ann Young (Anita); Tommy Bupp (Young Tommy); Betsy Gay (Young Betty Lou); John Peters (Carl); Sayre Dearing (Fred); and William Carlton, John Elliott, Bruce Mitchell, Mickey Martin, Jerry Jerome

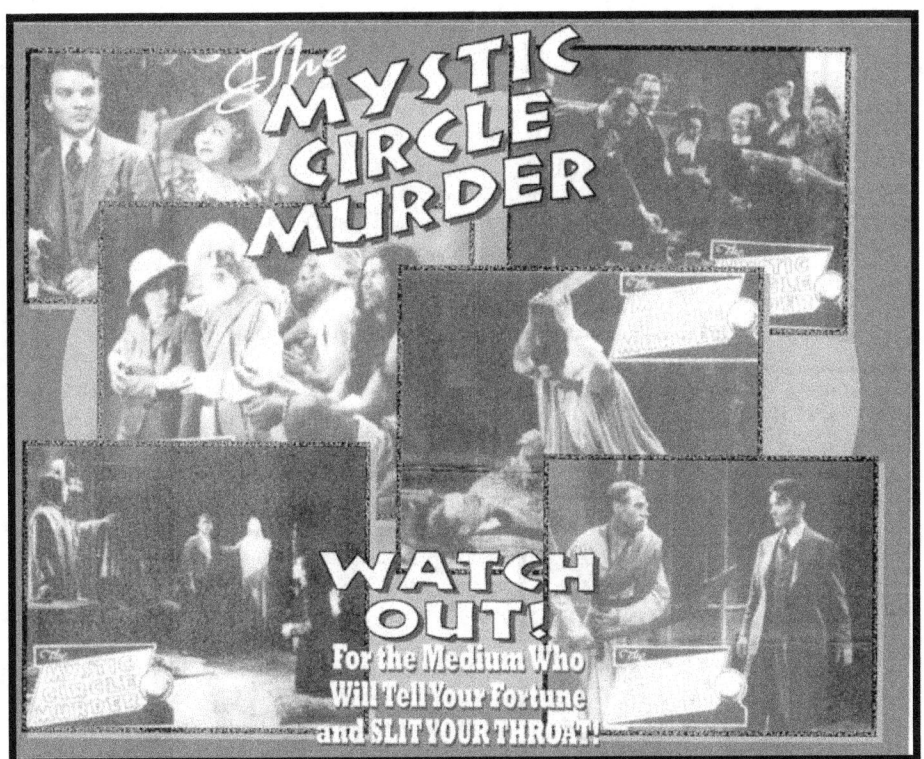

THE MYSTIC CIRCLE MURDER
a.k.a.: RELIGIOUS RACKETEERS
(Fanchon Royer Features, Inc./Continental Pictures, Inc./Merit Pictures, Inc.)

Fanchon Royer, one of the most independent of independent producers, raised and spent some $35,000 to make *Religious Racketeers* or *The Mystic Circle Murder*. (The title would vary, depending upon when and where the picture was playing.) This investment was a bundle for a company whose previous pictures (including the 1936 *Death in the* Air, a.k.a. *Pilot X* and *Mysterious Bombardier*) had been brought in for $23,000, tops.

Here we have an earnest social-agenda film, jazzed up with some mock-exotic thrills, that is calculated to convince the viewer that spiritualism is a load of banana oil. The attitude is bolstered by an extended cameo from the widow of the stage magician Harry Houdini, who had spent much of his career debunking crystal-gawkers, spook-walkers, hoodoo-hawkers and spirit-talkers.

Murder is less the point here than a great deal of aimless globetrotting accomplished by faded silent star Betty Compson, as a minion, and Helen LeBerthon, as a willing sucker, in the service of fake fakir Robert Fiske. Arthur Gardner plays an impatient newspaperman who spends the picture trying to draw the curtain on Fiske's crooked game. All concerned appear ill at ease with the stilted dialogue, and Frank O'Connor's direction is lacking in the tension that should arise from such situations.

Royer tried to lend spectacle to the presentation with scenic footage of the Egyptian Pyramids, but the stock frames are absurdly matched with the in-studio material. We have not seen the original hour-and-a-half cut—but given the overall qualities of forced performances and sloppy pacing in the surviving version, the preview edition must have been a mess and a half.

CREDITS: Producer: Fanchon Royer; Director: Frank O'Connor; Story: Frank O'Connor; Adapted by: Charles R. Condon; Dialogue: Don Gallaher; Production Manager: Ray Nazarro; Photographed by: Jack Greenhalgh; Art Director: Paul Palmentola; Sound: Cliff Ruberg; Editor: George Halligan; Technical Advisors: Dr. Edward Saint and Bhogwan Singh; Produced at: Grand National Studios; Distributed by: Merit Pictures, Inc.; Running Time: 90 Minutes at Preview, April of 1939; Release Version: 69 Minutes; Released: During October of 1939

CAST: Betty Compson (Ada Bernard); Robert Fiske (The Great LaGagge); Helen LeBerthon [in some sources, Helene LeBerthan] (Martha Morgan); Arthur Gardner (Elliott Cole); David Kerman (Wilson); Robert Frazer (Inspector Burke); Mme. Harry Houdini (as Herself)

EXILE EXPRESS
(United Players Productions, Inc./Grand National Pictures, Inc.)

Dr. Eugen Frenke forged through two decades of a hit-and-miss talking-picture career, missing more often than he hit but plugging right along with the occasional accomplished job. In late 1938, undaunted after the Pyrrhic victory of finagling his soap-operatic *Frankenstein* variant *Life Returns* away from big Universal Pictures, Frenke produced this unusual merger of espionage and science fiction. The project afforded the luminous beauty Anna Sten—Dr. Frenke was her second husband—a welcome Hollywood comeback after three years' self-exile with but scant prospects; she had graced only *A Woman Alone*, in England, since 1935. Miss Sten's energetic screwball heroism works ideally in the service of an audaciously comical thriller about a campaign to steal a powerful chemical weapon.

Nadine Nikolas (Miss Sten), soon to be Americanized, is an assistant to Dr. Hite (Harry Davenport), who has perfected a secret formula designed to wither the crops of enemy nations. Nadine is approached on the sly by an agent who wants her to steal this formula for her former country. She phones Hite, instead, to warn him, but Hite is murdered before he can make secure his papers. Nadine is arrested in connection with the slaying; though exonerated, she finds herself forced onto the Exile Express, a deportee train. Here, she finds herself encouraged to disembark illegally by a supposed friend (Jerome Cowan), who actually is the brains behind Hite's murder. A strange ploy to force Nadine into marrying an American (George Chandler) is foiled when newspaper reporter Steve Reynolds (Alan Marshall) barges in on the ceremony and, scaring away the *ad hoc* bridegroom with the threat of publicity, takes his place. After a wild chase involving the customary ill-placed trusts and inevitable betrayals; bogus news reports; a harrowing car crash; and a pursuit through the woods, the spy chief is exposed for the treacherous sort he really is. Nadine finally gets herself naturalized—as Mrs. Steve Reynolds.

Director Otis Garrett keeps all these complications pretty well on track, and there is just enough extra running time—a good 10 minutes more than the Poverty Row norm—to accommodate the necessary exposition. Miss Sten is delightfully defiant and determined as the wronged citizen-in-waiting, appearing "splendidly photographed by John Mescall," as *The Film Daily* told it. Alan Marshall makes a pleasantly heroic, however smart-mouthed and opportunistic, suitor. Jerome Cowan is a wonderfully treacherous schemer, and Leonid Kinsky plays a henchman as a bungler too faithful to dispose of. Good old Spencer Charters contributes an eerily humorous cameo as a small-town judge who finds himself obliged to perform a peculiar marriage ceremony.

The journalistic backdrop is the source of much of the comedy, with Jed Prouty as a hard-nosed editor and Walter Catlett (less grumpy than usual) as a chicken-hearted photographer. Feodor Chaliapin stands out among the exiles, as a double-talking Bolshevik orator, and rock-jawed Stanley Fields is plenty intimidating as a deportee who has proved too tough for Alcatraz. Suave Irving Pichel is a ranking enemy of the state who finds his racket undone by Miss Sten's rebellious nature. Vince Barnett, seven years after his scene-stealing performance in *The Death Kiss*, is still amusing as an inept authority figure.

Over the long haul, Russian-born Anna Sten gave better to Hollywood than she got in return. The big-time independent producer Samuel Goldwyn had brought her to America from Germany amid a barrage of hyperbole, but Stateside audiences did not take fondly to her, and after several features Goldwyn axed her contract. Though more interested in her other career as a painter, Miss Sten continued to tackle the occasional acting assignment on into the 1960s.

The reviews were largely enthusiastic for *Exile Express*: The Los Angeles *Times* called Miss Sten's absence from the screen "long and regrettable," and *The Film Bulletin* held the picture to be "swiftly paced... told with conviction." The *Daily Variety* critic found *Exile Express* "a definite box-office attraction...a decided credit to Eugen Frenke's careful preparation and showmanship," where *Weekly Variety* griped that "it won't satisfy even the most indulgent meller [melodrama, in archaic show-speak] fans."

CREDITS: Producer: Dr. Eugen [a.k.a. Eugene] Frenke; Director: Otis Garrett; Screenplay: Edwin Justin Mayer and Ethel La Blanche; Photographed by: John Mescall; Art Director: Ralph Berger; Assistant Director: Ray Nazarro; Editors: Edward Curtis and Robert Bischoff; Wardrobe: James Wade; Shoes: I. Miller; Musical Score: George Parrish; Dance Director: Buddy Harak; Production Manager: Gordon Griffith; Running Time: 70 Minutes; Released: May 27, 1939

CAST: Anna Sten (Nadine Nikolas); Alan Marshal (Steve Reynolds); Jerome Cowan (Paul Brandt); Walter Catlett (Gus); Jed Prouty (Hanley); Stanley Fields (Tony Kassan); Leonid Kinsky (David); Etienne Girardot (Catetaker); Irving Pichel (Victor); Harry Davenport (Dr. Hite); Addison Richards (Purnell); Feodor Chaliapin (Kaishevsky); Spencer Charters (Peace Justice); Byron Foulger (Serge); Don Brodie (Mullins); Henry Roquemore (Constable); Vince Barnett (Deputy); Maude Eburne (Mrs. Smith); Charles Richman (Judge); George Chandler (Marvin McGee)

ACROSS THE PLAINS
(Monogram Pictures Corp.)

Let's see, now—where have we heard this one before? Brothers Jimmy and Jack lose track of one another following a murderous raid on their family's wagon train. Sounds a whole lot like *The Rawhide Terror* and *Branded a Coward*, those long-obscured Frontier Gothics that we unearthed for our

1999 revision of the original *Forgotten Horrors*. This economical star vehicle for Jack Randall—kid brother of the *Three Mesquiteers* series' star, Bob Livingston—flogs that dead horse of a plot to a fare-thee-well but still justifies its modest investment of time and patchy resources.

Jack grows up to be a gunslinging hero known as Cherokee (Randall), so named on account of he has been rescued and raised by a band of Indians. Jimmy, kidnapped by his folks' killers, grows up to become the black-hearted Kansas Kid (Dennis Moore). Now, Cherokee and wagonmaster Buckskin (hard-working Hal Price) have joined forces to avenge the long-ago victims. The Kansas Kid, meanwhile, leads an unsuspecting wagon train smack into an ambush. Cherokee thwarts this plot, but later on Buckskin is abducted and overhears the outlaws reminiscing fondly about the time they did away with the Kid's parents. The Kid, bound for a showdown with his unsuspected brother, undergoes a transformation when Buckskin reveals to him the truth; seems the Kid had believed his Ma and Pa were killed by Indians. The brothers set aside their differences to wipe out the gang. The Kid, mortally wounded, accepts death philosophically, now that his parents have been avenged.

The antagonistic lead portrayals make *Across the Plains* a grimly uncompromising confrontation from start to finish. Randall socks enough anger into his model-citizen character to keep things credible, and Dennis Moore registers a genuinely bewildered anguish upon learning suddenly that everything he knows is wrong. Veteran thriller director Spencer Gordon Bennet orchestrates a harrowing shoot-out for the climax, and Moore's death scene seems an episode of the very sort that moved the old-time cowboy folk singers to compose all those heart-wrenching death-on-the-prairie ballads.

For those who may feel compelled to keep track of such things, another wagon-train massacre yarn occurs in Sam Newfield's *Valley of Vengeance* (1944), a *Billy Carson* series entry starring Buster Crabbe and Fuzzy St. John.

CREDITS: In Charge of Production: Scott R. Dunlap; Supervisor: Robert Tansey; Director: Spencer Gordon Bennet; Screenplay: Robert Emmett; Photographed by: Bert Longenecker and Henry Freulich; Art Director: E.R. Hickson; Assistant Director: W.B. Eason; Editor: Robert Golden; Wardrobe: Louis Brown; Sound Engineer: Glen Glenn; Production Manager: Charles J. Bigelow; Running Time: 54 Minutes; Released: June 1, 1939

CAST: Jack Randall (Cherokee); Frank Yaconelli (Lopez); Joyce Bryant (Mary Masters); Hal Price (Buckskin); Dennis Moore (the Kansas Kid); Glenn Strange (Jeff Masters); Bud Osborne (Lex); Dean Spencer (Rip); Wylie Grant (Rawhide); Rusty the Wonder Horse (Himself); Robert Card (Buff Gordon); and James Sheridan, Buddy Cox, Texi-Ray Cox

S.O.S.—TIDAL WAVE
(Republic Pictures Corp.)

S.O.S.—Tidal Wave concerns a hoax perpetrated by a corrupt political machine. (Photofest)

"Wells and Welles," sniped the *Variety* review, sarcastically pegging *S.O.S.—Tidal Wave* as a composite swipe from H.G. and Orson. The title disaster is, of course, a hoax, perpetrated by a corrupt political machine to distract the masses from a hotly contested election. The writers can only have been laboring under the influence of Orson Welles' October 31, 1938, radio adaptation of H.G. Wells' *The War of the Worlds*, whose real-time straight-faced documentary-like presentation had struck an excitable populace as a genuine news broadcast.

Where *Variety* trashed *S.O.S.—Tidal Wave* despite kind words for good guy Ralph

Byrd and several other players, *The Hollywood Reporter* likened the picture favorably to Welles' Halloween-invasion pageant and raved about the catastrophe scenes: "Process work, picturing the waterfront, then the entire city of New York, collapsing under...a surging tidal wave, is amazingly vital drama..."

Some memory these bums have. The "amazingly vital drama" of *S.O.S.*'s effects work actually belongs to a too-soon-forgotten 1933 epic called *Deluge*, which figures as a centerpiece of our first *Forgotten Horrors* collection. Republic had purchased the elaborate devastation footage, which it recycled here and in the serials *Dick Tracy vs. Crime, Inc.* (another Ralph Byrd-starrer, from 1941) and *King of the Rocket Men* (1949).

Sci-Films notes: "One manipulative sequence involving an injured child and a ventriloquist's dummy is about as badly handled as any scene I've ever see."

The larger story of *S.O.S.* is actually a great deal smaller than the *Deluge* excerpts that help to drive the plot: Byrd plays a television newsman—in those days when television was still popularly held to be a science-fictional concept—who helps an upstanding mayoral candidate prevail against the treacheries of a crooked politico. When Byrd comes up with an incriminating piece of film, kingmaker Marc Lawrence counters by broadcasting the tidal-wave footage in the guise of breaking news. Panic results, and Lawrence gets himself squashed by a truck whose driver is fleeing the make-believe disaster.

CREDITS: Associate Producer: Armand Schaefer; Director: John H. Auer; Screenplay: Maxwell Shane and Gordon Kahn; Story: James Webb; Additional Dialogue: Stanley Rauh; Photographed by: Jack Marta; Art Director: John Victor Mackay; Assistant Director: Tommy Flood; Editor: Ernest Nims; Supervising Editor: Murray Seldeen; Costumes: Adele Palmer; Musical Director: Cy Feuer; Production Manager: Al Wilson; Running Time: 62 Minutes; Released: June 2, 1939

CAST: Ralph Byrd (Jeff Shannon); George Barbier (Uncle Dan Carter); Kay Sutton (Laurel Shannon); Frank Jenks (Peaches Jackson); Marc Lawrence (Melvin Sutter); Dorothy Lee (Mabel); Oscar O'Shea (Mike Halloran); Mickey Kuhn (Buddy Shannon); Ferris Taylor (Clifford Farrow); Donald Barry (Curly Parsons); Raymond Bailey (Roy Nixon)

DEATH GOES NORTH
(Central Films, Ltd./Columbia Pictures Corp. of California/Warwick Pictures, Inc.)

An impersonation-and-murder yarn of considerable viciousness, the Canadian-made *Death Goes North* stars those Hollywood-based Poverty Row dependables, Rin Tin Tin, Jr., and Sheila Bromley (a.k.a. Sheila Manners and Sheila Manors), as canine sleuth and lady-in-distress. Rinty the Younger, for once, shows some of the fire of his old man, upstaging human heroes Edgar Edwards and Michael Heppell at every turn. There is a wealth of villainy and suspicious lurking-about, too,

R.C.M.P. Agent Edgar Edwards confronts uncle-impersonator Jameson Thomas with an incriminating clue in *Death Goes North*. Endangered heiress Sheila Bromley peeks out from the background. (Photofest)

from Walter Byron and Arthur Kerr as wicked brothers who are Miss Bromley's competitors in the lumber-mill industry; Reginald Hincks, as a deranged vagrant; and Dorothy Bradshaw and Jameson Thomas, as an English couple who may or may not be Miss Bromley's devoted kinfolks. The film was shot chiefly (and rather murkily) on interior sets—unaccountably failing to take full advantage of the North Woods setting.

After cabling her uncle, whom she has never met, to ship over and take charge of a troubled business, Elsie Barlow (Miss Bromley) learns that a dead man has been found in possession of her message. The worst is feared, until "Uncle Herbert" and "Aunt Martha" (Thomas and Bradshaw) arrive and identify the corpse as their emissary, Robert Druid. Borrowing the Barlow dog, King (Rinty, Jr.), to track the killer, Mountie Dan MacKenzie (Heppell) reaches a desolate barn, where he is slain by a hammer-wielding assailant. Bad lumberman Albert Norton (Byron) is arrested, but brother Bart (Kerr) engineers a jailbreak and the hoodlums sneak into the Barlow residence just as Elsie finds herself attacked by a would-be strangler. Mountie Ken Strange (Edwards) has done enough sleuthing to reveal the would-be uncle as Robert Druid. Strange calls upon King to point out Elsie's assailant, and the dog pounces on Druid. The bogus aunt almost pulls off a getaway—emphasis on that *almost*.

CREDITS: Producer: Kenneth J. Bishop; Production Supervisor for Columbia: Jack Fier; Director: Frank McDonald; Screenplay: Edward R. Austin; Photographed by: Harry Forbes and William Beckway; Editor: William Austin; Sound: Herbert Eicke; Technical Supervisor: Sgt. Walter Withers, R.C.M.P.; Running Time: 64 Minutes; Released: During July of 1939

CAST: Edgar Edwards (Ken Strange); Sheila Bromley (Elsie Barlow); Dorothy Bradshaw ("Aunt Martha"); Jameson Thomas (Robert Druid); Walter Byron (Albert Norton); Arthur Kerr (Bart Norton); James McGrath (Puffet); Vivian Combe (Maggie); Reginald Hincks (Freddie); Rin Tin Tin, Jr. (King); Michael Heppell (Dan MacKenzie); Harry Hay (Herbert Barlow); George Durham (Gordon Hayes); Fred Spencer (Griffin); Campbell Forbes (Bill Williams); A.A. Ransom (Messenger)

DAUGHTER OF THE TONG
(Metropolitan Pictures Corp.)

Evelyn Brent (1899-1975), born Mary Elizabeth Riggs in Tampa, Florida, was among the few established silent-screen stars who made a graceful segue into the talkers. Her menacing lead in *Daughter of the Tong* is a sad echo of her starring roles for Josef von Sternberg in *Underworld* (1927) and *The Last Command* (1928), but it is nonetheless consistent with her long-standing and perfectly appropriate typecasting as a seductive denizen of society's nether reaches.

Miss Brent, Dave O'Brien, Grant Withers, Richard Loo *et al.* are uniformly finer than the fabric of *Daughter of the Tong*, which suffers from simplistic hack writing, poorly staged stunt action—in situations where fights and pursuits are the order of the day—and unintentional hokum, as well as dialogue that casts the Asian sector of U.S. civilization in a wholly demeaning light. The photography, typical of Metropolitan Pictures, is extremely dim and lacking in tonal range. *Variety* was charitably willing to blame this muddiness upon the film stock, but the pictorial compositions and visual storytelling are lousy, too.

Miss Brent plays the Illustrious One, gangleader deluxe, who hides behind the name of Carney, quarry of an F.B.I. dragnet. Withers—soon to debut as a Monogram production honcho, with *Irish Luck* (coming right up)—is a federal agent who infiltrates the racket, and O'Brien is a former (legitimate) business partner who turns hostile after learning the real nature of the Illustrious One's dealings. Dorothy Short, as O'Brien's sister and a vengeful former captive of the gang, gets to help lead the inevitable crackdown.

CREDITS: Presented by: Henry S. Webb; Producer: Lester F. Scott, Jr.; Director: Raymond K. Johnson; Story: George H. Plympton; Continuity: Alan Merritt; Photographed by: Elmer Dyer; Assistant Director: Ray Nazarro; Editor: Charles Diltz; Musical Score: Lee Zahler; Sound Technician: Clifford Ruberg; Running Time: 56 Minutes; Released: During August of 1939

CAST: Evelyn Brent (the Illustrious One); Grant Withers (Ralph Dickson); Dorothy Scott (Marion Morgan); Dave O'Brien (Jerry Morgan); Richard Loo (Wong); Dirk Thane (Slade); Harry Harvey (Muggsy); Budd Buster (Lefty); Robert Frazer (Williams); Hal Taliaferro (Lawson); James Coleman (Hardy)

IRISH LUCK
(Monogram Pictures Corp.)

Here we have Frankie Darro and Mantan Moreland's first shot at a loosely connected comedy-thriller series that not only would mature strikingly over the course of an all-too-brief run, but also would cement a lifelong friendship. No one among the published critics seems to have remarked on the groundbreaking ploy of a white-guy/black-guy comedy team. Perhaps this oversight is because the stories placed Darro and Moreland on an equal social standing, usually portraying servants of various types, aspiring to become hot-stuff detectives. Or perhaps it is because Monogram neglected to pitch the team *as* a team. A simple ampersand connecting Moreland & Darro—Frankie & Mantan, whatever—would have worked wonders at announcing a distinctive identity.

Darro is Buzzy O'Brien, a Hotel Royale bellboy and amateur detective whose nose for clue-chasing leads him into trouble straightaway. Mantan plays the Royale's baggage man, Jefferson, who

Irish Luck belongs thoroughly to Mantan Moreland and Frankie Darro. (Photofest)

plays right along (with eloquent misgivings) with Buzzy's dangerous escapades. Pretty Kitty Monohan (Sheila Darcy), a guest, is incriminated by a telegram warning the mysterious Thad Porter to keep an eye peeled for a woman with the initials K.M. Upon finding Porter slain, Buzzy helps Kitty elude the law; she had been seeking Porter, as it develops, for she had believed he might help find her missing brother, Jim, who stands accused in connection with a heist at Porter's bank.

Buzzy suspects that a hotel guest registered as one Mr. Elliott (Dennis Moore) must be Jim Monohan. Knocked unconscious while snooping in Elliott's suite, Buzzy wakes to find another corpse, along with a dazed Elliott, left to drown in a bathtub. Elliott admits he is Kitty's brother. Buzzy and Jefferson develop suspicions about Fluger (James Flavin), the hotel detective, who catches them just as they discover a cache of the Elliott bank's stolen securities. Jefferson, hiding in the next room, hears Fluger's threat against Buzzy and steals onto a ledge, where he creates a mock-suicidal commotion that draws the police.

It's a Monogram, which means of course that *Irish Luck* suffers from the customary deficiencies in production values, narrative sense, inventiveness in camerawork and overall polish. Such failings are compensated for by the sense of community that informs most of the studio's pictures, which though often desultory in technical and literary matters still radiate the fun that the things must have been for the participants. Director Howard Bretherton moves *Irish Luck* along briskly but dwells rewardingly on such bits of surprise as Darro's discoveries of the murder scenes and his abrupt confrontation with the killer.

Darro and Moreland are about equally matched in the google-eyes department when it comes to scared-silly reactions. Darro concentrates on the boyish impulsiveness that generates their close shaves, where Moreland is more the wise and resourceful party who has a philosophical quip for every occasion and an outlandish solution for the final desperate encounter. Even when shunted to the background of a scene, he makes himself the center of the audience's attention. How much of Moreland's banter is scripted, and how much improvised, is a matter for conjecture, for he was a master at making every utterance sound spontaneous. His long-term contract with Monogram was an actor/writer deal—the writing function involved no original screenplays, but rather his ability to make his characters say those things that nobody but Moreland would have the gumption to say.

Despite the sterner heroic presence of Dick Purcell and the vulnerably innocent beauty of Sheila Darcy, *Irish Luck* belongs thoroughly to Moreland and Darro, whose next such picture would be 1940's *Chasing Trouble* (see page 103). *Irish Luck* marked actor Grant Withers' debut as a producer.

CREDITS: In Charge of Production: Scott R. Dunlap; Associate Producer: Grant Withers; Director: Howard Bretherton; Screenplay: Mary C. McCarthy; Based upon: Charles Molyneaux Brown's *Detective Fiction Weekly* Story, "Death Hops the Bells"; Photographed by: Harry Neumann; Art Director: E.R. Hickson; Assistant Director: W.B. Eason; Editor: Russell Schoengarth; Wardrobe: Louis Brown; Musical Score: Edward Kay; Sound Engineer: Karl Zint; Production Manager: Charles J. Bigelow; Running Time: 58 Minutes; Released: August 22, 1939

CAST: Frankie Darro (Buzzy O'Brien); Mantan Moreland (Jefferson); Dick Purcell (Steve Lanahan); Lillian Elliott (Mrs. O'Brien); Dennis Moore (Jim Monohan); James Flavin (Fluger); Sheila Darcy (Kitty Monohan); Howard Mitchell (Hotel Manager); and Ralph Peters, Tristram Coffin, Pat Gleason, Gene O'Donnell, Donald Kerr

THE FIGHTING RENEGADE
(Victory Pictures Corp.)

Tim McCoy never found his way back to major-studio stardom after an impulsive mid-1930s decision to tether his fortunes along Poverty Row, but the community of smaller production companies treated him well in terms of one assignment after another. An upshot of this backfired career strategy was that McCoy got to make one of his best pictures, the Sig Neufeld-Leslie Simmonds production of *Lightnin' Bill Carson* (1936), a dire meditation on mortality and fate in a cruel frontier.

The *Carson* concept was picked up as a series in 1938 by Sam Katzman's Victory Pictures and continued down a long, dark trail under the original director, Sam Newfield. Although it would be misleading to claim an outright horrific impact for these quickies—indeed, there is more *mayhem* than outright *weird menace*, and McCoy's masquerades are often laughable—still the series honors the foreboding atmosphere of the original. These entries also foreshadow the brooding severity of producer Katzman's overt thrillers of the '40s—and of the soon-to-emerge noir style as a class. Film noir knows no genre.

The best and most representative of the lot, *The Fighting Renegade* gets down to some mighty offbeat vicious business: El Puma, supposedly a Mexican Robin Hood, is actually Lightnin' Bill Carson—not that the masquerade is evident to the archaeologists who hire El Puma to shepherd them through hostile territory.

Carson is alleged to have murdered a prior expeditioner. Using the slain Prof. Willis' diary as their guide to a lost treasure, the scientists run deep into trouble before the first reel has passed through the projector. Bill knows that Benson (Ted Adams), the party's foreman, is the real killer—but before Bill can act, a hired hand known as Old Dobie (Budd Buster) kills the professor in charge (Forrest Taylor) and frames Bill all over again. Benson plots to kidnap Willis' daughter, Marian (Joyce Bryant), because she can decipher a crucial map, but Bill abducts her as a safety measure. As good guys and bad converge on the stark mesa where the treasure lies hidden, Bill gets the drop on Benson and Old Dobie confesses all.

The others in the series are *Lightning Carson Rides Again* and *Six-Gun Trail* (both from 1938); *Code of the Cactus* (1939), which boasts a high-tech cattle-rustling racket; *Outlaw's Paradise* (1939), with McCoy playing both Carson and a notorious criminal; *Texas Wildcats* and *Trigger Fingers* (also from '39); and *Straight Shooter* (1940). Sig Neufeld and Sam Newfield (the artists were brothers)

Carol Davis and Monte Rawlins hold the symbolic death's-head pig-sticker in *Adventures of the Masked Phantom*. **(Photofest)**

liked the Bill Carson identity well enough that they later retooled Producers Releasing Corp.'s *Billy the Kid* series as a *Billy Carson* series for Buster Crabbe—of which 1944's *Wild Horse Phantom* is a splendid example that will figure in a third *Forgotten Horrors*.

CREDITS: Producer: Sam Katzman; Director: Sam Newfield; Story and Screenplay: William Lively; Photographed by: Art Reed; Assistant Director: Bert Sternbach; Editor: Holbrook Todd; Recording Engineer: Hans Weeren; Production Manager: Ed W. Rote; Running Time: 54 Minutes; Released: September 1, 1939

CAST: Tim McCoy (Lightnin' Bill Carson); Joyce Bryan (Marian Willis); Ben Corbett (Magpie); Ted Adams (Link Benson); Budd Buster (Old Dobie); Dave O'Brien (Jerry Leonard); Forrest Taylor (Prof. Lucius Lloyd); Reed Howes (Sheriff); John Eliott (Prospector)

ADVENTURES OF THE MASKED PHANTOM
(B.F. Ziedman Productions, Ltd./Equity Pictures, Inc.)

This peppy vehicle for the undeservedly obscure one-shot Western star Monte "Alamo" Rawlins pivots on a feisty grandmother's folk-tales about a Masked Phantom who once conquered the agents of evil with a terroristic dose of their own bitter medicine. Plenty of evil ranges at large in the film's

Here-and-Now, what with a string of killings, dismissed as accidents, plaguing a gold-mining operation run by Stan Barton (Matty Kemp) and his Grandma Mary (Dot Karroll). Foreman Murdock (George Douglas) is the secret ringleader, smelting hijacked gold for sale to the U.S. government. Wandering horseman Alamo (Rawlins) and his faithful dog, Boots, find Stan cornered in a Murdock ambush. Seeking reinforcements at Grandma's ranch, Alamo listens in fascination to the old lady's tales of the Phantom, who brandished a death's-head knife and put paid to all manner of old-time lawlessness. Alamo, cobbling together a Masked Phantom identity, announces himself to Stan's captors, so terrifying the racketeers that they clean forget to keep an eye on all that stolen gold. Regaining their wits sufficiently to ride in pursuit, Murdock and his men are captured with no little help from Grandma and her ranchhands.

Too bad nothing else came of *Adventures of the Masked Phantom*, which clearly fancied itself the start of a series, complete with a theme song and ready-made sidekicks. Rawlins makes a boisterous hero, and Dot Karroll—in her only documented feature-film appearance—is delightful as the plain-spoken Grandma Mary.

CREDITS: Director: Charles Abbott; Screenplay: Joseph O'Donnell and Clifford Sanforth; Photographed by: Marcel Le Picard; Special Effects: Howard A. Anderson; Music: David Chudnow; Songs: "The Masked Phantom," "Phantom Prairie Rose" and "A Rip-Snortin' Two-Gun Girl," by Johnny Lange & Lew Porter; Sound: Glen Glenn; Production Managers: Henry Spitz and Doc Merman; Running Time: 60 Minutes; Released: October 1, 1939

CAST: Monte "Alamo" Rawlins (Alamo); Larry Mason (Tooney); Betty Burgess (Carol Davis); Dot Karroll (Grandma Mary); Matty Kemp (Stanley Barton); George Douglas (Murdock); Jack Ingram, Merrill McCormick, Curley Dresden and Dick Moorehead (Henchmen); Boots (Dog); Thunder (Alamo's Horse); and Sonny Lamont

TORTURE SHIP
(Producers Distributing Corp.)

They sneered at the hangman, but a doctor's needle sent them screaming to their doom!– **From the Promotional Kit**

The actor and director Irving Pichel collaborated, if only just, with Ernest B. Schoedsack on the helming of *The Most Dangerous Game* (1932) and with Lansing C. Holden on *She* (1935). Pichel solo-directed the fine mystery *Before Dawn* (1933). He portrayed a memorable criminal mastermind in the 1933 *Oliver Twist* and an intense Josef Stalin in *British Agent* (1934); turned in an impressive pinch-hitter job of villainy in the stead of an ailing Bela Lugosi in *The House of a Thousand Candles* (1936); and lent *Dracula's Daughter* (1937) its creepiest presence. By 1939, despite credentials as one of the industry's preeminent character actors, Pichel

Irving Pichel portrays Dr. Herbert Stander, a renegade surgeon who intends to prove that glandular tampering can eradicate the criminal instinct in *Torture Ship*. **(Photofest)**

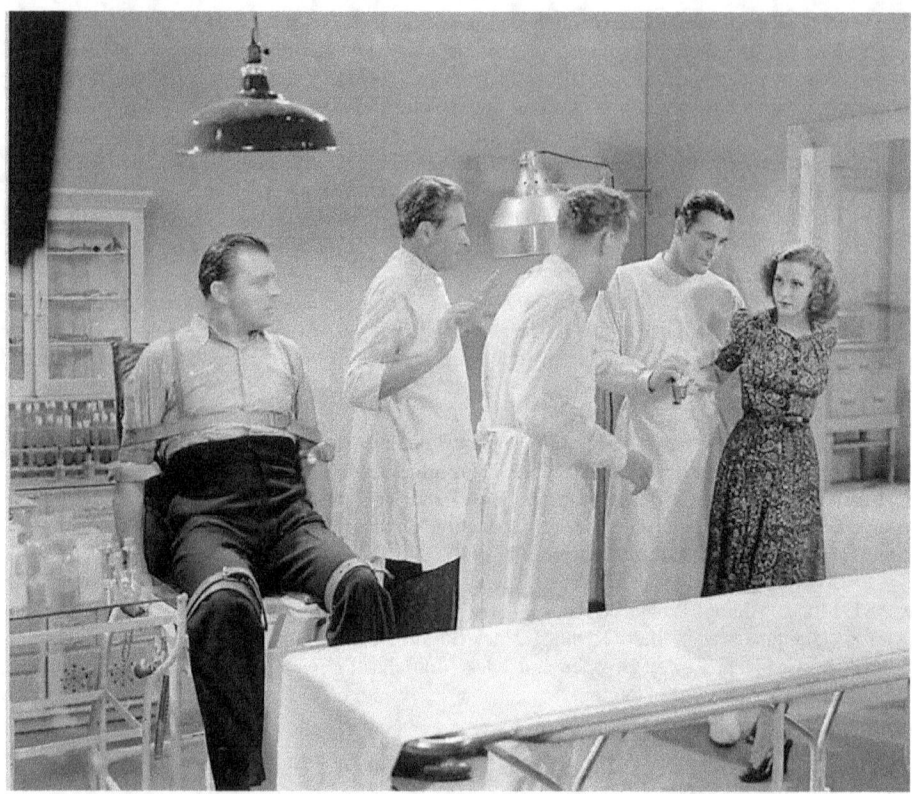

The foreboding look of *Torture Ship* is surprisingly well textured and suitably dressed, despite the necessarily small budget. Lyle Talbot braces himself for an overdose. (Photofest)

had determined to concentrate more intently on directing—at which he would prove consistently prolific and proficient until his death in 1954. He continued to act, however, as the occasion suited, showing an abiding preference for offbeat roles including a top-shelf job of villainy in *Dick Tracy's G-Men* (1939) and the sad, knowing off-camera narration that courses through John Ford's *How Green Was My Valley* (1941).

Little known even in its day, *Torture Ship* boasts a typically fine Pichel performance in the role of Dr. Herbert Stander, a renegade surgeon who intends to prove that glandular tampering can eradicate the criminal instinct. Adapted from one of Jack London's crueler short stories, the film finds Stander frustrated within the medical establishment. He outfits a yacht with a laboratory and hospital, promises asylum to several fugitives from justice and puts out to sea. His subjects include "Poison" Mary Slavish (Sheila Bromley), head of a murder-for-insurance racket; Joan Martel (Jacqueline Wells), who had been indicted as an accomplice to Mary; a modern-day Bluebeard named Ezra (Leander de Cordova); machine-gun assassin Jesse (Skelton Knaggs); the sadistic Ritter (Wheeler Oakman); and "Harry the Carver" (Russell Hopton), who has claimed six victims. Lyle Talbot plays Stander's nephew, Navy Lt. Bob Bennett, the heroic skipper who cannot quite develop a sympathy with the cause, and who falls in love with Miss Martel with only a passing concern as to her guilt or innocence.

The irony of the tale is grimly emphasized by director Victor Halperin (of *White Zombie* and *Supernatural*, among many other films outside that narrow realm) as it develops that Stander is no crackpot at all, but that his chosen subjects are becoming just as dangerously rebellious as if he really were a quack. Amid uprisings that eventually result in the doctor's slaying, Stander manages not only to vindicate his theory—by putting tough dame Sheila Bromley under the knife and rehabilitating her in the process—but also to reveal Miss Wells' innocence, to Talbot's relief. The film takes its dramatic center from Stander's dawning realization that he must experiment upon a normal person and chooses Bob. Talbot fares well with the character's growing desperation at this point, feigning helplessness from an injection and then freeing the killers.

Second-billed Pichel dominates a strong cast, conveying an Atwill-calibre intensity but stopping just short of thoroughgoing ruthlessness in his quest to alter the human species. Anthony Averill, as Pichel's assistant, seems better attuned to the outlawry implicit in so radical a quest for enlightenment. As the perfectly respectable doctor, Pichel is clearly chagrined to have been driven to such desperate measures, but his belief in a potential social boon is quite enough to settle any moral misgivings. Even so, Pichel displays sufficient megalomania to seem disturbingly akin to the vividly defined individual bad guys among his grotesque recruits. Their shared resentment comes across more as a seething, impersonal social force, and they manage a nice job of herd-instinct ensemble acting when, finally, panic drives them into Bob's custody. The romantic element is occasionally obtrusive, but Talbot and Miss Wells make a convincing match. Miss Bromley is properly brassy, but ultimately she gives in to sentimentality, as her nature proves altered, and delivers a dreadful speech asking Miss Wells' forgiveness. "She'll live—to prove my theory is right," says the dying surgeon. "I feel as though I've been born again!" says Miss Bromley.

Halperin had by now—too late to do his faltering career much good—finally overcome the silent-era style that had plagued his work as late as 1936's *Revolt of the Zombies*. He took on *Torture Ship* in the stead of the originally announced director, Rex Hale. Halperin's deployment of the various uprisings is calculated to unsettle the viewer with a sense of dangerous random menace. The foreboding look of *Torture Ship* is surprisingly well textured and suitably dressed, despite the necessarily small budget that was business as usual for the conjoined Producers Pictures Corp./Producers Distributing Corp. (soon to become Producers Releasing Corp., or PRC). Jack Greenhalgh's cameras capture a suitably dungeon-like atmosphere.

CREDITS: Producer: Sigmund Neufeld; Director: Victor Halperin; Screenplay: George Sayre [*The Hollywood Reporter* Also Credited Harvey Huntley]; Based upon: "A Thousand Deaths," by Jack London; Photographed by: Jack Greenhalgh; Art Director: Fred Preble; Editor: Holbrook N. Todd; Musical Score: David Chudnow; Sound Engineer: Hans Weeren; Produced at Grand National Studios; Running Time: 62 Minutes; Released: October 22, 1939

CAST: Lyle Talbot (Lt. Bob Bennett); Irving Pichel (Dr. Herbert Stander); Jacqueline Wells (Joan Martel); Sheila Bromley (Mary Slavish); Anthony Averill (Dirk); Russell Hopton (Harry); Julian Madison (Paul); Eddie Holden (Ole Olsen); Wheeler Oakman (Ritter); Stanley Blystone (Briggs); Leander de Cordova (Ezra); Dmitri Alexis (Murano); Skelton Knaggs (Jesse); Adia Kuznetzoff (Krantz); William Champan (Bill); Fred Walton (Fred)

HITLER—BEAST OF BERLIN
a.k.a.: BEASTS OF BERLIN; GOOSE STEP; BEAST OF BERLIN; HELL'S DEVILS
(Producers Distributing Corp.)

"It isn't the brutality of the Nazis that is their real evil," declared *Variety* on the occasion of the troubled release of Sam Newfield's *Beasts of Berlin*. "It's what's behind that brutality, the reason for it, that makes compassionate people shudder."

If the horror-ban zealots had worked as hard at banning real-life horrors as they did at suppressing horror movies, we might have had no *need* for such films as *Hitler—Beast of Berlin*—or 1934's *Dealers in Death* and *Hitler's Reign of Terror*, 1936's *I Was a Captive of Nazi Germany* and 1938's *Inside Nazi Germany*, to name only a few of the American cinema's long-unheeded documentary cries for intervention.

With the film they had intended to distribute as *Hitler—Beast of Berlin*, Ben Judell, Sigmund Neufeld and Samuel Newfield ran promptly afoul of attempts at repression: The Motion Picture Association's Production Code Administration, fearful of offending anyone—even the Nazi-sympathizer contingent—approved the title *Goose Step*, but the just-forming Producers (later, PRC) group

placed its advertisements as *Hitler—Beast of Berlin*. The Production Code objected on grounds that the title might prove inflammatory (precisely the intention) and in defiance of the industry's Politically Correct Rules & Regulations as to the respectful portrayal of other nationalities.

Provincial censor boards in New York and Massachusetts guardedly approved the title *Beasts of Berlin*, which the PCA also rejected. A Production Code seal finally came through for *Goose Step*, with the stern warning that no other title could be used. The censors looked beyond the title, too, to compromise the impact of a lengthy barroom scene: Carousing Nazis were one thing, but carousing Nazis lusting after female drinking companions—nope. Too inflammatory.

The short-memoried industry watchdogs, of course, failed to comprehend the bitter irony of the entire situation: The original title was a consciously Fuehrer-specific evocation of Rupert Julian's *The Kaiser, the Beast of Berlin* (1918), a wishful-thinking melodrama that ends with Kaiser Wilhelm's imprisonment at the hands of a vengeful Belgian citizen.

In *Hitler—Beast of Berlin*, Roland Drew plays Hans Manling, who leads an underground German resistance movement. The inner circle includes Hans' brother-in-law, Karl (Alan Ladd, in a near-breakthrough role); Gustav Schulz (John Ellis); Father Pommer (Frederick Giermann); and Albert (Hans H. von Twardowski), whose assignment is to infiltrate the Nazi ranks. Hans, whose pregnant wife (Steffi Duna) wants to flee to America, is arrested after a sympathetic tavern owner, Lustig (Vernon Dent), betrays him under torture. Albert loses his composure during a drinking bout with the Nazi loyalists and lets slip the names of the other undergrounders.

Everyone is imprisoned under Col. Hess (Walter O. Stahl), who had been Hans' commander in the last war. Hess might be forgiving, if only Hans would switch loyalties, but Hans is adamant—and suffers as a consequence. A guard, Braun (Hans von Morhart), is unexpectedly moved by Hans' plight. After Karl is slain in an escape attempt, Hans bides his time until he sees a way out. Braun pretends not to notice as Hans leaps into a farmer's wagon as it passes nearby. Hans is reunited with his wife and their infant son in Switzerland, where he swears he will carry on the resistance.

Hitler—Beast of Berlin is afflicted with some simplistic situational plotting and a tendency to concentrate more on the Nazis' overt thuggishness and less on any attempted insights into the society's perversely proud embrace of cruelty. The film is nonetheless a brilliantly delivered piece of received wisdom, more intuitive than intellectualized, from the Yiddish heart of the U.S. motion-picture industry. With the Nazis imposing their own blatantly self-glorifying movies, such as *Sieg im Westen/Victory in the West*, with impunity onto U.S. screens in that day of self-defeating fair-play isolationism, somebody in Hollywood sooner or later had to muster the gumption to mount a dramatic exercise in opposition. As usual, the responsibility fell to the risk-prone independent sector: Big-time MGM's purportedly revolutionary picture of a kindred nature, *Escape*, would not come until the autumn of the following year.

Director Sam Newfield handled *Hitler—Beast of Berlin* under his Sherman Scott pseudonym, which was hardly a bid for anonymity. Everyone in Hollywood knew that Newfield and Sig Neufeld were brothers, and that Sam (né Schmuel Neufeld) used the trade aliases of Scott and Peter Stewart to make less obvious his habit of accepting any and all low-rent assignments. If the Scott identity was meant to mask anything here, it probably was a distraction from the Newfield name's association with actionful escapism. Newfield's style here is under-obvious and often symbolic, making much of the shrouded underworld of the secret resistance and finding pleasing subtleties in characters (such as the oddly sympathetic Nazi guard) who would more easily have been rendered one-dimensional hoodlums. Roland Drew is quite affecting as the determined freedom fighter, and young Alan Ladd shows plenty of the star quality that mainstream Hollywood had yet to discover; a reissue would move Ladd up to star billing. Hans H. von Twardosky accounts well for the center of gravity of the crucial drunk scene, where he finks on his comrades amid a bout of Nazi revelry.

CREDITS: Producer: Ben Judell; Associate Producer: Sigmund Neufeld; Director: Sherman Scott [Sam Newfield]; Story and Screenplay: Shepard Traube; Photographed by: Jack Greenhalgh; Art Director: Fred Preble; Editors: Bob Crandall and Holbrook Todd; Costumer: Waldron Johnson; Musical Director: David Chudnow; Recording Engineer: Hans Weeren; Technical Director: Frederick Giermann; Makeup: Harry Ross; Running Time: 87 Minutes; Released: October 29, 1939

CAST: Roland Drew (Hans Manling); Steffi Duna (Elsa); Greta Granstedt (Anna); Alan Ladd (Karl); Lucien Prival (Sachs); Vernon Dent (Lustig); John Ellis (Gustav Schulz); George Rosener (Wunderlich); Bodil Rosing (Frau Kohler); Hans H. Von Twardowsky (Albert); Willie Kautman (Herr Kohler); Hans Joby (Herman Lippert); Frederick Giermann (Father Pommer); Clem Wilenchick (Klee); Henry von Zynda (Erlich); John Voight (Kleswig); Hans Schumm (Schaefer); John Peters (Kruger); Hans von Morhart (Braun); Walter O. Stahl (Col. Hess); Josef Forte (Berkley); Francisco Maran (Jouvet); Fred Mellinger (Ratig); Dick Wessel (Buchman); Alex Palasthy (Ruchtbein); Walter Thiele (Kalmeet); Paul Panzer (Brahm); Fred Vogeding (Wolff); Abe Dinovitch (Kopke); Bob Stevenson (Romholtz); Anna Lisa (Bertha)

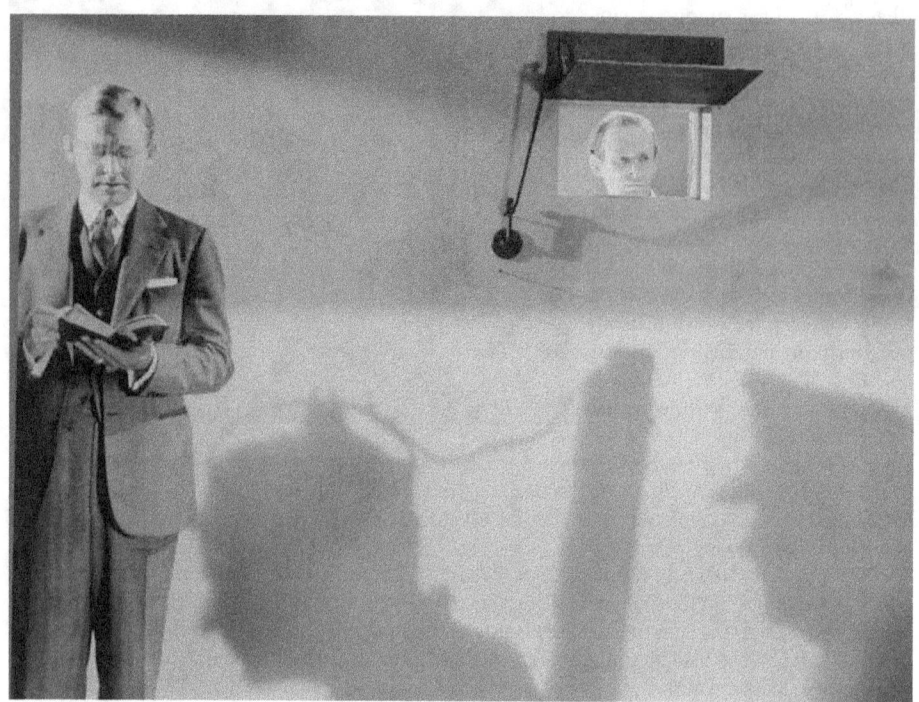

Robert Wilcox (in silhouette) settles in for a ride on Old Sparky at the climax of *Buried Alive*.

BURIED ALIVE
(Producers Pictures Corp.)

A crime melodrama of essential conventionality, Victor Halperin's *Buried Alive* gets a jazzy nudge toward the bizarre in the key elements of a career executioner driven to drink by the dehumanizing nature of his profession; an ill-balanced jailbird whose resemblance to the childlike brute Lenny Small, of Steinbeck's *Of Mice and Men*, is no happenstance; and a hard-luck hero whose random misfortunes make for a striking prefiguration of the soon-to-flourish noir school of narrative cinema.

Prison trusty Johnny Martin (Robert Wilcox) is caught up in a barroom brawl while trying to rescue executioner Ernie Mathews (George Pembroke). Manning (Wheeler Oakman), a mean-hearted newspaperman who had started the fight, publishes a story blaming Johnny and scandalizing the governor's office. Prison nurse Joan Wright (Beverly Roberts), while attempting to cushion Johnny from the letdown of a stalled parole, falls in love with him. Johnny's deranged cellmate, a childlike brute known as Big Billy (Don Rowan), kills an abusive guard during an attempted breakout. Johnny is wounded, accused in the slaying and condemned on false testimony from malicious inmate Gus Barth (Peter George Lynn). Mathews, presumably readying the execution chamber, has conspired instead with the Powers That Be to stage a bogus death. Barth, believing Johnny has been croaked, reveals his own lies—and Johnny gets an overdue crack at freedom.

Hackneyed on the one hand and yet quite progressive on the other, *Buried Alive* is a seethingly well-enacted little picture in need of recognition as a seminal film noir. Its very raggedness matches the suffocating desperation that courses through Robert Wilcox's figurative title portrayal, a pulp-magazine archetype sprung to life. Beverly Roberts is equally good as the nurse who represents Wilcox's every motivation to rejoin polite society, and George Pembroke delivers a tough-but-sensitive impersonation of the executioner who never forgets a kindness.

CREDITS: Producer: Ben Judell; Associate Producer: Sigmund Neufeld; Director: Victor Halperin; Screenplay: George Bricker; Story: William A. Ullman, Jr.; Photographed by: Jack Greenhalgh; Art Director: Fred Preble; Editor: Holbrook N. Todd; Music: Dave Chudnow; Sound: Hans Weeren; Running Time: 62 Minutes; Released: November 6, 1939

CAST: Beverly Roberts (Joan Wright); Robert Wilcox (Johnny Martin); George Pembroke (Ernie Mathews); Ted Osborne (Ira Hanes); Paul McVey (Jim Henderson); Alden Chase (Dr. Robert Lee); Don Rowan (Big Billy); Peter George Lynn (Gus Barth); Norman Budd (the Kid); Bob McKenzie (Al Garrity); Wheeler Oakman (Manning); Ben Alexander (Riley); Boyd Irwin (Rutledge); Edward Earle (Charlie Blake); Dave O'Brien (Carson); Gerald Storm (Robert Fiske); Mike Gurney (Joe McGuinn); Jack C. Smith (Mort Jarvis); Bob Sherwood (Holmes); Joe Caits (Rizinsky); James H. McNamara (Wegley)

THE DEVIL'S DAUGHTER
a.k.a.: POCOMANIA
(Lenwal Productions/Sack Amusement Enterprises, Inc.)

Pocomania is a Jamaicanized English slang term describing the frenzied thrall of Voodoo enchantment. Which might have been the state of mind that gripped veteran filmmaker George W. Terwilliger—one of those names W.C. Fields would have loved—when he recalled his perilous misadventures in shooting the bad-magic melodrama *Ouanga* (1936) on location in the West Indies. *Nothing* went right with *Ouanga*, not even the finished product (see *Forgotten Horrors: The Definitive Edition*). And even though Terwilliger must have enjoyed about all he could tolerate of the ooga-booga business, still he couldn't resist reconstituting his script as the basis of Arthur Leonard's *The Devil's Daughter*.

The Devil's Daughter, filmed on location around Kingston, Jamaica, takes a lighter approach than *Ouanga*, narrowing the class-and-color conflicts to a clash between sisters—one, an educated New Yorker; the other, a superstition-maddened Third Worlder and emphasizing funnyman Hamtree Harrington's portrayal of a dice-rattling Harlem con artist who tips his hand too quickly to the unexpectedly savvy Jamaicans.

New arrival Sylvia Walton (Ida James) is the cultured half-sister of banana farmer Isabelle Walton (Nina Mae McKinney). Isabelle has been running the family plantation in the long absence of Sylvia, the true heiress. Isabelle plots to terrorize Sylvia into leaving. Isabelle has her own home-grown problems, including a tense romantic

Beyond the Horror Ban

triangle involving her foreman, Phil Ramsay (Jack Carter), and longtime suitor John Lowden (Emmett Wallace). Elvira (Willa MacLane), Sylvia's maidservant, falls for Percy Jackson (Harrington) and subjects him to a love-charm hoodooing from Isabelle—who informs Percy that his soul has been transferred into a hog.

Phil proposes marriage to Sylvia. Sylvia proposes equal ownership of the estate to Isabelle. Isabelle proposes to subject Sylvia to a bloodthirsty ritual. Phil proves to have been plotting to scam Sylvia out of her fortune. John beats the truth out of Phil, who also reveals Isabelle's plot against Sylvia. John breaks in on the ritual, and the sisters are reconciled. Percy and Elvira, searching for the soul-harboring hog, are aghast to learn that the animal has been slaughtered for dinner. Isabel tells Percy she was just woofing him about the soul transference. Everybody chows down on a mess of barbecued pork.

Setting aside the crippling flaws of *Ouanga*, we might argue that the 1936 original at least nails a relentless severity that *The Devil's Daughter* could have used. The character portrayals are quite good—especially those of Harrington and Miss McKinney—and the pace cracks right along. But the everything's-all-right-now finale is as close to an ultimate cheat as a film can get, short of resorting to the old-standby just-a-dream cop-out. Speaking of which, see *Mr. Washington Goes to Town* and *Professor Creeps* and, on the ofay side of the equation, *The Man with Two Lives*.

CREDITS: Producer and Director: Arthur Leonard; Story and Screenplay: George W. Terwilliger; Photographed by: Jay Rescher; Assistant Cameraman: Tom Priestley; Editor: Samuel A. Datlowe; Wardrobe: Renie; Music: John Killam; Sound: Dean Cole, VariRay Blue Seal Recording; Narration: Leon Lee; Makeup: Richard Willis; Location Manager: Syl Priestley; Running Time: 65 Minutes; Released: During December of 1939

CAST: Nina Mae McKinney (Isabelle Walton); Jack Carter (Phil Ramsay); Ida James (Sylvia Walton); Hamtree Harrington (Percy Jackson); Willa MacLane (Elvira); Emmett Wallace (John Lowden)

1940
HIDDEN ENEMY
(Monogram Pictures Corp.)

Lighter than aluminum and more resilient than steel, an experimental metal developed by scientist George Cleveland stands to revolutionize warfare in this science-fiction-glazed espionage thriller. No mention is made of any particular foreign powers, but villains William von Brinken and William Castello play things with heavy Germanic and Italianate overtones.

The naive plotting would have the audience believe that Cleveland is working in a vacuum, fully aware of his invention's awesome potential but never suspecting that his breakthrough might be drawing spies. Warren Hull is better than the material as Cleveland's son, a newspaper reporter who is pressed into a heroic stance. Kay Linaker accounts for most of the twists and turns, as an out-of-town journalist who shows a decidedly un-journalistic interest in the discovery and at one point steals Cleveland's formula. Hull's approach to journalism is more of the conflict-of-interest variety: Fired for missing a big development, he regains his job by helping Miss Linaker dispose of von Brinken's character and then rushing into print with the lowdown on their role in protecting his dad's discovery.

CREDITS: Producer: T.R. Williams; Associate Producer: Fred Scheid; Director: Howard Bretherton; Screenplay: C.B. Williams and Marion Orth; Story: C.B. Williams; Photographed by: Harry Neumann; Assistant Director: W.B. "Breezy" Eason; Editors: Robert Golden and Russell Schoengarth; Sound Engineer: Karl Zint; Running Time: 63 Minutes; Released: January 20, 1940

CAST: Warren Hull (Bill MacGregor); Kay Linaker (Sonya Manning); William von Brinken (Prof. Werner); George Cleveland (John MacGregor); Fern Emmett (Aunt Mary); Edward Keane (Editor); William Castello (Eric Bowman); John Sheehan (Marden); Herbert Corthell (Pete); Vince Rush (Gruen); Hans Wollenberger (Mueller); and Paul Newland, Tris Coffin, I. Stanford Jolley

CHASING TROUBLE
(Monogram Pictures Corp.)

For their second run at a series that was shaping up as an anticipation of the soon-to-erupt Abbott & Costello comedies, Frankie Darro and Mantan Moreland tackled a novel but ill-developed twist on the old-standby espionage formula: Darro plays Cupid O'Brien, a floral-shop flunky and matchmaking fool who undertakes to find the proper sweetheart for his pal, Susie (Marjorie Reynolds). Cupid and his colleague, Jefferson (Moreland), allow themselves to be fooled into working for agents who use floral arrangements to transmit forbidden information.

The gimmick of *Chasing Trouble* is a running gag about the pseudo-science of handwriting analysis, which was quite popular at the time as a more nearly sophisticated twist on palm-reading and phrenology. Cupid, a novice at determining character via penmanship, at first mistakes the head spy, Morgan (Alex Callam), for a federal agent because of the crook's impressive signature. Later, he reappraises his analysis and realizes that Morgan is someone altogether more sinister.

Ultimately, Cupid hooks up with a reporter named Callahan (Milburn Stone), who not only proves to be the perfect beau for Susie—but also helps rescue her from the Morgan gang. Marjorie Reynolds' character has little more than a decorative role, leading us to wonder why the bad guys would want her put out of the way, except maybe for the old-standby gimmick of knowing too much. Moreland, too, has altogether too little to do in this one—an oversight corrected in subsequent teamings. Next up for Darro and Moreland: *On the Spot* and *Laughing at Danger* (see below).

CREDITS: In Charge of Production: Scott R. Dunlap; Associate Producer: Grant Withers; Director: Howard Bretherton; Screenplay: Mary McCarthy; Photographed by: Harry Neumann; Assistant Director: W.B. Eason; Sound Engineer: Karl Zint; Technical Director: E.R. Hickson; Running Time: 64 Minutes; Released: January 30, 1940

CAST: Frankie Darro (Cupid O'Brien); Mantan Moreland (Jefferson); Milburn Stone (Callahan); Marjorie Reynolds (Susie); Alex Callam (Morgan); George Cleveland (Lester); Lillian Elliott (Mrs. O'Brien); Tristam Coffin (Phillips); I. Stanford Jolley (Molotoff); Willy Costello (Kurt); Donald Kerr (Cassidy); Cheryl Walker (Phyllis); and Joe Devlin

The title menace of *The Invisible Killer* is no transparent human agent, but rather a poisonous substance hidden in a telephone receiver. (Photofest)

THE INVISIBLE KILLER
(Producers Distributing Corp.)

The title is honest enough, but still a come-on that can only have disappointed the fantasy-film enthusiasts of the day. The title menace of *The Invisible Killer* is no transparent human agent, but rather a poisonous substance hidden in a telephone receiver. Which is weird enough, especially when applied to a case of serial murder—but hardly as ferocious as the marquee would suggest.

There are other problems, including ill-at-ease supporting performances and an overall cheapness of presentation. The sense of danger is ever-present, however, and not even Joseph O'Donnell's stilted dialogue can defeat the desperation that propels the slight story.

The murders are piling up for members of a gambling syndicate, and news reporter Sue Walker (Grace Bradley) and homicide cop Jerry Brown (Roland Drew) are keen on breaking the case before a mob war can erupt.

Too late. The situation turns so ugly, so rapidly, that the law shuts down the betting houses, and racketeer Lefty Ross (Sydney Grayler) is murdered by an unseen force just as he is about to turn fink. A big-shot reformer (Boyd Irwin) is next to die—and this time, Sue wises up and confiscates a telephone receiver as evidence. The hideous mechanism is discovered. Finally, a trusted staff member (Harry Worth) is revealed as a snitch between the police and the underworld, and the gangsters' lawyer (Alex Callam) proves to be the Big Cheese himself.

Grace Bradley is efficiently relentless as the impulsive free-agent sleuth, and Jeanne Kelly has a nice lesser turn as the endangered daughter of a key victim. Roland Drew, the leading man of director Sam Newfield's watershed PRC picture, *Hitler—Beast of Berlin* (1939), is less impressive here as Miss Bradley's homicide-squad fiancé. Miss Bradley makes a fairly convincing gal-type news-hack until one of her published stories comes to light—an extraordinarily awful job of reportage that no self-respecting newspaper would inflict upon its readership. As on *Hitler—Beast of Berlin*, Newfield uses his open-secret identity of Sherman Scott.

Though no great shakes by any standard, *The Invisible Killer* is all the same a crucial title in the early development of the studio remembered today as Producers Releasing Corp. Ben Judell had launched the company in 1938 under the Progressive Pictures banner, renaming it Producers Distributing Corp. in 1939 and then ceding control to Sigmund Neufeld—who in 1940 changed the name to Sigmund Neufeld Productions. The change to Producers Releasing Corp., a branch of Pathé Laboratories, Inc., also came in 1940. The PRC identity would remain in force until 1946-47, when the company transmogrified itself into Eagle-Lion Studios.

CREDITS: Producer Ben Judell; Associate Producer: Sigmund Neufeld; Director: Sherman Scott [Sam Newfield]; Story: Carter Wayne; Adapted Screenplay: Joseph O'Donnell; Photographed by: Jack Greenhalgh; Assistant Director: Herman Webber; Editor: Holbrook N. Todd; Musical Director: David Chudnow; Sound Engineer: Hans Weeren; Technical Director: Fred Preble; Running Time: 61 Minutes; Released: January 31, 1940

CAST: Grace Bradley (Sue Walker); Roland Drew (Lt. Jerry Brown); William Newell (Pat); Alex Callam (Enslee); Frank Coletti (Martin); Sydney Grayler (Lefty Ross); Clem Wilenchick (District Attorney Sutton); Boyd Irwin (Cunningham); Jeanne Kelly (Gloria Cunningham); David Oliver (Worchester); Harry Worth (Tyler); Ernie Adams (Squint)

FRANKENSTEIN
(Pixilated Pictures)

We haven't enjoyed the luxury of viewing this labor-of-love production from San Antonio, Texas—but then, neither have we had the good fortune of seeing George E. Turner's own, somewhat later, amateur production of a *Frankenstein* takeoff in any reasonably coherent form. At least we know what became of the Turner *Frankenstein*, which was shot in 16-millimeter color in Amarillo, Texas, over a gradual span during the postwar 1940s and early 1950s: One of the Turner household's sons inadvertently destroyed the long-unedited footage around 1970 while attempting to project it without appropriate supervision. *Vita longa, ars brevis.*

We also can describe the Turner *Frankenstein*, in George's words, as "more Howard Lovecraft, really, than Mrs. Shelley...I used the *Frankenstein* identity, all right, but I was coming directly off ol' Lovecraft's serialized novel, *Herbert West: Reanimator*, rather than trying to adapt *Frankenstein* or do any kind of takeoff on the Universal movies. *Herbert*

The amateur company's businesslike approach included a fail-safe against no-shot talent—and ticket-selling duties for the actors. (Courtesy Interstate Theatres Collection, Austin, Texas)

Beyond the Horror Ban

On the backyard laboratory set of 1940's homegrown *Frankenstein*, with Henry Dielmann, Jr., as the Monster, Paul Meaders as Fritz and Glenn Alvey, Jr., as the renegade surgeon. The accomplishment would remain impressive even if the film's makers had not been schoolchildren.

West, naturally, owed its inspirations to *Frankenstein*. The Monster, as I played 'im, was closer to what Chris Lee wound up doing in the first Hammer *Frankenstein*—except for my being somewhat chubbier than ol' Chris ever was—than to any of the three Karloff interpretations."

So much for one of the mysteries of the missing *Frankenstein*s. The other remains a misplaced film, and—the proverbial Six Degrees of Separation notwithstanding—attempts to trace its crafters, or any surviving footage, have led to a *cul-de-sac*. But we know that this film and four other 16mm featurettes (see the 1937 *Dr. Jekyll and Mr. Hyde*) were completed and shown provincially, along with short subjects. And we know that the popular sensation these films caused in San Antonio led to some generous publicity on a national scale. We have turned up such artifacts as a production contract and several of the soundtrack discs, rendered unplayable by the passage of time and the forcible obsolescence of recording technology.

"Amateur movie-making is generally admitted to be 'a young man's game'—but down in Texas there's a group of movie-making amateurs for whose activities some new and super-youthful adjectives ought to be coined," wrote Wilton Scott in the April 1941 issue of *The American Cinematographer*. "Officially, they call themselves Pixilated Pictures..., [and] for five years these youngsters have operated a thriving 16mm production company." The journal of the American Society of Cinematographers was running over a year behind the activities in question, for Pixilated's *Frankenstein* had premiered in February of 1940 and had become, in turn, a sufficiently well-received attraction to merit showing in several of Texas' Interstate Circuit theatres.

In 1937, at the home of San Antonio's E. Humphrey Price family—no kinship to Mike Price, as far as we've determined—daughter Babe Price and several neighborhood chums staged a music-and-comedy revue. Babe's mother, a home-movie enthusiast, shot portions of the show with her Bell & Howell Filmo and then encouraged the kids to try making a picture of their own. Mrs. Price supplied the camera and film stock but recommended that the children—who ranged in age from 10 to 13 at the time—organize a company and sell shares in it.

Glenn Alvey, Jr., one of the older members, wrote a shooting script modeled after the 1932 Paramount version of *Dr. Jekyll and Mr. Hyde*. Completed in June of 1937, the production paid for itself and then some, enabling Pixilated Pictures to declare a stock dividend of 100 percent and mount a new issue at 20 cents a share—double the original price. Subsequent productions were *It's Laughter We're After* (December 1937), *Hollywood Ho!* (1938), *Snazzy Sixteen* (1939) and the 1939-40 production of *Frankenstein*. The company also made newsreels and a five-minute promotional film for a San Antonio dance studio.

Alvey derived his script for *Frankenstein* from the 1931 Universal version, embellished by a familiarity with the 1935 *Bride of Frankenstein* and the then-new *Son of Frankenstein*, whose striking wardrobe design for Boris Karloff was reflected in the shaggy pelt worn by Alvey's Monster, played by Henry Dielmann, Jr. Where surviving photographs show little in the way of makeup or elaborate costuming on Alvey (as Henry Frankenstein) or leading lady Edith Jarrell, considerable extravagance is obvious in the appearances of both the Monster and Dr. Frankenstein's helper, Fritz, played by Paul Meaders.

"As the youthful actor [playing the Monster] didn't particularly resemble Karloff, the foundation of the makeup had to be a mask," reported *Cinematographer*. "Yet... it must move naturally... and let the expressions show through..."

After several failed experiments with *papier-mâché* and paste, Alvey and a local taxidermist cast Dielmann's head in plaster, from which they built a mask of rubber, modeled after photographs of Karloff. A wig was fashioned from black goat-hair.

More elaborate yet were two sets representing Dr. Frankenstein's laboratory: One was built outdoors as a full-scale standing set, the better to take advantage of natural light and spare Dielmann the discomfort of wearing the mask under a Photoflood barrage. The other was an intricate miniature, complete with figurines of Dielmann, Alvey and Meaders and a pulley apparatus that would allow the raising of the operating table through the ceiling. "The two [sets] matched up surprisingly well," said *Cinematographer*. Another miniature was built of the windmill where the climactic confrontation and fire take place. Mrs. Price's Model 121 magazine-loading Filmo was used for most of the shooting, but camera operator Jack Locke resorted to a Model 70D-A Filmo to accommodate the higher speed necessary to make the miniatures appear more nearly convincing. Dialogue and sound effects were captured on home-recording discs, with musical scoring selected from commercial phonograph records. The final production tab was reported at $100.

Alvey, Locke and Babe Price edited the film and shot titles in a combination office-and-studio in the attic of the Price residence. Alvey, Russell Bertsch and Tish Walker designed posters. *Frankenstein* had its premiere in the ballroom of San Antonio's St. Anthony Hotel before an audience of 400 people. The presentation required as much organic stagecraft as it did mechanical projection, with staffers manning multiple phonographs to keep the canned music and custom-recorded dialogue and sound effects—at 78 r.p.m., which allowed only three to five minutes' playing time per side of a disc—in synch with the picture. The San Antonio newspapers contributed abundant promotional space. The Interstate Circuit Theatres not only supplied production resources but also played *Frankenstein* and a re-edited *Jekyll & Hyde*, jazzed up with sound effects, on a limited basis.

CREDITS: President: Howard Hudson; Director, Screenwriter and Designer: Glenn Alvey, Jr.; Photographed by: Jack Locke; Settings and Promotional Materials: Glenn Alvey, Jr., Russell Bertsch and Tish Walker; Makeup: Adrian Hines Taxidermy; Production Assistant and Supervising Editor: Babe Price; Script Supervisor: Elizabeth Kenney; Sound-on-Disc Engineered by: Glenn Alvey, Jr.; Director of Company: Joe McMoodie; Running Time: Approx. 30 Minutes; Publicly Shown: Beginning in February 1940

CAST: Glenn Alvey, Jr. (Henry von Frankenstein); Elizabeth Mortix (Edith Jarrell); Fritz (Paul Meaders); Little Maria (Tish Walker); Maria's Father (Russell Bertsch); Henry Dielmann, Jr. [Given as Harry Dielmann, Jr., in Some Reports] (the Monster)

SON OF INGAGI
(Hollywood Productions/Richard C. Kahn Productions./Sack Amusement Enterprises, Inc.)

Spencer Williams, Jr., the writer and outstanding player of *Son of Ingagi*, landed the role of a lifetime in 1950, when the influential entertainers Freeman Gosden and Charles Correll chose him to play Andrew Halt Brown in a CBS-Television series based upon their long-running radio serial, *Amos 'n' Andy*. Gosden and Correll, white men who impersonated black characters on radio and in off-screen voices for two animated cartoons, also had appeared in blackface in a 1930 feature-film spin-off called

A captive ape-man named N'Gena (Zack Williams) is the *Son of Ingagi*. (Photofest)

Check and Double Check. A generation later, they knew that the greasepaint gimmick would no longer wash, and so they peopled their teevee version with some of the finest black talent Hollywood had to offer: Loquacious Tim Moore weighed in as the exuberant schemer, George "Kingfish" Stevens, and mild-mannered Alvin Childress became Andy's conscience and hard-working business partner, Amos. Many of Gosden & Correll's authentically black supporting players carried over from radio, lending the transplant continuity and substance, but the real casting coups lay with Williams and Moore.

Since 1928, *Amos 'n' Andy* had virtually defined the popular view of middle-class black community life. The show was as popular in black households as it was with white folks. To the credit of Gosden and Correll, *Amos 'n' Andy* was an affectionate and often sentimental program, however broad in its strokes, and the creators sought a greater cultural weight in bringing *Amos 'n' Andy* to television. Though most episodes dealt with situations among the black characters, the series took occasional pains to introduce white players on equal social footing, with reciprocal displays of respect. Despite this progressive attitude, many voices were raised against *Amos 'n' Andy*. A blast from the National Association for the Advancement of Colored People, obviously based upon no familiarity with the stories, finally sunk the show in 1953, although syndicated reruns continued into the 1960s. The CBS Television Network repressed its *Amos 'n' Andy* archive for years, until saner thinking prevailed and the program found an appreciative new audience on the video market. The series remains more socially uplifting than the loudly mediocre and blatantly pandering spate of Afrocentric programming that has cropped up to feed the television monster in recent years.

What had seemed a bold strategy for Spencer Williams, proved at length to have been a misstep. He could not turn back, for producer Al Sack—who had allowed Williams a tightly budgeted creative autonomy from the late '30s through 1946—had edged away from the movie business, sensing the approaching collapse of the black neighborhood theatre circuits that had been his marketplace. Nor could Williams move forward in the major leagues, for though the film-and-television industry was quick to cancel a popular weekly sitcom in the face of hysterical protests, it was damnably reluctant to blaze new trails. For generations, mainstream Hollywood fooled itself into believing it had room for perhaps one black A-list star at a time—Lena Horne during the 1940s, Eartha Kitt and Dorothy Dandridge by turns during the '50s and Sidney Poitier and Sammy Davis, Jr., during the '60s, when things finally loosened up a bit. Not only was the portly Williams better suited physically for comedy relief than for leading-man duties, but he also was too diversified in his talents to be conveniently categorized. A black writer- director-actor holding forth at a major studio? Not bloody likely.

But such chances finally began improving in 1970, when Melvin Van Peebles and Gordon Parks broke through with the major-league releases of *Watermelon Man* and *Shaft*. Spencer Williams had died in obscurity just the year previous, at age 76. No particularly lofty opportunities opened up as a consequence of the coups for Van Peebles and Parks—except for the low-budget "blaxploitation" craze, which was hardly a case of cultural uplift—but when Spike Lee followed along during the 1980s with the independent *She's Gotta Have It* and the major-studio releases of *School Daze* and *Do the Right Thing*, he worked plenty hard to keep the door open.

Williams' prime period of 1937-46 had begun finding its shape in 1910, when the Louisiana-born entertainer made his way to New York and landed a messenger job with Oscar Hammerstein. Williams meanwhile studied acting and struck up a friendship with the black vaudevillian Bert Williams (no kin). Spencer served in the Army during World War I, then returned to show business, briefly as a recording artist. His OKeh Records duet with the singer-guitarist Lonnie Johnson, a bawdy hokum blues tune called "It Feels So Good," bespeaks a passion for music that would surge throughout his films.

By the close of the '20s, Warners' part-talker *The Jazz Singer* had convinced the industry to edge closer to a talking-picture standard. Williams, who took his craft more seriously than he took his ego, responded to a call for technical talent by signing with Christie Studios as an audio engineer; stardom could come in due course. While developing a reputation for knowing his way around the recording console, Williams also impressed studio boss Al Christie with his story ideas, his deep and resonant voice, his expressive face and his crackerjack comic timing.

The timing was more right than Williams could have guessed, for during 1927-28 Christie Studios hired the Yiddish-American humorist Octavus Roy Cohen to adapt his several novels about black community life in Alabama and Harlem. In a bid for a heightened realism, Christie promoted Williams to co-writer. Williams reserved the right to act in his own yarns. It is anybody's guess whether Williams may have ghost-directed any of these (which bear such spoofing titles as *The Melancholy Dame* and *Music Hath Harms*), for the official documentation identifies such white-guy directors as Archie Mayo and Arvid Gillstrom. But these pictures bear stylistic flourishes and cultural nuances that also figure in Williams' *auteur* films of 1940-46. If the Cohen series geared itself toward white audiences and indulged in blatant stereotypes, still Williams' involvement kept them grounded in an authenticity that is lacking in the larger studios' few black-ensemble pictures of the same period.

Williams met the Depression years as an actor, primarily, appearing in such black-ensemble indies as *Georgia Rose*, *Bad Boy* and *Virginia Judge*. He contributed dialogue and played support to jazz crooner Herb Jeffries for a series of Westerns—*The Bronze Buckaroo*, *Harlem Rides the Range*, *Two-Gun Man from Harlem* and *Harlem on the Prairie*—which brought Williams to the attention of

Beyond the Horror Ban

Son of Ingagi has to do with a hidden fortune in African gold, which is sought by the scientist's crooked brother (Arthur Ray, the "dark-skinned Bela Lugosi" of 1942's *Professor Creeps*) with homicidal results.(Photofest)

the Dallas-based producer Al Sack. Sack, a Jewish businessman with an eye for neglected niche-markets, bought Williams' script for *Son of Ingagi* and hired him to play a bumbling but ultimately helpful police detective. Sack was so pleased with the result that he enlisted Williams as a one-man producer-director-writer-star combination.

Among the historic filmmakers of color, only Oscar Micheaux enjoyed a greater creative freedom—for which Micheaux paid severely, given his distaste for integrated business partnerships. Williams was more an integrationist, and a pragmatist to boot, and in Al Sack he found a *laissez-faire* backer who afforded him prominence in a limited orbit; money to spare, given Williams' dollar-stretching abilities; and the freedom to develop his own stories. The result is a legacy of nine splendidly rough-hewn motion pictures (10, if one counts *Son of Ingagi*, which Williams did not direct), all filmed on budgets of between $10,000 and $15,000. The Williams films possess a slightly finer commercial gloss than the generally threadbare work of Micheaux. They sidestep the somber bitterness on which Micheaux preferred to dwell, and they show black community life of the era, by turns, at its most prosaic, its most glamorous, its most good-humored, its most brutal and its most devout. They seem to represent a variety of genres (one horror fantasy, two comedies, three spiritual exercises and four melodramas), but in fact each is *sui generis*, each a worthy example of what a Hollywood outsider can achieve when he reconciles his own ideas with a knowledge of what his fixed audience wants.

The Herb Jeffries "all-colored" Westerns are very much of the same formulas that had served the likes of Ken Maynard, Gene Autry, Bob Steele and John Wayne. *Son of Ingagi* is, by contrast, no more a conventional mad-doctor yarn than it is a sequel to that notorious mock-expeditionary thriller of 1930, *Ingagi* (see *Forgotten Horrors: The Definitive Edition*). Laura Bowman, the distinguished stage actress, plays *Son*'s renegade physician as a surly schemer, plotting to lure a virginal young woman into a forbidden tryst with a captive ape-man named N'Gena (Zack Williams). There are hints, of course, that the creature hails from Africa, so he might very well be the long-lost offspring of a gorilla and some sacrificial tribal maiden, given the forbidden notion of interbreeding that had given *Ingagi* its million-dollar box-office clout. Dame Bowman seems careless to the point of harboring a death-wish, for she allows the monster the run of the house and finally croaks at its hands before her plans can be fulfilled.

Williams' screenplay concerns itself more with establishing a lifelike domestic state between the romantic leads, Daisy Bufford and Alfred Grant, and with Williams' own comical portrayal of an overbearing cop who seems incapable of detecting the monster at close range. In a choice sequence that would fit nicely into a Hal Roach two-reeler, Williams putters about the kitchen of the benighted house while the ape-man hovers just out of sight. No sooner has Williams built himself a sandwich and turned away for a moment, than the beast darts in and devours the delicacy. Williams finds himself more interested in the case of the missing sandwich than with tracking down the cause of the mayhem.

The story has much to do with a hidden fortune in African gold, which is sought by the scientist's crooked brother (Arthur Ray, the "dark-skinned Bela Lugosi" of 1942's *Professor Creeps*) with homicidal results. Finally, N'Gena abducts Miss Bufford but accidentally torches the house before he can get on about his business with her. Williams and Grant save the day—and Williams saves the gold, in a twist ending.

Williams' deft comic presence accounts for much of the charm here, and so does Dame Bowman's formidable but too-brief portrayal of the grouchy renegade doctor. Williams' script is rich in the finer points of citified black folklife, dwelling on the hospitable details of a wedding reception, reveling in a love of music and establishing early on that the doctor has deep reasons—some friendly, some sinister—for wanting to see the young lady inherit the mysterious old house-*cum*-laboratory. Miss Bufford and Grant make convincingly devoted newlyweds, even to a bickersome outbreak.

The lead photographer on *Son of Ingagi* is Roland C. Price, the "Vagabond Cameraman" responsible for that cruel Southwestern docu-drama, *The Penitente Murder Case*—and a distant relative of *Forgotten Horrors*' Mike Price. A comic-strip version of *Son of Ingagi* appears in Price's 1998 anthology, *Southern-Fried Homicide*.

CREDITS: Producer and Director: Richard C. Kahn; Supervisor of Production: Dr. Herbert Meyer; Story and Continuity: Spencer Williams, Jr.; Photographed by: Roland C. Price and Herman Schapp; Editor: Dan Milner; Sound Engineer: Cliff Ruberg; Production Manager: Dick L'Estrange; Running Time: Surviving Prints Vary from 60-70 Minutes; Released: During 1940; Distributed on a State-by-State Basis on into the 1950s

CAST: Zack Williams (N'Gena); Laura Bowman (Dr. Helen Jackson); Alfred Grant (Bob Lindsay); Daisy Bufford (Eleanor Lindsay); Arthur Ray (Zeno Jackson); Spencer Williams, Jr. (Det. Nelson); Earl J. Morris (Bradshaw); Jesse Graves (Chief of Detectives); and the Four Toppers (Vocal Group)

PHANTOM RANCHER
(Colony Pictures, Inc.)

Indiana born but claiming native Texan citizenship in a savvy studio publicity ploy, Ken Maynard (1895-1973) was the roughest, toughest, straight-shootin'est, picture-makin'est *hombre* who ever laid siege to Old Hollywood. An unnervingly proud and plain-spoken artist, Maynard had come to the screen in 1924 as a veteran of the rodeo and Wild West exposition circuits, rapidly winning a devoted following even as he estranged himself from one studio after another with his intimidating martinet tactics and his insistence upon creative autonomy. *Phantom Rancher*, with its impoverished production values and spotty release via the sub-distributor states'-rights system, is a sobering example of how far Maynard had fallen since the middle 1930s, when he alienated Mascot Pictures honcho Nat Levine. Levine had rescued Maynard from a sacking at Universal, amply aware of the star's volatile combination of marquee value and irascibility. Levine ultimately found Maynard insufficiently grateful and replaced him on desperate impulse with a then-struggling Gene Autry in a manic science-fiction/musical/Western serial, 1935's *The Phantom Empire*. This project was a genre-bender experiment whose unanticipated runaway success might have put Maynard at the top of the game for years to come; at any rate, *Empire* certainly had that effect on Autry's career.

And while Autry zoomed to a massed acclaim—thanks, in great measure, to a parallel hit-record and radio career that Maynard could scarcely have matched—the mighty Ken turned anew to the rodeo arena. He certainly wasn't "out of films" by this time, as Ephraim Katz's *The Film Encyclopedia* categorically declares. Indeed, the Maynard résumé contains 24 features spanning 1935-44. But Maynard's big-screen fortunes had diminished noticeably. The 1938 *Phantom Ranger* that Katz lists as a Maynard picture, incidentally, is actually a Tim McCoy starrer, dealing with a counterfeiting racket.

Certainly easy to mis-read *Phantom Ranger* as *Phantom Rancher*. But *Rancher* proves to be an out-and-out weirdie, in which Ken Mitchell (Maynard) inherits both the ranch and the bad reputation of an uncle who had been suspected of provoking a disastrous outbreak of stampedes. The distrustful ranchers will have none of Ken's help, so he insinuates his way into a murderous outlaw gang; learns that a big-shot cattleman named Collins (Ted Adams) is secretly the real pain-in-the-neck; and suits himself up as the Phantom Rancher—thwarting Collins' takeover plans by helping the locals meet their mortgages.

The masquerade is more Robin Hood than Phantom of the Horse Opera, but Maynard's very anger and indignation render this Phantom a figure of menace, at least to those who deserve menacing. Maynard may have lapsed beyond recovery of his star power and behind-the-scenes authority, but his attitude is still that of the rambunctious, hard-riding Westerner, and his magnificent charger, Tarzan, is still the smartest horse in the movies, Roy Rogers' Trigger notwithstanding.

This long, final exile on Poverty Row found Maynard's appetite for slugfests—and for verbally abusing his opponents, rather like Popeye the Sailor Man, while thrashing them—undiminished. Another 1940 Colony entry featuring Maynard, *Death Rides the Range*, boasts a garnish of eeriness in the person of a homicidal land-grabber named Baron Starkoff (Sven Hugo Borg). Colony Pictures executives Max and Arthur Alexander were cousins of Universal's former production chief, Carl Laemmle, Jr., who in 1934 had clashed bitterly with Maynard over the perceived debacle of the offbeat Western *Smoking Guns*—and fired Maynard in retaliation.

A long span of reclusiveness, coupled with a taste for strong drink, had left Maynard a shadow of his larger-than-life self by the time he cropped up in a 1970 exploitation picture called *Bigfoot*. Maynard died of malnutrition at age 77.

CREDITS: Producers: Max Alexander and Arthur Alexander; Director: Harry Fraser; Story and Screenplay: Bill Lively; Photographed by: William Hyer; Art Director: Fred Preble; Editor: Fred Bain; Music: Lew Porter; Sound: Clifford Ruberg; Running Time: 61 Minutes; Released: Beginning in March of 1940 on a States'-Rights Basis

CAST: Ken Maynard (Ken Mitchell); Dorothy Short (Ann Markham); Harry Harvey (Gopher); Ted Adams (Collins); Dave O'Brien (Luke); Tom London (Parker); John Elliott (Markham); Reed Howes (Lon); Steve Clark (Burton); Carl Matthews (Hank); Sherry Tansey (Joe); Tarzan (Himself)

DRUMS OF FU MANCHU
(Republic Pictures Corp.)

From the pages of fiction steps the most sinister figure of all time—Fu Manchu. Schooled in the ancient mysteries of the Orient, he is as modern as tomorrow! Ruthless, ageless, holding himself above human law, he embarks upon his most stupendous crime—the conquest of Asia! And with him comes the thunder of his summons to death... the Drums of Fu Manchu!– From the Prologue

For its 17th serial and its first big splash of 1940, Republic Pictures turned to Sax Rohmer as a heavy-duty pop-literary source: The world-beating Dr. Fu Manchu, ageless mandarin and master of a thousand tortures and treacheries, had been a hit with the mass audience ever since his debut in *Story Teller* magazine in 1912—the wicked protagonist of many of Rohmer's novels and short stories, to

Drums of Fu Manchu **is unique among Republic's serials, playing out more like an extraordinarily long feature film with chapter breaks.**

say nothing of earlier motion pictures, a syndicated comic strip and a radio program. Dr. Fu had outlived the Yellow Peril subgenre that had spawned him to become as recognizable a name as Mickey Mouse or Superman. And here, Republic was dead-set upon restoring the big-screen popularity of a character whose novels had made Rohmer (professional name of Arthur Sarsfield Ward) a millionaire many times over.

In arranging to latch down the film rights during 1939, Republic bought more than just the then-new book *Drums of Fu Manchu*. The title was just right, but so were elements from several other Rohmer yarns, which a team of eight screenwriters wove into one of the studio's more nearly perfect chapter-plays. The adaptation boasts as much striking originality as Republic had shown during 1936-37 in transforming the title character of *Dick Tracy* from a plainclothes cop into an F.B.I. agent. Fu Manchu, as played by Henry Brandon, and his poisonous daughter, Fah Lo Suee (Gloria Franklin), are sufficiently loyal to the source. But Fu's Scotland Yard Nemesis, Sir Denis Nayland Smith (William Royle), and Sir Denis' chronicler Dr. Petrie (Olaf Hytten) become more in the way of sideline characters, yielding much of the actionful heroism to a written-for-the-screen youngster named Allan Parker (Robert Kellard). The action itself is surprisingly subdued for a Republic, giving way to an unusually great deal of plot development and characterization. *Drums of Fu Manchu* is unique among Republic's serials, playing out more like an extraordinarily long feature film with chapter breaks—which is the way most fans today watch the serials, as a sustained block of time on video—than a typically episodic pageant of cliffhangers.

Republic may have had in mind merely a cosmetic adjustment in making Fu's elite guard of 17 blindly obedient hoodlums—known as *dacoits*—something more or less than human in appearance. But the massed impact of the servants is more substantial, underscoring the film with a visceral, unreasoning horror in counterpoint to Fu's thoroughly rational malice. These dacoits, as fashioned from a corps of fine stuntmen and character actors by makeup artist Bob Mark, are nightmare-inducing

Beyond the Horror Ban

Fu Manchu's (Henry Brandon) nightmare-inducing henchmen each bear a ghastly arrow-point scar on the forehead to signify brain surgery performed by Dr. Fu. The lead dacoit, Loki (played by John Merton), is distinguished further by snakelike fangs. (Photofest)

creatures, each bearing a ghastly arrow-point scar on the forehead to signify brain surgery performed by Dr. Fu. The lead dacoit, Loki (played by John Merton), is distinguished further by snakelike fangs. As Fu Manchu, veteran movie villain Henry Brandon, who had been discovered on the Los Angeles stage by Hal Roach, is a study in restraint—a quality all the more impressive in light of his flamboyant Oriental-deco wardrobe—and displays a mingled sense of menace and droll humor that is fully consistent with the defining portrayals of years past by Boris Karloff, Warner Oland and Harry Agar Lyons. Gloria Franklin is at once delectable and creepy as Fah Lo Suee.

The story finds Fu searching for the sceptre of Genghis Khan, which the superstitious Himalayans will accept as his credential as the New World Conqueror. At the command of Fu and Fah Lo Suee are the merciless, zombie-like dacoits. Sir Denis Nayland Smith of the British Foreign Office sets out to put the kibosh on his chronic enemy, Dr. Fu. Joining Sir Denis are Allan Parker, son of an early victim, and Mary Randolph (Luana Walters), daughter of a museum curator who had lost a priceless artifact to Fu. After any number of desperate encounters, Parker places the sceptre in safe hands, proving to the rebellious Himalayans that Fu does not bear following. The dacoits have been destroyed, but Dr. Fu Manchu survives to begin plotting new treacheries.

Republic was all set to get cracking on those new treacheries and promptly announced a sequel. At the onslaught of World War II, a twist was added: Fu Manchu would shelve the conquering urge and place himself—however grudgingly—at the service of the Allies. National sensitivities intruded, however, and on July 19, 1942, the *New York Times* carried the following article:

Phooey, Dr. Fu

International protocol has disturbed Republic Pictures Corp. a good deal this week. Fu Manchu Strikes Again, *a photoplay in which Sax Rohmer's indestructible Chinese villain was to have switched over to the side of the angels and harried the Japanese, had to be shelved "out of deference to the Chinese people." Dr. Fu has long been a source of displeasure to the Chinese government, Republic learned, and he is not even wanted as an ally.*

The *Times'* account, lifted from a drier dispatch in *The Hollywood Reporter*, was followed with a late-July *Reporter* announcement that Republic would proceed, after all, with *Fu Manchu Strikes Again*, emphasizing the anti-Axis stance. Nothing came of the project, after all, but that did not stop Republic from issuing a feature-length condensation of *Drums of Fu Manchu* in 1943. The studio hardly did so with impunity, however, for that fall the U.S. government denied a clearance for export on grounds of *Drums'* "derogatory picturization of our Chinese allies."

And so where Nayland Smith and all the might of the British Empire had succeeded only in frustrating Fu Manchu's ambitions, the forces of Political Correctness put the *quietus* on the villain's movie career for the duration. Only after the Axis had fallen and the ensuing Cold War had resurrected the "Yellow Peril" as a fashionable component of a larger "Red Menace," could Fu come back into vogue as a screen character.

CREDITS: Producer: Hiram S. Brown, Jr.; Directors: William Witney and John English; Screenplay: Franklyn Adreon, Morgan B. Cox, Ronald Davidson, Norman S. Hall, Barney A. Sarecky and Sol Shor; Original *Fu Manchu* Stories and Characters created by: Sax Rohmer; Photographed by: William Nobles; Editors: Edward Todd and William Thompson; Musical Score: Cy Feuer; a Serial in Twelve Chapters, 269 Minutes; Released: March 15, 1940; Condensed Version, Running Time: 68 Minutes; Released: November 27, 1943

CAST: Henry Brandon (Dr. Fu Manchu); William Royle (Sir Nayland Smith); Robert Kellard (Allan Parker); Gloria Franklin (Fah Lo Suee); Olaf Hytten (Dr. Petrie); Tom Chatterton (Prof. Randolph); Luana Walters (Mary Randolph); Lal Chand Mehra (Sirdar Prahni); George Cleveland (Prof. Parker); John Dilson (Howard); John Merton (Loki); Dwight Frye (Anderson); Wheaton Chambers (Dr. Humphrey); George Pembroke (Crawford); Guy D'Ennery (Rang Sang).

MR. WASHINGTON GOES TO TOWN
(Dixie National Pictures, Inc./Consolidated National Film Exchanges)

Moreland & Miller, one of the finer comedy teams of black Vaudeville, stuck together in pictures as well, even though Mantan Moreland's fortunes as a solo artist in Hollywood proved greater than those of Flournoy E. Miller. Their co-starring movies, including the Harlem-out-West cowboy adventures of Herb Jeffries, were aimed expressly at African-American audiences. These contain a larger measure of stereotypical business than the mainstream pictures that Moreland graced without Miller.

Three Moreland & Miller movies in particular capture the artists' teamwork pretty much as it must have appeared in the black neighborhood nightspots where they perfected their dead-solid-perfect combination of slapstick *shtick* and absurd wordplay. These are *Mr. Washington Goes to Town* and 1942's back-to-back *Lucky Ghost* and *Professor Creeps*, all from the white producer Jed Buell. Buell's *Up Jumped the Devil* is an interim effort, minus Miller.

Buell, who was as much a well-intentioned huckster as he was a picturemaker, publicized *Mr. Washington* to the black newspapers as "the first all-Negro comedy feature ever made." Of course, most of the talents at work behind the cameras were white—and black actors and singers had been making comedy films since the silent era, both among themselves and with integrated ensemble casts.

But neither Buell's extravagant claims nor his amateurish filmmaking skills can diminish the fun of *Mr. Washington Goes to Town*. It all starts in the jailhouse, where a prisoner named Schenectady (Moreland) learns that he has inherited a hotel. Next thing he knows, Schenectady has arrived at the Hotel Ethiopia, where he puts himself to work as an elevator operator and hires his jailbird pal, Wallingford (Miller), as his assistant.

The hotel proves to contain more unnerving surprises than Schenectady can handle: A gorilla shows up, accompanied by a man in formal attire. Headless men prowl the place, and a knife thrower, an invisible man and a magician terrorize Schenectady and Wallingford. A menacing character named Brutus Blake (Maceo B. Sheffield) challenges Schenectady's ownership of the place and begins dis-

Mantan Moreland looks more indignant than scared as a gorilla-pelted Clarence Morehouse goes rampant in *Mr. Washington Goes to Town*.

mantling the hotel in search of hidden treasure. The situation has grown intolerable when Schenectady suddenly wakes. The entire misadventure has been a dream.

Wallingford wants to visit the hotel once the pals are sprung, but Schenectady nixes the idea: He has already been there, he says, and he finds the place none to his liking.

There is no other cop-out quite as infuriating as the just-a-dream resolution, but at least the ending of *Mr. Washington Goes to Town* is a foregone conclusion. Too many such finales—including those of the otherwise superior film noirs *The Strange Affair of Uncle Harry* (Universal; 1945) and *Fear* (Monogram; 1946)—have come about as hasty afterthoughts to placate the censors. *Mr. Washington*'s dream setting places the film more nearly on a par with the phantasmagorical newspaper cartoons and silent films of Winsor McCay (including *Little Nemo in Slumberland* and *Dream of a Rarebit Fiend*). Buell's customarily shabby production values serve to emphasize the otherworldly ambiance without detracting from the work of Miller & Moreland. The pals' funny business renders it immaterial whether there is a story to be found here.

Curiously, there is no reference to anybody named Washington in Dixie National's pressbook or in either of the rather choppy prints screened in preparation for this book. Maybe Washington is supposed to be Schenectady's last name.

CREDITS: Producers: Jed Buell and James K. Friedrich; Associate Producer: Maceo B. Sheffield; Director: Jed Buell; Screenplay: Walter Weems and Lex Neal; Story: Walter Weems; Photographed by: Jack Greenhalgh; Art Director: Fred Preble; Editor: William Paris; Musical Director: Harvey Brooks; Sound Engineer: Hans Weeren; Sound Effects: Treg Brown; Production Manager: Bert Sternbach; Assistant Production Manager: Charles Wayne; Running Time: 65 Minutes; Released: Following Los Angeles Preview on April 11, 1940

CAST: Flournoy E. Miller (Wallingford); Mantan Moreland (Schenectady); Maceo B. Sheffield (Brutus Blake); Arthur Ray (Blackstone); Margaret Whitten (Lady Queenie); Clarence Morehouse

(Gorilla); Monte Hawley (Stiletto); Zerita Steptean (Mrs. Brutus); Florence O'Brien (Chambermaid); Vernon McCalla (Invisible Man); John Lester Johnson (Tall Headless Man); DeForrest Covan (Short Headless Man); Edward Boyd (the Lonesome Ranger); Clarence Hargrave (Man in White Tuxedo); Johnnie Taylor (Magician); Walter Knox (Crippled Man); Geraldine Whitfield (Glamour Girl); Sam Warren (Barber); Cleo Desmond (Old Maid); Charlie Hawkins (Goldberg); Nathan Curry (Cop); Slick Garrison (Barbershop Patron); Henry Hastings (Uncle Utica)

Prof. Lewis (Joseph Stefani), who fancies himself to be working on a defense weapon invents a deadly beam for a master smuggler. Alert viewers will get a kick out of spotting *Dracula*'s Dwight Frye among *Sky Bandits*' players. (Photofest)

SKY BANDITS
(Criterion Pictures Corp./Monogram Pictures Corp.)

Grand National, one of the last surviving Poverty Row studios in that waning Depression era, had struck a resonant chord in 1937 by bringing Laurie York Erskine's long-popular novels-and-radio character, Sgt. Renfrew of the R.C.M.P., to the screen. The series soon lapsed to a production-distribution deal between Criterion and Monogram, sustaining a remarkable consistency under a variety of creative talents. Generously sprinkled with heroic ballads in a Canadian-copper twist on the singing-cowboy school of Westerns, the *Renfrew*s also boast an appetite for bizarre mortal perils.

George Turner, who cared little for cowboy-crooner movies and even less for baritone-Mountie movies, once suggested that there should have been a *Renfrew* picture called *Yukon Have It*. Personal tastes aside, George admitted there was plenty to like about the *Renfrew*s, "if you can get around all that pseudo-operatic caterwauling."

Sky Bandits, from a screenplay by *White Zombie*'s Edward Halperin, stands out as the *Renfrew* that pays off most generously for the science-fantasy fans: Renfrew (radio singer James Newill) and Constable Kelly (series regular Dave O'Brien) go airborne to connect an outbreak of plane wrecks

Beyond the Horror Ban

to a gang of smugglers. Renfrew's pal, Buzz Murphy (Eddie Featherstone), is ready to take off with a payload for the Yukon Gold Mining Co. The lurking evil takes the sunniest possible guise: A radio personality known as Uncle Dimwitty has wiretapped the mining company and is sneaking encrypted information into his children's-hour broadcasts. The most devoted listener is master smuggler Morgan (William Pawley), who on a cue from Uncle Dimwitty zaps Buzz's plane with a radio beam. Renfrew watches in horror as his friend crashes.

The deadly beam's inventor is Prof. Lewis (Joseph Stefani), who fancies himself to be working on a defense weapon. When he learns otherwise and complains accordingly, Morgan threatens him. Renfrew finds the machinery but is forced to scram before he can collect evidence. When he returns with backup, the lab has been dismantled, and Refrew's colleagues begin to question his state of mind. Obsessed with vengeance, Renfrew takes to the air—with the professor's daughter (Louise Stanley) as a stowaway. Morgan prepares to blast Renfrew, but the professor steers the ray toward Morgan's plane. Kelly and the professor make short work of the rest of the gang.

The *Renfrew*s found little critical respect in their day, and they are seldom even acknowledged in the rash of guides aimed at the video audience. (Most such guides, of course, are mostly good at steering folks toward self-evident landmarks.) But this forgotten series had its loyalists when the titles were fresh out of the projector, and some first-generation *Renfrew* fans still recall a pang of sadness on realizing that the rip-snorting *Sky Bandits* would be the final adventure. Until the day we see a *Collected Renfrew* on DVD or whatever flavor-of-the-moment medium crops up next, the Sinister Cinema videocassette catalogue makes a respectable accounting of the entries. Alert viewers will get a kick out of spotting *Dracula*'s Dwight Frye among *Sky Bandits*' players.

For the record, the other installments are *Renfrew of the Royal Mounted* (1937), a counterfeiter-thriller with a literally chilling set-piece in a frozen-meat locker; *Renfrew on the Great White Trail* (1938), with Richard Alexander as a likably drunken physician harboring a grim secret; *Fighting Mad* (1939), with Sally Blane as a kidnap victim-turned-suspect and Milburn Stone as a gang boss; *Crashing Thru* (1939), in which Stone plays a mining-company chief leading a murderous secret life; *Danger Ahead* (1940), scripted by Ed Halperin, with Renfrew taking charge of an armored-truck fleet to find a vanished driver and payload; *Yukon Flight* (1940), from another Halperin script, with James Newill's Renfrew baiting bad-guy mail-service boss William Pawley into an airborne confrontation; and *Murder on the Yukon* (1940), in which Newill and O'Brien, en route to a peaceable retreat from crimebusting, find instead the corpse of a newly wealthy miner.

CREDITS: Producer: Phil Goldstone; Director: Ralph Straub; Screenplay: Edward Halperin; Based upon: Laurie York Erskine's 1928 Novel *Renfrew Rides the Sky*; Photographed by: Mack Stengler; Assistant Director: Ben Chapman; Song, "Mounted Men," by Betty Laidlaw & Robert Lively, and selections by Lange & Porter; Editor: Martin Cohn; Running Time: 62 Minutes; Released: April 15, 1940

CAST: James Newill (Renfrew); Louise Stanley (Madeleine Lewis); Dewey Robinson (Swiddie); William Pawley (Morgan); Joseph Stefani (Prof. Lewis); Jim Farley (Inspector Warner); Dave O'Brien (Kelly); Karl Hackett (Hawthorne); Jack Clifford (Whispering Smith); Bob Terry (Hutchins); Eddie Featherstone (Buzz Murphy); and Ted Adams, Dwight Frye, Ken Duncan

ON THE SPOT
(Monogram Pictures Corp.)

Soda-fountain jerk and hotel porter are the respective stations in life of Frankie Darro and Mantan Moreland in this continuation of their astonishingly progressive comedy-team series. Nothing particularly comical about the story itself, whose serial-murder case serves to provoke the pals into rising good-humoredly above their stations to out-perform the local police as crimebusters. The film is an effortlessly (and inadvertently) near-perfect illustration of Mark Twain's definition of humor as a necessary response to the fundamental wretchedness of human existence. Even the partners' shared

Mantan Moreland and Frankie Darro take the buddy-comedy tradition to the next level in *On the Spot*. (Photofest)

impulsive interest in amateur sleuthing is an adventurous rebellion against the numbing drudgery of their second-class citizenship: Better to risk mortal peril than to succumb to the unfeeling nothingness of wage slavery. This attitude of tacit Existentialism, perhaps more so than the trailblazing integrationism of the partnership, is what distinguishes the Darro-Moreland pictures from even the more finely developed work of Laurel & Hardy and Abbott & Costello. Where Stan Laurel and Oliver Hardy exist on-screen in a state of grace however downtrodden ("the *shabby* gentlemen," as a supporting character dismisses them in one early talking picture), and where Bud Abbott and Lou Costello are patently stage-and-screen stars playing at fringe-dweller buffoonery, Frankie Darro and Mantan Moreland seem almost documentary representations of the serving class, bent upon benevolent subversion. *On the Spot* is particularly emphatic in this regard, what with the victims being mobsters whom the law prefers dead and the elusive criminal ringleader turning out to be a pillar of Social Respectability.

Amateur Detective was the work-in-progress title of *On the Spot*, and as such it ably defines the tone of almost the entire series. Darro and Moreland are throughout—whatever their character identities from picture to picture—simply Darro and Moreland, a fast-talking, quick-thinking buddy act. When the pictures are (too rarely) unearthed today, Darro impresses modern eyes as almost a genetic template for Michael J. Fox. Moreland remains incomparable, despite the best funny business of such late-20th Century breakout talents as Robin Harris, Eddie Murphy, Jamie Foxx and Martin Lawrence. Darro and Moreland's ensemble work retains an insurgent freshness.

Frankie (Darro) is minding the counter at a small-town pharmacy's soda fountain when a big-city mobster lurches into the shop, dying from gunshot wounds. Frankie and his chum, Jefferson (Moreland), are quickly assumed to have become the Men Who Know Too Much, for both the police and the underworld—not to mention the press—believe that the victim must have told them about a hidden fortune from a bank robbery. Another gangster turns up dead. Frankie decides to flush out the killer, convincing Jefferson to pretend to possess crucial information while Frankie lurks in wait for an attack. Jefferson nervously topples a pallet of shipping cartons, however, and the approaching murderer escapes. But among the shattered crates, Frankie finds hidden clues that betray local banker Cyrus Haddon (Robert Warwick) as the brains behind the crimes.

The sense of menace is palpable, and Robert Warwick—who had been a key figure in the transition from silents to talking pictures—is just right as the stuffed-shirt mastermind. Darro and Moreland seem particularly pleased with themselves at having found triumph amid a disastrous bungle. Far more than just a rediscovered oddity from the Depression-into-wartime years, this series sheds new light on Hollywood's comedy-thriller genre as a class.

CREDITS: In Charge of Production: Scott R. Dunlap; Associate Producer: Grant Withers; Director: Howard Bretherton; Screenplay: Joseph West (from His Story) and Dorothy Reid; Photographed by: Harry Neumann; Editor: Russell Schoengarth; Sound: Karl Zint; Running Time: 62 Minutes; Released: June 11, 1940

CAST: Frankie Darro (Frankie); Mantan Moreland (Jefferson); John St. Polis (Doc Hunter); Robert Warwick (Cyrus Haddon); Mary Kornman (Ruth Hunter); Maxine Leslie (Gerry); Lillian Elliott (Mrs. Kelly); Leroy Mason (Smilin' Bill); Jeffrey Sayre (Hype Innes); Gene O'Donnell (Slates Eckert); and Russell Hopton, Dave O'Brien

THE LEOPARD MEN OF AFRICA: AN EXPOSÉ OF UNRECORDEDSAVAGE RITUALS IN THE CONGO
(Paul L. Hoefler/Walter A. Futter/Zeidman International, Inc.)

"It's a thriller," declared *Variety*, whose severe box-office bias more commonly led its crix to denounce the goona-goona exploitationers as tedious fakes. *The Leopard Men of Africa*—whose bigger mouthful of a title appears on-screen but is not part of the copyright record—is of course largely a fake in its own right. But at least the film has the gumption to announce up front that its ticket-selling "cannibal" "rituals" were enacted for the camera. There is a helpful basis in authenticity, and the natural and staged sequences dovetail impressively, thanks to the assured continuity by Allyn Butterfield, a respected editor of big-screen newsreels.

A generous 65 minutes of green-hell horrors, *The Leopard Men of Africa* starts with a search by Dr. Paul L. Hoefler, a veteran explorer, to put the kibosh on a society of cannibalistic Leopard Men. These fiends dress in cat skins and wear gloves rigged with steel blades. New recruits to the cult must suffer a branding in silence, lest their outcries mean instant death.

The British government wants the Leopard Men out of commission, and Hoefler treks toward a confrontation. Ali, Hoefler's scout, witnesses a prelude to a ritual disemboweling, then hurries to summon help. Hoefler and his guardsmen charge to the rescue, but the Leopard Men charge right back at them, driving the would-be protectors away. The Leopard Men proceed with their unholy deed. Hoefler, vowing better results the next time, rather ineffectually denounces the savagery of those no-account good-for-nothing Leopard Men.

Where some Republic serial version would have assured a safe-and-sound finale, Dr. Hoefler's dire account dares inform the audience that his heroic forces are no match for this band of killers. The attitude only amplifies the film's ring of authenticity, which benefits from a documentary-like travelogue framework, punctuated by a destructive siege from swarming locusts.

A screen credit indicates color photography. The two prints we've turned up over the last 30-odd years are entirely in black-and-white. The Production Code Administration demanded scissorings of some of the more explicit depictions of cannibalism and nudity, but our viewings reveal abundant harrowing detail, and abundant toplessness. Dr. Paul Hoefler was better known for the 1930 expeditionary picture, *Africa Speaks*.

CREDITS: Presented by: B.F. Ziedman; Producer, Director and Scenarist: Dr. Paul L. Hoefler; Adapted Screenplay: Allyn Butterfield; Research: Walter Futter; Photographed by: Herman Schopp; Special Effects and Color Cinematography: Howard Anderson; Film and Soundtrack Editor: E.H. Schroeder; Music Composed and Conducted by: James Dietrich; Recording Engineer: Peter Decker; Running Time: 65 Minutes; Released: June 20, 1940

CAST: Dr. Paul L. Hoefler and Central African and Ethiopian Ensemble Casts

THE LAST ALARM
(Sherwill Productions, Inc./Monogram Pictures Corp.)

Movies about pyromaniacs are a fairly common staple for the action market, but *The Last Alarm* is the only one we've found whose firebug worships Vulcan and starts the conflagrations as sacrifices to that Ancient Roman god of flame. (Another worthy title of similar concern—though altogether conventional by crime-melodrama standards—is Joe Kane's *Arson Gang Busters*, from 1938.)

As portrayed by George Pembroke, the Irish-American actor who did a nifty job of projecting disordered mentality for the smaller studios, this creature of *The Last Alarm* keeps a statuette of Vulcan at hand and laughs with mordant glee as he peers through pop-bottle eyeglasses at each new atrocity. Pembroke adds a pleasingly chilling dimension to an old-fashioned family-circle yarn centering on the problems of a veteran fireman who is forced into a premature retirement.

Ted Williams, heading a unit company for Monogram, made this one for the supporting second-feature market, but *The Last Alarm* stands on its own as a solid hour of action, staged straightforwardly with human-interest sequences alternating with the weird machinations. Footage of genuine conflagrations is matched well with the staged action.

After 40 years as a firefighter, Jim Hadley (J. Farrell MacDonald) is pensioned off but proves restless in retirement, especially now that a pyromaniac seems intent upon razing the city. Jim's daughter, Joan (Polly Ann Young), tries to convince him to join forces with her fiancé, Frank Rogers (Warren Hull), an insurance investigator, to track down the menace. When Jim's best friend, Burt Stanford (Joel Friedkin), is killed in one of the fires, Jim gets on the case. The audience is informed early on that the firebug is actually a dealer in antiques named Wendell, who believes himself the living instrument of the god of fire. While watching one blaze, Wendell accidentally drops his Vulcan effigy, which Hadley finds. Wendell sees Jim hide the evidence in his car and retrieves it. When Jim describes the clue to Frank and Joan, they remember having seen it at the an-

George Pembroke, who had played a sympathetic executioner in *Buried Alive*, lays it on thick as one of the more flamboyant villains of the 1940s in *The Last Alarm*. (Photofest)

tiques store. Armed with a warrant, Jim searches the shop and finds sawdust that matches the wood used in setting the fires. Wendell evades capture and vengefully sets a firebomb in the basement of the Hadley home. Jim and Frank find the culprit holding Joan and Mrs. Hadley (Mary Gordon) hostage in the burning house. They rescue the women, and Wendell is trapped. The city appoints Jim honorary fire chief.

J. Farrell MacDonald should have obtained a patent on his role as the heroic old-timer, which he also played as a policeman, a railroad engineer, a tramp, a frontier sheriff, a cavalryman, a factory bull-of-the-woods and a sea captain. Here he is as expert as ever—one of the dependables. Mary Gordon, soon to become the perennial Mrs. Hudson to Basil Rathbone's Sherlock Holmes, and Polly Ann Young offer good support as MacDonald's family. Warren Hull, who portrayed the Spider, Mandrake the Magician and the Green Hornet so ably for the serial fans, is overqualified for his part here as the juvenile lead. As for Pembroke, he lays it on thick, which is precisely what the part wants.

CREDITS: Producer: T.R. Williams; Director: William West; Associate Producer: T.H. Richmond; Original Screenplay: Al Martin; Director of Photography: Harry Neumann; Sound Recording: Karl Zint; Editor: Russell Schoengarth; Music: Lee Zahler; Assistant Director: Glen Cook; Production Manager: Chris A. Beute; Sound: Western Electric; Running Time: 61 Minutes; Released: June 25, 1940

CAST: J. Farrell MacDonald (Jim Hadley); Polly Ann Young (Joan); Warren Hull (Frank); Mary Gordon (Mrs. Hadley); George Pembroke (Wendell); Joel Friedkin (Burt Stanford); Bruce MacFarlane (Jack); Eddie Hart (Dick Roberts); Edward Kane (Chief); Charles A. Hughes (Lt. King); Willard Hall (Briggs); Charles Phipps (Stevens); James Coughlin (Cummings)

BOYS OF THE CITY
a.k.a.: THE GHOST CREEPS
(Four Bell Pictures, Inc./Monogram Pictures Corp.)

Monogram's *East Side Kids* series began in 1940, carrying on an ensemble-comedy pattern that had begun under more grimly earnest dramatic circumstances: Sidney Kingsley's Broadway play *Dead End* (filmed in 1937) had cast a reformer's eye on the big-city slum conditions that could transform children into criminals. The stage and screen versions went over so well with the mass audience that the original players—including Huntz Hall, Bernard Punsley, Leo Gorcey, Billy Halop, Gabriel Dell, Hally Chester and Bobby Jordan—became the Dead End Kids, stars of half a dozen social-problem sequels including *They Made Me a Criminal* and *Angels with Dirty Faces*. A loose-knit batch of *Dead End Kids/Little Tough Guys* features and serials followed at Universal, becoming ever more adventurous and comical and less concerned with blaming society for juvenile delinquency; it was society, after all, that was buying all those movie tickets to watch the kids act like delinquents. By the time Gorcey, Jordan and Chester joined producer Sam Katzman at Monogram, the template had been struck for a slapstick franchise that would last well into the 1950s, finally evolving into the *Bowery Boys* films. Hall would remain with the Little Tough Guys long enough for the rival series to overlap confusingly, but he soon joined the East Siders for the long stretch.

Boys of the City, second of the *East Side Kids* pictures, harks back to the original *Dead End* with an unexpectedly serious opening note—the pals face a hitch in detention for a simple act of mischief that had veered out of control—but soon hits a more adventurous and comical stride. It delivers throughout "more than the usual serving of suspense," as the tradepaper *Exhibitor* remarked.

As an alternative to reform school, the East Side Kids accept a court order to visit a wealthy do-gooder's summer camp in the Adirondacks. Meanwhile, the notoriously crooked Judge Parker

The East Side Kids recoil from a shrouded annoyance—not necessarily to say a ghost—in *Boys of the City.*

(Forrest Taylor) is bound for the same region—intent upon hiding out from both the law and the underworld.

After Parker's car is bombed by a mob bent on his destruction, the East Siders offer Parker and his ward, Louise (Inna Gest), a lift. The kids' station wagon breaks down not far from Parker's mansion—a gloomy place where the boys find themselves obliged to spend the night. Hovering about menacingly is Agnes (Minerva Urecal), the housekeeper, who bears an old grudge against Parker and seems to be in touch with the spirit of the judge's late wife.

During the night, Louise is abducted through a hidden panel. Judge Parker is found strangled. Giles (Dennie Moore) and Simp (Vince Barnett), Parker's bodyguards, accuse Knuckles (Dave O'Brien), a grown-up East Sider who once had been wrongfully convicted in Parker's court, but the kids help Knuckles get away and begin a search for the culprit. In a hidden passageway, they find Louise and encounter Harrison (Alden Chase), a detective who has been trailing Parker.

The murderer make a sudden appearance, clubbing Knuckles and pursuing Louise. The kids and Harrison give chase and capture the slayer, revealing him as Simp—least likely of the suspects on hand, a mobster who had infiltrated the judge's inner circle.

The dangers seem convincingly real, and Forrest Taylor is just right as the disgraced big shot whose creepy old homestead serves as the backdrop. (The house is genuine, a huge, castle-like residence situated above Sunset Boulevard near Beverly Hills. The mixed studio and location interiors vary from opulent to jury-rigged, but the nighttime exteriors are top-notch, especially a finely detailed graveyard setting.) Taylor's death scene is a jewel of shocker in the *Cat and the Canary* tradition, photographed in silhouette. The discovery of an incidental victim behind a doorway also harks back to the mystery-farce tradition that the silent screen and early talkers had appropriated from Broadway. Minerva Urecal is every bit the classic-manner sinister housekeeper until she changes her tone for a blackout gag at the finale.

Dave O'Brien is right in his element as a heroic sort who hasn't forgotten his origins as a tenement ruffian. Leo Gorcey has yet to assume the brash dominance he would come to show as the series progressed. The inclusion of Sunshine Sammy Morrison is an inspired touch; the expressive black player had been a mainstay of Hal Roach's *Our Gang* comedies in the silent years, and he fits in well despite the film's tendency to temper its tacit argument for integration with an overabundance of "Negro" gags. A similarly broad strain of comedy relief comes from Vince Barnett, as a squirmy lunkhead who proves rather surprisingly to be the phantom killer. Leading lady Inna Gest, whom Katzman had noticed while she was working on a Tex Ritter Western, shows a fair amount of gumption as the judge's defiant ward, although the screenplay gives her little more to do than be menaced and rescued, by turns.

CREDITS: Producer: Sam Katzman; Director: Joseph H. Lewis; Story and Screenplay: William Lively; Production Manager: E.W. Rote; Photographed by: Robert Cline and Harvey Gould; Assistant Directors: Robert Ray and Arthur Hammond; Settings: Fred Preble; Sound Engineering: Glen Glenn; Editor: Carl Pierson; Running Time: 65 Minutes; Released: July 15, 1940

CAST: Bobby Jordan (Danny); Leo Gorcey (Muggs); Dave O'Brien (Knuckles); George Humbert (Tony); Hally Chester (Boy); Sunshine Sammy Morrison (Scruno); Frankie Burke (Skinny); Donald Haines (Pee Wee); Jack Edwards (Algy); Vince Barnett (Simp); Dennie Moore (Giles); Alden Chase (Harrison); Minerva Urecal (Agnes); Inna Gest (Louise); Forrest Taylor (Judge Parker); David Gorcey (Pete; Mentioned as "Ike" in Studio Papers); Jerry Mandy (Cook)

HAUNTED HOUSE
(Monogram Pictures Corp.)

All of a sudden, Monogram starts looking intolerably shabby, on the flimsy evidence of one annoying picture. Our acceptance of sub-par production values and incoherent storytelling ordinarily has a forgiving threshhold, on condition that the film under scrutiny convey an Attitude with a capital "A." It might be an attitude of solemnity or disorientation (as in *Invisible Ghost*), of defiant hilarity or adventurous desperation (both bases covered, among others, throughout the *Range Busters* pictures) or one of sheer cockamamie fershlugginer lunacy (see, at peril of mental equilibrium, the *Private Snuffy Smith* features). In other words, Monogram earns considerable slack because so many of its pictures pack an emotional resonance, a certain "set of the jaw" and a conspiratorial glint in the eye that bespeak a communion with the viewer.

Attitude, in the sense beyond the textbook definition, is scarcely a new invention. Attitude, beyond mere sex appeal, is probably what the Jazz Age had in mind when it christened Clara Bow "the 'It' Girl." One either has "It" or one doesn't, and the point is beyond negotiation. It matters not what the Attitude is, just so long as it figures in one's art, one's work, one's being. In cinema, the artist who cannot announce an Attitude before the first reel has lapsed is foredoomed to failure.

By such a standard, it barely makes sense that Robert McGowan's *Haunted House* should have survived into the present day, much less attracted fresh interest. Stultifyingly overlong and as blandly irritating as a Jell-O buffet, the film is utterly lacking in anything resembling Attitude. Give it the opportunity to show compassion, and it sits there waiting for the occasion to pass. Present its protagonists with a crisis, and they fritter away the time until the urgency has evaporated. The line of least resistance gets pursued throughout, in terms of plot, thespic energy and that all-important Attitude. It is a wonder that the juvenile leads even venture inside the "haunted" house of the title—not that they accomplish much while on the premises.

The collapse of Marcia Mae Jones' once-promising Hollywood career can be traced to such pictures as this one and the following year's *The Gang's All Here*, and if Jackie Moran's career had not already collapsed, his work alongside Miss Jones in these same two films would have sunk him straightaway. Moran continued in small parts while pursuing a parallel career in music, on through the 1940s, and Miss Jones kept puttering about in film into the '50s. Neither ever recaptured the plateaus they had known, such as Miss Jones' terror-stricken role in *These Three* (1936) and Moran's Huckleberry Finn in *The Adventures of Tom Sawyer* (1938).

Well, yes, and aren't they all cute when they're little? Here, Moran clings embarrassingly to a lapsed air of cuteness as a small-town newspaper reporter named Jimmie Atkins. When a laborer named Olaf (Christian Rub) is charged with robbing and murdering his boss, Jimmie rushes to the accused man's defense in an ill-advised article. Jimmie's insipid arrogance is compounded when Mildred (Miss Jones), niece of the publisher, arrives to spend the summer in town. These little snots have nothing better to occupy their interests than to "investigate" the murder; their irksome meddling gets Jimmie fired. As the kids' misgivings focus on lawyer Cy Burton (Henry Hall), they find themselves drawn to the murder victim's abandoned farmhouse, where cryptic messages are

found that lead to the lawyer's office, to another reprimand for the youngsters and back to the farmhouse. Finally, Burton gives himself away as the culprit, after all, and Jimmie gets to perform a bit of mild heroism before the real authorities arrive to close the case. Mildred is so pleased with the way things have turned out that she throws a great big party in Jimmie's honor, and Jimmie gets his job back at the newspaper. Which only reminds us of the passive-aggressive, invasive state of journalism in the present day—but no, we have more interesting ground to cover just now.

CREDITS: In Charge of Production: Scott R. Dunlap; Associate Producer: William T. Lackey; Director: Robert McGowan; Screenplay: Dorothy Reid; Original Story: Jack K. Leonard and Monty Collins; Photographed by: Harry Neumann; Assistant Director: Glenn Cook; Art Director: E.R. Hickson; Editor: Russell Schoengarth; Music: Edward Kay; Sound Engineer: Karl Zint; Production Manager: Charles J. Bigelow; Running Time: 70 Minutes; Released: July 22, 1940

CAST: Marcia Mae Jones (Mildred); Jackie Moran (Jimmie); George Cleveland (Albert Henshaw); Christian Rub (Olaf Jensen); Henry Hall (Cy Burton); John St. Polis (Simkins); Jessie Arnold (Mrs. Henshaw); Marcelle Ray (Lucy); Buddy Swann (Junior); and Clarence Wilson, Mary Carr, Hooper Atchley

BILLY THE KID OUTLAWED
(Sigmund Neufeld Productions, Inc./Producers Releasing Corp.)

Nobody knows for certain when he was born, or where,... how many men he killed..., or what ratio of evil distorted the good that was in him... He has been depicted as a sort of Robin Hood of the Wild West, an outlaw only because the law was corrupt. An opposing faction, overreacting to such fantasy, goes to the other extreme and brands him a sadistic monster. A third view is often expressed that he was nothing more than a "punk," a pimply and degenerate juvenile delinquent deserving of no more attention than is accorded any other such creature. One thing only is beyond disputing: The desperado... known as Billy the Kid has become the most popular and fascinating legend in American folklore.– George E. Turner *Secrets of Billy the Kid* (1974)

We had wanted a good, representative selection from Bob Steele's *Billy the Kid* series for the present volume, and this dark fable of the Great Plains fills the bill admirably. It is easy to get carried away with looking for the grislier elements in Hollywood's low-budget horse operas—especially when the authors of the moment happen to be born-and-bred Texans who share a fondness for the Cowboy Way—and so we've reined ourselves in, you should pardon the expression, and tried to keep the Western selections from predominating. Anyone who wants to explore a vaster range of the sagebrush Gothics is herewith directed to the catalogues of Sinister Cinema and Grapevine Video (see the Appendices), which offer horseback horrors out the wazzoo, and thus save us a great deal of verbiage.

Billy the Kid Outlawed is the first of 18 *Billy the Kid* features that Sig Neufeld produced during 1940-43. The first half-dozen feature Bob Steele, that emotive "horseback Hamlet," whose outlandish starring picture *Big Calibre* (1935) is a linchpin of the first *Forgotten Horrors* collection. Buster Crabbe picked up the role for the remainder of the *Kid* series, then continued it, more or less, in Neufeld's vaguely related *Billy Carson* series that spanned 1943-46. Neither incarnation boasts a factual communion with the Billy the Kid who ranged the Southwestern frontier late in the 19th Century, but Steele pretty well nails the tormented, distrustful nature that has come to light in the diligent research of times more recent.

This striking melodrama blames the prevailing lawlessness around Lincoln City, New Mexico, on storekeepers Pete Morgan (Joe McGuinn) and Sam Daly (Ted Adams), who are pushing to have Daly elected as sheriff. Enter Billy the Kid (Steele), who stops to visit two rancher friends while passing through with a cattle drive—only to learn that they have been murdered by a gang led by the brutal Lije Ellis (John Merton), a shadowy enforcer of the Morgan-Daly interests. After a gun battle with the more obvious thugs, Billy encounters Judge John Fitzgerald (Walter McGrail), arriving on federal orders to clean up the territory. Daly and Morgan order Fitzgerald slain, and Daly's ascent to office enables him to brand Billy and his pals Jeff Travis (Carleton Young) and Fuzzy Jones (Al St. John) as outlaws.

Billy accepts this insult with a defiant indignation, becoming so devoted a terrorist against the entrenched racket that the crooked partners turn to the slain judge's daughter (Louise Curry) and law partner (Ken Duncan) to engineer a pardon for Billy. Finally, an ambush against Billy backfires fatally on Daly and Morgan. His trust in "law and order" damaged beyond repair, Billy rejects the pardon and hightails it into the wilderness.

The *Billy the Kid* Westerns, like the kindred *Lone Rider* series, proved a welcome hard-bitten alternative to the cowboy-crooner pictures that had become all the rage since Gene Autry's rise to stardom during the middle 1930s. At 34, Steele may have been a bit long in the tooth to be impersonating a legendary owl hoot who lived only to the age of 21, but the actor's attitude is precisely right. This picture set a pace that seldom flagged as long as Steele occupied the role, rendering the inescapably cheap hastiness of production irrelevant to the essentially crisp storytelling. Director Sam Newfield (Sig Neufeld's brother, working here under the pseudonym of Peter Stewart) fixes the darkening mood right off the bat and confronts Steele with enough menacing characters—some, out-and-out outlaws; others, human monsters cloaked in respectability—to drive any self-respecting cowpoke to a righteous rage. Joe McGuinn and Ted Adams are suitably loathsome as the brains behind the killings, and John Merton makes a terrifying principal thug. Carleton Young and Al St. John lend a helpful leavening as Steele's loyal sidekicks, and Louise Curry shows plenty of gumption as a determined survivor. A more merciful story would have permitted some mushy business, but the film would have proved less honest as a consequence.

Steele's other *Billy the Kid* entries include *Billy the Kid in Texas* and *Billy the Kid's Gun Justice* (both from 1940); and *Billy the Kid in Santa Fe*, *Billy the Kid's Fighting Pals* and *Billy the Kid's Range War* (all from 1941).

CREDITS: Producer: Sigmund Neufeld; Director: Peter Stewart [Sam Newfield]; Screenplay: Oliver Drake; Photographed by: Jack Greenhalgh; Settings: Fred Preble; Assistant Director: Melville DeLay; Editor: Holbrook N. Todd; Musical Director: Lou Porter; Sound Engineer: Hans Weeren; Production Manager: Bert Sternbach; Running Time: 52 Minutes; Released: July 29, 1940

CAST: Bob Steele (Billy the Kid); Al St. John (Fuzzy Jones); Louise Curry (Molly Fitzgerald); Carleton Young (Jeff Travis); John Merton (Lafe Ellis); Joe McGuinn (Pete Morgan); Ted Adams (Sam Daly); Walter McGrail (John Fitzgerald); Ken Duncan (David Hendricks); Reed Howes (Whitey); George Chesebro (Tex); Budd Buster (Clem); Steve Clark (Shorty); Karl Hackett (Sheriff Long); Sherry Tansey (Outlaw); and Jack Ingram, Carl Sepulveda

THE RANGER AND THE LADY
(Republic Pictures Corp.)

Speaking of cowboy-crooner pictures—as we were, right up above, in the piece on that anti-crooner entry *Billy the Kid Outlawed*—here we have one that reconciles the tuneful and romantic aspects with a good bracing shot of monstrous terror. Roy Rogers may have nurtured a clean-cut and wholesome image, but he enjoyed a good scare as much as the next guy. He told us as much in 1970:

"I enjoy a good scare as much as the next guy," said Rogers. "And there's no rule that says you can't have your harmonies and your yodeling and your smooching on your leading lady in the same picture where there's a monster on the loose. I reckon there must have been plenty of monsters on the loose, back in the frontier days. Most of 'em were thieves and murderers who, really, must have seemed about as normal as the guy next door—but there must have been some subhuman brutes around, too.

"'Course, now, Republic wanted me to deliver a certain quota of pictures that'd play things mostly light and adventurous, with lots of singin' and smoochin' and comedy relief, along with the shootin' and fistfightin'.

Roy Rogers and Trigger, the Smartest Horse in the Movies (except for Ken Maynard's steed, Tarzan, of course).

But once in a while they'd let me make something really *dark*. I remember those exceptions very fondly: There was one I did in the late '40s called *Eyes of Texas*, which had this mean ol' crooked lawyer-woman with a pack of trained-killer dogs.

"And in 1940, we did a kind of a *Most Dangerous Game* type of thing. It was called *The Ranger and the Lady*, except I reckon maybe we should have called it *The Ranger and the Lady and the Monster*. Because we even had Noble Johnson in it, playing the kind of brute he had played in the real *Most Dangerous Game*—only scarier, I like to think."

We reckon that Rogers' reminiscent rambles were as great a delight as his movies. This particular interview started backstage one afternoon at the Tri-State Fairgrounds in Amarillo, Texas, and continued into the evening, resuming the next morning over a round of golf with Rogers, Dale Evans and Pat Brady—and it covered more ground than we have room for here.

So we cut to the relentless chase that is *The Ranger and the Lady*: Henry Brandon is a study in abusive authority as Gen. LaRue, the crooked head of the Texas Rangers, who in 1836 declares the wide-open Santa Fe Trail as a toll road. Jacqueline Wells, that A-list star among B-movie leading ladies, is Jane Tabor, an indignant trader who protests the scam by finding a detour. Rogers is Capt. Colt, a good-guy Ranger who chafes at the necessity of enforcing LaRue's crooked orders. After Jane surprisingly aligns her interests with LaRue to develop a monopoly, Colt and Sgt. Gabby Whittaker (good ol' George "Gabby" Hayes) resign in disgust and start conspiring to unseat LaRue. Jane eventually is revealed to have a conspiracy of her own going against LaRue. With Roy's help, she finally takes vengeance on the man who had killed her father.

Heightening the tensions throughout—though in a role that proved expendable under the editing shears—is Noble Johnson, playing a monstrous thug named El Lobo. The distinguished black actor, as an Indian marauder whose viciousness indeed recalls his *Most Dangerous Game* performance, is a sure-fire scene-stealer in what prints his performance was left intact.

Missouri-born in 1881 and raised in Colorado Springs, Noble Mark Johnson (1881-1978) attended school with Lon Chaney; they renewed their friendship as fellow actors during the early years of feature-filmmaking. Technically a mulatto, six-foot-two and heavily muscled, Johnson could appear primitively cruel in one film and immensely sympathetic in another. Johnson left the movies in the early 1950s—with a fleeting return, via television's *Lost Island of Kioga*, during the 1960s—and invested in Nevada real estate.

A 1950s television-syndication cut of *The Ranger and the Lady* so marginalizes El Lobo that the film's horrific essence is lost; this is the version that has become prevalent on the video market. Just take our word, and Roy Rogers' word, for it: *The Ranger and the Lady* is as terrifying as they come, if seen in its 1940 cut.

CREDITS: Associate Producer and Director: Joseph Kane; Screenplay: Gerald Geraghty and Stuart Anthony; Story: Bernard McConville; Photographed by: Reggie Lanning; Assistant Director: William O'Connor; Editor: Lester Orlebeck; Musical Director: Cy Feuer; Songs: "As Long as We're Dancing" and "Chiquita," by Peter Tinturin; Production Manager: Al Wilson; Running Time: 59 Minutes; Released: July 30, 1940

CAST: Roy Rogers (Capt. Colt); George "Gabby" Hayes (Sgt. Gabby Whittaker); Jacqueline Wells (Jane Tabor); Harry Woods (Kincaid); Henry Brandon (Gen. LaRue); Noble Johnson (El Lobo); Si Jenks (Purdy); Ted Mapes (Kramer); Yakima Canutt (McNair); Trigger, the Smartest Horse in the Movies (Himself); and Chuck Baldra, Chick Hannon, Herman Hack, Art Dillard

LAUGHING AT DANGER
(Monogram Pictures Corp.)

A devil-made-flesh with the heavenly name of Celeste makes life a hell-on-Earth for Frankie Darro and Mantan Moreland in this continuation of the partners' comedy-thriller series. Monogram was drawing such vast popular support for *anything* featuring Moreland that the studio moved the artist's billing up a few notches and made his expressive mug even more prominent than that of Darro on the promotional materials.

Laughing at Danger makes no bones about its horrific circumstances: At Celeste's Beauty Shop, a laundry chute yields the grisly discovery of the mortal remains of an operator named Florence (Maxine Leslie). Mary Baker (Joy Hodges), the last person to have visited with the victim, is accused. Page boy Frankie Kelly (Darro) and his pal, Jefferson (Moreland), set out to prove Mary's innocence.

The amateur sleuths learn that Florence had intended to give information on a blackmail racket to a detective named Dan Haggerty (George Houston). Then, the body of Florence's fiancé is discovered in a dumbwaiter. Then, one of Mary's clients (Kay Sutton) turns up dead. A phonograph recording is found of a blackmail message between the latest victim and someone at the beauty parlor. Frankie determines that the boss, Celeste (Veda Ann Borg), has been recording some of her customers' more embarrassing moments and then using the Dictaphone documents to coerce hush-money payments. A vengeful Celeste and her lawyer (Guy Usher) imprison Frankie and Jeff, but the friends stall their intended execution long enough for the cops to come barging in.

The danger here is nothing at which to laugh, of course—which is what makes the Darro-Moreland pictures so funny *and* so hair-raising. Veda Ann Borg is fine as the schemer-turned-killer, and her final show of malice (at first, merely intending to skip town, then deciding upon blood vengeance) makes for a delectably cold twist.

CREDITS: Producer: Lindsley Parsons; Director: Howard Bretherton; Screenplay; Joseph West (from His Story) and John Kraft; Photographed by: Fred Jackman, Jr.; Editor: Jack Ogilvie; Sound Engineer: William Fox; Running Time: 63 Minutes; Released: August 15, 1940

CAST: Frankie Darro (Frankie Kelly); Mantan Moreland (Jefferson); Joy Hodges (Mary Baker); George Houston (Dan Haggerty); Kay Sutton (Inez Morton); Guy Usher (Alvin Craig); Lillian Elliott (Mrs. Kelly); Veda Ann Borg (Celeste); Betty Compson (Mrs. Van Horn); Rolfe Sedan (Pierre); Maxine Leslie (Florence); Ralph Peters (Dugan); Gene O'Donnell (Chuck Benson)

THE RANGE BUSTERS
(Phoenix Productions, Inc./Monogram Pictures Corp.)

In Louis Weiss's 1932 production of *The Night Rider*, Harry Carey hits the trail in search of the flesh-and-blood causes behind a ghostly reign of terror. Gunfire, seemingly from nowhere, figures strongly here—being a favorite element of the frontier folk-tale tradition from which so many Western movies had sprung—and would keep on figuring, in such striking examples of the Cowboy Gothic cinema as *The Star Packer* (1934) and *Desert Phantom* (1936).

Some authorities regard *Desert Phantom*, starring the easygoing Johnny Mack Brown in a delightfully grim avenging role, as a remake of *The Night Rider*. It is at least an echo, but an altogether more severe picture than the essentially comical Weiss production. Certainly, however, *The Range Busters* is an unattributed remake of *Desert Phantom*—even a plagiarism, for the story credits thoroughly ignore the 1936 film's writers, E.B. Mann and Earle Snell. Director S. Roy Luby handled both *Desert Phantom* and *The Range Busters*. The 1940 version's chief alteration is to pitch three heroes instead of one.

Serial murder plagues the Circle T Ranch, whose owner, Homer Thorpe (Horace Murphy), is the latest victim. Into the benighted village come the Range Busters (Ray "Crash" Corrigan, John "Dusty" King and Max "Alibi" Terhune), heroic plainsmen who immediately rescue Thorpe's daughter, Carol (Luana Walters), from an abusive rival rancher named Torrence (LeRoy Mason). Carol rewards the pals with work at the Circle T, and friendly Doc Stengle (Frank LaRue) tells Crash about a legendary Phantom that supposedly haunts the rangeland.

Crash and Dusty dodge a barrage supposedly fired by the Phantom. Chasing after the mysterious assailant, they find a mineshaft where Torrence is stashing contraband weapons. Crash evades an ambush and helps Dusty get away from Torrence's thugs. Meanwhile, Alibi becomes curious about the supposed blindness of Carol's crotchety Uncle Rolf (Earle Hodgins). After several tense encounters, Torrence is captured and seems ready to reveal the truth about the fabled haunting—but he is felled by a shot from Rolf's room.

In the abandoned mine, Dusty and Alibi find a shaft leading into Rolf's quarters at the ranchhouse. Doc Stengle, who has held the uncle captive, begins firing at Crash. Subdued by Dusty and Alibi, the lovable physician proves to have found a hidden vein of gold; he was exploiting the "Phantom" myth to gain control of the ranch.

This first in a series of 22 *Range Busters* pictures is a winner whose ties to *Desert Phantom* run even deeper than the presence of director Luby and the appropriated storyline: Karl Hackett, who had played the disabled rancher in the 1936 version, holds forth here as the sheriff.

CREDITS: Producer: George W. Weeks; Director: S. Roy Luby; Associate Producer: Anna Bell Ward; Screenplay: John Rathmell; Photographed by: Eddie Linden; Production Manager, Melville Shyer; Musical Director: Frank Sanucci; Sound: Glen Glenn; Editor: Roy Claire; Song: "Git Along, Cowboy," by Lew Porter and Johnny Lange; Running Time: 56 Minutes; Released: August 22, 1940

CAST: Ray Corrigan (Crash); John King (Dusty); Max Terhune (Alibi and Elmer); Luana Walters (Carol); LeRoy Mason (Torrence); Earl Hodgins (Uncle Roy); Frank LaRue (Doc Stengle); Kermit Maynard (Wyoming); Bruce King (Wall); Duke Matthews (Rocky); Horace Murphy (Thorpe); Karl Hackett (Sheriff); Ed Brady (Ranch Hand); Eddie Dean (Singing Cowboy)

MARKED MEN
(Sigmund Neufeld Productions, Inc./Producers Releasing Corp.)

The brother act of Sigmund Neufeld and Sam Newfield had an undeniable taste for terror, even in their outdoor-adventure melodramas. The chilling element of *Marked Men*—an otherwise conventional revenge melodrama about a wrongly accused man's quest for vindication—takes place in the withering heat of the Arizona desert. A splendidly trained dog named Gray Shadow helps things along, with the antagonistic support of a marauding, strategically little-seen wolf pack.

Railroaded into prison on a frame-up by rackets boss Joe Mallon (Paul Bryar), innocent Bill Carver (Warren Hull) is carried along with the mob in a jailbreak staged by Mallon. Bill alone reaches freedom and is rejoined by his dog, Wolf. Prospects are looking better for Bill, who has settled in with two newfound friends, Dr. Harkness (John Dilson) and daughter Linda Harkness (Isabel Jewell).

Meanwhile, the re-jailed Mallon busts out once again and implicates Bill in a new crime. Finding this new insult intolerable, Bill takes up the trail, intending to capture Mallon and force a confession from him. The enemies meet in the desert, and an uneasy truce is formed when Mallon comprehends that he and his henchmen cannot reach the safety of the border without Bill's guidance. Starving wolves attack the party, and Mallon at length kills his accomplices (Art Miles, Ted Erwin and Eddie Featherstone) as the struggle for survival drives them to madness. Finally, only Bill and Mallon remain. Mallon agrees to sign a confession, but he turns murderous once again when suddenly Dr. Harkness and Linda drive up in their motorcar. Mallon takes aim on Bill, but the courageous Wolf attacks just in time.

Warren Hull's performance varies from indifferent to very good, with the intensity of his character deepening as the desert trek commences. Isabel Jewell never quite registers the depth of affection that supposedly materializes between her character and Hull's wronged fugitive. Paul Bryar is downright scary as the unhinged mobster, and Gray Shadow steals the show as the smart, ferocious police dog. Sam Newfield directed *Marked Men* as Sherman Scott, although advertising materials list the director as Peter Stewart—another Newfield pseudonym.

CREDITS: Producer: Sigmund Neufeld; Director: Sherman Scott [Sam Newfield]; Screenplay: George Bricker; Story: Harold Greene; Photographed by: Jack Greenhalgh; Assistant Director: Melville de Lay; Settings: Ernest Graber; Editor: Holbrook N. Todd; Musical Director: David Chudnow; Sound Engineer: Hans Weeren; Production Manager: Bert Sternbach; Running Time: 66 Minutes; Released: August 28, 1940

CAST: Warren Hull (Bill Carver); Isabel Jewell (Linda Harkness); John Dilson (Dr. Harkness); Paul Bryar (Joe Mallon); Charles Williams (Charlie Sloan); Lyle Clement (Marshall); Budd L. Buster (Marvin); Al St. John (Gimpy); Eddie Featherstone (Marty); Ted Erwin (Mike); Art Miles (Blimp)

UP IN THE AIR
(Monogram Pictures Corp.)

Mantan Moreland and Frankie Darro served their comedy-team thrillers as working stiffs who aspire to more glamorous careers. The running irony of the pictures is that these ill-respected citizens are perfectly capable of rising to whatever desperate occasion should arise. In the shining instance of *Up in the Air*, the guys' reality is to labor as a porter and a messenger-boy at a Hollywood broadcasting studio, where they would relish a crack at becoming entertainers.

After they land in trouble for helping another toiler, Anne Mason (Marjorie Reynolds), seek an audition as a singer, Frankie Ryan (Darro) and Jeff (Moreland) find themselves pressed into a more heroic state after an ill-tempered vocalist, Rita Wilson (Lorna Gray), is murdered during a rehearsal. The likeliest suspect is Tex Barton (Gordon James), a pathetic nobody who fancies himself a glamorous cowboy singer but lets show a darker nature in an unguarded moment. Producer Farrell (Tristram Coffin) wants Frankie to keep mum about an argument between Farrell and Miss Wilson; Frankie has

A staged publicity shot for *Up in the Air*. The script says nothing about any harmonizing ambitions on the part of Frankie Darro and Mantan Moreland.

Farrell promise to give Anne an audition. Frankie discovers the hiding place of the murder gun—which is traced to Tex, and to an unsolved case in Wyoming. Tex turns up dead.

Following through on evidence found in Tex's quarters, the police arrest Anne, believing her tied to the Wyoming case. It develops that the mystery woman was in fact Rita—who had cuckolded her husband, Tex, for a radio-station boss. An unobtrusive character, radio emcee Van Martin (Alex Callam), confesses to the murders while holding the assembled station brass at gunpoint. Jeff suddenly intrudes, throwing open a door and toppling Martin for an easy capture.

Darro and Moreland not only get to handle the heroics in high style—with Darro as the impulsive fools-rush-in type and Moreland as the hesitant voice of reason who cannot help becoming involved. While scouring a crime scene, Darro teases Moreland about being afraid of ghosts—a curious confrontation, rather than an exploitation, of stereotype. "It ain't the ghost," Moreland replies. "It's the person that *made* her a ghost—that's what's botherin' me!" The actors also are allowed some pure-comedy showcases apart from the mystery, in scenes where they try to prove what a hit they could be on radio. Darro's brief appearance in blackface might seem offensive today, but in 1940 the *shtick* was still a norm of the waning Vaudeville tradition: Like Al Jolson, Emmett Miller and Bing Crosby before him, Darro is not lampooning African-American sensibilities, but rather trying (a bit too strenuously) to *become black*, while playfully acknowledging a fraction of the debt that white America owes to black America. As the men prepare for a rehearsal, Moreland asks, indignantly: "You don't expect me to speak in no dialect, do you?" When Darro's rapid-fire delivery proves *too* rapid for Moreland's tastes, Mantan halts the routine to tell his overeager partner to slacken the pace. Like the white rock-and-roll acts, from early-day Fleetwood Mac to Eric Clapton, that would attempt almost to *become* the Deep Blues artists they admired, Darro is forcing the process. (Muddy Waters found it necessary to ask Paul Butterfield to slow things down a bit, too, when their paths crossed during the 1960s.) When boss-man Tris Coffin angrily swipes at the black makeup on Darro's face and then glances at Moreland, Mantan snaps: "Don't touch *me*! *I* don't rub off!" In such subtextual insights into a cross-cultural shadowland, perhaps more so than in its conscious humor, the Darro-Moreland combo is a marvel of quick-wittedness and spontaneous patter. What makes it work is the sense of friendship between players.

Story-wise, *Up in the Air* is a muddle of coincidence and contradiction—standard Monogram fare—that keeps crucial clues well out of the audience's reach. If the unmasking of the killer comes off as less than a satisfactory resolution, then Moreland's inadvertent capture of the culprit compensates plenty well.

CREDITS: Producer: Lindsley Parsons; Director: Howard Bretherton; Story and Screenplay: Edmund Kelso; Photographed by: Fred Jackman, Jr.; Art Director: Charles Clague; Editor: Jack Ogilvie; Decor: Al Greenwood; Musical Director: Edward Kay; Songs: "By the Looks of Things" and "Somehow or Other," by Edward Kay and Harry Tobias, and "Doin' the Conga," by Edward Kay, Lew Porter and Johnny Lange; Sound Engineer: Edward Fox; Running Time: 64 Minutes; Released: September 9, 1940

CAST: Frankie Darro (Frankie Ryan); Marjorie Reynolds (Anne Mason); Mantan Moreland (Jeff); Gordon James (Tex Barton); Lorna Gray (Rita Wilson); Tristram Coffin (Farrell); Clyde Dilson (Marty Phillips); Dick Elliott (B.J. Hastings); John Holland (Sam Quigley); Carleton Young (Stevens); Alex Callam (Van Martin); Maxine Leslie (Stella); Ralph Peters (Delaney); and Jack Mather, Dennis Moore, Phil Kramer

THE APE
(Monogram Pictures Corp.)

It was during 1936-39 that Boris Karloff, Bela Lugosi and Peter Lorre—the original triumvirate of horror-movie stars—found their careers compromised by the British and European embargo on films of the very sort that had defined the actors' popular appeal. Karloff retrenched by signing with Monogram to star in a series of mysteries based on Hugh Wiley's tales of an Oxford-educated detective named James Lee Wong. The *Mr. Wong* pictures (no kin to Monogram's *Mysterious Mr. Wong*, a 1934 starrer for Lugosi) were designed to compete with Fox's *Charlie Chan* series. Lorre took refuge in the *Mr. Moto* detective pictures at Fox. Lugosi, less well attuned to strategy, found himself reduced to poverty during this long dry spell—although he managed subversively to make one serial in 1937, Republic's *S O S Coast Guard*, which is as much a horror thriller as an action-adventure piece. The chapter-a-week cliffhangers got away with considerably more mayhem than was permitted in the feature-film sector, even during the official span of the ban.

Karloff held forth in five *Wong*s. By 1940, horror was back in style, and Karloff fulfilled his six-film contract at Monogram by starring in *The Ape*. Keye Luke, who had graced Fox's *Charlie Chan*s as Number One Son to Warner Oland's Chan, replaced Karloff in the final *Wong* entry, *Phantom of Chinatown*. William Nigh, who had directed the Karloff *Wong*s, took charge of *The Ape*.

Although *The Ape* is a lesser entry for Karloff, it is a cut above most of his others at Monogram. (*Mr. Wong, Detective*, that

Delightful behind-the-scenes study from the circus set for *The Ape*. Ray Corrigan, at camera, in full gorilla regalia, with camera operator Fleet Southcott, assistant cameraman Roy Ivey and director of photography Harry Neumann.

series' opener, is a jewel.) But of course, Monogram seldom made remarkably fine pictures; it was a true Poverty Row company, having neither the money nor the talent pool of the majors.

Karloff serves *The Ape* as the kindly Dr. Bernard Adrian, who in his obsession with finding a cure for infantile paralysis has resettled in a small town, far removed from the medical community that has rejected his theories. His small-town neighbors shun Adrian. An uncommonly friendly neighbor, Frances Clifford (Maris Wrixon), is confined to a wheelchair and makes a trusting if hesitant subject for Adrian's sudden breakthrough.

A circus gorilla escapes after fatally mauling a sadistic trainer (I. Stanford Jolley). Adrian takes the opportunity to extract a vial of spinal fluid. He prepares a serum and administers it to Frances with promising results. When the gorilla breaks into Adrian's laboratory, the doctor kills the beast. And yet an ape remains on the prowl, attacking the town's most despised citizens. Frances' treatments continue. Finally, an intended victim stabs the ape, which staggers toward Adrian's house. The sheriff arrives and fires on the ape—then finds the dying creature to be Adrian. The doctor lives just long enough to see Frances rise and walk toward him.

Selmer Jackson, right, attempts to persuade Boris Karloff to rejoin the Society of Respectably Ordinary Physicians in *The Ape*. But only after Karloff's renegade methods have proved revolutionary, of course.

Exteriors for *The Ape* were filmed on the long-standing Western town set at Newhall. The gloomy interiors were shot at Monogram's own studio in East Hollywood. A surprisingly big name is that of screenwriter Curtis (sometimes billed as Kurt and Curt) Siodmak, the German-born author whose novel *Donovan's Brain* has yielded a variety of movie adaptations and knockoffs, and whose many stories and screenplays for Universal include the first two *Wolf Man* films. The basis of *The Ape* is an unspecified play by Adam Hull Shirk—possibly the same work that Monogram had adapted as *The House of Mystery* in 1934. *The Ape* resembles *The House of Mystery* only in its menacing use of a gorilla. Shirk also had written continuity for the notorious gorilla-hunt mock-documentary, *Ingagi* (1930).

The Ape boasts one of Karloff's more driven portrayals, a gentlemanly monster who confines his killing rage to rascals, rotters and nincompoops whose passing can only serve to improve the human species. The first victim is a malicious carnival hand, played by that Grand Manner bad-guy specialist, Stan Jolley. Later on, Karloff's counterfeit ape does away with a wife-beating loan shark, done to a repulsive turn by Philo McCullough. Karloff's patient, Maris Wrixon, tells him, "You're so intense, you frighten me sometimes," but it is a crippling flaw that the story neglects to explain why the townspeople should harbor such a fearful hatred of Karloff's Dr. Adrian. He seems a sad, kindly sort who rides about on a bicycle, heals an injured dog and treats the skinned knee of a local brat who has vandalized Adrian's house. (That boy, incidentally, is Buddy Swan, who also portrays Charles Foster Kane as a child in *Citizen Kane*.)

It defies reason that the elderly physician could mangle his victims with such ferocity, or that he might fashion the pelt of the gorilla so handily into a suit approximating the ape's size and proportions.

Boris Karloff contemplates a maverick cure for polio in *The Ape*.

But whatever its failings, *The Ape* anticipated a staggering medical breakthrough by more than a decade. The film's generalized prediction of the Salk vaccine against polio is as striking as the prophecies of cryogenics and artificial-organ technology in which Karloff participated during the same period as the star of a series of mad-doctor pictures at Columbia.

The title creature is played by Ray "Crash" Corrigan, who at the time was also a Western star within the independent sector. His other contracts allowed Corrigan to carry on with his lucrative gorilla-suit sideline as long as it did not conflict with his heroic portrayals and he did not receive cast billing. Corrigan's several ape outfits are far from realistic, but they are plenty scary.

Maris Wrixon contributes a nice portrayal of the apprehensive patient. The slender blonde had registered impressively at Warners, but she seems not to have minded her sojourn on Poverty Row. She spoke with us in 1984 about *The Ape*: "I liked it. It wasn't so much a horror picture, as it was a tragic drama about a man obsessed with the desire to benefit mankind. Boris Karloff was wonderful to work with."

Philo McCullough has a rousing prelude to his demise, in a cruel scene with his abused wife, touchingly played by Mary Field. Gertrude W. Hoffman, in her youth a pioneer in modern dance, is most effective as Karloff's housekeeper, whose silent comings and goings are punctuated strikingly by one whispered line. Gene O'Donnell is a stock small-town juvenile lead, serving chiefly to embody the locals' hateful intolerance. The atmospheric cinematography is by Harry Neumann, who usually shot Westerns. Edward Kay's elaborate musical score ranges from blaring martial cues, to sentimental melodies, to the requisite menacing passages.

CREDITS: Production Supervisor: Scott R. Dunlap; Associate Producer: W.T. Lackey; Director: William Nigh; Screenplay by Kurt Siodmak and Richard Carroll; Adaptation: Kurt Siodmak; Suggested by a Play by: Adam Hull Shirk; Director of Photography: Harry Neumann; Editor: Russell Schoengarth; Musical Director: Edward J. Kay; Technical Director: E.R. Hickson; Assistant Director: Al Wood; Sound: Karl Zint; Production Manager: Charles J. Bigelow; Makeup: Gordon Bau; Operative Cameraman: Fleet Southcott; Assistant Cameraman: Roy Ivey; Stills: Warner Crosby; Running Time: 62 Minutes; Released: September 30, 1940

CAST: Boris Karloff (Dr. Bernard Adrian); Maris Wrixon (Frances Clifford); Gertrude W. Hoffman (Housekeeper); Gene O'Donnell (Danny Foster); Henry Hall (Sheriff Jeff Holiday); Jack Kennedy (Tomlin); Dorothy Vaughan (Mrs. Clifford); Philo McCullough (Mason); Selmer Jackson (Dr. McNulty); George Cleveland (Head Trainer); Jessie Arnold (Mrs. Brill); I. Stanford Jolley (Trainer); Pauline Drake (Girl); Buddy Swan (Injured Boy); Donald Kerr (Townsman); Mary Field (Mrs. Mason); Harry T. Bradley (Druggist); Gibson Gowland (Posse Member); Ray Corrigan (Ape)

MIDNIGHT SHADOW
(George Randol Productions/Sack Amusement Enterprises, Inc.)

Here, in certain communities, the life of which is found nowhere else in all the world, these people of darker hue have demonstrated their abilities in self-govern-

Buck Woods (foreground) and Richard Bates are the comic-relief detectives, efficient in spite of themselves, in *Midnight Shadow*. (Photofest)

> *ment by the orderly processes of law of which they are capable when unhampered by outside influences.*
> —**From the Prologue, Which Might Be Read as a Manifesto-in-Miniatur of Black Separatism**

Today, the eerie malice of *Midnight Shadow* would fall under the fashionable heading of "black-on-black crime." In 1940, in a picture whose cultural isolation was at once a blessing and a curse, the story emerged as a portrait of African-American community life that could never have been realized—or even visualized, for that matter—by any conventional Hollywood studio, small or large.

A Southwestern town receives a visit from a showman known as Prince Alihabad the Great: "Mind Reader, Wonder Worker," his billing declares. Alihabad (John Criner) takes lodging with the Wilson family—and takes a romantic interest in daughter Margaret (Frances Redd). The entertainer assures Dan Wilson (Clinton Rosemond), Margaret's father, that his intentions are honorable. Mama Emma Wilson (Ollie Ann Robinson) is less easily convinced. Margaret's hometown beau, Buster Barnett (Edward Brandon), is nonplussed to find Alihabad beating his time. Mrs. Wilson, sensing the truth without actually knowing the prince is a charlatan, advises Buster to stand his ground with Margaret.

Dan makes the mistake of showing Alihabad an oilfield deed that he plans to give Margaret as a wedding present. Margaret balks at the interloper's offer to take her along on an ocean voyage. Meanwhile, a shadowy figure watches the house—and later breaks in, overwhelms Emma and Dan with fumes from a vial, and steals the deed.

Next morning, Margaret finds her mother unconscious and her father dead. She calls on the wealthy Langleys (Napoleon Simpson and Ruby Dandridge), friends whose mama's-boy grown-up son Junior (Richard Bates) is an aspiring but incompetent detective—complete with Sherlock Holmes-style deerstalker hat. Buster is jailed as a suspect.

Junior and his shuck-and-jive Watson, Lightfoot (Buck Woods), stake out the scene of the crime and find the paw-prints of a pet housecat. "Could've been one of them were-cats!" says Junior. After a run-in with the police, Junior comes up with a better idea: He and Lightfoot journey to Shreveport,

Louisiana, to meet with an oil company executive (Pete Webster) who had once tried to purchase the Wilson deed. Finally, a stranger approaches the oilman and demands money for the deed. "The man I stole [it] from is dead," mutters the stranger, "and one more murder won't make much difference." A local detective arrives to nab the killer.

Back home, Buster is freed. Prince Alihabad, who is innocent of the crime but whose presence had helped to trigger the slaying, is revealed as a fraud and loses Margaret to Buster.

The rescue and restoration of *Midnight Shadow* began in August of 1983, spearheaded by a preservation team including Dr. G. William Jones, of Dallas' Southwest Film & Video Archive, and Mike Price, then of the Fort Worth *Star-Telegram*'s entertainment desk. *Midnight Shadow*, along with more than 100 other titles, was found in a long-neglected warehouse in the East Texas city of Tyler. "Roughly a third of these were perhaps the last—or the best—remaining prints of a little-known but important group of films made from the 1920s through the early 1950s, strictly for black audiences," as Jones explained the discovery in his 1991 book, *Black Cinema Treasures: Lost and Found*.

Midnight Shadow certainly borrows from a broader tradition of melodrama—the skulking killer, the bumbling amateur sleuths, the red-herring charlatan seeking to barge in on an innocent romance—but it renders things in such decidedly black-American shades as to seem fresh. The unattributed screenplay doesn't exactly play fair with the element of mystery, but it does come up with a reasonable conspiracy to capture the killer. Richard Bates and Buck Woods are delightful as the would-be Holmes-and-Watson team, and John Criner makes a particularly oily Prince Alihabad. Ruby Dandridge, who plays the proud mother of the aspiring Sherlock, was the mother of the major-league star-to-be Dorothy Dandridge.

CREDITS: Producer and Director: George Randol; Photographed by: Arthur Reed; Assistant Director: Charles Hawkins; Editor: Robert Jahns; Musical Directors: Johnny Lange and Lew Porter; Sound Engineer: Corson Jowett; Production Manager: Wilfred Black; Produced at: International Studios, Hollywood; Running Time: 57 Minutes; Released: During October of 1940

CAST: Frances Redd (Margaret Wilson); Buck Woods (Lightfoot); Richard Bates (Junior Langley); Clinton Rosemond (Dan Wilson); Jessie Lee Brooks (Sgt. Ramsey); Edward Brandon (Buster Barnett); Ollie Ann Robinson (Emma Wilson); John Criner (Prince Alihabad); Pete Webster (John Mason); Ruby Dandridge (Mrs. Langley); Napoleon Simpson (Mr. Langley)

WHO KILLED AUNT MAGGIE?
(Republic Pictures Corp.)

Atlanta, Georgia, had gone world-premiere crazy in 1939 with the first official showing of MGM's epic soap-opera *Gone with the Wind*. The opportunity to land another such gala event in rapid order was tremendously appealing to the City Fathers—especially so, if the picture in question bore the localized title *Belle of Atlanta*.

And *Belle of Atlanta* was indeed the work-in-progress title of this solidly crafted but less than remarkable multiple-murder yarn. A rechristening to the more lurid-sounding *Who Killed Aunt Maggie?*—which was, after all, the title of the popular source-novel—occurred after the premiere agreement had been reached, but Atlanta went through with the occasion. Republic Pictures sent in several members of the cast and a number of studio executives, and *The Hollywood Reporter* described a festive scene in which "excited thousands thronged the streets."

Premieres tend to have more to do with people-watching, the communal act of seeing and being seen, that with earnest movie-watching, and so it is scarcely a matter of record what those "excited thousands" thought of *Who Killed Aunt Maggie?* The tradepaper *Variety*, which screened the film privately in New York a week after the Atlanta presentation, found it "a sufficiently tight entertainment" that was nonetheless "for the duals"—a since-extinct bit of exhibitor lingo for double-feature engagements.

The yarn starts in New York, where radio advertising salesman Kirk Pierce (John Hubbard) and his fiancée, Sally Ambler (Wendy Barrie), get into a terrible row provoked by his contempt for a play she has written. He says her tale of a forbidden secret room in a shadowy old mansion is so much hogwash. She calls off their wedding.

The most winning performance in *Who Killed Aunt Maggie?* belongs to the fine black comedian Willie Best. Granted that the role is a stereotype of the most extreme and indefensible kind, but Best gives it full measure of trepidatious hilarity. (Photofest)

Summoned home to Atlanta on orders from her Aunt Maggie (Elizabeth Patterson), Sally finds herself in precisely such a situation as she has been fictionalizing. Another mysterious summons, from meddling in-law Dr. George Benedict (Walter Abel), moves Kirk to follow along.

At the Ambler estate, the body of a freshly deceased great-uncle has disappeared. Maggie, the lone heir, insists that a secret room somewhere on the premises contains a treasure. Kirk arrives and learns that Sally is next in line as heir. A storm strands everyone within the isolated grounds. A stranger who presents himself as John Lloyd (Milton Parsons), a gravestone salesman, claims to have been injured in an auto wreck—but goes skulking about the place, anyway. Maggie is found strangled. Sally learns that "John Lloyd" is an impostor. Her cousin Eve finds the hidden room—but is soon found slain. Maggie's corpse vanishes. Eve's husband, Dr. Benedict, attacks Sally and reveals himself as the killer. The fake Mr. Lloyd proves to be a detective in pursuit of Benedict, who is captured just in time. Back in New York, Sally and Kirk resume sparring, but they make up long enough to get married and start turning their misadventure into a radio program.

A frenzy of action keeps things clicking along, but *Who Killed Aunt Maggie?* adds little to the Old Dark House tradition. Director Arthur Lubin—teamed here with the veteran script doctor and novice producer Albert J. Cohen—had been helming pictures competently but often unremarkably since 1934. Lubin's splendid Universal picture, *Black Friday*, dates from the same year as *Who Killed Aunt Maggie?* The following year, Lubin would register strikingly as one of the savvier directors of the Abbott & Costello comedies, and in 1943 he would deliver his masterpiece of a long and uneven career: *The Phantom of the Opera*, with Claude Rains.

The performances in *Who Killed Aunt Maggie?* are energetic but rather more stock-fictional types than sharply defined characters, and too much is made of the bickering-sweethearts angle, which leads to a forcibly cute finale. The most winning performance belongs not to a participant in the terrors, but to a talkative observer—a terrified butler named Andrew, played by the fine black comedian Willie

Best. Granted that the role is a stereotype of the most extreme and indefensible kind, Best gives it full measure of trepidatious hilarity.

CREDITS: Associate Producer: Albert J. Cohen; Director: Arthur Lubin; Screenplay: Stuart Palmer; Based on: the Novel and Associated Press Newspaper Serial *Who Killed Aunt Maggie?* by Medora Field; Additional Dialogue: Frank Gill, Jr., and Hal Fimberg; Photographed by: Reggie Lanning; Art Director: John Victor Mackay; Assistant Director: Phil Ford; Editor: Edward Mann; Supervising Editor: Murray Seldeen; Wardrobe: Adele Palmer; Musical Director: Cy Feuer; Production Manager: Al Wilson; Running Time: 70 Minutes; Released: November 1, 1940, Following World Premiere on October 24, 1940, in Atlanta

CAST: John Hubbard (Kirk Pierce); Wendy Barrie (Sally Ambler); Edgar Kennedy (Sheriff Gregory); Elizabeth Patterson (Maggie Ambler); Onslow Stevens (Bob Dunbar); Joyce Compton (Cynthia Lou); Walter Abel (Dr. George Benedict); Mona Barrie (Eve Benedict); Milton Parsons (John Cartigan, a.k.a. John Lloyd); Tom Dugan and William Haade (Troopers); Joel Friedkin (Coroner)

PHANTOM OF CHINATOWN
(Monogram Pictures Corp.)

This sixth and last of the *Mr. Wong* pictures is the one minus Boris Karloff. It is also the only *Mr. Wong* without William Nigh as director or Harry Neumann as cinematographer, and it is shorter than the others.

What happened was this: The series was going downhill at the box office, and—with one last entry to be filmed and with Karloff committed to one more picture for Monogram—the management decided to put Karloff where he'd attract the most money: in an old-fashioned horror picture. Thus Karloff's last Monogram became the moderately successful *The Ape* (which see), to which the usual *Mr. Wong* crew members were assigned.

Phantom of Chinatown was probably intended as a throwaway, an easy way out of a deteriorating situation. Keye Luke brings in some needed pep with his younger, more romantically inclined interpretation of Mr. Wong, although the character has been diluted somewhat from Karloff's severely dignified reading. The crucial subtext here is that Luke was still smarting from a crass bait-and-switch ploy that 20th Century-Fox had pulled on him two years earlier in connection with the *Charlie Chan* series. Luke was grateful to land the *Mr. Wong* assignment, which he regarded as "a kind of a circuitous consolation prize, you might say."

"You see, Fox had promised me a shot at the title role in the *Charlie Chan* series, should anything ever happen to Warner Oland," Luke told us in 1989. "I'd been playing Number One Son to Mr. Oland for a good while, there, and it seemed like a reasonable graduation for me, especially with Mr. Oland's health failing as he couldn't seem to lay off what he called his 'tiger tea'—his martinis, y'know. Well, the inevitable happened [Oland died in 1938], and the *Chan*s showed no sign of stopping as a series, so I reminded Fox of their promise—and they told me to get lost. Just like that.

"So I landed back playing Number One Son, in that cameo in that *Mr. Moto* picture [1938's *Mr. Moto's Gamble*], which Fox had originally intended as a *Chan*. Sidney Toler wound up 'carrying on,' as it were, and made a perfectly okay Charlie Chan, himself, but it was a double heartbreaker for me—first, to lose Mr. Oland, who for me remains the *real* Charlie Chan, and then to lose a crack at succeeding Mr. Oland. But anyhow, yes, I was very grateful to drop some hints of what I might have done as Chan for that little *Mr. Wong* picture." (Many years later, Luke would supply the voice of a stiffly animated cartoon version of Charlie Chan, for network television's *Amazing Chan and the Chan Clan*.)

With a fresh script by George Waggner (slumming under the pseudonym of Joseph West), and Phil Rosen's snappier-than-Nigh direction, *Phantom of Chinatown* has considerably more to offer than either *The Fatal Hour* or *Doomed To Die*. The indoor atmosphere is abundantly mysterious, and there is a fair measure of outdoor adventure involving an expedition into Mongolia, intercut via sophisticated flashback technique.

An invaluable scroll is discovered along with the tomb of an ancient Chinese ruler in an oil-rich desert region. The safari's photographer (John H. Dilson), intent upon claiming the discovery as his own, commits murder. The expeditionary film itself, shown during a meeting of scientists in San Francisco, figures in the unraveling of the mystery. The new Mr. Wong is called upon to investigate the poisoning of the chief archaeologist (Charles Miller). Suspicion falls upon practically everyone, even Mr. Wong, until the Oxford-educated detective pulls all the clues into place.

Series veterans Grant Withers and Lee Tung Foo are back, and welcome. The Eurasian actress Lotus Long, who had served earlier *Mr. Wong* entries as a victim, makes an attractive semi-leading lady opposite Luke, but too little is made of what is patently a romantic attraction. Conspicuously missing is series regular Marjorie Reynolds, but she had a good excuse: A well-deserved breakthrough to the big time lay in store for her at Paramount.

CREDITS: Producer: Paul Malvern; Director: Phil Rosen; Screenplay: Joseph West [George Waggner]; Story: Ralph Bettinson; Based upon: Characters from Hugh Wiley's *James Lee Wong* Stories in *Collier's* Magazine; Photographed by: Fred Jackman; Special Effects: Jackman Process Corp.; Art Director: Charles Clague; Assistant Director: Mack Wright; Editor: Jack Ogilvie; Decor: David Milton; Musical Score: Edward Kay; Sound Engineer: Edward Fox; Running Time: 61 Minutes; Released: November 15, 1940

CAST: Keye Luke (Jimmy Lee Wong); Grant Withers (Capt. Street); Lotus Long (Win Len); Charles Miller (Dr. John Benton); Huntly Gordon (Wilkes); Virginia Carpenter (Louise Benton); John H. Dilson (Charles Fraser); Paul McVey (Grady); John Holland (Mason); Dick Terry (Toreno); Robert Kellard (Tommy Dean); William Castello (Jonas); Victor Wong (Charley One); and Lee Tung Foo

THE DEVIL BAT
a.k.a.: KILLER BATS
(Producers Releasing Corp.)

We have caught *The Devil Bat* on screens large and small over the long stretch, under pristine first-run conditions; in late-show teevee recyclings during the 1960s, complete with lopsided framing and commercial interruptions every quarter-hour for salvage-carpet warehouses and miracle-diet scams; in big-screen revivals in the 1980s, invariably tainted by the reactionary "badfilm" craze that mistakes cheap ridicule for responsibly enlightening criticism; and finally in ever-improving video restorations that pretty well recapture the ragged beauty of the piece. Here is a

Bela Lugosi touts his latest designer fragrance in *The Devil Bat*.

film that wears its age increasingly well, proving to have intended itself all along as a dark comedy.

In its day, which fell just slightly outside Bela Lugosi's heyday, *The Devil Bat* provided the actor with his most sardonic role apart from all those triumphant portrayals of the 1930s. Today, in a newly appreciative climate for the maverick, even anti-Hollywood, filmmaking imperative, *The Devil Bat*'s mocking contempt for corporate America is enough to transcend its technical and literary failings:

Bela Lugosi's façade of cordiality slips perceptibly in *The Devil Bat*.

When Lugosi's Dr. Paul Carruthers rails against the company that has treated him with such dismissive condescension, it might as well be Lugosi himself, brooding over the halt-and-go stardom he had known at the hands of opportunistic Universal Pictures.

Lugosi is Dr. Paul Carruthers, a beloved small-town physician, whose cosmetic formulas have made a fortune for the local manufacturing company of the Heath and Morton families. Not that Carruthers has reaped much in the way of benefits: He had sold out, rather than accept a partnership. Maddened by a festering resentment, Carruthers has developed a remarkable new designer fragrance—designed, that is, to attract a bloodthirsty mutated bat. The slaying of son Roy Heath (John Ellis) brings onto the scene a big-city newspaperman, Johnny Layton (Dave O'Brien), and his smart-mouthed photographer, One-Shot Maguire (Donald Kerr). As the victims accumulate, Layton perceives a connection between their wounds and the pungent scent that clings to the bodies. Carruthers gives Layton a bottle of the stuff, which Maguire tries. Layton kills the bat when it swoops toward Maguire, but the doctor has another creature ready to turn loose.

Before Carruthers can dispose of daughter Mary Heath (Suzanne Kaaren), Layton steals into the laboratory. Dousing Carruthers with the potion, Layton holds the doctor at gunpoint and awaits the attack. Carruthers bolts, and the bat makes short work of him. The bat is killed as it bears down on Mary.

Lugosi's ability to convey a conflicted personality, torn between benevolence and resentful malice, had been put nicely to the test in his British-made extravaganza, *Dark Eyes of London* (a.k.a. *The Human Monster*; 1939). This gift would figure on into his lengthy span of restored star appeal at Monogram, even as the bigger studios kept putting the artist to lesser use. But it is *The Devil Bat*—a morbid delight, warts and all—that gives him the greatest latitude in using his friendlier nature to cinch the trust of the very people he means to harm. Lugosi frets and fumes with profound indignation when alone but seems the soul of affability when presenting his intended victims with a sample of the deadly cologne, beaming as he recommends the liquid be placed on "the *tender* part of your neck." And what other actor could make the simple expression, "*Good*bye," sound so much like a death sentence?

DIGRESSION FROM MIKE PRICE: *In the earlier years of my long collaboration with George E. Turner, around 1968-75, I frequented a barber shop operated by George's father, George A. Turner, a lanky former cowboy who hardly seemed the type to make with the jokes. One afternoon, the elder George offered me a splash of after-shave lotion for "the tender part of your neck"—never cracked a smile. Later on, I mentioned the line to George E., who chuckled: "Yeah, Pop's a big fan of* The Devil Bat—*been using that routine on his customers for years. Most of 'em don't 'get' it, of course." Later on, I caught George's dad adapting a bit from Tod Slaughter's* Sweeney Todd, the Demon Barber of Fleet Street *(England; 1936): After administering the shave-and-a-haircut treatment, he'd say: "Now—let me polish you off!"*

The end is near for *The Devil Bat*, but Bela Lugosi's span of Poverty Row prominence is just beginning.

The Devil Bat provided a striking showcase for director Jean Yarbrough, who proceeded through a long career of, mostly, more of the same—budget-bound spookers, slapstick comedies and action yarns—with the occasional remarkable highs and remarkable lows. Yarbrough would hit his stride more confidently in 1941's *King of the Zombies*. Going 'way beyond treating *The Devil Bat* as just a vehicle for Lugosi, Yarbrough renders it a fairly involved ensemble piece. The victims are an engaging, well-intentioned lot of self-absorbed fat cats, especially Guy Usher as perfume tycoon Henry Morton and boyish Gene O'Donnell as a doomed offspring. In later years, O'Donnell developed the habit of autographing photos of himself under attack with: "Hey! Watch out for that [*expletive deleted*] bat!" Suzanne Kaaren is precisely the type to make the men in the audience want to rescue her from Lugosi's Devil Bat, and Dave O'Brien makes the heroic newspaperman an identifiably regular guy. As a counterpoint to Lugosi's droll wit, Donald Kerr so overplays the comedy relief that it would be a greater relief merely to see the creature do away with him. Arthur Q. Bryan, Elmer Fudd himself, has a nice bit as a gwouchy newswoom boss—though without the diawect.

An official (sort-of) sequel, 1946's *Devil Bat's Daughter*, neutralizes the gleeful animosity of the now-absent Lugosi character, characterizing the late Dr. Carruthers as merely a misunderstood genius. *The Devil Bat* was remade, too, in 1946, as *The Flying Serpent*, starring George Zucco. The Devil Bat, its own seedy-looking self, took an encore in 1944, swooping down to menace Fuzzy St. John in PRC's *Wild Horse Phantom*.

CREDITS: Producers: Jack Gallagher and Sigmund Neufeld; Associate Producer: Guy V. Thayer, Jr.; Director: Jean Yarbrough; Screenplay: John Thomas Neville; Story: George Bricker; Photographed by: Arthur Martinelli; Art Director: Paul Palmentola; Editor: Holbrook N. Todd; Musical Director: David Chudnow; Sound Engineer: Farrell Redd; Production Manager: Melville DeLay; Running Time: 68 Minutes; Released: December 13, 1940

CAST: Bela Lugosi (Dr. Paul Carruthers); Suzanne Kaaren (Mary Heath); Dave O'Brien (Johnny Layton); Guy Usher (Henry Morton); Yolande Mallott (Maxine); Donald Kerr (One-Shot Maguire); Edward Mortimer (Martin Heath); Gene O'Donnell (Don Morton); Alan Baldwin (Tommy Heath); John Ellis (Ray Heath); Arthur Q. Bryan (Joe McGinty); Hal Price (Chief Wilkins); John Davidson (Prof. Raines); Wallace Rairden (Walter King); Billy Griffith (Coroner)

1941
THE BLOOD OF JESUS
(Sack Amusement Enterprises)

Spencer Williams leapt in short order from a screenwriter-actor job on *Son of Ingagi* (which see) to a full-fledged directing assignment, along with writing and acting, on *The Blood of Jesus*. These oddly matched films marked the beginning of a lengthy and mutually beneficial collaboration between Williams, an ambitious black artist with many stories worth the telling, and Alfred Sack, a Dallas-based Jewish entrepreneur who was keen on tapping the well-hidden but lucrative market in black neighborhood theatres. The abrupt change in subject matter may seem more drastic than the heightened responsibility—for Williams had long since learned how to take charge of a movie shoot—but in fact *The Blood of Jesus* is far and away a weirder piece of work than *Son of Ingagi*, whose mad-doctor shenanigans and comic-relief slapstick routines themselves defy convention.

Few accepted conventions of feature-film storytelling intrude on *The Blood of Jesus*, which plays out today like some rough-sketch prototype for Steven Spielberg's *The Color Purple* (1985), with the grace-notes of a literal nod to Georges Mèliés' pioneering special-effects fantasies of the early-day French cinema. Williams' simplistic, redeemingly ardent view of black Southern spiritual life is distinguished throughout by a sense of immersion in the society, complete with its perpetual struggle between piety and profanity.

Williams plays Ras Jackson, a backslider who makes himself conspicuously absent from the riverside baptism of his bride, Martha (Cathryn Caviness). When Martha returns home, one of the more pious churchwomen confronts Ras. He claims to have been hunting, but in fact he has been poaching on a nearby hog farm. Ras' gun falls—discharging and wounding Martha. The naturalism of the film lapses into supernatural fantasy as her disembodied soul finds itself traveling to a cosmic crossroads that separates the celestial realm from Hades. Satan (James B. Jones), lurking along the way, sends a suave badman (Frank H. McClennan) to tempt Martha. After some harrowing detours, Martha reaches the crossroads—only to run blindly into the hell-bound pathway. She backtracks and drags herself to the base of a cross, where she is anointed in blood.

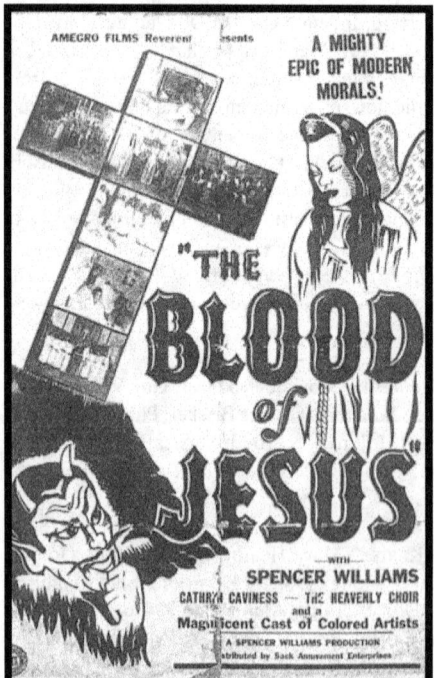

Back at the house, Martha wakes to finds her husband in mourning. She assures Ras that she will recover. The neighbors revel in Martha's return.

Williams' artistry is as raw and rudimentary as the production values, but his film's deliverance is an earnest piety and a flat-out bizarre narrative sense that overcomes the obvious lack of polish. The dime-store Halloween costume that identifies Satan is so lacking in artifice that it becomes its own kind of artifice, a defiance of the very limitations that would have defeated a less determined filmmaker. Williams had a keen technical advantage, however, in Dallas-based Jamieson Film Company, a processing laboratory that handled footage for projects large and small. In years to come, the Jamieson labs would serve interests as disparate as Oral Roberts' evangelical tent-revival troupe, many Southwestern television stations and Larry Buchanan's minimalist horror thrillers and exploitation-as-art pictures of the 1960s.

When Dr. G. William Jones, who headed the restoration campaign for this and other long-mislaid black-ensemble films, titled his book about the project *Black Cinema Treasures: Lost and Found* (University of North Texas Press; 1991), he was thinking primarily of *The Blood of Jesus*.

CREDITS: Producer: Alfred Sack; Screenwriter and Director: Spencer Williams, Jr.; Photographed by: Jack Whitman; Sound Engineer: R.E. "Dick" Byers; Music: The Honorable Rev. R.L. Robertson & the Heavenly Choir and Henry Thacker Burleigh; Film Laboratory: Jamieson Film Co., Dallas; Film Laboratory Technician: Gordon Yoder; Running Time: 68 Minutes; Released: During 1941 to Black Neighborhood Theatres on a Region-by-Region, or States'-Rights, Basis

CAST: Spencer Williams, Jr. (Ras Jackson and Narrator); Cathryn Caviness (Martha Jackson); Juanita Riley (Sister Jenkins); Heather Hardeman (Sister Ellerby); Rogenia Goldthwaite (Angel); James B. Jones (Satan); Frank H. McClennan (Judas Green); Eddie DeBuse (Rufus Brown); Alva Fuller (Luke Willows)

THE LONE RIDER RIDES ON
(Sigmund Neufeld Productions, Inc./Producers Releasing Corp.)

Sig Neufeld's *Lone Rider* series originated with this very picture as a *Lone Ranger* knockoff, trusting in a sound-alike character name and a mysterious maverick hero to siphon popular interest from the more polished genuine article, which Republic Pictures had treated definitively as a serial in 1939. The *Lone Rider* concept quickly developed a distinctively darker attitude, however, where the *Lone Ranger* pictures veered away from the shadows and into a sun-drenched wholesomeness.

George Houston introduces the character here as Tom Cameron, who in 1901 has become known as the Lone Rider—a determined cuss, who still vividly recalls the childhood episode in which he seems to have been the lone survivor of a massacre at his family's campsite (a chronic, if not acute, plot device). Upon encountering a new campsite murder, the Rider finds a ranchland deed among the effects of the victim, Richard Brown, and decides to look into the matter after a flashback to the trauma of his youth. The ranch is in foreclosure, and crooked Frank Mitchell (Frank Hagney) and his accomplice, Curly (Lee Powell), are now ready to evict Brown's sister, Sue (Hillary Brooke). Mitchell frames Tom for Brown's slaying, but a friendly general-store proprietor, Fuzzy Jones (Al St. John), volunteers to help Tom. While on trial, Tom recognizes the presiding judge (Karl Hackett) as the mob leader responsible for the attack on Tom's family. Tom is sentenced to hang, but Fuzzy executes a jailbreak. Amid the resulting mayhem, Tom finally recognizes the brutal Curly as his long-lost brother. Curly softens, revealing that Mitchell had adopted him and told him that his family had been killed by Indians.

In an attack by a Mitchell thug, Curly stops a bullet meant for Tom, who cleans up the territory. The gang routed, Fuzzy pitches Tom as a candidate for judge. Tom declines the offer and rides on in search of new wrongs to set right.

As the series progressed, of course, the Lone Rider would take on Fuzzy as a recurring sidekick. George Houston eventually relinquished the lead to Bob Livingston, but St. John remained a constant. The supposedly original screenplay in this premiere adventure is scarcely original, what with such stock-in-trade plot elements as the campsite massacre, the murderers assuming positions of respectable authority and the recognition of the long-lost brother by a birthmark. *The Lone Rider Rides On* is, withal, a promising launch for a franchise that helped keep the Western film true to its Gothic roots for a goodly while.

CREDITS: Producer: Sigmund Neufeld; Director: Samuel Newfield; Screenplay: Joseph O'Donnell; Photographed by: Jack Greenhalgh; Art Director: Fred Preble; Assistant Director: Melville DeLay; Editor: Holbrook N. Todd; Sound Engineer: Hans Weeren; Songs: "I'm the Lone Rider," "Roll Along, Prairie Wagon," and "Nobody's Fault but My Own," by Johnny Lange & Lew Porter; Production Manager: Bert Sternbach; Running Time: 61 Minutes; Released: January 10, 1941

CAST: George Houston (Tom "Lone Rider" Cameron); Hillary Brooke (Sue Brown); Al St. John (Fuzzy Jones); Karl Hackett (Judge Graham); Lee Powell (Curly); Forrest Taylor (Sheriff); Frank Hagney (Mitchell); J. Wilsey (Bill); Frank Ellis (Pete); Curly Dresden (Jerry); Buddy Roosevelt (Joe); Al Bridge (Bob Cameron); Isabel la Mal (Ma Cameron); Harry Harvey, Jr. (Jim Cameron); Don Forrest (Eddie); Bob Kortman (Dave); and Bobby Winkler, Wally West, Steve Clark

YOU'RE OUT OF LUCK
(Sterling Productions, Inc./Monogram Pictures Corp.)

The lowly-but-noble big-city elevator man has seldom been recognized as the driving force he used to be in high-rise community and corporate life. Before automation made *everybody* an elevator operator for better or worse, these dedicated professionals—who were, economically speaking, just a step or two up from Skid Row—took a distinct tribal pride in seeing to it that each passenger, no matter how crowded the car or how impatiently abusive the riders, reached the appropriate floor in due time.

It is safe to say that few real-life elevator men harbored a desire to play detective, and this quirk is precisely what makes the Frankie Darro-Mantan Moreland team in *You're Out of Luck* such a delight. These guys know their way around the inner chambers of a ritzy hotel, and thus do the actors ground their more extravagant deeds in an unerring practical reality.

If Mantan Moreland is the great unacknowledged comedian of Old Hollywood (see *King of the Zombies*, below), then Moreland and Frankie Darro must certainly want consideration as one of the better comedy teams, ill-recognized. Their starring series of desperate mystery-farces for Monogram holds up as a kind of poor man's Abbott & Costello (whose big-screen teaming Moreland and Darro foreshadowed), and the combination of Darro's overzealous boyishness and Moreland's never-at-a-loss wisecracking wisdom is still a wonder to behold. That they formed—and sustained—an integrated comedy-adventure act long before Robert Culp and Bill Cosby (network television's *I Spy*) or Danny Glover and Mel Gibson (the *Lethal Weapon* pictures) makes their work all the more ripe for rediscovery.

Darro was born Frank Johnson in 1917 in Chicago, the son of circus aerialists. Small of frame and as agile as a prairie catamount, he started out playing adventurous roles as a youngster; a good sustained example of his teen-age work occurs in 1935's *The Phantom Empire* (see *Forgotten Horrors: The Definitive Edition*). Darro was still being (aptly) cast as a kid, for all practical purposes, even into adulthood.

Which brings us to *You're Out of Luck*, which Darro serves as a hotel elevator operator and bellman named Frankie O'Reilly. Frankie and Jeff (Moreland), a garageman and mechanic for the same Carlton Arms, chance to witness a mob hit—latest outburst of a crime wave that has found Frankie's brother, police detective Tom O'Reilly (Richard Bond), hard-pressed to nail a mastermind. Tom considers Frankie a nuisance, but the kid tags along anyhow as they trace Dick Whitney (Tris Coffin), a playboy resident of the hotel, to criminal elements. Tom grudgingly accepts help from Jeff and Frankie in trailing Whitney.

Whitney pulls off a shakedown on a gangster named Johnny Burke (Willie Costello) and passes an envelope full of money to Frankie, with orders to deliver it to the murder victim's sister. Whitney calls for a police raid. Tom breaks into a now-deserted nightclub, only to find himself humiliated by a mocking newspaper report.

Frankie has hidden the envelope within the hotel. Later, when ordered to repair a sluggish lift, Jeff and Frankie find Whitney's body atop the elevator car. It develops that Burke is responsible for the slayings, which were provoked by gambling shenanigans. Burke's hoodlums capture Jeff and Frankie and Sonya (Vicki Lester), a *femme fatale* who had been involved with both Burke and Whitney. Burke herds the captives into a freight elevator, the better to hold off a police siege. Jeff and Frankie save the day by freezing the elevator via an emergency control panel.

The complications run needlessly thick, what with Vicki Lester walking a fine line between helping the cops and bum-steering them as she tries to lay her mitts on a small fortune in illicit loot, while still seeming a dutiful gang moll; Moreland carrying on an affair with the moll's housekeeper; detective Richard Bond tackling the underworld while fending off an abusive press corps; and a cash-laden envelope defying all attempts to keep track of it. Moreland and Darro keep the messy scenario under control with brisk wordplay and whiplash slapstick reactions—and ultimately, a heroism born of their unique knowledge of the inner workings of an elevator.

CREDITS: Producer: Lindsley Parsons, for Sterling Productions; Director: Howard Bretherton; Story and Screenplay: Edmund Kelso; Photographed by: Fred Jackman, Jr.; Assistant Director: Mack Wright; Art Director: Charles Clague; Settings: David Milton; Editor: Jack Ogilvie; Sound Engineer: William Fox; Running Time: 62 Minutes; Released: January 20, 1941

CAST: Frankie Darro (Frankie O'Reilly); Mantan Moreland (Jeff); Kay Sutton (Margie); Vicky Lester (Sonya Varney); Richard Bond (Tom O'Reilly); Janet Shaw (Joyce); Tristram "Tris" Coffin (Dick Whitney); Willie Costello (Johnny Burke); Alfred Hall (Haskell); Paul Maxey (Pete); Ralph Peters (Mulligan); Billy Snyder (News Photographer) and Paul Bryar, Jack Mather, Gene O'Donnell

THE GREAT TRAIN ROBBERY
(Republic Pictures Corp.)

Although only its title betokens a kinship with the watershed Edison film of 1903, Joseph Kane's *The Great Train Robbery* is nonetheless an old-fashioned rip-snorter. "Old-fashioned" in this case means more of a welcome throwback to the 1930s—that age of grimmer, less tunefully romanticized Westerns. Republic's production values are many notches above those of Bob Steele's Depression-era shoot-'em-ups, but there is a tremendous fidelity here to Poverty Row's style and attitude of the early-talkie years.

Steele plays a hard-bitten, short-fused railroad detective—a fellow by name of Tom Logan—who lands the high-profile job of guarding a million-dollar gold shipment. Though Tom is a fair-and-square straight-shooting sort, his family's wicked reputation catches up with him at an awkward crucial moment. Another detective (Hal Taliaferro, a.k.a. Western stalwart Wally Wales) develops suspicions that Tom's train-robber father might have passed along some crooked genes. It helps none at all that Tom's brother, Duke (Milburn Stone), is the operator of a low-down drinking and sporting establishment. Tom shows up almost too late for duty, looking rather like something the cat dragged in, and the departure takes place even though one of Duke's "entertainers," Kay Stevens (Claire Carleton), has followed Tom aboard.

Signaling ahead to have Kay removed at the next stop, the railroad superintendent (Monte Blue) learns only that the passengers have already been robbed and dropped off. A search for the train turns up only a phantom whistling, even though there is but one track on the line.

In a flashback to the night previous, we see that Duke had ordered his men to waylay Tom, who escaped in time to make the run. Kay, who is in love with Tom in spite of Duke's affections for her, had followed out of legitimate concern. Duke's gang had overtaken the train, taking advantage of Tom's hesitation to fire on his brother. Steering the train onto an abandoned mining spur and covering their path with a landslide, the mobsters played a recording of a whistle to make it appear the cargo had gone through.

Tom and Kay escape, and amid a wild running battle Tom crashes the train through the landslide. Pierce arrives and mows down Duke, who in a dying confession clears Tom's reputation once and for all.

Director Joseph Kane's sharp deployment of mystery and near-spectacle make this particular *Great Train Robbery* a delight, with a pleasing hint of supernatural interference and a chilling cur-

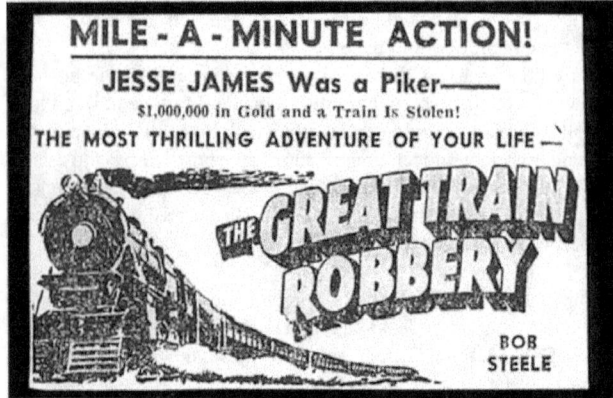

rent of deadly tensions between estranged brothers. Steele perks right along with his familiar intense indignation, becoming more handsome and heroic with every frown that creases his brow. Future TV Western favorite Milburn Stone, who alternated gracefully between sympathetic and villainous parts as a B-movie dependable, is Steele's (melo)dramatic match as the despicable brother; Stone also was pursuing a secondary career at the time as a big-band singer, often pinch-hitting for Frank Sinatra with the Tommy Dorsey Orchestra. Saucy Claire Carleton completes the triangle as something more than a dance-hall floozy. Old-timer Si Jenks is delightful as an eccentric prospector who comes along at just the right moment, and Helen MacKellar has a telling small role as the careworn mother of the warring Logan boys.

The box-office success of *The Great Train Robbery* prompted Republic to plan a series of "melodramas in the old-time style," as *The Hollywood Reporter* noted. The idea got only as far as Joe Kane's *Rags to Riches* (1941), an underworld adventure with musical interludes.

CREDITS: Associate Producer and Director: Joseph Kane; Screenplay: Oliver Cooper, Garnett Weston and Robert T. Shannon; Photographed by: Reggie Lanning; Art Director: John Victor Mackay; Assistant Directors: William O'Connor and Mel Tucker; Supervising Editor: Murray Seldeen; Editor: Lester Orlebeck; Wardrobe: Adele Palmer; Musical Director: Cy Feuer; Production Manager: Al Wilson; Running Time: 62 Minutes; Released: February 28, 1941

CAST: Bob Steele (Tom Logan); Claire Carleton (Kay Stevens); Milburn Stone (Duke Logan); Helen MacKellar (Mrs. Logan); Si Jenks (Whiskers); Monte Blue (Superintendent); Hal Taliaferro (Pierce); Jay Novello (Santos); Dick Wessell (Gorman); Lew Kelly (Dad Halliday); Guy Usher (Barnsdale); Yakima Canutt (Klefner).

THE FORGOTTEN VILLAGE
(Pan-American Films/Mayer-Burstyn, Inc.)

Noteworthy in the present context for its prominent element of backwater superstition, this dramatized documentary feature is of greater interest as a little-known original work by John Steinbeck. The Great Man's epic novel *The Grapes of Wrath* and its kindred novella, *Of Mice and Men*, had recently been adapted to cinema, and the acclaim that greeted these pictures encouraged Steinbeck to write a piece directly for the screen. Burgess Meredith, who had co-starred in Lewis Milestone's 1939 filming of *Of Mice and Men*, signed on as narrator for *The Forgotten Village*. Principal photography was completed over a period of 10 months on location in a mountainous region of Mexico.

The greater point here is to urge a heightened awareness of the enforced ignorance that (even today) holds rural Mexico in poverty and vulnerability to disease. In the town of Santiago, a conjurer named Trini uses her bewitchments and potions to foretell a long and distinguished life for a child yet unborn. A boy named Paco falls ill, and Trini casts a spell that supposedly will drive the disease into a clutch of eggs. A local schoolteacher blames the malady on contaminated water, but Paco's mother insists that Trini alone can bring about a cure. Paco dies, and a greater outbreak follows. As the townspeople pray in vain for protection, the teacher and Paco's surviving brother, Juan Diego, risk ostracism to bring in a doctor from the outside world. The physician purifies a dank well. Trini accuses him of poisoning the water. Juan Diego, now rejected by his own family despite evidence of a cure, decides he must journey to civilization to study medicine.

Steinbeck and producer/director Herbert Kline promptly found themselves frustrated by the very conditions they meant to examine and indict: In an article published long after the fact, the *New York Herald Tribune* reported that the company had arranged to pay its amateur actors more than they were earning as fieldhands, and the local farm owners, finding such generosity a threat to their feudal dominion, threatened to disrupt the filming. Only after the wealthiest of the region's farmers gave his blessing did the project proceed unhampered, according to the newspaper's account. The picture works better as a documentary account than as (melo)drama, but the conjure-woman is suitably intimidating and the portrayal of Juan Diego is pleasingly natural.

The company also ran afoul of the New York censors, who banned *The Forgotten Village* in view of its depictions of childbirth and breast-feeding. An appeal cleared the film for distribution in New York State by December of 1941. *The Forgotten Village* was later published as a book, illustrated with photographs from the motion picture.

CREDITS: Producer and Director: Herbert Kline; Associate Producer: Rosa Harvan Kline; Written for the Screen by: John Steinbeck; Co-Director and Director of Photography: Alexander Hackensmit; Assistant Director and Interpreter: Carlos L. Cabello; Cameramen: Augustín Delgado and Felipé Quintanar; Musical Score: Hans Eisler; Conductor: Jascha Horenstein; Production Manager: Mark Marvin; Running Time: 65-67 Minutes in English and Spanish Versions; Released: Following Previews during February-March of 1941

CAST: Burgess Meredith (Narrator) and a Native Mexican Ensemble Cast

MR. DISTRICT ATTORNEY
(Republic Pictures Corp.)

Peter Lorre was hardly the type to do a Dr. Jekyll, but he did get to play a memorably wicked Mr. Hyde in this ambitious but deeply flawed attempt at launching a series.

Mr. District Attorney, one of Phillips H. Lord's more successful radio programs, began airing in 1939 and long remained a Wednesday-night staple of NBC, eventually spawning a teleseries and even a run of comic books. Republic tackled this big-screen spin-off during 1940-41, starting out modestly but yielding such good-looking early results that studio boss Herbert J. Yates was moved to boost it to the "Republic Special" class. The radio writers had favored offbeat, noir-ish themes, and scenarists Karl Brown and Malcolm Stuart Boylan followed suit, pitting greenhorn prosecutor Dennis O'Keefe against a corrupt politician named Mr. Hyde—an allusion, nothing more, to R.L. Stevenson—with a troublesome Mrs. Hyde as a climactic garnish.

Leading man Dennis O'Keefe has too ineffectual a role—and a laughable character name, to

Beyond the Horror Ban

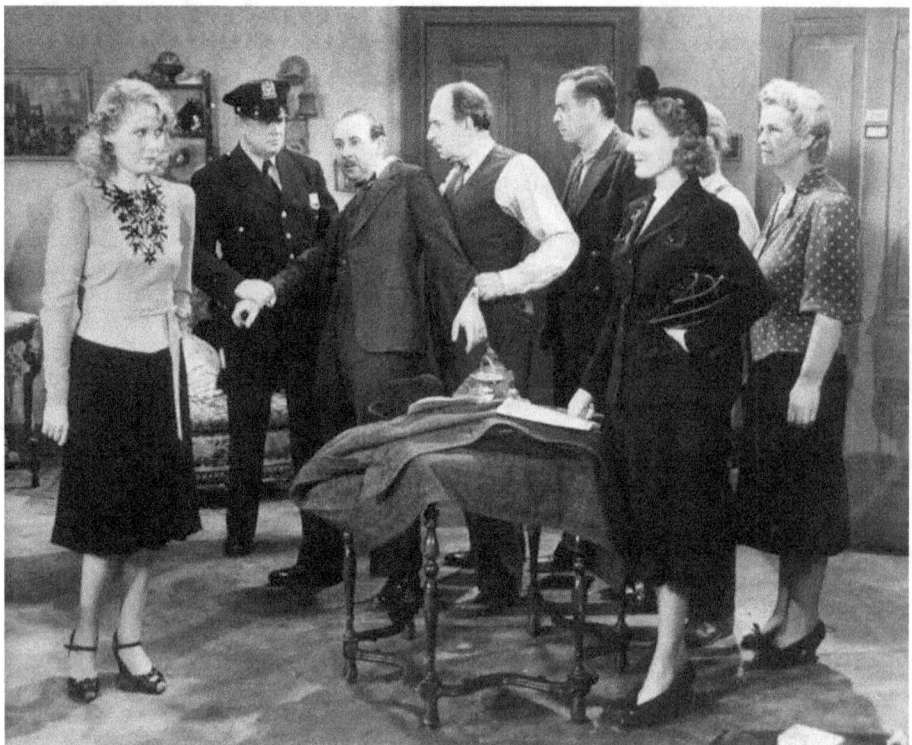

Dennis O'Keefe, Florence Rice, Charles Arnt and Joan Blair are entwined in a mystery in *Mr. District Attorney.* (Photofest)

boot—to pose much of a threat to Lorre's murderous scheming. As novice prosecutor P. Cadwallader Jones, about the only edge O'Keefe can muster is with the help of the muddled script, whose convenient coincidences and overobvious plot developments leave plenty to be desired. Pre-production censorship plagued the project, too—to such an extent that an obviously prostitutional character is dismissed as merely a tough dame.

Lorre's fugitive Mr. Hyde represents a dead-end investigation to the office of District Attorney Winton (Stanley Ridges). So when bungling novice Jones, fresh out of Harvard, causes a mistrial in a gangland case, he finds himself saddled with finding out whatever became of Mr. Hyde, who vanished four years ago with a fortune in your tax dollars and ours, too.

But then, Jones stumbles onto a real clue when marked currency connected to Hyde is found among the bets at a racetrack. D.A. Winton sidelines Jones, hoping to tie the loot to a political enemy named Barrett (Minor Watson). Jones and newspaperwoman Terry Parker (Florence Rice) look into a seemingly unrelated case involving crusty Betty Paradise (Joan Blair) and a crooked bank clerk named Herman Winkle (Charles Arnt). Hyde makes a furtive appearance, apparently as Winkle's benefactor—but then kills the clerk, who has been lifting cash from one of Hyde's false-name depositories. Hyde then does away with Betty.

Barrett fails in an attempt to have Jones killed but persuades Hyde's long-abandoned wife (Helen Brown) to murder Hyde. Helen Brown's abrupt confrontation with Lorre is a jewel, but she lays things on a bit thickly with a hysterical confession in follow-through. Jones and Terry, thoroughly humiliated by their own meddling, set matters right by catching Barrett in the act of ransacking Hyde's safe-deposit box. Better the yarn should have concentrated more on Lorre's suave and soft-spoken brand of evildoing and less on Minor Watson's altogether conventional show of villainy.

Despite so flawed a beginning, the series would continue later in 1941 with the far more impressive *Mr. District Attorney in the Carter Case* (which see), and with *Secrets of the Underground* (see our 1942 section). *Secrets of the Underground* was conceived and filmed as a *Mr. District Attorney* entry, but not released as such. Columbia would attempt to revive the series in 1947, but a successful long-term picturization of *Mr. District Attorney* would have to wait until NBC's television version of 1951-54.

CREDITS: Associate Producer: Leonard Fields; Director: William Morgan; Screenplay: Karl Brown and Malcolm Stuart Boylan [*The Hollywood Reporter* Credits Hugh Herbert with Additional Dialogue and Eve Green as Script Doctor]; Photographed by: Reggie Lanning; Assistant Director: Tom Flood; Art Director: John Victor Mackay; Supervising Editor: Murray Seldeen; Editor: Edward Mann; Wardrobe: Adele Palmer; Music: Cy Feuer; Production Manager: Al Wilson; Running Time: 69 Minutes; Released: March 27, 1941

CAST: Dennis O'Keefe (P. Cadwallader Jones); Florence Rice (Terry Parker); Peter Lorre (Mr. Hyde); Stanley Ridges (District Attorney Winton); Minor Watson (Barrett); Charles Arnt (Herman Winkle); Joan Blair (Betty Paradise); Charles Halton (Hazleton); Alan Edwards (Grew); George Watts (Judge White); Sarah Edwards (Miss Petherby); Helen Brown (Mrs. Hyde); and Grady Sutton, Ben Welden, Emmet Vogan, Dewey Robinson, Charles Williams, Eddie Gribbon, Frederick Burton, Dick Elliott

CITY OF MISSING GIRLS
(Select Attractions, Inc./Merrick-Alexander Productions)

White slavery and serial murder hold a promise of thrills that are never satisfactorily delivered in this tale of feigned respectability, journalistic persistence and hamstrung law enforcement. Astrid Allwyn plays a hell-bent-for-bylines reporter who has no inkling that her father (Boyd Irwin), a theatrical agent, is in cahoots with a shady racket involving a nightclub and a "school" of "fine" "arts." Girls who enroll in the academy are in peril of winding up shanghaied as "entertainers" at procurer Philip Van Zandt's nitery, and the vanished beauties keep turning up dead. It falls to a tough cop (H.B. Warner) to connect the underworld with the academic realm, but Miss Allwyn charges into a maverick investigation of her own—intent upon beating an assistant district attorney (John Warner) to a solution.

Warner and Miss Allwyn spend altogether too much time pursuing an antagonistic romantic attraction to allow the film to concentrate on its own underlying horrors. The motivating tragedies seem almost incidental to Warner's frame-up for one murder and Miss Allwyn's risky ploy of enrolling herself in the bogus school. Veteran director Elmer Clifton, late of the D.W. Griffith company and amply represented in the prior volume of *Forgotten Horrors*, allows a lax pace that finally snaps taut when the crooked agent has a change of heart—only to fall prey to mobster Van Zandt. H.B. Warner is the soul of determination as the gruff but benevolent detective. Future teevee sitcom star Gale Storm can be spotted in a small role.

CREDITS: Producers: Max Alexander and George M. Merrick; Production Executive: Alfred Stern; Director: Elmer Clifton; Story: George Rosener and Elmer Clifton; Screenplay: Oliver Drake; Additional Dialogue: George Rosener; Photographed by: Edward Linden; Editor: Charles Henkel, Jr.; Settings: Fred Preble and James Altweis; Sound Engineer: Clifford Ruberg; Running Time: 73 Minutes; Released: Following New York Opening on March 27, 1941

CAST: H.B. Warner (Police Capt. McVeigh); Astrid Allwyn (Nora Page); John Archer (James Horton); Sarah Padden (Mrs. Randolph); Philip Van Zandt (King Peterson); George Rosener (Officer Dugan); Katherine Crawford (Helen Whitney); Patricia Knox (Kate Nelson); Walter Long (Officer Larkin); Gale [Billed Here as *Gail*] Storm (Mary Phillips); Boyd Irwin (Joseph Thompson); Danny Webb (William Short)

Tom Tyler is caught off-guard in *Adventures of Captain Marvel.*

ADVENTURES OF CAPTAIN MARVEL
(Republic Pictures Corp.)

Among the more polished and relentlessly entertaining of Republic's serials, though hardly in a class with Universal's splendid *Flash Gordon* chapter-plays, is *Adventures of Captain Marvel*. The project was undertaken by default when an attempt to adapt *Superman* to live-action cinema fell through in pre-production. Republic's switch can only have exacerbated a war of nerves between the characters' rival publishers, whose lawyers sniped at one another for years over the simplistic accusation that Captain Marvel was an imitation of Superman. The Superman camp finally won—a feeble victory, after all that sabre-rattling—driving Captain Marvel out of print while gaining control of the character's trademarks in the process, and then neglecting to do anything constructive with the properties until many years after the fact.

Of course, *all* the comic-book superheroes, from whatever publishing companies, were imitations of one character or another; Superman merely claimed pride of place as a takeoff on heroic legends dating from antiquity and pop-literary world-beaters dating from recent times. Captain Marvel's great originality is that his stories had a redeemingly playful sense of humor about them—courtesy of the principal creator, a thoughtfully mature and droll cartoonist named C.C. Beck—where Superman and most of his kind were caught up in self-serious juvenile power fantasies. The distinction between Marvel's child*like* wit and Superman's scowlingly child*ish* bluster went sailing right over the heads of the hell-bent-for-litigation trademark wranglers.

An aftertaste of Republic's abortive *Superman* serial ironically found its way into *Adventures of Captain Marvel*. Veteran Western star Tom Tyler, who landed the title role, was quite the image of a funnybook superhero, but only in the generic sense. Lacking the beefy and bumpkin-like aspect of Beck's character, Tyler proved a leaner, sterner Captain Marvel than the comics audience had known.

This Marvel's ruthlessness in dealing with criminals can be quite scary, and Tyler's clipped delivery is calculated to intimidate. And what a grim Superman Tyler would have made!

The story retells the familiar fantasy about an urchin named Billy Batson (Frank Coghlan, Jr.), who is granted the ability to transform himself into the "world's mightiest mortal," Captain Marvel, on pronouncing the name of an ancient wizard, Shazam. In the flim's closest resemblance to the comic-book yarns, Nigel de Brulier looks as though he might have stepped directly from one of Beck's drawings of Shazam.

The tale concerns a forbidden expedition into a burial ground near the Burmese border—where a simmering volcano, a long-dormant curse involving the secrets of alchemy, and the mixed blessing of Shazam's gifts lie in wait. The otherworldly thrills become gradually more attuned to modern-day civilization as the serial progresses, what with a cloaked badman called the Scorpion on a rampage, Billy Batson's chums in near-constant peril and Billy/Marvel himself subjected to explosions, falling blades, floods of lava, electrocution, bombs, machine-gun barrages and the like.

Tom Tyler as the World's Mightiest Mortal.

Any pretense at plot is frankly beside the point: The real reason to watch, to remember, and to rediscover *Adventures of Captain Marvel* in particular among the serials of the Depression-into-WWII years, is to relish its splendid pageantry of effects, the stirring musical cues that lend dramatic momentum where there is no actual "drama," to speak of, and the breathless pacing that kept the kids of 1941—and of 1953, when a full-scale reissue took place—coming back, week after week. The masked villain known as the Scorpion only looks hokey; his voice, courtesy of Gerald Mohr, is plenty menacing, and his murderous devices bring out the best in Republic's crackerjack special-effects team. Bud Thackery's process photography is as convincing as usual. The special props by the Lydecker brothers, Howard and Theodore, include an astonishingly realistic larger-than-life mannequin, which represents Captain Marvel in flight. Dave Sharpe's action stunting as Marvel includes numerous bone-rattling drops and leaps, with a particularly impressive display of acrobatics in Chapter No. 1.

Later on in 1941, Superman fared impressively in a series of animated cartoons, launched by the Fleischer brothers studios for Paramount. A 1948 *Superman* serial and its 1950 sequel, *Atom Man vs. Superman*, produced by Sam Katzman for Columbia, proved almost thoroughly disappointing.

CREDITS: Producer: Hiram S. Brown, Jr.; Directors: William Witney and John English; Screenplay: Ronald Davidson, Arch B. Heath, Joseph Poland, Sol Shor and Norman S. Hall; Based upon: the *WHIZ Comics* Series; Photographed by: William Nobles; Special Effects: Bud Thackery (Process Shots), with Howard and Theodore Lydecker (Special Props); Assistant Directors: Louis Germonprez and R.G. "Bud" Springsteen; Editors: Edward Todd and William Thompson; Musical Supervisor: Cy Feuer, Incorporating Original Scoring with Dramatic Cues from the Serials *Drums of Fu Manchu* and *Mysterious Doctor Satan*; Composers: Mort Glickman, Ross DiMaggio, Cy Feuer and William Lava; Location Shooting at: Chatsworth and Lake Sherwood, Calif.; a Serial in 12 Chapters, Total Running Time: 216 Minutes; Released: March 28, 1941; Reissued as *Return of Captain Marvel* on: April 15, 1953

CAST: Tom Tyler (Captain Marvel); Frank Coughlan, Jr. (Billy Batson); William Benedict (Whitey); Louise Curry (Betty Wallace); Gerald Mohr (Voice of the Scorpion); Robert Strange (John Malcolm); Harry Worth (Prof. Luther Bentley); Bryant Washburn (Henry Carlyle); John Davidson (Tal Chotali); George Pembroke (Dr. Stephen Lang); Peter George Lynn (Dwight Fisher); Reed Hadley (Rahman

Bar); Jack Mulhall (James Howell); Kenneth Duncan (Barnett); Nigel de Brulier (Shazam); John Bagni (Cowan); Carleton Young (Martin); Leland Hodgson (Maj. Rawley); Stanley Price (Owens); Ernest Sarracino (Akbar); Tetsu Komai (Chan Lai); Augie Gomez (Native No. 1); Al Taylor (Native No. 2); Eddie Dew (Cavalry Lieutenant); Carl Zwolsman (Sentry); Marten Lamont (Radio Sergeant); Maj. Sam Harris (Col. Hudson); Curley Dresden (Native No. 3); Loren Riebe (Lab Heavy and Curio Heavy No. 1); Fenton Taylor (Lab Heavy No. 2); Jerry Jerome (Brandon); James Fawcett (Curio Heavy No. 2); Francis Sayles (Carter); Kenneth Terrell (Hawks); Bud Geary (Pete); Frank Marlowe (Gus); Lynton Brent (Lefty); Wilson Benge (Benson); Frank Wayne (Steve); Edward Cassidy (Captain Dodge); Chuck Morrison (Carlson); Ted Mapes (Sailor); Al Kikume (Native Chief); Paul Lopez (Ali); Armand Cortes (Hamid); Dave Sharpe (Captain Marvel Stuntman); and Earl Bunn, George Suzanne

FEDERAL FUGITIVES
(Producers Releasing Corp.)

An officially deceased madman posing as a distinguished financier makes a worthy quarry for a dyspeptic undercover agent in this crisp thriller from director William Beaudine and producer John T. Coyle.

Silent-era star Neil Hamilton plays Capt. James Madison, who is trailing Capitol Hill lobbyist Bruce Lane (Charles Wilson) on suspicion of international shenanigans. At a restaurant, with his supply of antacid tablets at the ready, Madison spots a ringer for the master criminal Otto Lieberman, long supposed dead. It becomes evident that Lieberman had staged a false demise, only to re-invent himself as Dr. Frederic Haskell (Victor Varconi), a Lane crony. Haskell and Lane conspire to buy the rights to an experimental aircraft from its inventor, Henry Gregory (George Carleton), but Madison convinces Gregory to take part in a ruse to trap the crooks.

Madison, posing as a partner of Gregory's, is distracted by Lane's seductive cohort, Rita Bennett (a since-forgotten actress with the unforgettable name of Doris Day). Meanwhile, Haskell snoops out the G-Man's true identity and slips a poisonous pill into Madison's supply of heartburn remedy. Rita switches loyalties when she learns of the plot to kill Madison, but she is knocked unconscious in an auto accident before she can deliver a warning. She regains her wits days later, slips away from her hospital room and catches up with a captive Madison just as Haskell—who has lost patience with his game of medicinal Russian roulette—is about to force the agent to swallow the poison. While Madison's helper, Chuck (Lyle Latell), and his pal, Ox (Frank Moran), battle Haskell's thugs, Madison chases after the villain, who takes a fatal plunge down an elevator shaft. All ends romantically for Madison, who has developed a new variety of heartburn—for the reformed Rita.

The charm of *Federal Fugitives* lies in its canny balance between murderous menace and lunkheaded comedy. The latter is supplied by Lyle Latell and Frank Moran, as the brawn-over-brains types who enable Hamilton to concentrate on taking out the chief heavy. Hamilton, seen here at age 41, still radiates the star power he commanded as Paramount's biggest box-office name of the late 1920s. More than a generation later, Hamilton would find an entirely new mass audience as Commissioner Gordon on the teleseries *Batman*.

The charm of *Federal Fugitives* lies in its canny balance between murderous menace and lunkheaded comedy

The chemistry between Hamilton and this particular Doris Day is of the bittersweet variety, but their final clench rings true enough. (The other, more enduringly famous, Doris Day was still several years away from her own movie breakthrough, but was just then on the verge of becoming a popular big-band vocalist.) Victor Varconi, whose career ran a less prominent parallel to that of his fellow Hungarian Bela Lugosi, plays the brains of the racket with suave Continental malice.

Producer Coyle had been a busy talent on Poverty Row during the Depression years, and this project impressively marked his arrival at PRC. The material must have inspired Beaudine, as well, for the old-timer generates an unaccustomed wealth of suspense. Pre-production press notices, by the way, identify the director as William X. Crowley—a Beaudine alias—but the screen credits use the artist's genuine name.

CREDITS: Executive Producer: George R. Batcheller; Producer: John T. Coyle; Director: William Beaudine; Story and Screenplay: Martin Mooney; Photographed by: Arthur Martinelli; Art Director: Frank Sylos; Assistant Director: Edward Monfort; Editor: Guy V. Thayer, Jr.; Musical Director: Alberto Colombo; Sound Engineer: Ferol M. Redd; Production Manager: Peter Jones; Running Time: 63 Minutes; Released: March 29, 1941

CAST: Neil Hamilton (Capt. James Madison); Doris Day (Rita Bennett); Victor Varconi (Dr. Frederic Haskell); Charles Wilson (Bruce Lane); George Carleton (Henry Gregory); Lyle Latell (Chuck); Frank Shannon (Col. Hammond); Betty Blythe (Marcia); Gerald Oliver Smith (Hobbs); Frank Moran (Ox)

BRIDE OF BUDDHA
(Record Pictures/WAFilms)

Bride of Buddha was a Futter Corp. production of 1933, originally issued by major-league RKO-Radio Pictures as *India Speaks*. (Photofest)

A *Variety* critic was treated on April 14, 1941, to a double-bill program at New York's Central Theatre: *Kidnapping Gorillas*—a rechristened *Love Life of a Gorilla*, still cluttering up the film exchanges from its late-'30s release—along with the somewhat more enjoyable *Bride of Buddha*. Both reviews missed the boat in a big way, here, neglecting to tie either film to its earlier incarnations and thus helping only to confuse matters for generations of movie buffs down the line. The reviewer faked his way through the *Bride* review as "apparently... a compilation of material from a Walter Futter trek through India," failing utterly to spot the film as a Futter Corp. production of 1933, originally issued by major-league RKO-Radio Pictures as *India Speaks*.

This Poverty Row condensation scraps a quarter-hour of exposition but retains the more harrowing discoveries: Director and narrator Richard Halliburton, appearing as an explorer fascinated with legends of the White Goddess of a remote Himalayan outpost, remarks with revulsion on a ceremony in praise of the deity Kali; rituals of self-torture and encounters with jungle snakes and vampire bats, which are presumed to harbor the souls of wicked men, follow. After a respite from the horrors in the Shalimar Gardens of Srinigar, the explorer forges ahead into taboo territory, beholding soul-cleansing

Beyond the Horror Ban

ceremonies including cremations; a lion-vs.-tiger fight; and a ritual where he is exposed as an outsider and pursued by a bloodthirsty horde of the faithful. Finally, he reaches the forbidden valley. Here, despite his marginal acceptance as an emissary to the White Goddess, he proves incapable of rescuing her from a sacrificial rite. An earthquake interrupts the ceremony, and the explorer and a sympathetic priest escape, but the Goddess goes through with her sacrifice as the Bride of Buddha.

"Too gruesome for the screen," complained the *Variety* critic in 1941, admitting nonetheless to finding much of this version entertaining.

Although Richard Halliburton was a *bona fide* globetrotter, he had acknowledged during the 1933 New York premiere that he did not accompany the filming crew to India. The RKO cut of *India Speaks* originally featured a scrolled prologue explaining that fictionalized Hollywood sound-stage footage is intercut with the documentary scenes; this acknowledgment of fakery is missing from the print we have seen of *Bride of Buddha*. By the time Walter Futter premiered this recycled version, Halliburton had died at sea, during a voyage from Hong Kong to San Francisco in 1939.

CREDITS: Producer: Walter A. Futter; Director of Studio Footage: Richard Halliburton; Narration Written by: Norman Houston; Novelized Version by: Will C. Murphey, Published 1933; Photographed by: Peverell Marley, Robert Connell and H.T. Cowling; Musical Supervisor: Samuel Wineland; Technical Director: David Miller; Running Time: 63 Minutes (as *India Speaks*, 78 Minutes); Originally Issued as: *India Speaks* on April 28, 1933, by RKO-Radio Pictures, Inc. and the Futter Corp., Ltd.; New York Opening as *Bride of Buddha*: April 14, 1941

CAST: Richard Halliburton (Narrator and Explorer)

INVISIBLE GHOST
(Monogram Pictures Corp.)

Indecision plagued the christening of *Invisible Ghost*, Bela Lugosi's first of nine starring pictures for the "new" Monogram, which had reorganized during the late 1930s following the forced absorption of the Depression-era Monogram into Republic Pictures. Announced variously as *The Maniac*, *Murder by the Stars* and *Phantom Monster* but then launched into production in March of 1941 as *Phantom Killer*, the film was completed in April and issued as *Invisible Ghost*, a title that at least captures the haunting incoherence of the story. Monogram might have been better advised to swipe the title of MGM's *Mad Love* (1935), for here we have a deranged passion of a high order. (*Phantom Killer* at length became the name of a 1942 remake of Monogram's *The Sphinx* [1933].)

As meandering and defiant of logic as a dream, *Invisible Ghost* trades with utter conviction on the crackpot assumption that a cuckolded and bereaved husband could be driven to a killing rage when reminded of his loss. Lugosi is Charles Kessler, a warm-hearted country squire living in denial, as the pop-shrinks would put it, of his departed wife's disloyalty. Long presumed dead, Mrs. Kessler (Betty Compson) is actually alive but far from well—a passive nutcase, sheltered in a nearby cellar by Kessler's secretive gardener, Jules Mason (Ernie Adams). Mrs. Kessler has taken to roaming by night, and her fleeting appearances have so unsettled her husband that he has committed murder while in a trance-like state.

Forgotten Horrors 2

Clarence Muse (left) and Bela Lugosi in a staged situation that does not figure in *Invisible Ghost*.

A chauffeur had been the first to get croaked, and while that case remains unsolved, the household's new cook, Cecile (Terry Walker), is strangled. When Ralph Dickson (John McGuire), sweetheart of Kessler's daughter, Virginia (Polly Ann Young), is learned to have quarreled with Cecile over a bygone affair, Dickson finds himself railroaded into prison and executed on circumstantial evidence.

Invisible Ghost surges ahead with a regal assurance wholly at odds with these rampant implausibilities. Lugosi attributes his refusal to vacate the accursed mansion to "sentimental reasons," even as Ernie Adams hopes against hope for the day when he can reunite the mad Mrs. Kessler with her husband. The wrongly convicted lover proves to have a look-alike brother named Paul (McGuire, again), whose sudden arrival tests the film's confidence in its own unremittingly grim attitude. Somberness prevails, thanks to a tiny, gemlike scene between Adams and the fine black actor Clarence Muse, who plays the butler with a stern authority: The twin shows up unannounced, unnerving all concerned. Muse approaches Adams and asks quietly, "Do I look pale?" A lesser film would have used the line as a set-up for a dismissive color gag, but here Adams merely appears caught off-guard. Muse finishes by declaring solemnly: "I *feel* pale."

The killings continue with an attack on Adams, whose sudden revival and expiration in the coroner's lab reinforces the prevailing sense of helpless terror. (This scene is frustratingly incomplete in the best available video edition, a Roan Group laserdisc assembled from several surviving prints; the missing footage appears more-or-less intact, however, in an Astor Pictures reissue trailer, which also is contained on the Roan disc.) Finally, as suspicion is trained on the butler, Mrs. Kessler is found and brought before her husband, who unwittingly cracks the case by losing control in view of witnesses. Mrs. Kessler is escorted to a nearby room, where she collapses in death. At this moment, her husband regains his senses—only to learn too late of his uncomprehending secret life as the killer.

Beyond the Horror Ban

Bela Lugosi—possessed by the urge to kill in *Invisible Ghost*.

All of which developments render the story beyond belief, but director Joseph H. Lewis subdues the extravagant conceits of the script with an even greater extravagance of style: Too much is never enough on Poverty Row. This tactic, coupled with an unerring sense of character definition and narrative pace, was Lewis' trademark as a budget-bound and highly productive director from 1937 until the late 1950s, when he began a distinct second career in television. Massive, quivering shadows loom forebodingly over the players, whose more intimate exchanges are framed by flames from within a fireplace. Lugosi's transformations are accomplished with subtle facial expressions, emphasized by sophisticated camera angles and ominous lighting, as he gazes in disbelief from the house while a haggard-looking Betty Compson prowls about outside.

Miss Compson, a lapsed romantic star of the silent era, plays the figurative "ghost" with a generous avoidance of vanity. She establishes her character's lunacy with a trembling, resentful voice and a wild stare and exhibits the courage at one point to stand alongside a large glamour portrait of herself in better days—a prominent prop in the Kessler house. All concerned, especially Muse, Adams and Polly Ann Young, match the sincerity with which Lugosi distinguishes the picture.

CREDITS: Producer: Sam Katzman; Director: Joseph H. Lewis; Screenplay: Helen and Al Martin; Photographed by: Marcel Le Picard and Harvey Gould; Associate Producer: Pete Mayer; Production Manager: Ed W. Rote; Assistant Directors: Edward M. Saeta and Harry Slott; Set Decorator: Fred Preble; Musical Directors: Johnny Lange and Lew Porter; Editor: Robert Golden; Sound Engineer: Glen Glenn; Running Time: 62 Minutes; Released: April 25, 1941

CAST: Bela Lugosi (Charles Kessler); Polly Ann Young (Virginia Kessler); John McGuire (Ralph Dickson and Paul Dickson); Clarence Muse (Evans); Terry Walker (Cecile); Betty Compson (Mrs. Kessler); Ernie Adams (Jules Mason); George Pembroke (Williams); Ottola [mis-billed as "Ollola"] Nesmith (Mrs. Mason); Fred Kelsey (Ryan); Jack Mulhall (Tim)

KING OF THE ZOMBIES
(Monogram Pictures Corp.)

Originally announced during early 1941 as a starring picture for Bela Lugosi, this wild fantasia on an anti-Nazi propaganda theme wound up instead as the most elaborate showcase Mantan Moreland ever found during his short but emphatic movie career. Henry Victor inherited the Lugosi role, as a scientist bent on raising the dead for warmongering purposes, and he brought to it a perfectly serviceable competence that has none of the good-humored subtleties or mournful intensity one would have expected from Lugosi. Meanwhile, Lugosi lavished his gifts upon *Invisible Ghost*.

Moreland, who had come to Hollywood during the 1930s from the Southland's Chitlin' Circuit of black-neighborhood nightclubs and Vaudeville theatres, brought a distinctive wit and energy to bear here, transforming an incidental comic-relief assignment into the heart and soul of the picture while rendering *King of the Zombies* one of the few most memorable of the Poverty Row spookers. It might be argued that the 39-year-old Moreland also transformed the film into an outright comedy. In any case, the picture cinched Moreland's credentials early on as a uniquely dependable supporting player and led to consistent employment if not bigger opportunities.

Moreland plays Jefferson "Jeff" Jackson, valet to Naval Intelligence Agent Bill Summers (John Archer). They are airborne with pilot James "Mack" McCarthy (Dick Purcell) over the Caribbean in search of a vanished plane when forced to land on a jungle island. The crack-up strands the party in a cemetery, where the men regain their bearings and proceed to a forbidding castle occupied by Dr. Miklos Sangre (Victor). Sangre seems hospitable enough—although he insists that Jeff be lodged with the servants lest they become resentful, and he seems amused that Jeff finds the butler, Momba (Leigh Whipper), downright creepy.

Jeff, who has a wisecrack for even the most unnerving occasion, pretends to mistake Momba for a fellow lodge member and then mutters, "Harlem never was like *this*!"

Prowling about, Jeff begins flirting with a pretty servant, Samantha (Marguerite Whitten). Nearby lurks Tahama (Madame Sul-Te-Wan), a cadaverous-looking cook. "I know a *mu*seum that would give a *for*tune just to have her under *glass*," Jeff observes. Samantha tells him of the zombies that stalk the grounds; Jeff is disinclined to believe her until Samantha summons a few of the living-dead creatures. Jeff hightails it for safety. He cannot get Bill or Mack to believe his account, and Sangre holds Jeff up to ridicule.

It develops—and so what else is new?—that Sangre is "cultivating" zombies for the Third Reich. The idea derives from an earnest Real World interest among some of the more superstitious Nazi chieftains to learn whether the dead might be reanimated as a "*todenkorps*" of unquestioning cannon fodder. But of course the Nazis could never have imagined an Allied secret weapon like Mantan Moreland.

The final showdown between Nazi Voodoo and allied normalcy in *King of the Zombies*.

An incidental bit of ghastliness comes to light in *King of the Zombies*.

Suffice that the screenplay contains such trappings as come with the turf for pulp-magazine horrors and B-as-in-budget Hollywood spookers—the captive military official, the wraithlike wife of the renegade scientist, the Voodoo ritual, the inevitable loss of control of the massed zombies—and let it be known that Moreland overwhelms the clichés and subverts all manner of black-comedian stereotypes at every turn. The Louisiana-born actor speaks in a richly Southern dialect, which renders his subversions all the more disarming. He admits to being fearful and makes a run for cover when discretion so dictates, but instead of lapsing into the expected scared-silly act, Moreland laughs in the face of danger, demands that the menace be confronted and gives the white guys plenty of jovial back-talk in protesting his second-class citizenship. He also indulges to an unusually great extent in flirtatious banter with the beautiful Marguerite Whitten, bringing his characterization nearer the romantically robust, fully rounded performances that the great Paul Robeson had given in Dudley Murphy's *The Emperor Jones* (1933) and James Whale's *Show Boat* (1936) while moving away from the buffoonish and figuratively impotent portrayals that were the stock-in-trade of Lincoln "Stepin Fetchit" Perry and Willie "Sleep'n' Eat" Best.

Upon learning that he has competition for Miss Whitten's attentions, Moreland seems relieved to learn that his potential rival is dead. Miss Whitten explains that her sweetheart had been killed in an accident involving "a revolving crane." Moreland absorbs this revelation and then comments: "Mmmm-*mmm*! Y'all *sho'* have some fierce *birds* around this country!" He is less pleased to learn that the victim has been revived as a zombie. Later on, Victor decides that Moreland belongs among the zombies. Giving in to Victor's hypnotic influence, Moreland joins the ranks of the living dead with, "*Move* over, boys—I'm one of the *gang*, now." Later, when Miss Whitten challenges his zombiehood on grounds that "zombies can't talk," Moreland replies, "Can *I* help it 'cause I'm lo*qua*cious?"

As tempting as it is to call *King of the Zombies* Moreland's movie, plain and simple, even a cursory viewing will point up the brisk pacing, the conversational flow of dialogue and the keen stylistic technique that director Jean Yarbrough brought to the table. A particularly fine visual invention illustrates the speed with which Moreland reacts to his first encounter with the zombies: The camera exaggerates the comedian's takeoff, then dashes around and ahead of him, seemingly through the very foundations of the castle, and catches him arriving in his boss' room.

Edward Kay's original music, too, is broadly distinctive, built upon tribal chant-like rhythms and incorporating a breezy, jazz-tinged *leitmotif* for Moreland in effective contrast to the low-brass martial cues for the zombies. In a watershed year for acknowledged great movies, the Kay score gave Monogram a rare crack at an Academy Award: It made the final cut of 20 nominees (the Oscars' field was broader then), in competition with works by Alfred Newman (*How Green Was My Valley* and *Ball of Fire*); Bernard Herrmann (*All That Money Can Buy* and *Citizen Kane*); Miklos Rosza (*Lydia* and *Sundown*); Edward Ward (*Cheers for Miss Bishop* and *Tanks a Million*); Franz Waxman (*Dr. Jekyll and Mr. Hyde* and *Suspicion*); Frank Skinner (*Back Street*); Morris Stoloff & Ernest Toch (*Ladies in Retirement*); Meredith Willson (*The Little Foxes*); Cy Feuer & Walter Scharf (Republic Pictures' *Mercy Island*, another of our *Forgotten Horrors* rediscoveries); Louis Gruenberg (*So Ends Our Night*); Victor Young (*Hold Back the Dawn*); Werner Heymann (*That Uncertain Feeling*); Richard Hageman (*That Woman Is Mine*); and Max Steiner (*Sergeant York*). Herrmann won the Oscar, for *All That Money Can Buy*.

Yarbrough had weighed in modestly as a director, with a string of broad comedies (including 1934's *Kentucky Kernels* and 1936's *Silly Billies*) to his credit. He joined the formative PRC with 1938's *Rebellious Daughters*, but found his truer niche with PRC's blackly humorous Lugosi-starrer *The Devil Bat* (which see) and by 1941 had established himself as a stylish director of low-budget comedies. Yarbrough spent the 1940s and 1950s alternating between humor and horror, building a résumé distinguished by the two starring pictures of the tragic Rondo Hatton (*House of Horrors* and *The Brute Man* [both 1946]) and two of the Bud Abbott–Lou Costello team's better entries (*Here Come the Co-Eds* and *The Naughty Nineties* [both 1945]). He also handled two of the least effective Abbott & Costellos, *Jack and the Beanstalk* and *Lost in Alaska* (both 1952) and bowed out at age 67 in 1967 with that legendarily dreadful hybrid of a horror spoof and a country-music concert, *Hillbillies in a Haunted House* (1967).

Henry Victor (1898-1945) had been a silent-era leading man in England but delivered his best-remembered portrayal in early-talkie Hollywood, as the cruel circus star Hercules in Tod Browning's *Freaks* (1932). Dick Purcell is not quite his two-fisted heroic self in *King of the Zombies*, which keeps him somewhat on the sidelines. Purcell proceeded through such assignments as *Phantom Killer* (which see) and *The Mystery of the Thirteenth Guest* (which also see) in 1942-43 and died of a heart attack in 1944 at age 36 after completing Republic's *Captain America* serial. John Archer, who plays Moreland's boss, seems more the heroic type, although conventional heroism is almost beside the point here. Joan Woodbury, who had been the leading lady in *The Eagle's Brood* (1935), the best of William Boyd's many *Hopalong Cassidy* series features, has rather too little to occupy her time as a reluctant inmate of Victor's benighted household. Leigh Whipper and Madame Sul-Te-Wan, as glowering servants, and Patricia Stacey, as Victor's entranced wife, lend appropriately macabre touches.

Moreland was already on a roll in cinema, having left a strong impression as early as 1936 with an unbilled part in *The Green Pastures*. By 1939, he was asserting a genuine mastery of screen acting, particularly in the black-ensemble feature *One Dark Night*—which, the title notwithstanding, is not a chiller but a domestic comedy with faint undertones of crime melodrama and science fiction. Moreland had handled more than 30 scene-stealing bit parts and featured appearances by the time he landed in *King of the Zombies*. He became a favorite with the critics at *Variety*, whose

various notices raved that "he works with remarkable ease and at all times is natural" and "never fails to garner a laugh, no matter how feeble the line." Among Moreland's many assignments to come, at studios large and small, was a similarly conceived role in Monogram's *Revenge of the Zombies* (1943, to be covered in *Forgotten Horrors 3*), which is more an elaboration than a sequel or a remake.

Moreland sustained a relentless pace through the Monogram resumption of the *Charlie Chan* series but hit a *cul-de-sac* during 1949-50, when he became a target of an N.A.A.C.P.-spearheaded campaign to "eliminate demeaning stereotypes" from the movies. A more subdued Moreland appeared in a handful of pictures during the mid-'50s; again in the mid-'60s (including a brief turn in Jack Hill's *Spider Baby*); and again from 1970 until 1973, the year of his death.

Melvin Van Peebles, who cast Moreland strikingly in the 1970 satire *Watermelon Man*, has called it "a tragedy...that Mantan was left out in the cold in his prime, that the studios let themselves be bullied into thinking his image fostered some sort of 'racism.'" The perennially boyish white-guy actor Frankie Darro (1917-1976), who teamed with Moreland for a Monogram series of mystery-comedies, recalled the comedian fondly as "anything *but* a stereotype. Mantan was unique among humanity, and as great a pal as he was an actor." Darro served as an honorary pallbearer at Moreland's funeral.

CREDITS: Producer: Lindsley Parsons; Director: Jean Yarbrough; Screenplay: Edmund Kelso; Musical Score: Edward Kay; Photographed by: Mack Stengler; Production Manager: Mack Wright; Editor: Richard Currier; Settings: Dave Milton; Sound Directors: William Fox and Glen Rominger, Western Electric; Art Director: Charles Clague; Running Time: 67 Minutes; Released: May 14, 1941

CAST: Dick Purcell (James "Mack" McCarthy); Joan Woodbury (Barbara Winslow); Mantan Moreland (Jefferson "Jeff" Jackson); Henry Victor (Dr. Miklos Sangre); John Archer (Bill Summers); Patricia Stacey (Alyce Sangre); Guy Usher (Adm. Wainwright); Marguerite Whitten (Samantha); Leigh Whipper (Momba); Madame Sul-Te-Wan (Tahama); Jimmy Davis (Lazarus); Laurence Criner (Dr. Couille); and Josephine Whitten

THE SHARK WOMAN
(B.F. Ziedman Productions/World Pictures Corp.)

A little beauty of a nature-in-the-raw melodrama, *The Shark Woman* captures thrills aplenty in its struggles between Malaysian pearl divers and various beasts of the wild, both on land and in the sea. A romantic subplot between boy and girl villagers plays out with a disarming naturalism, but the greater substance of the film is its crystalline photography—especially in a battle between a shark and an octopus. The underwater footage is particularly fine; it is the work of Stacy Woodard, who with his brother Horace Woodard made that excellent dramatized documentary of 1938, *The Adventures of Chico*.

CREDITS: Producers: Charles Hunt and B.F. Ziedman; Director: Ward Wing; Story: Lori Bara; Photographed by: John C. Cook; Underwater Photography: Stacy Woodard; Editor: Tom J. Geraghty; Musical Supervision: Abe Meyer; Running Time: 59 Minutes; Released: Following New York opening on May 30, 1941

CAST: Ahmang (Pearl Diver); Sai-Yu (His Sweetheart); Ko-Hai (His Brother); Mamounah (His Mother); Chang-Fu (Sea Captain)

THE GANG'S ALL HERE
(Sterling Productions, Inc./Monogram Pictures Corp.)

Here we have another of those crackerjack Frankie Darro–Mantan Moreland mysteries, a truck-wrecker melodrama that finds the pals saving the day through a combination of dumb luck and courageous resourcefulness. Although the film represents a lapse for the series overall, the stars are right on the money.

Good ol' Pop Wallace (Robert Homans) is in danger of losing his freight company to a campaign of sabotage and murder. Frankie (Darro) and Jeff (Moreland) are anything but professional drivers, but Pop's desperate situation moves them to apply. Patsy Wallace (Marcia Mae Jones), the boss's opportunistic daughter, intends to use Frankie to provoke her unassertive sweetheart, a greasemonkey named Chick (Jackie Moran), to jealousy.

Patsy's scheming is nothing compared with what Pop has been hiding: He and his insurance agent, Saunders (Irving Mitchell), have been splitting the payoffs from the wrecks—but Pop is appalled that the incidents have turned deadly. He pleads with Saunders to call off the wreckers.

Meanwhile, Frankie and Jeff hit the road with a payload and run straightaway into saboteurs. They are saved inadvertently when a traffic cop pulls Frankie over for speeding, and the shipment comes through.

Novice trucker George Lee (Keye Luke) seems so eager to learn the trade that he becomes an intolerable snooper around the Wallace depot. George reveals himself as an undercover insurance investigator after Frankie and Jeff are kidnapped and imprisoned by trucking boss Norton (Ed Cassidy) and his mechanic, the brutal Ham Shanks (Laurence Criner). Pop threatens Saunders with exposure unless Frankie and Jeff are freed safely, but the buddies escape—only to find Pop beaten nearly to death. Frankie comprehends that Pop was strong-armed into playing along with the sabotage racket. After an outlandish last-minute hostage situation involving Jeff, Frankie, Patsy, Chick and the crooked insurance agent, the good guys are saved by another speeding citation.

Probably the least of the Darro-Moreland comedy-thrillers, *The Gang's All Here* takes an inappropriately wide turn into sentimentality with the plight of Robert Homans' "Pop" character, and it allows the irritating Marcia Mae Jones a scene-stealing role that she comes ill-equipped to justify. Jackie Moran, better remembered as Huck Finn in 1938's *The Adventures of Tom Sawyer*, serves here chiefly to prompt Miss Jones to a nagging frenzy. Keye Luke's character wavers between needless comedy relief and real heroism, and the nature of his mission is given away rather too abruptly. Jean Yarbrough's direction meanders badly by comparison with his purposeful handling of *King of the Zombies*, and the photography seems hastily composed. Darro and Moreland are delightful, especially in a scene where Frankie tries to teach his reluctant chum the finer points of truck driving.

Darro and Moreland would wrap things up with the fall-of-'41 release of *Let's Go Collegiate*—a decidedly un-murderous situation comedy.

CREDITS: Producer: Lindsley Parsons; Director: Jean Yarbrough; Screenplay: Edmund Kelso; Photographed by: Mack Stengler; Art Director: Charles Clague; Editor: Jack Ogilvie; Settings: Fred Milton; Musical Director: Edward Kay; Sound Engineer: Glen Glenn; Production Manager: Glen Cook; Running Time: 63 Minutes; Released: June 11, 1941

CAST: Frankie Darro (Frankie); Mantan Moreland (Jeff); Marcia Mae Jones (Patsy Wallace); Jackie Moran (Chick); Keye Luke (George Lee); Robert Homans (Pop Wallace); Irving Mitchell (Saunders); Ed Cassidy (Jack Norton); Pat Gleason (Marty); Jack Kinney (Dink); Jack Ingraham (Matt); Laurence Criner (Ham Shanks); Paul Bryar (Bob)

MURDER BY INVITATION
(Monogram Pictures Corp.)

This savvy throwback to *The Cat and the Canary*'s Old School of murder farces makes up in sheer generosity what it lacks in subtlety. The *Variety* reviewer complained that the film "rings in sliding panels, hidden passageways and secret doors in such corny proportions that it will have to struggle holding onto the lower rung of a dualer." (A "dualer" is a double feature of the type once

Murder by Invitation fairly revels in its hokum, confronting and embracing one Jazz Age-into-Depression Era cliché after another. (Photofest)

programmed by most urban theatres, back in the day when 70 minutes was a lengthy running time for a B-unit movie.)

The point that *Variety* missed is that *Murder by Invitation* fairly revels in its hokum, confronting and embracing one Jazz Age-into-Depression Era cliché after another, then filtering the accumulation through the altered sensibilities of the war era. The film closes on a blistering clinch between Wallace Ford and Marian Marsh—in flat-footed defiance of the forces of institutionalized censorship that had taken hold in 1934—only to upstage the smooch with a wisecracking character (Herbert Vigran) who barges right in and announces to the audience: "The Hays Office ain't gonna like that long kiss!"

But to begin at the beginning: Old maid Cassandra Denham (Sarah Padden) defies all attempts to have her declared incapable of managing the fortune she claims to possess. Her grasping nephew, lawyer Garson Denham (Gavin Gordon), is among relatives invited to attend a midnight gathering at Aunt Cassie's mountainside estate, with instructions to be there or be disinherited. Despite Garson's concern that Cassie plans to do away with the heirs, they all arrive—only to learn that Cassie wants to weed out the undeserving souls among them. Garson is the first to die.

Newspaperman Bob White (Wallace Ford) and his girlfriend Nora O'Brien (Marian Marsh) learn of the murder and visit the estate, along with a photographer named Eddie (Vigran). Despite the presence of a sheriff (George Guhl), another relative soon turns up croaked. The corpses begin disappearing and reappearing at the least convenient moments. After a chance encounter in a revolving bookcase, Cassie promises Eddie a reward for protecting a strongbox. Another relative dies. Cassie reveals her plan to torch the house—assuming that the killer will rush inside to nab the loot. As fire consumes the place, Cassie's niece and resident helper, Mary Denham (Hazel Keener), reveals herself and her secret husband, Cassie's chauffeur, Michael (Dave O'Brien), as the plotters. Michael attempts to lam out through a hidden tunnel, but Bob heads him off. Cassie springs another surprise when she

Wallace Ford and Marian Marsh brace for an onslaught in *Murder by Invitation*.

proposes marriage to neighbor Trowbridge Montrose (J. Arthur Young), a longtime admirer who had been a likely suspect. Eddie collects his reward—a worthless Confederate bank note. It develops that all of Cassie's money is Confederate tender, but Montrose seems more interested in Cassie than in her supposed fortune.

Wallace Ford had been playing this type, the impatient smart-aleck hero, since the Depression years, but he seems not to have outgrown it by so late a date. He and Marian Marsh—the John Barrymore discovery who had been such a knockout in the 1931 *Svengali*—make an appealing pair. Miss Marsh's career was fast winding down, with only *Gentleman from Dixie* (1941) and *House of Errors* (1942) yet to go. Sarah Padden seems by turns deranged and sweet-natured as the dotty aunt, and although she is too easy a suspect—still, one can't help wondering. The creepy old house is one of the better Monogram sets, tricked out with all the sinister gadgets and secret tunnels one could hope to spot, and its occupants react appropriately. Stuntman-turned-actor Dave O'Brien has a nice bit as the cowardly, hidden menace, and Hazel Keener shows a suitably self-justifying indignation when revealed as the brains behind the murders.

CREDITS: Producer: A.W. Hackel; Director: Phil Rosen; Screenplay: George Bricker; Photographed by: Marcel Le Picard; Settings: Dave Milton; Assistant Director: Mack Wright; Editor: Martin G. Cohn; Sound Engineer: Glen Glenn; Production Manager: Ben Gutterman; Running Time: 67 Minutes; Released: June 30, 1941

CAST: Wallace Ford (Bob White); Marian Marsh (Nora O'Brien); Sarah Padden (Aunt Cassandra Denham); Gavin Gordon (Garson Denham); George Guhl (Sheriff Boggs); Wallis Clark (Judge Moore); Minerva Urecal (Maxine Denham); J. Arthur Young (Trowbridge Montrose); Herbert Vigran (Eddie); Philip Trent (Larry Denham); Dave O'Brien (Michael); Hazel Keener (Mary Denham); Isabelle LaMal (Martha Denham); Lee Shumway (Eric); John James (Tom Denham); Kay Deslys (Katie)

CRIMINALS WITHIN
a.k.a.: ARMY MYSTERY
(Producers Releasing Corp.)

A veneer of top-secret science-fiction mumbo-jumbo and a frenzy of harrowing events scarcely can camouflage the ordinariness of this spy melodrama from George R. Batcheller's sector of the PRC group. The standout elements lie in the extraordinary casting, with I. Stanford Jolley in top form as an outwardly meek Fifth Column menace, Constance Worth as a seductive spy and Eric Linden as a heroic Army man on a mission combining patriotism with indignation and vengeance. The West Texas-bred actress Ann Doran, ostensibly cast as a love interest for Linden, becomes a strong heroic presence in short order.

Cpl. Greg Carroll (Linden) is imprisoned at Camp Madison after he acknowledges having read a forbidden document involving his scientist-brother and four other researchers in a secretive experiment. A recreation-hall hostess named Alma Barton (Miss Worth) hides a coded message in a pair of shoes to be delivered to a cobbler named Carl Flegler (Jolley). Greg, who has mysteriously been handed a key to his cell, escapes the guardhouse and attempts to telephone his brother—who has already been murdered.

Greg's commander, Bryant (Robert Frazer), is found dead in the rec hall after an attempt to interrogate Alma. Greg is accused in connection with the officer's slaying but manages to escape from the base grounds after he sneaks into Bryant's office and memorizes a list of the scientists attached to the guarded project. The complications pile up rather haphazardly as a reporter-turned-Army sergeant (Weldon Heyburn), a newspaperwoman named Linda (Miss Doran), a determined lieutenant (Don Curtis) and another sergeant (Ben Alexander) enter the fray. The murder of Miss Worth's character takes a great deal of the steam out of the story too early, and the unmasking of Alexander's friendly and helpful topkick as a fiend comes as rather a puny revelation.

Ann Doran is terrific as the spirited journalist, and Eric Linden rises just enough above the morass of outlandish developments to deliver a pleasing portrayal of desperate heroism. The tension finally reaches a critical mass at the finale, when Linden becomes the captive of Jolley's assembled foreign agents and Alexander locks Miss Doran inside a suffocating chamber. The final turning of the tables is too simply handled, but for a moment there, *Criminals Within* generates a powerful sense of dread.

CREDITS: Executive Producer: George R. Batcheller; Producer: E.B. Derr; Director: Joseph Lewis; Story: Arthur Hoerl; Screenplay: Edward Bennett; Photographed by: Arthur Martinelli; Assistant Director: William Strobach; Editor: Howard Dillinger; Wardrobe: Emanuel Glussman; Sound Engineers: Benjamin Winkler and Arthur Smith; Production Manager: Earl Sheffer; Running Time: 70 Minutes; Released: June 27, 1941

CAST: Eric Linden (Cpl. Greg Carroll); Ben Alexander (Sgt. Paul); Don Curtis (Lt. Harmon); Ann Doran (Linda); Constance Worth (Alma Barton); Weldon Heyburn (Sgt. Blake); Dudley Dickerson (Sam Dillingham); Bernice Pilot (Mamie); Ray Erlenborn (Pvt. Norton); I. Stanford Jolley (Carl Flegler); Emmett Vogan (Harold); Robert Frazer (Capt. Bryant); Boyd Irwin (Col. Longstreet); William Ruhl (Capt. Grey); and Dennis Moore, John Holland, Peter George, Earl Hodgins

THE DEADLY GAME
(Monogram Pictures Corp.)

Nothing singularly horrific about this spy melodrama from Phil Rosen, but the fans will want to take note of its science-fictional garnish about an endangered scientist (J. Arthur Young) who is developing a gizmo to spot nighttime raiding flights. Charles Farrell is the F.B.I. agent who gets on the case of Nazi troublemakers David Clarke, Hans von Morhart and John Miljan. June Lang is well worth protecting as the scientist's daughter, and Bernadene Hayes is treachery made flesh as a *frau fatale*.

The Deadly Game **features Charles Farrell and June Lang trying to save the world from Nazi troublemakers. (Photofest)**

CREDITS: Producer: Dixon R. Harwin; Associate Producer: Barney Sarecky; Director: Phil Rosen; Screenplay: Wellyn Totman; Photographed by: Arthur Martinelli; Art Director: Charles Clague; Assistant Directors: George Webster and Edward Monfort; Editor: Martin G. Cohn; Set Dresser: David Milton; Recording Engineer: Glen Glenn; Running Time: 65 Minutes; Released: August 8, 1941

CAST: Charles Farrell (Barry Scott); John Miljan (Henri Franck); J. Arthur Young (Dr. Reisner); June Lang (Christina Reisner); David Clarke (John Brandt); Bernadene Hayes (Mona Brandt); Dave O'Brien (Ralph Spencer); Fred Gierman (Carl Nash); Hans von Morhart (Fritz); John Dilson (Harkness); Byron Foulger (Lodge Manager); Kurd Kreuger (German Lieutenant); and Tom Herbert, Kenneth Duncan, John Harmon, Jack Gardner, Ottola Nesmith, Walter Bonn, William Vaughn, Harold Daniels

PEER GYNT
(David Bradley/The Willow Corp.)

"I was just 18 when I made my first picture, there in the summer of 1941," Charlton Heston told us in 1996. "It was an amateur concoction based on Ibsen's *Peer Gynt*, which a classmate of mine named David Bradley, there at Northwestern University's speech and drama department, put together as an experimental thing. David used Grieg's suite for the musical scoring, pacing the drama to the compositions. He shot it mostly by himself in 16 millimeter on various locations in Illinois and Wisconsin, including this incredibly accurate Norwegian-type little village he had found. Turned out pretty well, but not what you'd call Hollywood calibre.

The teenaged Charlton Heston, shown with Rose Andrews, already radiates star quality in

"David and I made another one, later, a *Julius Caesar* in 1949, after I'd already graduated to Broadway and to live-on-the-spot television," Heston continued. "David's *Caesar*—where I played Marc Antony—actually got some kind of limited theatrical release. *Peer Gynt*, now, it had to wait quite a long time before it got formally finished. David was hurrying so as to get on with going into the Army. He tampered with it some more during the 1960s and got it shown in some of the art-house theatres."

Indeed, few films have known such a long gestation between the making and the definitive showing as David Bradley's *Peer Gynt*. The weird Norwegian legend, as dramatized by Ibsen in the 1867 play *Peer Gynt: A Dramatic Poem*, was a natural for the screen, and had accounted for one of the early-day cinema's more important productions: A 1915 version by the Oliver Morosco Photoplay Co. appears to be the first film for which a musical score was expressly composed and arranged.

The play withstands even the 21-year-old Bradley's amateurish limitations. Heston is Peer Gynt, the good-for-nothing lout whose disrespectful nature turns downright antisocial when, spurned by a lovely newcomer (Katherine Elfstrom) to his village, he abducts and ravishes his former sweetheart (Betty Barton) just before she is to marry a worthier citizen (Alan Eckhart). Gynt finds himself imprisoned by a troll and confronted by a hag and a deformed child that may be his own offspring—only to be transformed into a wealthy man of influence. His evils catch up with him, however, and after witnessing a vision of his funeral, Peer is allowed one last chance to justify his existence.

Heston went on to bigger and better things—and so what else is new?—including high recognition from the Motion Picture Academy's Oscar Awards; a lasting political prominence that has varied wildly from left-of-center to right; and a range of "larger-than-life characters from Moses to Michelangelo," as the historian Ephraim Katz once put it.

Peer Gynt gets a last crack at redemption, whether or not he deserves it. (Photofest)

David Bradley took a stranger path into a movie career, with spotty results. He finally escaped the amateur ranks after the 1949 *Caesar*, then weighed in as a promising director-in-earnest with the MGM noir programmer *Talk About a Stranger* (1952). His sparse résumé also includes *Dragstrip Riot* (1958) and *Twelve to the Moon* (1960), but the more remarkable centerpiece of Bradley's body of work must be a freakish patched-together hodgepodge called *Madmen of Mandoras* (1963), better known as *They Saved Hitler's Brain*.

In 1965, Bradley re-edited *Peer Gynt* significantly from the rough cut he had premiered in Wisconsin in 1941. The venerable Francis X. Bushman added his voice, speaking for the troll. Bradley retained the tinting process that had washed the black-and-white image in greens, blues and reds during the supernatural sequences. The Willow Corp. mounted a limited theatrical release.

CREDITS: Producer and Director: David Bradley; From *Peer Gynt: A Dramatic Poem* by: Henrik Ibsen; Photographed by: David Bradley, Richard Roth and Robert Cooper; Property Master: Roy Eggert, Jr.; Costumers: Sally Hyde, Elizabeth Cole, Katherine Elfstrom; Makeup: Roy Eggert, Jr.; Technical Staff: Rod Maynard, John Jerrard, Philip McConnell, George B. Moll; Music: Selections from *Peer Gynt Suite* by Edvard Grieg; Running Time: 85 Minutes; Premiered: August 25, 1941, in Winnetka, Wisc.

CAST: Charlton Heston (Peer Gynt); Betty Hanisee (Aase); Mrs. Herbert Hyde (Old Woman); Lucielle Powell (Kari); Charles Paetow (Aslak); Alan Eckhart (Mads Moen); Katherine Elfstrom (Solveig); Morris Wilson (Haegstad); George B. Moll (Drunkard and Bedouin Chieftain); Betty Barton (Ingrid);

Audrey Wedlock (Woman in Green as a Youth); Sarah Merrill (Woman in Green as a Hag); Alan Heston (Hideous Child); Roy Eggert, Jr. (Dovre-King, Mr. Ballon and Priest); David Bradley (Herr Trumpeterstralle and Bailiff); Warren MacKenzie (MacPherson); Rose Andrews (Anitra); Thomas A. Blair (Button Man and Skinny Man); Alice Badgerow (Cowherd); Francis X. Bushman (Voice of the Boyg/Voice from the Darkness); Robert Cooper (Bereaved Man); Rod Maynard (Boy); Jane Wilimovsky (Old Woman); and Katherine Bradley, Anty Ball

UP JUMPED THE DEVIL
(Dixie National Pictures, Inc./Consolidated National Film Exchanges)

Impressions from our long-ago and incomplete screening of this elusive black-ensemble comedy, coupled with sparse documentation by the American Film Institute and the Southwest Film & Video Archive, must suffice until the genuine article turns up intact. Mantan Moreland and Shelton (given elsewhere as Clarence) Brooks play a Laurel & Hardy-like combo of bickering pals who land jobs with a wealthy matron, only to learn that one of the positions requires a maidservant—which means that Moreland gets to spend much of the picture in drag. The villain of the piece is a phoney mystic (Maceo Sheffield), who intends to infiltrate the household for the sake of thievery. Nothing particularly horrific about the film, but the title and the soothsayer angle render it of marginal interest here. Oh, yes—Moreland gets back into manly attire by shooting dice with the luckless gents attending a ritzy party. So much for the notion that black stereotypes belong entirely to the Hollywood mainstream.

CREDITS: Producer: Jed Buell; Director: Undocumented in Files of American Film Institute and Southwest Film & Video Archive; Songs: "Dreams of You" and "Jump off the Springboard," Composers Unacknowledged; Running Time: 68 Minutes; Released: On a State-by-State Basis Beginning in August of 1941; Later in Distribution by: Toddy Pictures Co.

CAST: Mantan Moreland (Mr. Washington); Shelton [Elsewhere Given as Clarence] Brooks (Mr. Jefferson); Maceo Sheffield (Swami Reever, alias Bad News Johnson); Earl Morris (Hobo); Lawrence Criner (Sheriff); and Myrtle Fortune, Patsy Hunter, Millie Monroe, Suzette Harbin, Avanelle Harris, Doris Akes

SADDLE MOUNTAIN ROUNDUP
(Range Busters, Inc./George W. Weeks Productions/Monogram Pictures Corp.)

In *Forgotten Horrors: The Definitive Edition*, we rediscovered *Big Boy Rides Again*, in which Guinn "Big Boy" Williams crosses paths with a masked phantom-of-the-horse-opera and a skulking Chinese villain while attempting to take charge as heir to a ranch. *Saddle Mountain Roundup* is that film's remake, parceling out the leading-cowboy duties among a trio that was designed to become Monogram's answer to Republic's well-received *Three Mesquiteers* team—the Range Busters.

Saddle Mountain Roundup is a winner on all counts, directed with plenty of suspense and suspicion by S. Roy Luby. The picture showcases two-fisted Ray "Crash" Corrigan, balladeer John "Dusty" King and the comical voice-thrower and Mesquiteers alumnus Max "Alibi" Terhune for full measure of robust heroism and incidental humor. The adventurous lawmen are out stirring up trail dust on behalf of grouchy rancher Magpie Harper (John Elliott) when suddenly they are summoned back to his ranch. Alibi is left to herd Harper's cattle to market while Crash and Dusty return to headquarters—only to find the boss slain under creepy circumstances. Blackie (George Chesebro), the foreman, is a ready suspect, for he had objected to Harper's plan to have the Range Busters supervise the trail drive.

Harper had left a note revealing the location of a cache of money. The ranch's cook, Fang Way (Willie Fung), hides the note. Blackie attempts to incriminate Henderson (Steve Clark), a neighboring rancher who had formed an uneasy partnership with the victim. Meanwhile, Alibi is ambushed and imprisoned, and Crash learns that both Dusty and Blackie are missing. Dusty, finding himself lost in a tunnel beneath the ranchhouse, frees Alibi from captivity by pretending to be Harper's ghost. A mysterious intruder—the killer—proves to be Harper's trusted lawyer, Dan Freeman (Jack Mulhall).

The rambunctious spirit of *Big Boy Rides Again* is nicely recaptured here, with helpful amplifications. Screenwriters John Vlahos and Earle Snell improve on William Nolte's original continuity by making the foreman something more than a red herring and rendering the Chinese cook's furtive behavior more nearly explicable, if no more Politically Correct. Jack Mulhall is as formidable here as he had been in his star-player years, almost a decade earlier, and the Range Busters cover the bases from action to music to whimsy. Feisty Lita Conway is saddled with merely a decorative role, as the neighbor's daughter. Rural radio comedian "Cousin" Herald Goodman has a nice extended cameo, and Max Terhune's ventriloquism routines are strategically deployed. (Terhune's *Range Busters* moniker, Alibi, was coined as a sound-alike counterpart to his character Lullaby Joslin of the *Three Mesquiteers* pictures.) Ray Corrigan played host to the shooting at Corriganville, his well-equipped movie-location ranch at Chatsworth.

The *Range Busters* entries for 1941 also include *Trail of the Silver Spurs*, *The Kid's Last Ride*, *Tumbledown Ranch in Arizona*, *Wrangler's Roost*, *Fugitive Valley* and *Tonto Basin Outlaws*.

CREDITS: Producer: George W. Weeks; Associate Producer: Anna Bell Ward; Director: S. Roy Luby; Original Story: William Nolte; Dialogue and Continuity: John Vlahos and Earle Snell; Photographed by: Robert Cline; Editor: Roy Claire; Musical Director: Frank Sanucci; Songs: "The Doggone Dogie That Got Away" and "That Little Green Valley of Mine," by Jean George & John "Dusty" King, and "Little Brown Jug," by Joseph E. Winner; Sound Engineer: Glen Glenn; Production Manager: William L. Nolte; Running Time: 60 Minutes; Released: August 29, 1941

CAST: Ray "Crash" Corrigan (Crash); John "Dusty" King (Dusty); Max "Alibi" Terhune (Alibi and His Mannequin, Elmer); Lita Conway (Nancy Henderson); Jack Mulhall (Dan Freeman); Willie Fung (Fang Way); John Elliott (Magpie Harper); George Chesebro (Blackie); Jack Holmes (Sheriff); Steve Clark (Henderson); Carl Mathews (Bill); "Cousin" Herald Goodman (Himself)

MERCY ISLAND
(Republic Pictures Corp.)

We had remembered this unusual Oscar-bait Republic as a merciless study of gathering madness in the midst of a desperate adventure. The rediscovery proves *Mercy Island* even meaner than our memories had allowed us to recall.

A big-game fishing party sets out from Key West. Aboard are the respected prosecuting attorney, Warren Ramsey (Ray Middleton); his wife, Leslie (Gloria Dickson); his longtime pal, Clay Foster (Don Douglas); the skipper, Captain Lowe (Forrester Harvey); and a dockhand and guide known as the Kid (Terry Kilburn). Bent upon pursuing a particularly large fish, Ramsey recklessly strands the party on distant Mercy Island with a damaged boat and no provisions. Ramsey's irritability has already put everyone on edge, but things start looking up when the island's lone inhabitant, one Dr. Sanderson (Otto Kruger), proves helpful. Sanderson is a physician who had fled a mercy-killing rap in the States. Ramsey recognizes Sanderson, whom he had prosecuted, and is so appreciative of the doctor's help that he volunteers to bring him back to civilization and clear his name.

Ray Middleton gives a commanding portrayal of gathering madness in *Mercy Island*. (Photofest)

But Ramsey's erratic behavior reasserts itself. Later on, he becomes equally determined to send Sanderson to the electric chair and put the Kid in prison for harboring the fugitive. He needles Leslie and Clay unmercifully, until Clay slaps him. "You shouldn't have hit him," Leslie says. "Yes, I know—particularly with my open hand," Clay snarls.

Ramsey becomes an outcast, despised by everyone but his loyal wife, and hating even her. Sanderson finally tells Leslie, "I've known hundreds of him, Mrs. Ramsey, in the learned professions, in prison. Who's to say where sanity ends and insanity begins? The borderline is as imaginary as the equator." Meanwhile, a hungry alligator has moved into the key and almost grabs Ramsey but is distracted by a school of fish. Soon, the creature has eaten all the fish in the lagoon. The party is saved from starvation days later when they catch a huge grouper. Hoping to spare Sanderson, the others refuse to help Ramsey signal an airplane. Ramsey knocks Leslie down and tears off her dress. Clay fights with him. Ramsey tries to knife Clay but is disarmed. At length, the alligator kills Ramsey.

The dominating character of Ramsey is played in fine style by Juilliard graduate and Chicago Opera baritone Ray Middleton, who doesn't sing a note while portraying a respected courtroom spellbinder whose mind deteriorates alarmingly and in short order. It is an unusual touch of casting, in that Middleton is the tallest, handsomest and most charismatic of the group, but he handles his embittered dialogue and increasingly despicable scheming so well that it works. Early along, he seems affable enough, although he lets a few subtle signs of megalomania show through the seams: He has an imperious manner in dealing with the local fishermen, and he develops a burning need to land one certain fish whose pursuit can only mean disaster.

After he suffers a head wound and his wife sews it up, Ramsey says sardonically, "Well, there's a dutiful wife for you—in sickness and in health." Sizing up the situation, he mutters, "Only 20 miles from civilization, and we might as well be struggling in the mud of the Eocene." At one point,

"...might as well be struggling in the mud of the Eocene." Ray Middleton in *Mercy Island.*

he declares: "I'm going to be the greatest criminal attorney since Clarence Darrow." When Ramsey announces he plans to accuse Clay as co-respondent in a divorce because "I can't afford to have it known I have an unfaithful wife," Leslie protests, "I have not been unfaithful to you in any way." He retorts: "Then let's say you've been merely disloyal." Middleton accentuates Ramsey's descent to the brute with a repulsive scene in which he gobbles fish fat. After several years as a leading man in the more expensive dramas and musicals at Republic, Middleton moved on to greater popular acclaim as a star of Broadway shows.

The supporting players are a suitably befuddled and horrified lot, with Gloria Dickson delivering an outstanding show of patience and ultimate defiance and Otto Kruger anchoring the situation in heroic decency as the homesick hermit. Forrester Harvey and Terry Kilburn provide a helpful touch of coastal Southern folksiness, emphasizing the almost exotic setting. Director William Morgan uses the semitropical background to solid dramatic effect, emphasizing the citified characters' ill-preparedness to deal with nature.

The secondary menace is an unusually large and photogenic alligator that harasses the castaways. The monster eventually solves their biggest problem in one of the most gruesome comeuppances the Production Code would ever permit: We see the 'gator charge after Ramsey, who is holding the hideous, dripping fish-head, and after a splendid musical buildup and some horrendous screaming, we discover the saurian feasting on what's left of the madman.

Photographically, *Mercy Island* is top-drawer craftsmanship. Reggie Lanning, regarded by the Republic management as the studio's finest resident artisan, brings the location to life with ultra-sharp black-and-white images in which the judicious use of filters sharpens the tones and textures of sand, sea, sky and faces. The gorgeous underwater sequences were filmed at Silver Springs, Florida—the same location where the celebrated swimming scenes of MGM's *Tarzan Finds a Son!* were shot in

1938. There are some process projection shots made at Studio City, but the visual soul of the show lies in the natural scenic values and the glimpses of wildlife—the giant black grouper and birds, alligators and sea snakes—whose appearances are intercut with Ramsey's crazed actions.

Republic's musical director, Cy Feuer, and co-composer Walter Scharf put some of their best into *Mercy Island*, even to the use of a stirring choral refrain for the finale. The score received an Academy Award nomination.

CREDITS: Director: William Morgan; Associate Producer: Armand Schaefer (Listed as Producer in Some Sources); Screenplay: Malcolm Stuart Boylan; From the Novel by: Theodore Pratt; Photographed by Reggie Lanning; Underwater Scenes Photographed at Silver Springs, Florida; Musical Director: Cy Feuer; Music by: Cy Feuer and Walter Scharf; Art Director: John Victor Mackay; Supervising Editor: Murray Seldeen; Editor: Ernest Nims; Wardrobe: Adele Palmer; Photographic Effects: Ellis "Bud" Thackery; Sound: RCA Victor; Running Time: 72 Minutes; Released: October 10, 1941

CAST: Ray Middleton (Ramsey); Gloria Dickson (Leslie); Otto Kruger (Sanderson); Don Douglas (Clay Powell); Forrester Harvey (Captain); Terry Kilburn (the Kid); Ed Brady (Sailor)

JUNGLE MAN
(Producers Releasing Corp.)

Larry "Buster" Crabbe was a robust and athletic 34 when he played this intellectualized variant on Tarzan—a distinguished physician who has spent years attempting to defeat a plague among the tribes of Africa. In addition to developing a promising serum, Crabbe finds himself obliged to rescue a lovely, spoiled-brat heiress (Sheila Darcy) from lions; trek from village to village on a protracted errand of mercy; and dive into shark-infested waters to retrieve a cargo of medicine from a shipwreck.

The going is plenty tedious, what with all the stock-footage padding (easily half the running time) and a severe lack of *bona fide* thrills. Veteran action-picture villain Charles Middleton has an odd part as a priest whose pet tiger proves to be a man-eater. Crabbe is better than the picture deserves, but at least he manages to steal Miss Darcy away from her photographer fiancé (Weldon Heyburn). One can only hope that her various ordeals have made her a less self-centered and more honorable human being.

CREDITS: Executive Producer: George R. Batcheller; Producer: T.H. Richmond; Director: Harry Fraser; Story and Screenplay: Rita Douglas; Photographed by: Mervyn Freeman; Art Director: Robert Huff; Assistant Director: Robert Ray; Editor: Holbrook Todd; Recording Engineer: Ben Winkler; Technical Director: Marjorie Freeman; Running Time: 63 Minutes; Released: October 10, 1941

CAST: Buster Crabbe (Dr. Hammond); Charles Middleton (Father Jim Graham); Sheila Darcy (Betty Graham); Vince Barnett (Buck); Weldon Heyburn (Bruce Kellogg); Robert Carson (Andy); Paul Scott (William Graham); and Hal Price, Floyd Shackelford

SPOOKS RUN WILD
(Banner Pictures Corp./Monogram Pictures Corp.)

Often confused with *Ghosts on the Loose* (1943) on account of a curiously shared star billing for Bela Lugosi and the East Side Kids, *Spooks Run Wild* is a distinctive picture. It allows Lugosi the mixed-nuts opportunity to act scary, act scared and finally turn out to be—but no, don't let's give everything away all at once. And the picture raises the ante on the prevailing slapstick by pitting Leo Gorcey, Huntz Hall *et al.* against a prowling murderer who means business. Somebody could get slaughtered here, just any minute now, and therein lies the quality that keeps the yarn's essentially humorous tone at such a keen and well-sustained pitch.

Bound for summer camp, the East Siders—Muggs, Danny, Glimpy, Scruno, Skinny and Peewee—hear a radio newscast warning of a "monster killer" at large. A cloaked stranger named Nardo (Lugosi) and his dwarf helper, Luigi (Angelo Rossitto), stop at a filling station to ask the way to an abandoned mansion, site of a long-ago murder. Later, there arrives another car bearing a popular mystery writer, Dr. von Grosch (Dennis Moore). The local constable (Guy Wilkerson) pegs Nardo as a suspect.

Nardo and Luigi, prowling about a cemetery, draw gunfire from a gravedigger. The East Siders wander into the graveyard. Peewee (David Gorcey) is wounded, and the pals take him to the creepy old house, where Nardo treats the boy's injury and invites the kids to stay the night. While most of the guys are unable to doze off, Peewee dozes off and goes sleepwalking. The stock complications—hidden passageways, convenient and/or inconvenient disappearances—lead the authorities to conclude that the East Side Kids have fallen prey to the fiend. The boys frighten Nardo with a ghostly masquerade.

Spooks Run Wild **is a smooth and brisk little slapsticker.**

Camp nurse Linda Mason (Dorothy Short) arrives with von Grosch, who suddenly turns menacing. Muggs (Leo Gorcey), drawn by Linda's screams, tackles von Grosch, the sought-after killer. Nardo, who has turned out to be a stage magician and a perfectly okay sort, entertains the gang. One such trick caps the film with a blackout gag.

Shot during the late summer of 1941 as *Ghosts in the Night*, this smooth and brisk little slapsticker is pure formula for the East Side Kids and little more than a lurk-through for a clearly delighted Lugosi. Everyone on hand, in fact, seems to be enjoying the pageantry. Dennis Moore makes a properly troublesome celebrity author, who seems—rather like Michael Gough in 1958's *Horrors of the Black Museum*—the sort who commits murder just to keep his muse stimulated.

The *East Side Kids* entries of 1941 also include *Pride of the Bowery*, *Flying Wild* and *Bowery Blitzkreig*.

CREDITS: Producer: Sam Katzman; Associate Producer: Pete Mayer; Director: Phil Rosen; Story and Screenplay: Carl Foreman and Charles R. Marion; Additional Dialogue: Jack Henley; Photographed by: Marcel Le Picard; Assistant Directors: Art Hammond and Herman Pett; Settings: Fred Preble; Editor: Robert Golden; Music: Lange & Porter; Recording Engineer: Glen Glenn; Production Manager: Ed W. Rote; Running Time: 65 Minutes; Released: October 24, 1941

CAST: Bela Lugosi (Nardo); Leo Gorcey (Muggs); Bobby Jordan (Danny); Huntz Hall (Glimpy); Sunshine Sammy Morrison (Scruno); Dave O'Brien (Jeff Dixon); Dorothy Short (Linda Mason); David Gorcey (Peewee); Donald Haines (Skinny); Dennis Moore (Dr. von Grosch); P.J. Kelley (Lem Harvey); Angelo Rossitto (Luigi); Guy Wilkerson (Constable); Rosemary Portia (Margie)

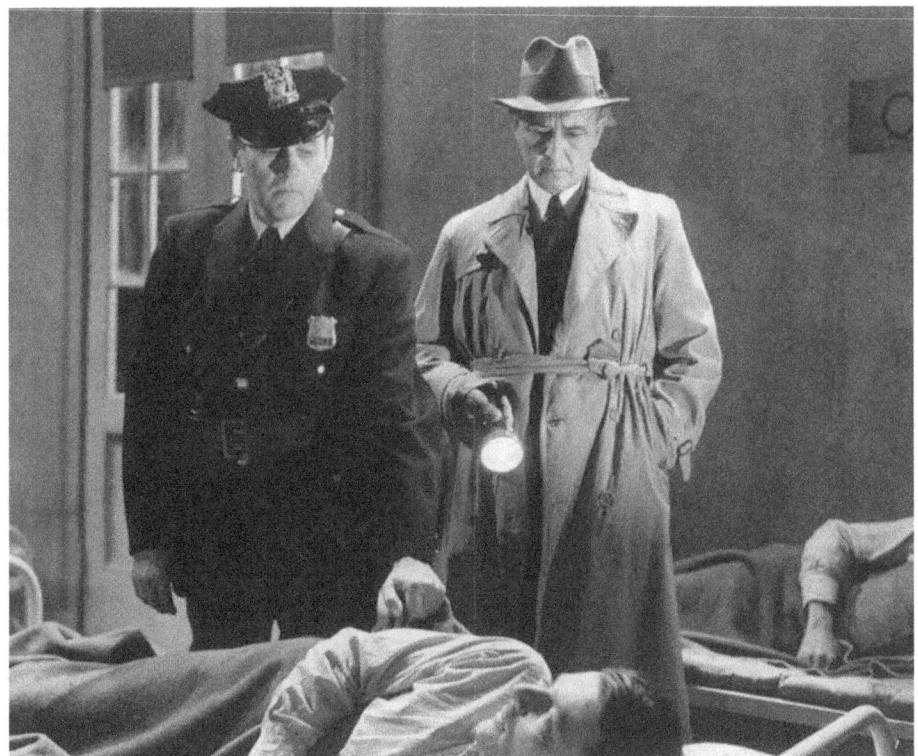

The Devil Pays Off is a convoluted tale of a ship-hijacker's hijinks, augmented with adulterous treacheries and illicit dope usage. (Photofest)

THE DEVIL PAYS OFF
(Republic Pictures Corp.)

Forgotten he-man actor William Wright plays a hard-drinking, disgraced Navy man who gets a backhanded chance at redemption in this convoluted tale of a ship-hijacker's hijinks, augmented with adulterous treacheries and illicit dope usage.

Chris Waring (Wright) is insulted to learn it is not his bravery the Navy wants to press back into service—but rather his bad reputation as a playboy. Seems that a shady shipping magnate, Arnold DeBrock (J. Edward Bromberg), has this trifling wife, Valerie (Osa Massen), who might prove vulnerable to an undercover sting.

Chris rejects the bid to play the infiltrator, but later he cozies up to a mysterious woman and invites her to his shipboard cabin—only to find Joan Millard (Margaret Tallichet), secretary to Naval Admiral Curtiss (Selmer Jackson), waiting there and pretending to be his wife. The woman identifies herself as Valerie DeBrock and leaves in a huff. Joan presses Chris to get cracking on "their" investigation. A rescued castaway proves to be Captain Jonathan Hunt (Charles D. Brown), who had rebelled against DeBrock's crooked orders. A menacing Captain Brigham (Ivan Miller) and his shipboard doctor (Ronald Varno) try to make Hunt talk by administering a drug, but Hunt stands his ground and is ordered slain. Brigham consigns Hunt's coffin to Davy Jones' Locker—but Chris has secretly rescued Hunt.

The betrayals, beatings, befuddlements and beratings pile up from here with a blessed randomness, peaking when DeBrock is confronted by Hunt—whom he mistakes for a ghost. DeBrock at length

The betrayals, beatings, befuddlements and beratings pile up with a blessed randomness in *The Devil Pays Off*. (Photofest)

maneuvers himself into a fatal fall, closing the case now that the misappropriated seagoing vessels have been accounted for. Somewhere along the meandering way, Chris and Joan have fallen in love.

All of which add up to a cram-packed seven reels, with the transgressions well deployed among sadistic brains-heavy J. Edward Bromberg, snarling muscle-heavy Ivan Miller and eager-to-please dog-heavies Martin Kosleck and Richard Varno. (The grades of heavy, or villain, once were a standard measure used among the fans of action-adventure films to distinguish, literally, intellect from brawn from sniveling misguided loyalty.) Osa Massen is an alluring mystery-woman, and Margaret Tallichet is quite good as her wholesome and no-nonsense opposite number. Wright's heroism is convincingly reluctant, but once he rises to the occasion he stays there for the duration. Abner Biberman has a good turn as a secondary hero, a Cuban Military Intelligence agent in disguise as a deckhand.

CREDITS: Associate Producer: Albert J. Cohen; Director: John H. Auer; Screenplay: Lawrence Kimble and Malcolm Stuart Boylan; Story: George Worthing Yates and Julian Zimet; Photographed by: John Alton; Art Director: John Victor Mackay; Assistant Director: Harry Knight; Supervising Editor: Murray Seldeen; Editor: Howard O'Neill; Wardrobe: Adele Palmer; Music: Cy Feuer; Production Manager: Al Wilson; Running Time: 70 Minutes; Released: November 10, 1941

CAST: J. Edward Bromberg (Arnold DeBrock); Osa Massen (Valerie DeBrock); William Wright (Chris Waring); Margaret Tallichet (Joan Millard); Abner Biberman (Carlos); Martin Kosleck (Greb); Charles D. Brown (Capt. Jonathan Hunt); Ivan Miller (Capt. Brigham); Roland Varno (Doctor); Robert Frazer (Detective); Selmer Jackson (Adm. Curtiss); John "Skins" Miller (Gilhooley); Tim Ryan (First Mate); Roy Darmour and William Newell (Stewards); Hugh Prosser (Purser); José Pérez (Bellhop); John Mylong (von Eltzen); Dwight Frye (Radio Man).

The stark opening scene of *I Killed That Man*.

I KILLED THAT MAN
(K-B Productions, Inc./Monogram Pictures Corp.)

Phil Rosen's *Devil's Mate* (Monogram; 1933) is one of the jewels of the original *Forgotten Horrors* canon, a work of such cold ferocity as to defy improvement. Rosen gave it another go, all the same, with the formal remake, *I Killed That Man*.

New screenwriter Henry Bancroft efficiently reworks the Leonard Fields–David Silverstein script, retaining the structure and exposition—from the poison-dart murder of a condemned killer (Ralf Harolde) within the execution chamber; through the discovery of a cigarette holder that might be used as a dart-gun, the planting of a contaminated spike in an automobile horn and the customary threats and cryptic messages; to the unveiling of an ambitious candidate for the Parole Board, played by George Pembroke, as the killer. Pembroke's guilt comes as less of a surprise than that of squeamish Hobart Cavanaugh in *Devil's Mate*—or maybe that only goes for those of us who are familiar with the source-film. The critics at large in 1941 tended to hail *I Killed That Man* as a thriller without precedent.

Ricardo Cortez steps ably into the Preston Foster role of a determined investigator, and Joan Woodbury seems better prepared than *Devil's Mate*'s leading lady, Peggy Shannon, to take care of herself in the desperate finale. The reworking is a worthy variation, helped along in the exposition department by a generous running time, but hardly a match for its model in terms of meanness. The King Brothers' painstaking deployment of higher-than-usual production values holds the promise of greater things ahead in the long term for Monogram.

CREDITS: Producer: Maurice King; Associate Producer: Franklin King; Director: Phil Rosen; Screenplay: Henry Bancroft; Story: Leonard Fields and David Silverstein; Photographed by: Harry Neumann;

The critics at large in 1941 tended to hail *I Killed That Man* as a thriller without precedent. (Photofest)
Art Director: Frank Dexter; Assistant Director: Arthur Gardner; Editor: Martin G. Cohn; Set Dresser: Glen P. Thompson; Music: Johnny Lange and Lew Porter; Sound: Glen Glenn; Production Manager: Mack V. Wright; Running Time: 71 Minutes; Released: November 28, 1941

CAST: Ricardo Cortez (Roger Phillips); Joan Woodbury (Geri Reynolds); Pat Gleason (Bates); George Pembroke (Lowell King); Iris Adrian (Verne Drake); Herbert Rawlinson (Warden); Ralf Harolde (Nick Ross); Jack Mulhall (Collins); Vince Barnett (Lush); Gavin Gordon (Reed); John Hamilton (District Attorney); Harry Holman (Lanning); George Breakston (Tommy)

FOUR SHALL DIE
(Million Dollar Productions, Inc.)

Dorothy Dandridge was already poised for major-league stardom—which proved to be long in coming—when she graced this little-seen chiller/comedy about restless spirits and omens of doom. Encouraged by her mother, the stage-and-screen actress Ruby Dandridge, Dorothy had been performing since age four, first in a song-and-dance routine with her sister, Vivian Dandridge. Dorothy broke through in Hollywood at 24 with a notable bit part in the Marx Brothers' hit, *A Day at the Races* (1937). Her busiest year over the long haul was 1941, which brought her modest parts in *Lady from Louisiana* at Republic; *Sun Valley Serenade* at Fox; *Bahama Passage* at Paramount; and a showy romantic lead in *Four Shall Die*.

Four Shall Die is a black-ensemble piece from a studio of predominantly black ownership. The picture finds Miss Dandridge in the role of an heiress, Helen Fielding, whose crooked former sweetheart, Covey (Jack Carr), plots to regain her affections and her fortune. A spiritualistic medium (Vernon McCalla) summons a disembodied voice foretelling doom.

Upon the apparent fulfillment of the prophecy, Helen's new boyfriend (Johnny Thomas) falls under suspicion. No sooner have detective Pierre Toussaint (Pete Webster) and his boisterous helper, Beefus (Mantan Moreland), arrived, however, than another slaying is reported. One beneficiary prepares to leave the country on the medium's advice, but Toussaint establishes that the supposed victims are alive and well—and awaiting the outcome of a scam to terrorize the heirs.

Its sheer scarcity is reason enough to take an interest in *Four Shall Die*, but the film is neither particularly well made nor original in concept. The credits show an overabundance of producers, suggesting a too-many-cooks situation. Among the players, only Miss Dandridge and Mantan Moreland proved to possess that elusive spark of star quality over the long haul. Moreland had already begun proving his worth at the larger, nearer-the-mainstream studios. Miss Dandridge's big breakthroughs, despite steady work all along, would have to wait until *Carmen Jones* in 1954 and *Porgy and Bess* in 1959. By 1960, she was among the world's most popular film personalities but died by her own hand after losing a fortune in an oil-investment scam.

CREDITS: Executive Producer: Harry M. Popkin; Associate Producer: Sara Francis; Producer: Clifford Sanforth; Production Supervisor: George D. Ringer; Assistant Production Supervisor: Arthur C. Ringer; Director: Leo C. Popkin; Screenplay: Ed Dewey; Photographed by: Marcel Le Picard [Given Here as Picard]; Art Director: Paul Palmentola; Assistant Director: George Hippard; Second Assistant Director: Eddie Saeta; Editor: Martin G. Cohn; Prop Master: Bill Billings; Sound: Cliff Ruberg and Earl Hiller; Production Manager: Alfred Westen; Publicity: Harry Levette; Running Time: 72 Minutes; Released: Following New York Opening on Dec. 12, 1941

CAST: Pete Webster (Pierre Toussaint); Mantan Moreland (Beefus); Alfred Grant (Roger Fielding); Dorothy Dandridge (Helen Fielding); Vernon McCalla (Dr. Ronald Webb); Jesse Lee Brooks (Dr. Hugh Leonard); Reginald Fenderson (Hickson); Jack Carr (Lew Covey); Johnny Thomas (Bill Summers); Edward Thompson (Sgt. Adams); Earl Hall (Jefferson); Guernsey Morrow (Attendant)

MR. DISTRICT ATTORNEY IN THE CARTER CASE
a.k.a.: THE CARTER CASE
(Republic Pictures Corp.)

More a matter of selfishly motivated amateur sleuthing than official investigation, this second entry in a radio-spinoff series is noteworthy for its outlandish means of extracting clues from what Smiley Burnette, a busy sidekick/comedian in an entirely different class of Republic productions, would have called "one of them ol' dead corpses." The film also pitches a convincing argument that Franklin Pangborn—the movies' finest prissy meddler and a favorite foil of W.C. Fields—was possessed of a range broader than persnickety comedy.

Assistant District Attorney P. Cadwallader Jones (James Ellison, picking up where Dennis O'Keefe had left off) tackles the murder of Elliott Carter (Bradley Page), a big-shot publisher, by railroading the likeliest suspect, Andrew Belmont (John Eldredge), into a death sentence. The evidence holds that Carter had seduced Belmont's wife, actress Joyce Belmont (Lynne Carver), and that Carter's colleague Charley Towne (Pangborn) had seen Belmont confront the victim shortly before the slaying. Jones' fiancée, newspaper reporter Terry Parker (Virginia Gilmore, subbing for Florence Rice), is demoted for filing a premature report of acquittal.

Otto Strucker (John Bleifer), who prints Carter's *Society Spotlight* magazine, phones Terry with a promise of new evidence. She finds Strucker murdered, lying against a press containing fragments of a typeset article involving Carter and Mrs. Belmont. Nosing about further, Terry learns that Carter had withdrawn a huge sum from his business account without Towne's okay. Jones agrees to reopen the case, demanding that Terry stop meddling. She promises but reneges by calling on Joyce Belmont—who is killed suddenly by an unseen assailant.

Vincent Mackay (Douglas Fowley), one of Joyce's more persistent admirers, comes out of hiding to explain his situation to Terry. He had known that Strucker was printing an article that could have been used to blackmail the actress; the anonymous blackmailer must be the killer. Because Strucker had fallen against the type form, the text may have been pressed into his flesh. Mackay and Terry visit the morgue and find the entire message imprinted on the corpse—along with the name of Charlie Towne. No sooner has Terry passed this information along to Jones, than Towne traps her and Mackay, glibly admitting to the murders and herding them out to be killed. Jones and a police squadron get on the trail just in time. Belmont is freed, and Towne is bound over for trial.

Pangborn gives a splendidly cold-blooded reading of the vengeful businessman. His snarling arrogance when exposed comes as a revelation—not merely to the plot, but also to all those who picture the actor chiefly in light of his many portrayals of flustered bureaucrats, floorwalkers, bean-counters and hotel managers over a 30-year career. Even the studio's press materials made a big deal of this change-of-pace for Pangborn, but like ZaSu Pitts, another capable dramatic player who became too good at the fidgety mannerisms, he was typecast for the long haul.

James Ellison and Lynne Carver make an appealingly combative pair of leads, but Miss Carver—fresh from her well-received appearance in *Swamp Water*—carries the bulk of the investigation with an impetuous manner and a willingness to venture into dark places that Ellison's snooty Ivy League prosecutor would probably shun. Douglas Fowley serves an admirably heroic supporting function, as a rather pathetic star-struck type who helps Miss Carver seize upon the grisly clue in the morgue. The movies have used autopsies, séances and reanimation as a means of forcing the dead to give up their secrets, but this may be the only time that a printer's handset-type block, pressed into a murder victim's carcass, has yielded the solution to a crime.

Its essential grisliness aside, however, *Mr. District Attorney in the Carter Case* also packs a wealth of breezy comedy, thanks largely to Eddie Acuff as a brash photographer and to the crisp overall dialogue. Old-timer Paul Harvey, whose career in film dated from the nickelodeon days, is impressive as the senior district attorney. Director Bernard Vorhaus, a German who had worked extensively in England, was as adept with comedy and sentimental fare (including the heartwarming *Dr. Christian* series) as at suspense; his Hollywood career ended in 1951, when the House Committee on UnAmerican Activities branded him a Communist.

In what may be the most ephemeral bit of "movie trivia" ever to cross our desks, *Mr. District Attorney in The Carter Case* accounts for the 145th appearance of Oscar, sturdiest of the many life-size mannequins that Republic used to represent corpses. No kin to the Motion Picture Academy's Oscar.

CREDITS: Associate Producer and Director: Bernard Vorhaus; Original Screenplay by: Sidney Sheldon and Ben Roberts; Based upon: the Phillips H. Lord Radio Program, *Mr. District Attorney*; Photographed by: John Alton; Supervising Editor: Murray Seldeen; Editor: Edward Mann; Art Director: John Victor Mackay; Musical Director: Cy Feuer; Wardrobe: Adele Palmer; Sound System: RCA Victor; Running Time: 67 Minutes; Released: December 18, 1941; Shown During 1942 as: *The Carter Case*.

CAST: James Ellison (P. Cadwallader Jones); Virginia Gilmore (Terry Parker); Franklin Pangborn (Charley Towne); Paul Harvey (District Attorney Winton); Lynne Carver (Joyce Belmont); Spencer Charters (Judge White); Douglas Fowley (Vincent Mackay); John Eldredge (Andrew Belmont); Eddie Acuff (Hypo); John Sheehan (Beanie); Bradley Page (Elliott Carter)

Claude Rains is taken into custody in *Strange Holiday*. (Photofest)

1942
THE "STRANGE HOLIDAY" OF "THIS PRECIOUS FREEDOM"
(General Motors Corp./Sound Masters, Inc./Elite Pictures Corp./
Mike J. Levinson/Producers Releasing Corp.)

Present-day viewers of this bold patchwork curiosity have remarked that it reminds them of a *Twilight Zone* television episode, what with its Kafkaesque attitude of disorientation and persecution and its air of humanistic righteousness. Rod Serling would have been proud to hear the connection made, for the *Twilight Zone* mastermind owed much to the radio pioneer Arch Oboler. Oboler's NBC-Radio series, *Lights Out*, proved a decisive influence on *The Twilight Zone*—more so, perhaps, on Serling's much later *Night Gallery*—and *Strange Holiday* derives directly from an Oboler broadcast called *This Precious Freedom*. The tale concerns a returning vacationer's grim discovery that America has been taken over by a foreign oppressor.

The history of *Strange Holiday* is as unusual as the film itself: The 1940 airing of *This Precious Freedom*, starring Raymond Massey, had caught the ear of a General Motors executive named Paul Garrett. Garrett arranged for GM to finance a movie version, which at one point was to be called *Terror on Main Street*. Like most gigantic manufacturers, the company made many films for exclusive showing to its employees, but these were by-and-large training and motivational shorts. *This Precious Freedom* would be different: Garrett intended a morale-booster entertainment for GM's homefront workforce. Oboler was enlisted to write, produce and direct, and a non-theatrical studio-plus-laboratory, Sound Masters, Inc. of New York, submitted the low bid to specifications to handle turn-key production. Garrett appointed himself supervisor. The casting tapped some well-established

Claude Rains gives one of his very best—and least seen—performances as a victim of totalitarian invaders in *Strange Holiday*. (Photofest)

Hollywood names—unusual among the institutional/industrial moviemaking sector—including Claude Rains, Gloria Holden, Milton Kibbee and Martin Kosleck. Accounts vary as to whether the featurette clocked in at 20 minutes or 40 minutes; we viewed a 20-minute version during the 1960s. *International Photographer* magazine reported that "thousands of General Motors war workers and their families" were treated to screenings. Sensing a broader popular appeal, MGM acquired the short but then allowed it to languish unseen.

    Bigger developments, and bigger disappointments, lay in store: Oboler and Rains, being understandably proud of their work, contracted with the low-budget producer A.W. Hackel and his partners, Max King and Edward Finney. Together, they formed Elite Pictures Corp. as an *ad hoc* studio that would buy back *This Precious Freedom* from MGM and expand the film. (Oboler had something of an inside track, having co-scripted MGM's anti-Nazi epic of 1940, *Escape*, and having directed the psychological thriller *Bewitched* at MGM during 1944.)

    The expanded version of *This Precious Freedom* (rechristened *Strange Holiday* for enhanced marquee appeal) is a mess, and so was the attempt at theatrical distribution. But then, what you see is what you get:

    John Stevenson (Rains), a victim of torture-in-captivity, recalls the carefree life he had known. In a flashback, we see John as a devoted family man, fed up with the instability of the wartime homefront. John takes a wilderness vacation with a friend, Sam Morgan (Kibbee). Sam is ready to head for home after three weeks, but John insists upon staying. On remembering his wedding anniversary, John agrees to return. Stranded after their light plane develops mechanical problems, the men approach a farmer, who seems afraid even to talk to them. Leaving Sam to keep the plane secure, John pays an apprehensive trucker for a ride into town. John is astonished to find the community all but abandoned. The people he encounters will speak only of "the way things are," without explanation. John's family has vanished. Attacked by two hoodlums, John wakes in a cell and complains of his "rights" being "violated." His cellmate, a philosophically inclined black man (Thaddeus Jones), explains vaguely that "they" have eliminated human rights.

John receives the third-degree treatment by an inquisitor (Martin Kosleck), who demands in a German-accented snarl that John explain himself. John protests that he has nothing to do with any resistance movement, but beyond a brief reunion with John's wife (Gloria Holden), his captor allows no quarter. Finally, John is informed that America's complacency had allowed some brutal New Order to take over the country with scarcely a struggle. John vows to become a freedom fighter—at which point, he wakes up at the campsite and tells Sam it is time they returned home.

Gloria Holden gives an impassioned portrayal of Claude Rains' wife in *Strange Holiday*. This image comes from the later additions, which rendered explicit the Nazi-menace element. (Photofest)

The Hollywood Reporter announced early in 1944 that new scenes were being filmed to reflect "recent events" for what was still being called *This Precious Freedom*. The new shooting, re-editing and rechristening were completed within a year, and in March of 1945 *Daily Variety* announced that Elite was on the hunt for "a major distributor" for *Strange Holiday*. No such luck, though: The decidedly minor-league distributor Mike J. Levinson ended up in possession of the film and opened it only sporadically after New York and Los Angeles premieres during October of 1945. A year later, *The Hollywood Reporter* ran a notice that Producers Releasing Corp.—now in want of product "to fill in for the lapse in production plans brought on by the organization of Eagle-Lion [Films, Inc.]," had agreed to distribute *Strange Holiday*.

The troubled little picture deserved a better handling, but Oboler's story also had deserved a more painstaking transformation. The avoidance of explicit references to Nazi Germany may have been merely disingenuous in the 1942 filming, but it is purely a case of intellectual dishonesty in the 1944-45 footage. Continuity problems are damaging, as well: The dialogue refers to a state of war here, a postwar setting there. These lapses serve inadvertently to compound the tale's essence of disorientation.

The acting is first-rate. Claude Rains' anguished performance is as fine as anything else the great actor ever did, and Martin Kosleck matches Rains for intensity as the torturer. Gloria Holden is an impassioned wonder as Rains' wife, as affectionately devoted in the flashbacks as she seems haggard and broken in the reunion scene. Thaddeus Jones, in a début that should have led somewhere better, is most effective as Rains' cellmate; the casting here of a black player is an unusually progressive touch, typical of Oboler. Jones followed through with small appearances in Oboler's own *The Arnelo Affair* (1947) and Robert Z. Leonard's political drama *B.F.'s Daughter* (1948) before dropping out of the industry.

Oboler's greater fortunes lay in radio, but he forged boldly into the occasional movie project, favoring offbeat subject matter and novelty gimmicks. He contemplated the collapse of civilization in *Five* (1951); helped to pioneer the use of three-dimensional cinematography in the feature-film sector with *Bwana Devil* (1952); and satirized the dehumanizing threat of television in *The Twonky* (1953). For an early-1960s record album called *Drop Dead! An Exercise in Horror!*, Oboler remade several of his radio scripts in a beautifully designed panoramic-stereo mix. Oboler died in 1987.

CREDITS: Producers: Arch Oboler, Claude Rains, A.W. Hackel, Frank R. Donovan, Edward Finney and Max King; Director and Screenwriter: Arch Oboler; Production Supervisor (Short Version): Paul Garrett; Photographed by: Robert Surtees; Production Stills: Fred Parrish; Montage Effects: Howard Anderson and Ray Mercer; Art Director: Bernard Herzbrun; Editor: Fred Feitshans, Jr.; Musical Score: Gordon Jenkins; Assistant Director: Sam Nelson; Sound Engineer: W.H. Wilmarth; Running Time as *This Precious Freedom*: Variously Reported as Either a Two-Reeler (Approx. 20 Minutes) or a Four-Reeler (Approx. 40 Minutes); *This Precious Freedom* Shown: During 1942; Revamped Feature Version, *Strange Holiday*, Running Time: 61 Minutes; Released: During October of 1945

CAST: Claude Rains (John Stevenson); Bobbie Stebbins (John, Jr.); Barbara Bate (Peggy Lee Stevenson); Paul Hilton (Woodrow Stevenson); Gloria Holden (Jean Stevenson); Milton Kibbee (Sam Morgan); Walter White, Jr. (Farmer); Wally Maher (Trucker); Tommy Cook (Newsboy); Griff Barnett (Regan); Ed Max and Paul Dubov (Detectives); Helen Mack (Secretary); Martin Kosleck (Inquisitor); Charles McAvoy (Guard); Priscilla Lyons (Miss Stevenson); David Bradford (Joe); Thaddeus Jones (Cellmate).

PRIVATE SNUFFY SMITH
(Capital Pictures Corp./Monogram Pictures Corp.)

If it should strike anyone as weird that a slapstick comedy based on a big-nose/big-foot comic strip should make the cut for a *Forgotten Horrors* playbill, then consider: *Forgotten Horrors* is about weird choices, to begin with, and the process of choosing is hardly any simple matter of talking to death the better-known such movies. Weirdness comes no weirder than *Private Snuffy Smith*, whose semblance of a plot contains the science-fictional notion of an invisibility potion. Its prompt sequel, *Hillbilly Blitzkrieg*, is only somewhat less peculiar.

Snuffy Smith (played here by Bud Duncan) is a backwoods moonshiner who originated as a supporting character in the newspaper cartoon *Barney Google*, created in 1919 by Billy DeBeck and carried on over the longer haul by Fred Lasswell and assorted syndicate ghost-artists. The character of Barney Google has long since been overshadowed by the upstart supporting player Snuffy Smith—whose published misadventures continue apace.

Snuffy and his boisterous wife, Lowizie (a.k.a. Loweezy), were ripe for the movies by 1942, for backwoods comedies had become quite the rage. *Grand Ole Opry* stalwart Roy Acuff had launched his own movie career, the cornball-comedy act of the Weaver Brothers & Elviry had nailed a popular series at Republic, and Chester Lauck and Norris Goff had parlayed their hick-town radio program, *Lum & Abner*, into a successful string of sentimental chucklers distributed by RKO-Radio.

Private Snuffy Smith opens as Snuffy, weary of a constant war with a "revenooer" named Cooper (Edgar Kennedy), gets a hankering to join the Army. Disqualified for being too short, and appalled to learn that Cooper is now a sergeant, Snuffy nonetheless becomes the camp's yardbird (which is G.I.-speak for janitor). He is accompanied by an invisible dog, rendered thus by a liquid concocted by Lowizie.

Had more been made of the invisibility angle, and less of a routine sabotage plot, *Private Snuffy Smith* would be a more rewarding picture. There are treats to be had, nonetheless, in the jovial antagonism between bulb-nosed Bud Duncan and grouchy Edgar Kennedy and in a boondocks war-games exercise that turns comparatively serious. Sarah Padden makes an ebullient Lowizie, who gets to count coup on an invading party of Axis troublemakers captive after all else has failed. *Private Snuffy Smith* was intended as a comeback vehicle for the diminutive Duncan (1886-1960), who had been absent from the screen since the *Ham & Bud* series of comedy-team shorts, co-starring Lloyd Hamilton, of the 1910s. The series-in-miniature of *Snuffy* and *Hillbilly Blitzkreig* led only to a lasting obscurity for Duncan. The pictures, acquired by Monogram from an even smaller production company, were given the sparsest of provincial distribution, although a sub-distributor, Astor Pictures, kept them in play on into the 1950s as a double feature—the very definition of superfluous redundant overkill.

CREDITS: Producer: Edward Gross; Associate Producers: Jack Dietz and Dan Keefe; Director: Edward Cline; Screenplay: John Grey, Jack Henley, Lloyd French and Donoho Hall; Based upon the Comic Strip, *Barney Google & Snuffy Smith*, Created by Billy DeBeck; Photographed by: Marcel Le Picard; Assistant Director: Chris Beute; Art Director: Richard Irvine; Editor: Robert Crandall; Musical Director: Rudy Schrager; Songs: "Time's a-Wastin'," by Ole Olsen, Chic Johnson, Jay Livingston and Ray Evans, and "The Yard Bird," by Jimmie Dodd; Sound: William Fox; Makeup: Ern Westmore; Production Manager: Dan Keefe; Assistant Production Manager: Nelson L. Gross; Running Time: 67 Minutes; Copyrighted: January 16, 1942; Released: On a State-by-State Basis

CAST: Bud Duncan (Snuffy Smith); Edgar Kennedy (Sgt. Cooper); Sarah Padden (Lowizie); J. Farrell MacDonald (General); Doris Lindsey (Cindy); Jimmie Dodd (Don); Andria Palmer (Janie); Pat McVeigh (Lloyd); Frank Austin (Saul)

LAW OF THE JUNGLE
(Monogram Pictures Corp.)

Mantan Moreland raises this Nazis-in-the-jungle adventure well above the ordinary. Top-billed Arline Judge is no slouch, either, as a disgraced nightclub singer who has been snookered into helping the enemy. The story, too, allows a tribe of (fictional) native Africans to come to the rescue in a welcome inversion of stereotype.

Nona Brooks (Miss Judge), whose treacherous boss, Simmons (Arthur O'Connell), has made her instrumental in the slaying of a British agent, is wandering aimlessly through the bush-country when she encounters an explorer named Larry Mason (John King) and his helper, Jefferson Jones (Moreland). Simmons has already begun spreading unkind rumors about Nona, but Larry agrees to shelter her on condition she scram the next morning.

Stashed away in Nona's clothing are papers that had belonged to the slain Britisher. The Nazis (Victor

Kendall and Feodor Chaliapin) kill Simmons and begin tracking Nona. Larry begins to comprehend Nona's plight, but his bearers are slain by tribesmen in the employ of the Germans. Larry, Jeff and Nona take refuge in a cave littered with human remains, hiding the documents in a skull. The warlike tribespeople capture them, but Jeff saves the day, taking advantage of the kindnesses of a native woman who has developed a crush on him. Jeff and the chief discover that they are lodge brothers. Larry and the chief capture the Nazis.

Jean Yarbrough brings an almost impatient sense of timing to *Law of the Jungle*, dwelling primarily on Moreland's showcase scenes. The director and the show-stopping comedian had worked together to sharper advantage on *King of the Zombies*, but this one makes a nice companion-piece to that well-loved picture. The cave-of-bones sequence is suitably unnerving.

CREDITS: Producer: Lindsley Parsons; Director: Jean Yarbrough; Screenplay: George Bricker; Additional Dialogue: Edmond Kelso; Photographed by: Mack Stengler; Technical Director: Dave Milton; Assistant Director and Production Manager: William Strobach; Editor: Jack Ogilvie; Musical Director: Edward Kay; Sound Director: William Fox; Sound Engineer: Virgil Smith; Length: Six Reels, Approx. 60 Minutes; Released: February 6, 1942

CAST: Arline Judge (Nona Brooks); John King (Larry Mason); Mantan Moreland (Jefferson Jones); Arthur O'Connell (Simmons); C. Montague Shaw (Sgt. Burke); Guy Kingsford (Constable Whiteside); Lawrence Criner (Mojobo); Victor Kendall (Grozman); Feodor Chaliapin (Belts); Martin Williams (Bongo).

LUCKY GHOST
(Dixie National Pictures/Consolidated National Film Exchanges/Toddy Pictures Co.)

The Moreland and Miller comedy team followed through belatedly on *Mr. Washington Goes to Town* (1940) with this more literally supernatural yocker-with-chills, an improvement over *Washington*'s only-a-dream resolution. Producer Jed Buell planned a series of at least five additional titles but then took things only as far as *Professor Creeps*, which was shot and released almost simultaneously with *Lucky Ghost*. Mantan Moreland's burgeoning solo career took prior claim, and he wound up as both a long-term contract player for Monogram and a busy character man at most of the major studios.

Moreland and Flournoy E. Miller are squarely in their Negro Vaudeville element as career loafers Washington and Jefferson, who land in a posh sanitarium run as a gambling palace by the crooked Dr. Brutus Blake (Maceo B. Sheffield) and his partner, Blackstone (Arthur Ray). Soon, the ghosts of Blake's ancestors convene to lament their having left so grand a place to such a wastrel, and the spirit of Uncle Ezra (Henry Hastings) is sent to throw a good scare into Blake. Ezra arrives just after Washington and Jefferson have won the establishment in a game of dice; the pals win things just as wickedly as Blake had, and the ghosts lay siege to the property while Blake and Blackstone plot to regain control. Ezra confronts Blake while the other spirits send Washington and Jefferson packing.

The slight story benefits from a quick telling—three prints viewed range from 50 to 68 minutes—and from the wisecracking joviality of Moreland and Miller. The gagwriting dredges up such rancid corn as a reference to a nearby town called Goslow; this turns out to be a misread highway sign advising motorists to "Go Slow." Henry Hastings makes a suitably severe lead ghost, and burly Maceo Sheffield is fine as the badman in charge of things. The primitive special effects lend a stage-play sensibility to the crazy doings. A piano-playing skeleton accounts for the closing gag. *Lucky Ghost* has been acknowledged by Sherman Hemsley as an inspiration for the oddball comedy *Ghost Fever* (1984-87), which features Luis Avalos and Hemsley as cops who encounter an absurd haunting. But of course that jinxed picture had its more immediate origins as a stalled attempt to ride the coattails of 1984's *Ghostbusters*.

CREDITS: Producer: Jed Buell; Associate Producer: Maceo B. Sheffield; Director: William X. Crowley; Scenario: Lex Neal and Vernon Smith; Story Editor: Josephine Wickland; Photographed by: Robert Cline; Art Director: Eugene Stone; Assistant Director: Edwin Monfort; Editor: Robert Crandall; Musical Director: Don Swander; Music Composed by: Lorenza Flennoy; Sound Engineer: Hans Weeren; Production Manager: Peter Jones; Running Time: 68 Minutes; Released: February 10, 1942

CAST: Mantan Moreland (Washington Delaware Jones); Flournoy E. Miller (Jefferson); Maceo B. Sheffield (Dr. Brutus Blake); Arthur Ray (Blackstone); Florence O'Brien (Hostess); Harold A. Garrison (Brown); Jessie Cryer (Dawson); Nappy Whiting (Chauffeur); Jessie Brooks (Doorman); Ida Coffin (Checkstand Attendant); Nathan Curry (Farmer); Millie Monroe, Louise Franklyn, Lucille Battles and Aranelle Harris (Waitresses); Monty Hawley (Masher); Vernon McCalla (Guest); Harry LaVette (Diner); Henry Hastings (Uncle Ezra); Florence Field (Ezra's Wife); John Lester Johnson, Eddie Thompson, Leonard Christmas (Ghosts); Reggie Finderson (Dealer); and Buck Woods

PROFESSOR CREEPS
(Hollywood-Dixie National Pictures, Inc./Consolidated National Film Exchanges/ Toddy Pictures Co.)

"Our modern generation knows very little of the old minstrel show, which is a thing of the past, but we must give it credit for being the father of America's stage comedy and the element which promoted Vaudeville," wrote producer Jed Buell in the press materials for this Moreland and Miller gem. "The natural wit and fun of the Negro was personified in these minstrel shows, as the Negro is a natural-born comedian and entertainer...For more than a century...the humor of the Negro...was recognized as the essence of show business...We are trying to recapture...the true value of the old minstrel show and to put it into modern dress."

Its honky-fied condescension notwithstanding, Buell's appeal to the critics bespeaks a heartfelt sympathy with the very style he was exploiting in such pictures as *Mr. Washington Goes to Town*, *Lucky Ghost* and *Professor Creeps*. Although Buell insisted that *Professor Creeps* "was not...designed for Negro [theatres] alone," still it was black America that gave the picture a marketplace resilience in reissues that proceeded into the 1950s.

"Yes, it's a genuine cure for the wartime blues," wrote the Pittsburgh *Courier*'s Herman Hill, a pioneering civil-rights journalist who had taken many black-ensemble pictures to task for what he called "age-old *Amos 'n' Andy* business" and "dialected dialogue." Reporting from the South Central Los Angeles premiere for a mixed black-and-white audience, Hill raved: "Previewed in typical Hollywood fashion Thursday night at sepia town's leading

Arthur Ray, the "dark-skinned Bela Lugosi" (so said the *New York Times*) of *Professor Creeps*.

Mantan Moreland cops some Z's while Flournoy E. Miller makes like Sherlock Holmes in *Professor Creeps*. (Photofest)

theatre…Jed Buell's latest opus starring gawky F.E. Miller and button-eyed, ground-hoggish Mantan Moreland, [the] Mutt & Jeff of the cinema, all but convulsed the crowd with laughter." Hill may have been caught up in the jovial frenzy of the début ceremonies, or perhaps Jed Buell had picked up the tab for the coverage; in any event, the contrast of this story with Hill's more generally militant writing is of interest.

And yes, the "age-old *Amos 'n' Andy* business" is plenty much in evidence here—and it was an established black style before the white-guy talents behind *Amos 'n' Andy* appropriated the shtick—but the film's good-natured generosity with the scares and chuckles is undeniable.

Inept private eyes Washington (Moreland) and Jefferson (Miller) spend most of their time dodging bill collectors and the landlord (recurring tough-guy player Maceo B. Sheffield). The workload at their agency—where a sign proclaims: "Carrier & Stool Pigeons Furnished"—allows plenty of time for snoozing, and during one such interlude Washington dreams about a big case:

Harlem debutante Daffodil Dixon (Florence O'Brien) reports her boyfriend, Alexander (Clarence Hargrave), missing, and the detectives discover that Alexander is hardly the first of her admirers to disappear. At the home of Daffodil's uncle, the mysterious Prof. Whackingham Creeps (Arthur Ray), the partners attempt to reconstruct the circumstances that had led to Alexander's vanishment. Professor Creeps demonstrates his abilities to suspend gravity and change people into beasts. A disembodied voice—Alexander's—informs the sleuths that several of Daffodil's suitors have been transformed and hidden away, along with a Japanese fellow whom the professor had attacked as a matter of wartime principle. Jefferson is zapped into the shape of a gorilla. The professor gets a dose of his own medicine and is changed into a duck. A "real" gorilla, escaped from a circus, joins the fray, and its handlers capture Jefferson by mistake. Washington suddenly wakes up, unable to tolerate more of the absurd dream.

Such unapologetic silliness earned high marks from *Box Office* and *Motion Picture Daily*, which called Moreland and Miller a "sepia Abbott & Costello." Even *The New York Times* weighed in on

Arthur Ray subdues a mangy menace this a D.D.T.-atomizing gun in *Professor Creeps*. (Don Martin, one of *MAD* magazine's more celebrated cartoonists, told us that this film helped to inspire his early-'60s story "National Gorilla-Suit Day.") (Photofest)

a favorable note, likening title player Arthur Ray to "a dark-skinned Bela Lugosi" and noting of the Los Angeles premiere, "No Academy Award-winning production has ever received more enthusiasm." *The Hollywood Reporter* wrote: "It is a revelation to observe how Moreland, long regarded among the big three Negro comics in the industry, goes over with his own race." (The "big three" black comedians of the day would also have included Eddie "Rochester" Anderson and Willie Best.) The *Motion Picture Herald* likened *Professor Creeps* to *Hold That Ghost*, Universal's Abbott & Costello hit of 1941, and as though that weren't enough of a stretch, added: "Veteran William Beaudine's direction makes every foot of film count."

Such overzealous notices miss the point—which is merely that an able cast is having a great deal of fun with a silly story—but still it's keen to see a kind word written about good old William Beaudine. Practically the only nay-sayer was a humorless official of the Motion Picture Association's Production Code Administration, who challenged the film's original title.

Seems *Professor Creeps* had been shot as *Goodbye, Mr. Creeps*. MGM had made the uplifting drama *Goodbye, Mr. Chips* in England in 1939, and Production Code honcho Carl E. Milliken raised a red flag about how spoofs of "important titles" must be submitted for the approval of the "important" producer involved. Another PCA personage, Geoffrey Shurlock, replied that *Creeps'* standing as an "all-Negro" picture posed no threat to the eminence of *Goodbye, Mr. Chips*. So much for the notion of "separate but equal." Even so, Buell rechristened the film *Professor Creeps*. (No telling why the Production Code's Fun Police neglected to red-flag the earlier *Mr. Washington Goes to Town*, whose title is a patent take-off on Frank Capra's oh-so-important *Mr. Deeds Goes to Town*, from 1936.)

To this day, most people hearing the title of *Professor Creeps* for the first time don't know whether to take the word *Creeps* as a noun or a verb, and some sources have recorded the title as *The Professor Creeps*.

CREDITS: Producer: Jed Buell; Associate Producers: Dick L'Estrange and Maceo B. Sheffield; Director: William Beaudine; Screenplay: William X. Crowley, Roy Clements, Jed Buell and Robert Edmunds; Story: Robert Edmunds; Photographed by: Arthur Martinelli; Editor: Dan Milner; Sound Engineer: Ben Winkler; Running Time: 63 Minutes; Released: On a State-by-State Basis Following Los Angeles Opening on February 28, 1942

CAST: Flournoy E. Miller (Jefferson); Mantan Moreland (Washington); Arthur Ray (Prof. Whackingham Creeps); Florence O'Brien (Daffodil Dixon); Maceo B. Sheffield (Landlord); Margaret Whitten (Mrs. Green); Shelton Brooks (Jackson); Jessie Cryer (Mrs. Green); Billy Mitchell (Schenectady); Zack Williams (Telephone Man); Charles Hawkins (Pawnshop Man); Clarence Hargrave (Alexander); John Lester Johnson (Keeper); Nappy Whiting (Cabbie)

Bela Lugosi was the star of Monogram's *Black Dragons*

BLACK DRAGONS
(Monogram Pictures Corp.)

Attempts to exploit prevailing social conditions for the sake of entertainment value have never been so pronounced as during World War II, when the Axis menace proved a persistently bitter muse to Hollywood. No odder such result exists than William Nigh's *Black Dragons*, which is as fascinating for its suggestion of infiltration and sabotage via plastic surgery as it is for Bela Lugosi's ominously comical starring presence.

Lugosi lurks and muses with philosophical good humor through this one while waging a murderous war of nerves. The story concerns a larger menace for whose creation Lugosi proves to have been responsible. At a dinner-party gathering of captains of industry, commerce and politics, the jovial mood turns disturbing as we learn that six of these chaps aren't who they're supposed to be:

1. Stanford Jolley calls to order a meeting of the suicide squad in *Black Dragons*. Bela Lugosi, stealing the scene from a background vantage, makes with a heil-Hitler salute.

They are Japanese agents of the Black Dragon Society, transformed by courtesy of the Third Reich to resemble slain American big shots. Thus strategically placed, the cultists are free to undermine the Allied campaign.

Until Monsieur Colomb (Lugosi) shows up in Washington, that is. His unwelcome arrival in the household of the bogus Dr. Saunders (George Pembroke) touches off a low-key hostage situation in which Colomb settles in as a vaguely honored guest while his host becomes a forced recluse. The fake Kerney (Max Hoffman, Jr.) is first to die, ambushed in a taxicab and dumped on the steps of the barricaded Japanese Embassy, a ceremonial Japanese dagger clutched in one hand.

Doctor Saunders' niece—or is she?—Alice (Joan Barclay) chooses an awkward time to visit after a long absence. Her "uncle" refuses to see her, and Alice finds herself strangely attracted to Monsieur Colomb. Novice plainclothes cop Dick Martin (Clayton Moore) traces Kerney's path back to the Saunders residence, only to wait in vain to see the hidden master of the household. Martin finds himself not so strangely attracted to Alice.

Meanwhile, Colomb disables the ersatz Wallace (Edward Piel, Sr.) and uses him as bait for other impostors before killing him. He taunts the false Ryder (Bob Fiske) by sending an advertisement for a plastic surgeon, then lures Ryder and the substitute Van Dyke (Irving Mitchell) into a death trap. Colomb vanishes. Martin wises up late and catches a plane to meet the supposed banker Amos Hanlin (Robert Frazer), convincing him to come to Washington for protection.

But Colomb, too, has backtracked. The benighted Saunders household falls into sudden turmoil as Alice is revealed to be a government agent, sent to investigate matters on behalf of the real niece. "Saunders" comes out of hiding, keeping his head blanketed. Colomb kills "Hanlin" and is wounded in return. At length, "Saunders" makes with the explanations.

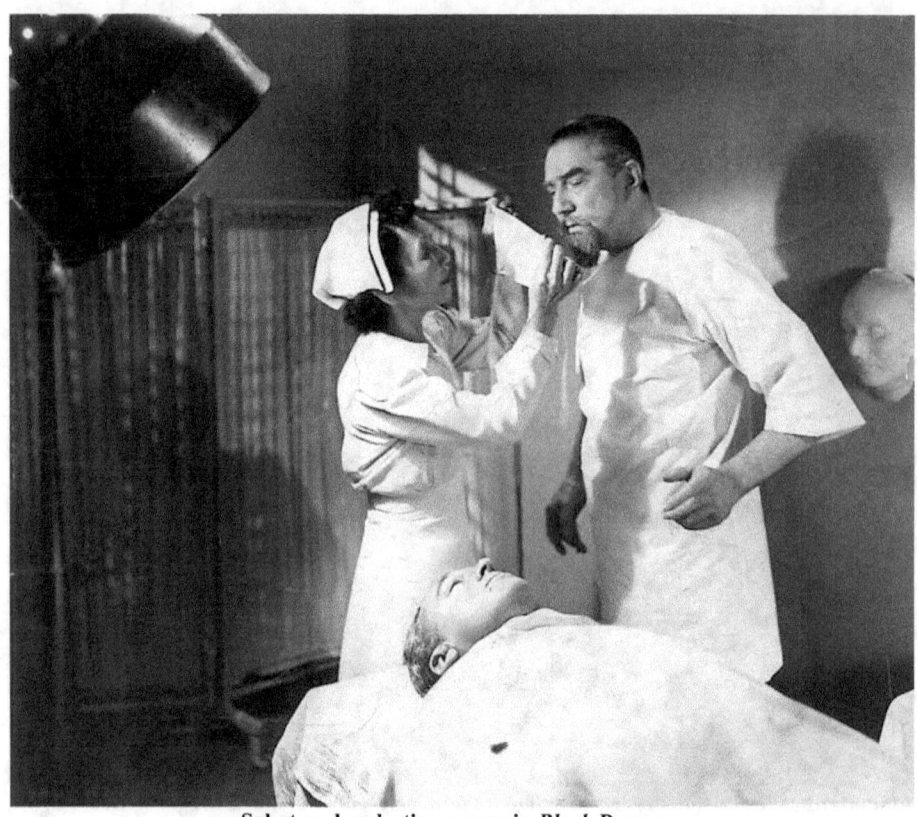

Sabotage by plastic surgery in *Black Dragons*.

For his help in altering the Japanese saboteurs to resemble death-masks of the real Americans, the Nazi surgeon Dr. Melcher—Colomb—was rewarded with imprisonment. Trading places with a conveniently look-alike captive, Colomb had gained freedom and trailed the agents to America. As he finishes his confession, the counterfeit Saunders reveals his face: Colomb has infected him with a disfiguring disease. Colomb gets in the last word—"And *you* must go on *living*!"—before collapsing in death.

Nazi though his character be, Lugosi comes across as a wholly sympathetic predator—a man betrayed, on a mission of vengeance, with a droll sense of humor about the ease with which he terrifies and manipulates his ungrateful former patients. Romance does not exactly figure here, but Lugosi engages in some ominously flirtatious banter with Joan Barclay, who plays another surrogate personage with nervy authority. Serial favorite and former aerialist Clayton Moore, the Lone Ranger-to-be, makes a boyishly arrogant cop, who seems astonished that Miss Barclay should find Lugosi alluring. Lugosi has by far the better come-on, even though he is clearly aloof from romantic complications. The hint of rivalry could have become a delicately balanced triangle with a little extra care and a heftier running time.

After Lugosi has throttled one of the false Americans within the Saunders house, Miss Barclay hastens to report she had heard a "gurgling." Lugosi has a ready explanation: "*Oh*! I was *humming*. Is my voice as bad as *that*?" While fleeing a shadowy intruder, Miss Barclay dashes smack into a collision with Lugosi. He muses, "When a young woman's nerves commence to give way, it is time she sought refuge in a strong man's arms." She replies, "I just ran into yours." He doesn't miss a beat: "*Mine* might be dangerous." When he packs out for parts unknown to mislead the authorities, she asks, "Will we see you again?" Lugosi: "Who knows, in this crazy world?" The killer's choice of an alias is a nice touch of wartime irony: *Colomb* connotes the French term for *dove*.

Bela Lugosi subdues George Pembroke in *Black Dragons*.

The complications of identity are a bit much for *Black Dragons*' brief running time, and director William Nigh is hardly a master of suspenseful pacing. There is one nifty surprise, when an airliner, bound for a meeting with the last intended victim, proves to be carrying Moore and not Lugosi. The change-of-pace role seems to delight Lugosi, and the five ghastly murders plus a shock-value finale make for a generously gradual payoff. Besides, any picture in which that championship bad-guy player, I. Stanford Jolley, impersonates a Japanese warlord, however briefly, is okay in our book. And this *is* our book, you know.

CREDITS: Producers: Sam Katzman and Jack Dietz for Banner Productions; Director: William Nigh; Story and Screenplay by: Harvey Gates; Photographed by: Art Reed; Production Manager: Ed W. Rote; Assistant Directors: Arthur Hammons and Gerald Schnitzer; Editor: Carl Pierson; Art Director: David Milton; Sound Engineer: Glen Glenn; Musical Directors: Lange & Porter; Running Time: 61 Minutes; Released: March 6, 1942

CAST: Bela Lugosi (Monsieur Colomb and Dr. Melcher); Joan Barclay (Alice); Clayton Moore (Dick Martin); George Pembroke (Dr. Saunders); Robert Frazer (Amos Hanlin); I. Stanford Jolley (the Dragon); Max Hoffman, Jr. (Kerney); Irving Mitchell (Van Dyke); Edward Peil, Sr. (Wallace); Bob Fiske (Ryder); Kenneth Harlan (Colton); Joe Eggenton (Stevens)

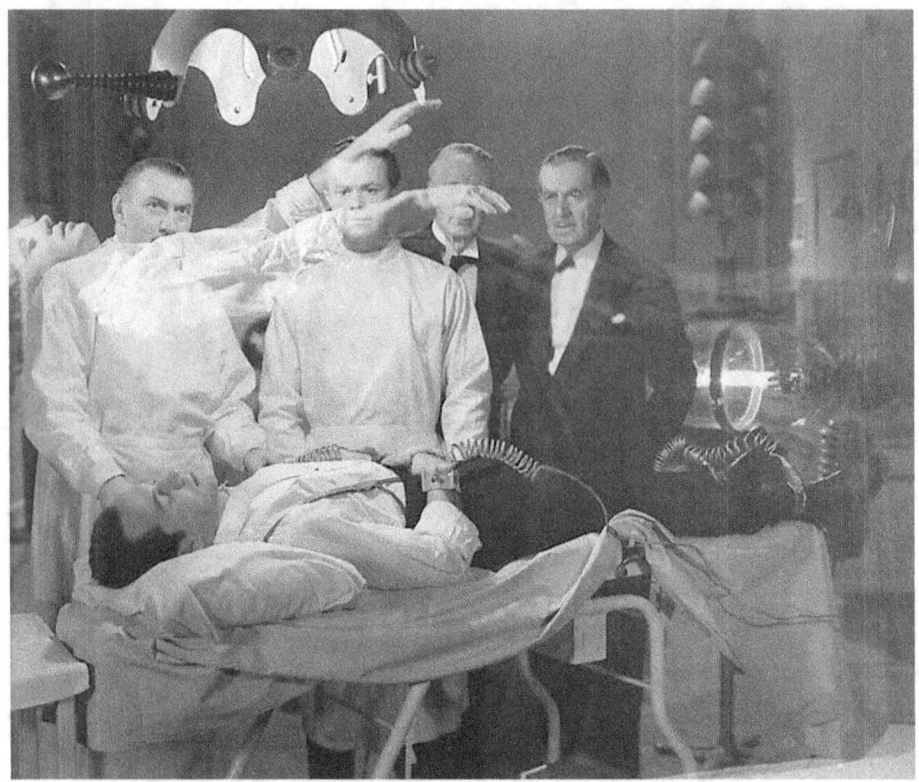

A ghostly resurrection in *The Man with Two Lives*. (Photofest)

THE MAN WITH TWO LIVES
(Monogram Pictures Corp.)

The *Frankenstein* myth colors this cheap sham from A.W. Hackel's Monogram unit in fascinating but ultimately false ways. Still, *The Man with Two Lives* deserves better than *Variety*'s cavalier dismissal: "What a nightmare!"

The engagement party of Philip Bennett (Edward Norris) and Louise Hammond (Eleanor Lawson) takes on a grimmer tone in an argument between Dr. Clark (Edward Keane) and Professor Toller (Hugh Sothern). Clark speaks matter-of-factly of his research into resurrecting the dead, but psychologist Toller is ill-impressed. Much talk concerns the approaching execution of Al Panino, a notorious criminal.

Then comes Phil's auto wreck. Phil's father (Frederick Burton) pleads with Clark to bring the youth back to life. The attempt takes place just at the moment of Panino's last gasp at the state prison. Phil is revived, but his mind seems a blank. He grows increasingly antisocial and begins visiting Panino's old haunts—eventually taking over the Panino mob. Things get so ugly that, at last, Clark is forced to take Phil's restored life. Phil suddenly awakes from the dream-state that has gripped him since the auto accident.

So much malice comes to flower within these several reels that it is difficult to dislike *The Man with Two Lives*. Edward Norris establishes his genial socialite character so efficiently that his resurrection and transformation make for some harrowing moments. Norris is equally effective as the criminalized youngster, especially in a deadly confrontation with the real mobster's former sweetheart (Marlo Dwyer) and in an ambush at a desolate warehouse. Director Phil Rosen makes much of Norris' immersion in the underworld and his family's inability to comprehend what has happened. The abrupt ending is more than a cheat—it is a cold and reprehensible denial of a pleasurably dour fantasy.

CREDITS: Producer: A.W. Hackel; Director: Phil Rosen; Screenplay: Joseph Hoffman; Photographed by: Harry Neumann; Assistant Director: Al Wood; Supervising Editor: Martin G. Cohn; Musical Director: Frank Sanucci; Sound Engineer: Glen Glenn; Production Manager: Ben Gutterman; Running Time: 67 Minutes; Released: March 13, 1942

CAST: Edward Norris (Philip Bennett); Marlo Dwyer (Helen Lengel); Eleanor Lawson (Louise Hammond); Frederick Burton (Hobart Bennett); Addison Richards (Lt. Bradley); Edward Keane (Dr. Clark); Hugh Sothern (Prof. Toller); Tom Seidel (Reginald Bennett); Elliott Sullivan (Eric); Anthony Warde (Hugo); Ernie Adams (Gimpy); Kenneth Duncan (Jess); George Dobbs (Tim); Lois Landon (Aunt Margaret); Frances Richards (Nurse); Jack Buckley (Mitch Larsen); Jack Ingraham (Ed Sporady); George Kirby (Butler)

SPY SMASHER
(Republic Pictures Corp.)

The comics hero Spy Smasher, from Captain Marvel's Fawcett Publications, had already fostered a strong popular dislike for the congealing Axis powers by the time a movie incarnation began taking shape in November of 1941. Republic nailed a shooting script only days before the Japanese invasion of Pearl Harbor, and it was with a newfound sense of propagandistic ferocity that the serial went into production on December 22.

The movie version takes savvy liberties with the source, providing the lead character of Alan Armstrong, alias Spy Smasher, with an entirely civilian twin named Jack—and thus obliging star player Kane Richmond to handle essentially three roles. A recurring villain called the Mask was literally un-masked for the screen, allowing Hans Schumm a richer opportunity for characterization.

The story starts off in bravura fashion, with Spy Smasher captured in occupied France while uncovering a Nazi plot to undermine the American economy. Over the dozen chapters, Spy Smasher faces certain doom from a gasoline explosion; machine-gun and torpedo volleys; a man-made flood; the crash of a futuristic flying machine; a descending elevator car; a brick-cutting blade and a blast of steam; a collapsing tower; a comparatively mundane auto crash; an industrial-strength pottery kiln; and a headlong fall from a rooftop amid a hail of bullets. Needless to say, the hero survives to win a medal for valor—although the story takes on a strong tragic resonance in the wholly unexpected death of the brother.

Richmond makes not only an impressive costumed crimebuster, but a winning pair of guys in street clothes, as well. A sophisticated combination of split-screen shots and body-double casting leaves no question but what there are two Kane Richmonds on the scene. There is a strong romantic interest in Marguerite Chapman, a striking beauty who usually graced the B-unit productions of Columbia Pictures, and Sam Flint is a classy Naval Intelligence honcho.

Veteran director William Witney pulls a curious departure from serial-shooting tradition here, handling the assignment solo rather than following the customary practice of sharing the helming chores. Over the course of 17 prior chapter-plays, Witney had co-directed with John English. The tactic of attaching two directors to one serial had become S.O.P. as early as 1932's *The Shadow of the Eagle*, enabling one director to prepare for the next day's shooting while his colleague was on the set. Witney brought *Spy Smasher* to completion in a brisk 38 days.

Typical of Republic is the magnificent variety of found locations, including an imposing brick-and-masonry factory in Temecula Canyon where Spy Smasher comes uncomfortably close to being sliced into pieces. Set designers Russell Kimball and John McCarthy provided magnificent interiors that would have been right at home in some top-of-the-line picture from MGM or Fox. The Lydecker brothers, Howard and Theodore, delivered their usual astonishingly realistic miniatures and life-size gizmos, including a fantastic flying machine that figures in one of the more dazzling escape stunts.

CREDITS: Associate Producer: W.J. O'Sullivan; Director: William Witney; Screenplay: Ronald Davidson, Norman S. Hall, William Lively, Joseph O'Donnell and Joseph Poland; Suggested by the Character in *WHIZ Comics* and *Spy Smasher* Magazines; Unit Manager: Mack D'Agostino; Photographed by: Reggie Lanning; Special Effects: Howard and Theodore Lydecker; Assistant Directors: R.G. "Bud" Springsteen and Louis Germonprez; Film Editors: Tony Martinelli and Edward Todd; Musical Supervisor: Cy Feuer; Musical Score: Mort Glickman, Incorporating Beethoven's *Fifth Symphony*; Running Time: 214 Minutes; Released: April 4, 1942

CAST: Kane Richmond (Alan "Spy Smasher" Armstrong and Jack Armstrong); Sam Flint (Adm. Corby); Marguerite Chapman (Eve Corby); Hans Schumm (the Mask); Tristram Coffin (Drake); Franco Corsaro (Pierre Durand); Hans von Morhart (Capt. Gerhardt); Georges Renavent (Gov. Le Conte); Robert O. Davis (Col. von Kahr); Henry Zenda (Ritter Lazar); Paul Bryar (Lawlor); Tom London (Crane); Richard Bond (Hayes); Crane Whitney (Hauser); John James (Steve)

HOUSE OF ERRORS
(Beaumont Productions/Producers Releasing Corp.)

The selection is not to be confused with *House of Horrors*. It is the unfortunate fashion to regard the great comedian Harry Langdon as a deserving casualty of both his own excesses and the talkie revolution, an egocentric has-been by 1928 who had estranged himself from an industry he helped to invent. But Langdon also bestowed upon the early-talkie years a wealth of short subjects and feature-film assignments that the film-snob elite has long chosen to ignore. The rediscovery today of Langdon's late-in-life pictures—including this gem-in-the-rough—proves the artist to have kept himself thoroughly well prepared for a resurgence that should have happened.

Langdon was doing more than going through the motions at PRC. *House of Errors*, from a Langdon original, is a brush with science fiction and hair-raising adventure that finds the childlike star player—at 57—as generously amusing as ever, and gifted with a piping, cartoonish voice that he uses to splendid effect. If Langdon's age tells—well, gosh, whose age *doesn't* tell?

Langdon and Charles Rogers play newspaper messengers who intend to become full-fledged reporters. Their crack at the big time comes via an eccentric inventor (Richard Kipling) who despises reporters. The chums wind up in possession of a fantastic new machine gun, which must be kept at all costs out of the hands of munitions racketeers. No such caveat about keeping the weapon out of the hands of nincompoops, and of course Langdon winds up causing a disaster with an unintended barrage. There is some welcome scary business during a violent storm. The lovely but fast-fading Marian Marsh makes an appealing leading lady whose affections might even be reserved for Langdon—no fair giving away too much—and John Holland and Ray Walker score as villain and hero, respectively. The teaming with Charles Rogers is gratuitous; this one is Langdon's show all the way.

Langdon died of a cerebral hemorrhage three days before Christmas of 1944, having fallen ill while on assignment at Columbia Pictures.

CREDITS: In Charge of Production: George R. Batcheller; Producer and Director: Bernard B. Ray; Story: Harry Langdon; Screenplay: Ewart Adamson and Eddie M. Davis; Photographed by: Robert Cline; Art Director: Fred Preble; Editor: Dan Milner; Musical Director: Lee Zahler; Sound Engineer: Corson Jowett; Production Manager: Robert Ray; Running Time: 65 Minutes; Released: April 10, 1942

CAST: Harry Langdon (Bert); Charles Rogers (Alf); Marian Marsh (Florence Randall); Ray Walker (Jerry Fitzgerald); John Holland (Paul Gordon); Betty Blythe (Martha Randall); Richard Kipling (Hiram Randall); Guy Kingsford (Drake); Robert Barron (Samson); Gwen Gaze (Molly); Roy Butler (Carr); Jim Mercer (Copy Boy); Monte Collins (Prof. Stark); Vernon Dent (White); Frank Hagney (Black); Lynn Starr (Waitress); I. Stanford Jolley (Cop)

THE PANTHER'S CLAW
(Producers Releasing Corp.)

Fulton Oursler, longtime editor of *Liberty* magazine and celebrated novelist, had created the potential for a crowd-pleasing movie series in his tales of a no-nonsense police commissioner named Thatcher Colt, published under the pseudonym of Anthony Abbot. This big-screen bow for Colt—nicely played by Sidney Blackmer—proved also to be the character's only such turn.

From its creepy opening in a cemetery to the unmasking of a money-mad criminal, *The Panther's Claw* proves to be a small jewel of a murder-and-blackmail thriller. It all begins with the arrest of a show-business wigmaker named Everett P. Digberry (mousy Byron Foulger) on charges of lurking about a graveyard after hours. Colt and his resident Watson, Anthony Abbot (played by Ricki Vallin), listen patiently to Digberry's account of how he had been ordered to leave $1,000 in the cemetery under threat of blackmail by a character known only as the Black Panther. Other members of Digberry's operatic company have received similar demands. A likely suspect would be tenor Enrico Lombardi (Joaquin Edwards), an unbalanced and violent sort. The police later catch Digberry in a lie, and it is revealed that Digberry's own pet cat had supplied a paw-print used on the blackmail notes. As Digberry hastens to explain himself, word comes in that one of his neighbors has been murdered. The victim proves to be a disguised singer, Nina Politza (Gerta Rozan), and Digberry is quick to remember threats made against her by both her former husband and Lombardi. A rival wigmaker named Wilkins (Frank Darien) turns up dead before he can shed light on the case, and yet Colt keeps an open mind as to Digberry's innocence. Finally, the commissioner accuses Nina's manager, Walters (Barry Bernard), of committing the murders and trying to frame Digberry, and then makes the charge stick. Digberry—whose secretive dealings with Nina can only mean trouble when his vacationing wife and children return home—takes solace in a reward that Walters had posted for the capture of Nina's killer.

Unusually lengthy for a PRC, *The Panther's Claw* boasts a well-tangled set of zigs and zags, almost forcing judgment upon Byron Foulger while piling complications upon complications. The revelation of Foulger as the mock-blackmailer is almost enough to seal his doom, and the real unveiling of self-important Barry Bernard as a thief, frame-up artist and killer comes breathtakingly late.

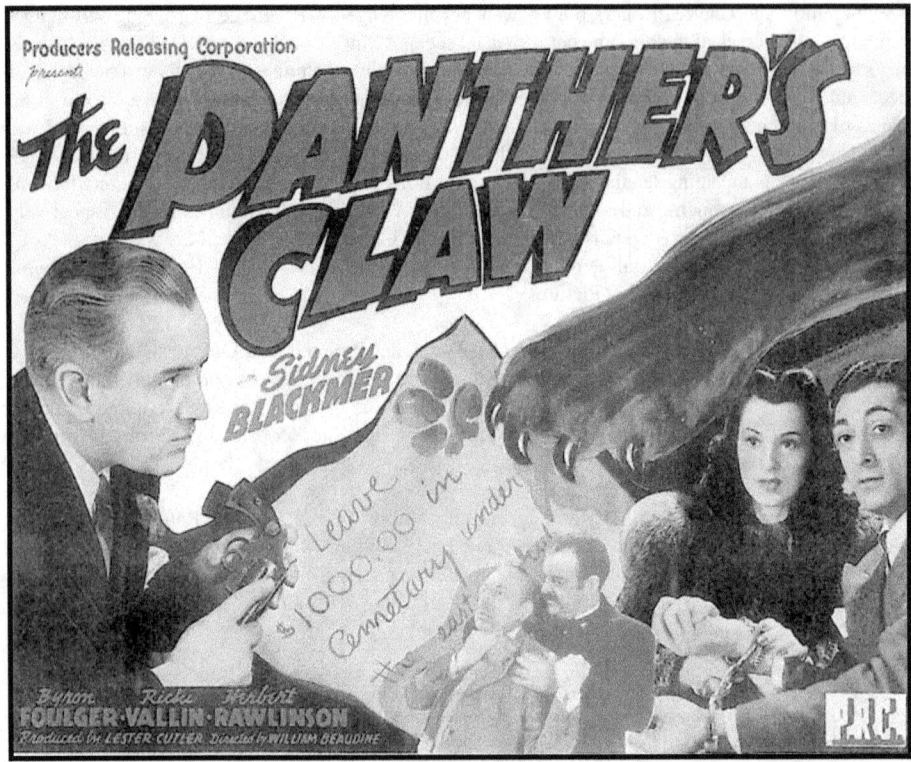

Why an intended series failed to take shape is anybody's guess. Could be because the absence of marquee-value star names prevented *The Panther's Claw* from catching on. Big names or not, Sidney Blackmer makes a fittingly stern Thatcher Colt; Foulger is surprisingly sympathetic as the squirmy little liar whose deceptions have masked his essential innocence; and Joaquin Edwards makes a menacing brute of a red herring.

The Anthony Abbot identity continued to be a moneymaker for Oursler, and a much later Abbot collection, *These Are Strange Tales* (published in 1948), has become an acknowledged classic of crime journalism and flat-out oddball raconteurism. Mike Price's comics adaptation of Abbot's "Vengeance Rents a House," illustrated by Mark Evan Walker, appears in the 1998 anthology, *Southern-Fried Homicide*. Abbot also had a hand in *The President's Mystery*, a multiple-author novel serialized in *Liberty* magazine, based on an idea by Franklin D. Roosevelt. Republic pictures filmed *The President's Mystery* in 1936.

CREDITS: In Charge of Production: George R. Batcheller for Motion Picture Associates, Inc.; Producer: Lester Cutler; Associate Producer: T.R. Williams; Director: William Beaudine; Dialogue Director: Edward Kaye; Original Story, "Shake Hands with Murder," by: Anthony Abbot [Fulton Oursler]; Screenplay: Martin Mooney; Photographed by: Marcel Le Picard; Editor: Fred Bain; Sound Engineer: Ben Winkler; Production Manager: C.A. Beute; Produced at: Talisman Studios; Running Time: 72 Minutes; Released: April 17, 1942

CAST: Sidney Blackmer (Thatcher Colt); Ricki Vallin [a.k.a. Rick and Rik] (Anthony Abbot); Byron Foulger (Everett P. Digberry); Herbert Rawlinson (District Attorney Bill Dougherty); Lynn Starr (Miss Spencer); Barry Bernard (Edgar Walters); Gerta Rozan (Nina Politza); Joaquin Edwards (Enrico Lombardi); John Ince (Capt. Flynn); Martin Ashe (Patrolman Murphy); Walter James (Capt. Henry); Frank Darien (Samuel Wilkins); Joseph M. De Villard (Antonio Spagucci); Jack Van (Giuseppe Bartarelli); William Castello (John Martin George)

Smiley Burnette (left) and Gene Autry in *Home in Wyomin'*.

HOME IN WYOMIN'
(Republic Pictures Corp.)

Gene Autry had found a shortcut to Hollywood stardom in 1935 with a bit part in a horrific Frontier Gothic, Ken Maynard's star vehicle *Mystery Mountain*, and a perhaps premature leading role in a science-fictional/musical Western, *The Phantom Empire*. No point in belaboring here what we've already laid down in *Forgotten Horrors: The Definitive Edition*; the greater point is that, despite his increasing popular acceptance in lighthearted cowboy-crooner fare, Autry still occasionally indulged a taste for the grimmer stuff.

Such a dark treat is *Home in Wyomin'*, an ostensibly nostalgic piece of tuneful rustic Americana that pivots on a finely etched portrayal of paranoid malice by the dependable character man Olin Howlin.

The picture starts off light and breezy, befitting Autry's image, but soon takes on a disturbing subtext: News photographer Clementine "Clem" Benson (Fay McKenzie) and reporter Hack Hackett (Chick Chandler) are hot on the trail of the famous singing cowboy Gene Autry. Gene wants nothing to do with the journalists, for they have made a habit of giving him the razz in print. Gene is more concerned with the troubled fortunes of Pop Harrison (Forrest Taylor), a Wild West show promoter who — according to the fiction of this script — gave Gene his break in show business. Pop's no-account son, Tex (James Seay), is wrecking the company with an appetite for booze and gambling.

Clem and Hack, arriving at the Harrison ranch, promptly bait the drunken Tex into a fight. Tex takes a beating and promises Gene he'll shape up. That evening, Hack slips away to follow three sneaky-looking guests.

A crusty prospector known as Sunrise (Howlin) loses a pouch of gold to Hack in a card game. The other players, Tex and the men Hack had shadowed, seem troubled when Hack boasts that he is aware of the three guests' bad reputations. Their leader, Crowley (George Douglas), is in fact a Chicago mobster named Luigi Scalese. Crowley orders his cohorts to kill Hack, who survives an attempt on his life.

Hack isn't so lucky the next day, when he is shot to death during a staging of Tex's marksmanship show. Tex had been firing blanks, but a sneak intruder now replaces the cartridges with live ammunition. While Gene and his pal, Frog Millhouse (Smiley Burnette), attempt to clear Tex, Clem advises Gene of Hack's suspicions about Crowley. Pop is wounded upon receiving a telegram concerning Crowley's real identity.

Meanwhile, Sunrise leads Clem on a tour of the abandoned gold-mine tunnels underlying the ranch. His eccentric manner becomes more threatening by degrees, and finally Clem learns that Sunrise had killed Hack and fired on Pop because he feared they knew where he had struck gold. Gene arrives just in time to save Clem, and Sunrise falls to his death in a mine shaft.

All ends happily, of course, with Tex making good on his promise to behave himself and Gene and Clem reconciling their differences romantically, but it is the Howlin performance that stays with the viewer. At first, Howlin's crazed miner could almost pass for one of the "ol' funny guy" sidekicks who graced so many matinee Westerns of the Depression and wartime years, but Howlin punctuates the grizzled eccentricities of the role with subtle facial tics and eyeball movements. The suggestion of dementia is easily dismissed at first, but director William Morgan keeps coming back to the character, who seems a bit more haggard, a bit more desperate, every time he shows up. The final confrontation, in an abandoned mine whose depths are as claustrophobically nightmarish as any stretch of Paris Opera catacombs, is a real chiller. Camera chief Ernest Miller gets maximum value out of the contrast between Autry's lighthearted musical sequences and increasingly capable horsemanship and the escalating desperation of the climactic scene.

Autry and sidekick Smiley Burnette are as spirited as ever, although one can only sense a darkness in Autry's portrayal of himself as a celebrity hounded by star-gawking gossip journalists—one of whom is, significantly, killed off while the other becomes a convenient love interest. Chick Chandler is right in his element as the reporter who learns too much for his own good. Fay McKenzie shows plenty of gumption, if not ethical sense, as the aggressive photographer. The question of whether the incognito mobster will be railroaded back to Chicago is left dangling, at least in the prints we've found.

Musical sequences are well placed to keep the story cracking along, but Autry's pre-recorded singing is not always in synch with his mouth. Irving Berlin's war-booster jingle, "Any Bonds Today?" debuts here as a pitch for U.S. Defense Bonds. Autry croons three countrified standards-to-be—his own "Be Honest with Me" and "Tweedle-O-Twill," and the Carter Family's "I'm Thinking Tonight of My Blue Eyes"—and Smiley Burnette contributes a satirical rib-tickler called "Modern Design." In a shortened version that Autry supervised for early-day television, several tunes were eliminated—leaving *Home in Wyomin'* looking altogether more forbidding than when it had graced the big screen.

CREDITS: Associate Producer: Harry Grey; Director: William Morgan; Screenplay: Robert Tasker and M. Coates Webster; Original Story: Stuart Palmer; Photographed by: Ernest Miller; Art Director: Russell Kimball; Assistant Director: George Blair; Editor: Edward Mann; Music Supervised by: Raoul Kraushaar; Running Time: 67 Minutes; Released: April 20, 1942

CAST: Gene Autry (Himself); Smiley Burnette (Frog Millhouse); Fay McKenzie (Clementine Benson); Olin Howlin [elsewhere, Howland] (Sunrise); Chick Chandler (Hack Hackett); Joe Strauch, Jr. (Tadpole Millhouse); Forrest Taylor (Pop Harrison); James Seay (Tex Harrison); George Douglas (Crowley); Charles Lane (Editor); Hal Price (Sheriff); Bud Geary and Ken Cooper (Henchmen); Ted Mapes (Bronc Rider); Jack Kirk (Cowboy); William Benedict (Receptionist); Cyril Ring (Monitor Man); Betty Farrington (Fan); Tom Hanlon (Commentator); Bill Kellogg (Rodeo Hand); Lee Shumway (Bartender); Champion (Autry's Horse); Spade Cooley (Musician); and Roy Butler, Rex Lease, Jean Porter, Stuart Palmer

THE CORPSE VANISHES
(Monogram Pictures Corp.)

Beyond its typically overstated advertising claim of being "unequaled for sheer horror," *The Corpse Vanishes* proves to be the most coherent and suspenseful of the Lugosi Monograms. It pivots on a plausible unfolding, so long as one buys into the implausible situation. It places the customarily

Bela Lugosi abandons Angelo Rossitto to the mercies of the law and/or the L.A. traffic as *The Corpse Vanishes* builds toward a climax.

cold gray weirdness of the loose-knit series at the service of a determined newspaperwoman's campaign to get to the bottom of things. And it gives Bela Lugosi a role that is convincingly torn between sympathetic devotion and sadistic malevolence.

One June bride after another is collapsing at the altar. Each in turn is pronounced dead, and each supposed corpse is stolen within moments. Each is duly delivered to the isolated mansion of Dr. Lorenz (Lugosi), a recluse who requires the young women for an extravagant experiment to restore beauty to his grotesquely aging wife (Elizabeth Russell). Lorenz' household also includes a hag of a servant, Fagah (Minerva Urecal), and her sons, the dwarf Toby (Angelo Rossitto) and the half-witted Angel (Frank Moran). Dr. Lorenz relies on Toby's loyalty, and he and the dwarf take delight in abusing Angel, who harbors a moronic fascination with the lovely, comatose brides whom Lorenz has collected.

Patricia Hunter (Luana Walters), a journalist possessed of ambitions bigger than covering weddings, finds that each of the vanished brides had received a peculiar hybrid orchid from some unknown person. She traces the exotic bloom to Lorenz, a renowned horticulturist, and visits him under the pretense of seeking an interview. Another visitor is Dr. Foster (Tris Coffin), a local physician who works with Lorenz but knows nothing of the secretive experiments. Lorenz' wife angrily rebuffs Patricia, but then becomes unnervingly friendly after a storm forces the reporter to stay the night. Terrified by an intrusion from Angel, Patricia roams the house and finds grim evidence of foul play. Half-convinced that she has dreamed the experience, she is as anxious to leave as she is eager to cinch a connection with the crimes. Lorenz finally loses all patience with Angel and kills him.

Foster helps Patricia persuade her paper to stage a spurious wedding. As the event nears, one of Lorenz' orchids—the source of a trance-inducing vapor—is delivered and confiscated. The case seems

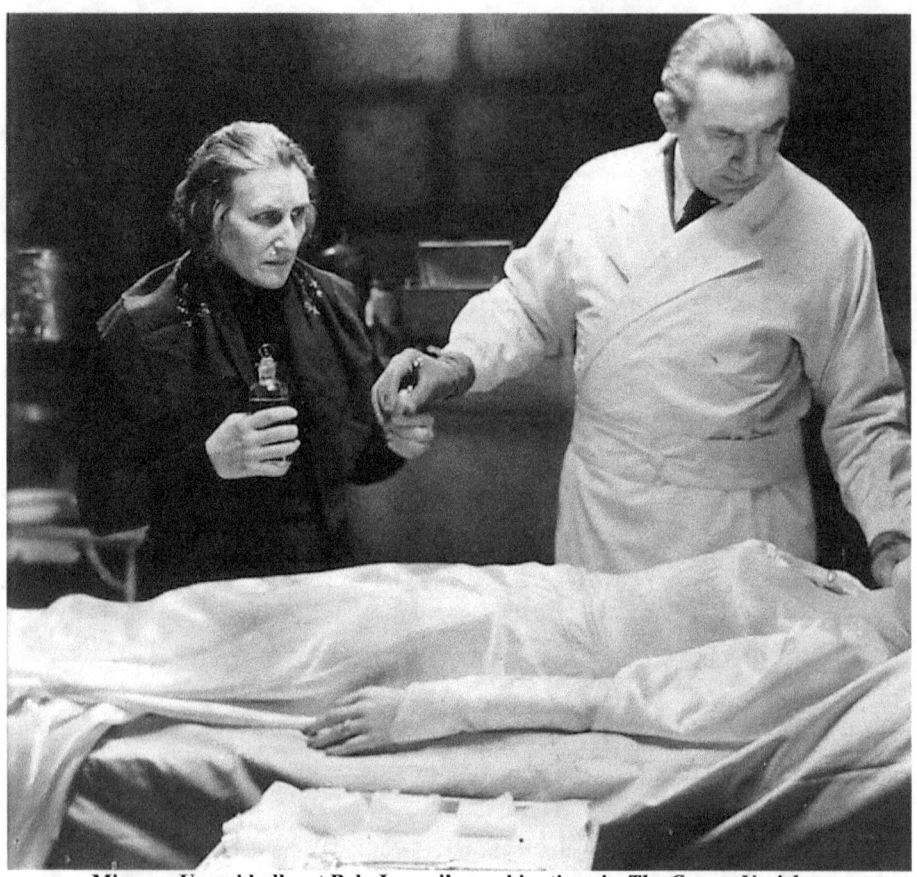

Minerva Urecal balks at Bela Lugosi's machinations in *The Corpse Vanishes*.

all but solved when a desperate Lorenz suddenly appears, accompanied by Toby, and nabs Patricia. Toby, felled by a policeman's gunfire, is abandoned by Lorenz, who rushes home to make Patricia an experimental victim. The vicious Mrs. Lorenz is impatiently awaiting another shot at rejuvenation when Fagah, angered at the loss of her sons, stabs Dr. Lorenz. He retaliates before collapsing in death, and Mrs. Lorenz attacks Patricia—only to be done in by the dying Fagah.

Director Wallace Fox keeps the telling reasonably straightforward for a Monogram spooker, but the eerie qualities are there in spades, too. Elizabeth Russell's introduction as the vain and malicious Mrs. Lorenz is particularly unsettling, punctuated by the most mournful cries of agony this side of Dr. Moreau's House of Pain. The dwarf actor Angelo Rossitto revels in a show of passive sadism, chuckling as a lamebrained sibling suffers a beating at Lugosi's hands. "I loved working with Bela Lugosi," Rossitto told us. "He was a very kind and humorous man, and those *el cheapo* pictures we did together [also including 1941's *Spooks Run Wild* and 1947's *Scared to Death*] were so much fun that we didn't really care whether they'd win us any awards."

Minerva Urecal's spirited performance as the hovering, antagonistic housekeeper is a far cry from her rather disoriented turn as Lugosi's sister in 1943's *The Ape Man*. Minimal comedy relief is entrusted to Vince Barnett, as a photographer who weasels in on the happy ending for a slapstick closing gag. Tris Coffin struggles valiantly with a blandly under-written romantic/heroic leading role; more could have been made of whether he might be in cahoots with Lugosi.

Luana Walters is pleasingly realistic as the frustrated journalist who risks her life to crack a police case—anything to escape a metropolitan newspaper's women's-page ghetto. Extreme as her

Elizabeth Russell, Angelo Rossitto and Bela Lugosi contemplate better living through illicit surgery in *The Corpse Vanishes*.

circumstances are, they echo the genuine experiences of a newspaperwoman named Joan Lowell, whose infiltration of several criminal rackets informed a fine, often lurid, memoir called *Gal Reporter*, published in 1933. Lugosi is his familiar suave-and-sinister self, with an air of world-weary paternalism giving way to a show of real vigor and desperation in the climactic kidnap scene.

Producer Sam Katzman, that *eminence grise* of Poverty Row, was still cranking 'em out on the quick-and-cheap when we encountered him during the mid-1960s on his frequent visits to West Texas. The occasions had less to do with show business than with long-standing friendships: In a classic instance of Small World Syndrome, these ties included Mike Price's theatre-manager uncle, Grady L. Wilson, for whom George Turner had worked during the prewar 1940s; and the retail clothiers Ben and Buck Altman, for whom Price worked as a fashion buyer during 1965-68. Katzman was ever ready to spin a movie-biz story, and he became especially animated when speaking of Lugosi.

"Ol' Bela—what a *mensch*!" Katzman said. "He was a handsome dog, and the picture of class with a capital *K*, I should tell you! Still had the matinee-idol magnetism, even at that 'advanced' age [Lugosi was 59, and Katzman 41, at the time of *The Corpse Vanishes*], and even though he was suffering with a chronic case of sciataca, so he told me, and had got saddled taking some kind of dope that some quack doctor had given him as a 'cure,' he was still smooth as you please, and full of pep as far as anybody could tell. Always ready for anything a picture called for—just give him a two-dollar cigar and let him know he's appreciated, and he's beaming. He sprained his back—threw it out of

"Ol' Bela—what a mensch!" Katzman said. "He was a handsome dog, and the picture of class with a capital K, I should tell you!"

joint, y'know, which had to be extraordinarily painful, in his condition—carrying Luana Walters off in the kidnap scene of *Corpse Vanishes*, but—like I said, a *mensch*. Never griped, and there's *always* been plenty to gripe about with *my* pictures. I wish Hollywood, its big-timers, had treated him better, 'cause there was no way Monogram could've given him what he deserved."

Corpse's photography makes efficient use of Hollywood real estate, especially in the street scenes and in the roadways (ostensibly rural) of Griffith Park. The unusually nuanced musical score includes a funereal organ rendition of Schubert's *Ave Maria*, as well as the bitterly ironic subtlety of a minor-mode version of the traditional wedding recessional.

CREDITS: Producers: Sam Katzman and Jack Dietz for Banner Productions; Director: Wallace Fox; Original Story: Sam Robins and Gerald Schnitzer; Screenplay: Harvey Gates; Production Manager E.W. Rote; Assistant Director: Arthur Hammond; Photographed by: Art Reed; Editor: Robert Golden; Art Director: David Milton; Sound Engineer: Glen Glenn; Musical Directors: Lange & Porter; Running Time: 64 Minutes; Released: May 8, 1942

CAST: Bela Lugosi (Dr. Lorenz); Luana Walters (Patricia Hunter); Tris Coffin (Dr. Foster); Elizabeth Russell (Mrs. [Countess] Lorenz); Minerva Urecal (Fagah); Angelo Rossitto (Toby); Joan Barclay (Alice Wentworth); Kenneth Harlan (Keenan); Gwen Kenyon (Peggy); Vince Barnett (Sandy); Frank Moran (Angel); George Eldredge (Mike); Patrick J. Kelly (Minister); Edward Kane (Police Inspector); Frank O'Connor (Policeman)

Glenn Strange (seated) earned a razzing-for-life from his pal Lon Chaney, Jr., with the title portrayal in *The Mad Monster*.

THE MAD MONSTER
(Producers Releasing Corp.)

"Producers turning out pictures for Producers Releasing Corp., do so on very low budgets," noted *Variety* in March of 1942, emphasizing that PRC's "rentals are proportionately less than for films from the majors." The point was that a cheaply acquired PRC production, though handicapped in terms of production values if not necessarily artistry, could ring the cash registers as surely as some prefabricated hit from the larger studios—if given sufficient general ballyhoo along with the proper push in the direction of its intended audience. A ticket to see something from PRC cost the same cash money as a ticket to see the latest star-power extravaganza from MGM; the little studio's product required extra promotion on the neighborhood-theatre front as a consequence. Where the major-league releases required a hefty guaranteed percentage of box-office receipts, even the newest pictures from PRC could be had for a flat rental of $20 to $25 a day from Oklahoma City-based Adams Film Exchange, which represented many of the Poverty Row studios.

Precisely such a PRC is veteran low-budget producer Sigmund Neufeld's *The Mad Monster*, directed by Neufeld's brother, Sam Newfield, and boasting enough prefabricated appeal in George Zucco to draw the very crowd that would turn out to see Zucco—or Bela Lugosi, or Lionel Atwill, or Boris Karloff or Lon Chaney, Jr.—in practically anything, irrespective of studio pedigree. Today, the tactic of identifying a core group of enthusiasts and catering to them is known as niche marketing, but it

Beyond the Horror Ban

Mild leading man Johnny Downs, at center, reacts appropriately as George Zucco, left, unleashes a transformed Glenn Strange in *The Mad Monster*.

thrived for generations before it received such a highfalutin name. Culturally and historically speaking, it is closely akin to the Southern evangelistic ploy of preaching to the choir in order to generate a frenzy that will attract and convert the curious. The pioneering film historian and lecturer William K. Everson wasn't woofing when he said, often and solemnly, "The cinema is my only religion," and he backed up that assertion with a missionary zeal.

For as any capable niche marketer (or revival preacher, for that matter) will tell you, the practice is ultimately limiting unless coupled with an attempt to broaden a niche by relentless degrees. No doubt some members of *The Mad Monster*'s built-in audience initiated friends into the pleasures of PRC's modest-but-audacious chillers—but it is just as certain that most of the theatres showing the film neglected to heed *Variety*'s advice about courting a more generalized trade.

Theatre managers are a peculiar breed, existing quite apart from normal humankind, and we mean that in the nicest way possible. The view from here is sympathetic as well as jaundiced, of course: George Turner and Mike Price have a combined experience in the picture-show business that stretches from the 1940s into the present day, and they have observed movie exhibition at its best and its worst in the theatremen of four generations. As a general rule, the operators neglect to accept the truth that Film Is Film, and they so compartmentalize their audiences that they lose sight of the fact that they have only *one* audience, a prospective audience that comprises everybody within shouting distance. There is a prevailing contempt toward genre pictures—the very pictures that will draw the most loyal paying customers—and a majority of movie-house operators from 'Way Back Then right up to the

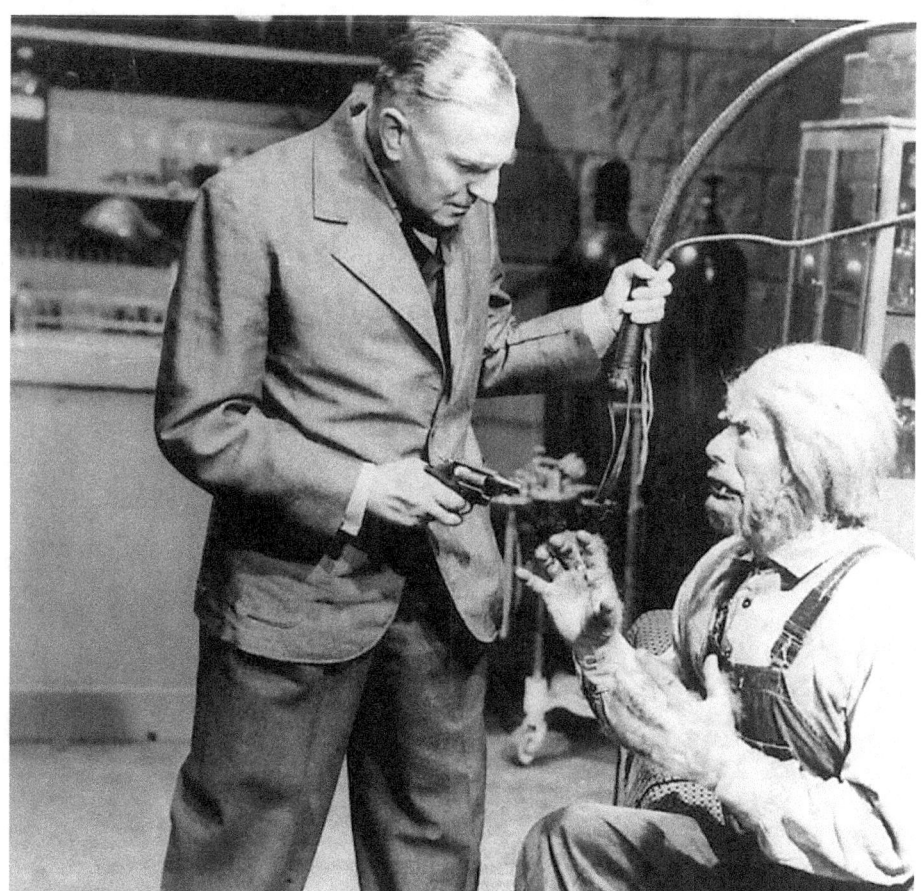

George Zucco pulls a Clyde Beatty routine on Glenn Strange in *The Mad Monster*.

Here-and-Now are as irritated with "having" to play "another damned horror picture" (or Western, or space opera or black-exploitation melodrama) as they are delighted to watch the fans queue up and shell out. This dichotomy reached some kind of a zenith in the summer of 1999, when thousands of managers cringed at the prospect of massed gatherings of fans, days in advance, for the opening of *Star Wars Episode I—The Phantom Menace*, even as they counted the inevitable hundreds of millions of dollars in paid admissions. George Lucas' intergalactic cash cow is an extreme example of niche marketing writ large, a phenomenon that can be traced all the way back to *Variety*'s good advice to push the enthusiasts' anticipation of a film beyond its likeliest customers.

Mike Price's uncle, the West Texas theatreman Grady L. Wilson, was among the few of that breed who actually looked forward to the next low-budget horror movie and took pains to court a general trade for such specialized fare. From the Depression years until his death in 1968, Grady ran his Interstate Circuit showplaces like the short-term getaway resorts they were meant to be, and he especially relished the challenge of pitching a genre-fied movie to a wider range of customers.

"Y'know how we hooked 'em in for *The Mad Monster* down at the ol' Rialto?" Grady asked his nephew after they had watched that very film on television one afternoon around 1960. "You can't depend on the ads to do more than just announce each new title as it comes along, and the critics are useless, more interested in showin' how snide they can be than in givin' their readers some useable information, except when they're suckin' up to some big-deal picture that they know they're *supposed* to get all gushy over.

Glenn Strange presses the advantage over George Zucco at the fiery climax of *The Mad Monster*. And why bother with any denouement when there's all this potential for conflagration?

"Anyhow, what we did with *The Mad Monster* was this: We traded on the bigger audience's fond memories of a somewhat earlier picture called *Of Mice and Men*, and we announced it right there in the lobby and the auditorium that we had this picture coming up soon called *The Mad Monster*, and that it featured this dead-solid impersonation of Lon Chaney, Jr.'s performance in *Of Mice and Men*, plus a takeoff on Chaney's *Wolf Man* in the bargain. This is why theatre managers should attend all the trade-show previews—not to decide whether they *want* to run the picture, but to understand what-all's coming out so they can deal with it when they wind up playing it. You've got no business selling a product if you haven't formed your own opinion of it.

"Now, you may hear people say how they 'hate' horror movies, but what they're *really* saying is that they *don't know how to watch* a horror movie—that they can't be bothered with givin' in to the scary business in the way that they'll give in to the exhilaration of a romantic comedy or the excitement of a war picture," Grady continued. "What it's *our* job to do, is to show people how every film they'll ever see ties in with every *other* film they'll ever see, as a body of accumulated experience, and that whether or not they like this particular movie, it's gonna give them a stronger background for appreciating the films they *do* especially like. Now, *Mice and Men* and *The Wolf Man* are far and away the classier pictures, but this li'l' ol' *Mad Monster* just shows you how lasting an impression Lon Chaney had made.

"See, back in the '40s, once you'd seen a movie in the theatre and it had run its course, the odds were that you'd never get a chance to see it again. No television, and very few official reissues. So for the people that had enjoyed *Of Mice and Men* and expected never to see it again, well, a little throwaway like this *Mad Monster*, it gave 'em a chance to see this other actor do his takeoff on ol' Chaney. Chances are they didn't even like *The Mad Monster* on its own, but we pulled a better box office on it by appealing to that more general audience than we would have if we'd just plastered up the posters and run the ad in the newspapers."

Sam Newfield and his ensemble cast clearly knew what they were doing in making *The Mad Monster* a composite knockoff of Lewis Milestone's *Of Mice and Men* (1939) and George Waggner's *The Wolf Man* (1941), with a twist on *Frankenstein* thrown in for good measure. PRC's publicists failed to pitch any exploitable connection here, however, and the critics of the day were more concerned with their usual gratuitous slamming of horror movies than with noticing the cunning subtexts of this superficially crude and over obvious shocker. Glenn Strange has scarcely the formidable presence of Lon Chaney, Jr., but he mimics the Chaney mannerisms well enough in portraying George Zucco's handyman as a slow-witted, compliant sort. Where the tragedies of Lenny Small in *Of Mice and Men* and Larry Talbot in *The Wolf Man*, both soulfully portrayed by Chaney, capture an Existential sense of doom, their curious amalgamation in *The Mad Monster* amounts dramatically to hardly more than an expendable plot device. Strange brings more to the role than is written, all the same, and the burly Irish-Cherokee actor registers genuine anguish upon finally comprehending his place in Zucco's vicious scheme. It helps to remember that Strange and Chaney were great pals—and that for years to come, Chaney would rib Strange mercilessly about the caricatured Chaney-isms of *The Mad Monster*.

Zucco, second-billed after the bland leading man Johnny Downs, is of course the crucial player here. As a disgraced medic, given the boot from the academic realm for radical experimentation, Zucco troops through the outlandish revenge-*cum*-propaganda yarn with utter conviction, his luminous eyes and resonant baritone voice conveying both the depths of his character's madness and the earnestness of his indignation. The objective here is to waken the beast in civilized humankind, and Zucco's means of doing so is a regimen of wolf-blood injections. Proof of his theories is no longer enough: Having planned originally to present the War Department with "an army of wolf-men," Zucco now will settle for doing away with the scientists who had engineered his ouster.

After a trial run in which the transformed Strange kills a backwoods child, Zucco takes his servant along to confront the estranged colleagues. The campaign of vengeance proceeds agreeably enough until Zucco's rebellious daughter (Anne Nagel) nearly falls prey to the monster. Her news-reporter sweetheart (Downs) stalls Strange long enough for them both to get safely away. The wolf-man strangles Zucco just as a fire, triggered by an electrical storm, sweeps through the scientist's rural Southern mansion.

Its plain production values serve *The Mad Monster* quite well, with a consistently oppressive atmosphere in the imposing house, a fogbound and moss-draped swampland exterior set and an austere and eerily dressed laboratory. Zucco's impassioned emoting would be just as effective on a bare stage: Ham, sliced thick and close-to-the-bone, without the baggage of side-dishes, can be a delicacy. The man-into-beast transformations are elementary time-lapse dissolves, but effective enough in their static way. More impressive, and just as simply accomplished, is a long sequence where Zucco fancies himself embroiled in an argument with his former associates, who appear as ghostly figments of his imagination via deliberately transparent double-exposure photography.

CREDITS: Producer: Sigmund Neufeld; Director: Sam Newfield; Screenplay: Fred Myton; Photographed by: Jack Greenhalgh; RCA Photophone Sound, Engineered by: Hans Weeren; Musical Score: David Chudnow; Art Director: Fred Preble; Makeup: Harry Ross; Editor: Holbrook N. Todd; Assistant Director: Melville DeLay; Production Manager: Bert Sternbach; Special Effects: Gene Stone; Running Time: 77 Minutes; Released: May 22, 1942

CAST: Johnny Downs (Tom Gregory); George Zucco (Dr. Cameron); Anne Nagel (Lenore); Sarah Padden (Grandmother); Glenn Strange (Petro); Gordon Demain (Prof. Fitzgerald); Mae Busch (Susan); Reginald Barlow (Prof. Warwick); Robert Strange (Prof. Blaine); Henry Hall (Doctor); Edward Cassidy (Father); Eddie Holden (Jed Harper); John Elliott (Prof. Hatfield); Charles Whitaker (Police Officer); Gil Patric (Police Lieutenant)

PRISONER OF JAPAN
(Atlantis Pictures Corp./Producers Releasing Corp.)

Arthur Ripley weighed in as a director with this dire hour-and-change of cold-blooded agonies within a microcosm of the Axis menace. As a vicious trifle, *Prisoner of Japan* serves admirably. As a foreshadowing of the doomy themes that Ripley would explore in finer detail in *Voice in the Wind* (1944), *Prisoner of Japan* is a revelation.

David Bowman (Alan Baxter) is known to furloughed sailors visiting the island of Nukuloa as a busy merchant and the husband of a Eurasian entertainer named Loti (Corinna Mura). Actually, Bowman is a prisoner in his own home under the secretive domination of a cruel Japanese spy named Matsuru (Ernest Dorian), whom Loti serves as both consort and agent. Ensign Bailey (Tommy Seidel), one of the guests, carelessly blabs the nature of his crew's mission to Loti, but she reassures him that the information will go no further.

Toni Chase (Gertrude Michael), an American who runs a café on the island, seeks David's help to return to the United States, but he seems strangely disinterested—even when informed of an impending threat to the American fleet just offshore. Matsuru gives himself away when he prevents Toni from transmitting a warning. Bailey's ship is destroyed in a Japanese attack; the ensign survives, but Matsuru orders his execution. Then, Maui (Billy Boya), a child who has given David information on how to escape, is found murdered. David, finally enraged, overpowers Matsuru with the help of Loti, whose loyalties have changed.

While David takes over a hidden radio communications center, Matsuru disposes of Loti. Raising no response from the cautious American convoy, David and Toni realize that they must order the U.S. ships to blast the island. Before Matsuru can break into the radio room, a bomb lands on the compound—killing everyone.

Pictures seldom come any bleaker than *Prisoner of Japan*, and just as well. The exception is usually more interesting than the rule it tests, and this exception is exceptional. Here is a picture in which everybody of consequence meets with foul play, and the cleanup scarcely matters because there is nothing left to clean up.

Ripley offers more than nihilism, however: Ernest Dorian, in his first assignment of a brief but impressive career, makes a grandly loathsome villain, a man of cunning as well as ferocity. Alan Baxter, in the heroic role, seems actually to have lost interest in his or anyone else's rescue—until, after one indignity too many, he transforms himself into an avenging force late in the game. Though necessarily hurried, the wrap-up accommodates a gathering tenderness between Baxter and Gertrude Michael, just enough to render bittersweet their act of self-martyrdom.

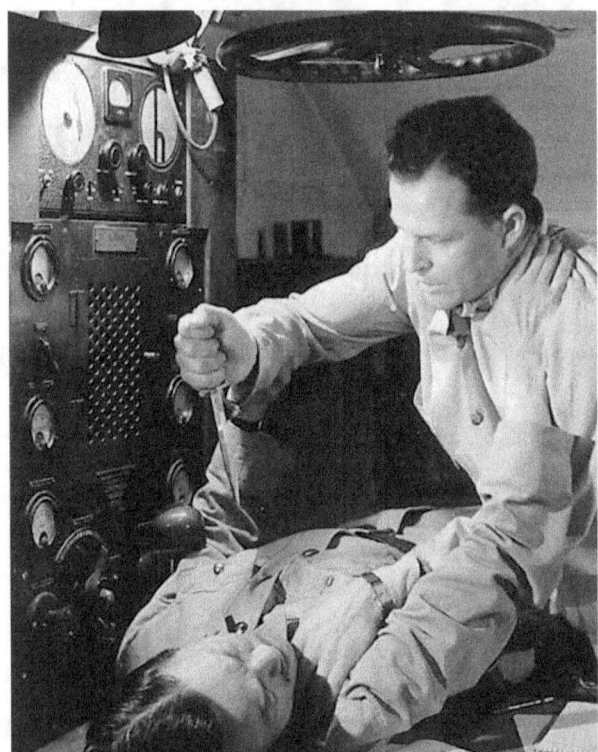

Alan Baxter gains an upper hand over Ernest Dorian in *Prisoner of Japan*. (Photofest)

CREDITS: In Charge of Production: Leon Fromkess; Producer: Seymour Nebenzal; Assistant to Producer: André Dumonceau; Director: Arthur Ripley; Story: Edgar G. Ulmer; Screenplay: Robert Chapin [Given Here as Chapman] and Arthur Ripley; Photographed by: Jack Greenhalgh; Assistant Director: Herman Pett; Editor: Holbrook N. Todd; Musical Score: Leo Erdody; Sound Engineer: Percy Townsend; Makeup: H. Ross; Running Time: 64 Minutes; Released: July 22, 1942

CAST: Alan Baxter (David Bowman); Gertrude Michael (Toni Chase); Ernest Dorian (Matsuru); Corinna Mura (Loti); Tommy Seidel (Ensign Bailey); Billy Boya (Maui); Ray Bennett (Lt. Morgan); Dave O'Brien (Marine); Ann Staunton (Edie); Beal Wong and Gilbert Frye (Radio Men); Kent Thurber (Commander. McDonald)

Ann Corio's burlesque-show fans can only have been disappointed with her limited display of epidermis in *Jungle Siren*. See photo on page 212. (Photofest)

JUNGLE SIREN
(Producers Releasing Corp.)

Nazis! Why does it always have to be Nazis? Because they were *there*, quite simply, and because without an Axis menace, fewer wartime pictures would have had an excuse to get made. Besides, it's not *always* Nazis. Just plenty often.

Ann Corio also was an excuse to make *Jungle Siren*. PRC knew the former burlesque dancer would be a draw, even if cast in a routine underbrush actioner, and the prospect of seeing Miss Corio cavorting in the wild was a sure-fire ticket-seller.

Such motivation can only have led to disappointment for the would-be oglers. *The Hollywood Reporter* lamented that "a handful of long shots...show the striptease queen swimming, but otherwise her display of epidermis is even less than one is accustomed to observing at the seaside."

However, the film does have its ogler-pleasing moments. Buster Crabbe told us in 1971 that he was delighted to have been Miss Corio's leading man in *Jungle Siren*. The rest of us can only envy him the opportunity. (Photofest)

Not much to get excited about in the action department, either. Buster Crabbe is a military officer tracking Nazis and tribal Fifth Columnists in Africa. Miss Corio is a female Tarzan whose parents were killed by a renegade chieftain (Jess Brooks). Crabbe and Miss Corio find romance almost in lieu of the limited mayhem. The handsome leads are well cast for mush and action, but too much of the former and too little of the latter make for a picture that drags when it should be getting on with its slight story.

A helpful sub-story involves a German woman (Evelyn Wahl) who becomes fed up with the treacheries of her sieg-heiler husband (Arno Frey) and suffers as a consequence of her rebellion. A touch of bogus zombieism comes from tribal ruler Jess Brooks' claim that he can return the dead to life; these "dead" are in fact victims of poisoning, stirred by an antidote. The corny finale finds Crabbe radioing for armed personnel—and a chaplain, by the way, so that he and Miss Corio can get hitched on the spot.

CREDITS: Producer: Sigmund Neufeld; Director: Sam Newfield; Story: George W. Sayre and Milton Raison; Screenplay: George W. Sayre and Sam Robins; Photographed by: Jack Greenhalgh; Art Director: Fred Preble; Assistant Director: Melville De Lay; Editor: Holbrook N. Todd; Sound Engineer: Hans Weeren; Makeup: Harry Ross; Production Manager: Bert Sternbach; Running Time: 68 Minutes; Released: August 21, 1942

CAST: Ann Corio (Kuhlaya); Buster Crabbe (Capt. Gary Hart); Evelyn Wahl (Anna Lukas); Paul Bryar (Sgt. Mike Jenkins); Milt Kibbee (Dr. Harrigan); Arno Frey (George Lukas); Jess Brooks (Selangi); Manart Kippen (Maj. Renault); James Adamson (Johnny); Greco (Chimpanzee)

Ricardo Cortez, fresh from a bullyragging by rival mobsters in Edgar G. Ulmer's *Tomorrow We Live*, finds no sympathy for his plight from Jean Parker. (Photofest)

TOMORROW WE LIVE
(Atlantis Pictures Corp./Producers Releasing Corp.)

Ricardo Cortez sets forth one hellacious menace in this rousingly warped gangster thriller. Persuasive to almost a supernatural extent and self-centered to the point of megalomania, the severe combination of villain and romantic lead seems so vastly larger than life that no conventional identity would suit him: Cortez is known simply as the Ghost, so called within the isolated underworld he dominates because he has defied any and all attempts to put him out of the way. And who better to call the Ghost's bluff than an ordinary small-town college girl with plenty of homespun gumption?

This audacious extended confrontation between suave evil and self-possessed common sense is as offbeat a piece as Edgar G. Ulmer ever delivered—in a career that was top-heavy with offbeat assignments. *Tomorrow We Live* is, likewise, as keen a showcase as Cortez ever found for his stock-in-trade arrogance, even during his Depression-era heyday.

Julie Bronson (Jean Parker) feels the stirrings of moral outrage on suspecting a business arrangement between her father, "Pop" Bronson (Emmett Lynn), and the Ghost. Pop tells her she is mistaken, even though his patch of Arizona desert real estate seems plenty busy as a storage depot for the Ghost's hijacking raids. Still tormented by doubts, Julie visits the Ghost at his nightclub—and finds herself enchanted with him. He reveals himself to her as the secret owner of Pop's roadside café. Certain he has Julie in his thrall, the Ghost proposes a romantic arrangement in exchange for her eventual inheritance of his estate. No such luck. But even though she turns down his offer, Julie cannot get the wicked charmer out of her mind.

Jean Parker resorts to brute force as a means of dealing with Ricardo Cortez in *Tomorrow We Live*. **(Photofest)**

Julie's former sweetheart, Lt. Bob Lord (William Marshall), who is stationed nearby, visits. A waitress, Melba, warns Bob that the Ghost has eyes for Julie. So Bob makes certain that he and Julie visit the Ghost's club. Julie and Bob restore their engagement.

The Ghost prevails in an altercation with thugs from a rival mob. When he tries to join Julie and Bob at their table, Julie snubs him. The Ghost retaliates by threatening to reveal Pop's past as an unpunished murderer. A violent intrusion by two thugs (Rex Lease and Jack Ingram) forces Pop and the Ghost to join forces to protect Jean. To placate the Ghost, Jean breaks up with Bob.

But the Ghost has lost too much ground in the mob war. His rivals torch the club and beat the Ghost nearly to death. The gangster accuses Pop of a double-cross, and the men fire on one another. Pop is killed outright, but the Ghost lives on just long enough to hear Julie berate him for his life of misdeeds. Julie decides to try another go at it with Bob.

The critics as a class despised *Tomorrow We Live*. Among the more articulate hostile reactions were *Daily Variety*'s dismissal of the film as "confusing to average minds" and *The Hollywood Reporter*'s claim that the yarn "confuses itself beyond... analysis." The only confused souls here were the critics, their own self-important dimwit selves. No such intolerant bourgeois sensibility, of course, has any business playing critic in the first place, which is why journalism—especially that which assumes a stance of cultural authority—should be a licensed profession. Not bloody likely, of course.

CREDITS: In Charge of Production: Leon Fromkess; Producer: Seymour Nebenzal; Assistant to Producer: André Dumonceau; Director: Edgar G. Ulmer; Story and Screenplay: Bart [Given Here as Bert] Lytton; Photographed by: Jack Greenhalgh; Assistant Director: Melville DeLay; Editor: Dan Milner; Settings: Fred Preble; Musical Score: Leo Erdody; Songs: "Juke Box Girl," by Leo Erdody, and "Señorita Chula," by Ann Levitt and Leo Erdody; Running Time: 64 Minutes; Released: September 29, 1942

CAST: Ricardo Cortez (the Ghost); Jean Parker (Julie Bronson); Emmett Lynn (Pop Bronson); William Marshall (Lt. Bob Lord); Roseanne Stevens (Melba); Ray Miller (Chick); Frank S. Hagney (Kohler); Rex Lease (Shorty); Jack Ingram (Steve); Barbara Slater (Blonde); Jane Hale (Dancer)

PHANTOM KILLER
(Monogram Pictures Corp.)

What few critics paid earnest attention to this small gem of a remake in its day, missed the point entirely by mentioning the "uniqueness" of its plot. *Phantom Killer* is, all the same, about as "unique" as a close copy can get, given its origins in one of the better independent shockers of the Depression years, Phil Rosen's *The Sphinx* (Monogram; 1933). Not that the hidden-twin motif is all that groundbreaking an idea to begin with, but the yarn is a treat in either version, an audacious variation on the theme. Where the story-and-screenplay credit goes to Albert DeMond in *The Sphinx*, Karl Brown is given as author and scenarist on *Phantom Killer*. What with Monogram's corporate ownership of the yarn, one can only suppose it could afford to have a short memory as to authorship. The studio had planned originally to keep *The Sphinx* as the remake's title; another work-in-progress title was the cryptic *Man and the Devil*. The final christening of *Phantom Killer*, which fits the film well enough, was a discarded working title of the Monogram picture that had become *Invisible Ghost*.

The remake's finest touch is the casting of Mantan Moreland, Old Hollywood's most dependable and yet most under-appreciated comedian, as a witness to the crime that sets things in motion. Luis Alberni had served the original quite nicely in the equivalent role of an immigrant janitor, but Moreland transforms an unnerving encounter with the murderer and a panicky discovery of the victim into a miniature showcase for his own scene-stealing efficiency. Here lies the truer uniqueness of *Phantom Killer*: Only his black ethnicity kept Moreland from finding acclaim in his day on a par with that of W.C. Fields and the Marx Brothers. A good test of that truism is to see how sorely Moreland is missed after *Phantom Killer* has dismissed his character.

A prominent citizen named John G. Harrison (John Hamilton, later to become indelibly identified with the Perry White role on television's *The Adventures of Superman*) is brought up on murder charges. Harrison is well known to be deaf and mute, but his accuser (Moreland) swears that the killer had asked him for a light and inquired about the time. The resulting humiliation in court drives an ambitious prosecutor (Dick Purcell) to quit his job.

Moreland's showcase comes in three stages: He reacts to the shock of discovering a corpse by heading straight for a quart bottle of booze and downing its contents in a guzzle. Then, while poring over a book of mug shots at headquarters, he renders a desultory scene at once hilarious and poignant: "Well, looka *there*—High-Pockets Johnson. I *wondered* what happened to *him*. Ol' High-Pockets. He wasn't a bad boy, at that. He was *awful* good to his mother." Finally, in the courtroom, he works the witness stand like a nightclub stage:

"Do you ever drink anything?" Moreland is asked under oath.

"Sho'. *Anything*."

"How much whiskey did you drink that night?"

"Not a *drop*."

"Now, think: That was six weeks ago. How can you be so sure?"

One of the recurring arrests of John Hamilton in *Phantom Killer*.

Beyond the Horror Ban

"Sure that I didn't drink any *whiskey*?"

"Yes."

"Well, *that* night, I was only drinkin' *gin*."

No sooner is the case against Harrison dismissed, however, than such killings resume. At length, it develops that the impaired big shot sets out to establish an alibi while his speaking-and-hearing twin goes about a secretive family trade of murdering for money and/or vengeance. John Hamilton is scarcely a match for the scowling intensity of Lionel Atwill, his dual-role counterpart in *The Sphinx*, but he pulls off the masquerade with a somber dignity and accounts grimly for the disclosure of the brothers' secret. The sudden appearance of twin Hamiltons, each with murder on his mind, gets the point across without recourse to tricky camera angles or extravagant lighting effects; the matter-of-fact presentation is enough.

Dick Purcell is fine as the determined prosecutor, and the delicious Joan Woodbury provides both a romantic function and a crucial narrative pivot as a newspaper reporter who endangers herself by taking a hand in the unraveling. Warren Hymer is right in his element of tough-talking comedy as a hard-boiled detective who is also a henpecked husband, and old-timer Kenneth Harlan stands out as a ranking plainclothesman. Director William Beaudine juggles gracefully the desperate urgency, the broad comedy and the bantering sweetheart business, moving things along briskly enough to sidestep the patent implausibility of the brothers' malicious scam.

CREDITS: Producer: A.W. Hackel; Director: William Beaudine; Story and Adaptation: Karl Brown; Story and Screenplay Credited to: Albert DeMond in the Original Version, 1933's *The Sphinx*; Photographed by: Marcel Le Picard; Editor: Jack Ogilvie; Running Time: 57 Minutes; Released: October 2, 1942

CAST: Dick Purcell (Edward Clark); Joan Woodbury (Barbara Mason); John Hamilton (John G. Harrison); Sgt. Corrigan (Warren Hymer); Lt. Brady (Kenneth Harlan); J. Farrell MacDonald (Police Captain); Nicodemus (Mantan Moreland); Gayne Whitman (District Attorney); George Lewis (Kramer); Elliott Sullivan (Dave Rigby).

THE DEVIL WITH HITLER
(Hal Roach Studios, Inc./United Artists Corp.)

Hal Roach, that beloved big-time producer who outlived most of his star players—even including many *Our Gang* youngsters—by a good many years, found himself reduced to a level nearer Poverty Row during the early 1940s. He had sold out some crucial trademarks to MGM, the big studio with which he had long enjoyed a prestigious releasing deal, and much of Hollywood believed Roach had sold himself out to the very devil in 1937, in an ill-advised filmmaking pact with Benito Mussolini.

The Board of Trustees of Hades goes head-hunting for Adolf Hitler in *The Devil with Hitler*. (Photofest)

"Mussolini wasn't getting a thing out of it," Roach told us shortly after his 100th birthday in 1992. "That is, nothing but a promise of fulfillment for his wish to see some Hollywood-calibre pictures made in Italy." Roach threw a welcoming party for the Italian dictator in Hollywood, whose influential Jewish population rebelled to an extent that Roach said he found "alarming."

"I mean, Mussolini wasn't particularly an anti-Semite, and I told him, going in, that I wouldn't have anything to do with him if he was," said Irishman Roach. "Because he *was* a Fascist, y'know. But I mean, it's like, Italy didn't even have anti-Jewish sanctions until Hitler imposed his 'Jewish problem' on Italy. But I backed out on the deal as it became so plain that our simple artistic and commercial arrangement was creating an international stinkeroo." Roach went on to make such big pictures as *Of Mice and Men* (1939) and *One Million B.C.* (1940), but his resources and his reputation had been diminished to such an extent that Roach became a low-budgeter merely for the sake of staying in the game. His *Streamlined Comedies* series of featurettes issues from this period—distinguished at first by a continuing distribution deal with United Artists (and later, with MGM), but nevertheless afflicted with lesser production values and even shorter running times than were the norm at PRC and Monogram.

Although the U.S. government commandeered many of Hollywood's production facilities as the war built toward an eruption, the Army Air Corps' occupation of the Roach Studios was accepted personally as "a penance, I suppose you might say," by the boss. It was during this period, while two sound stages were filled wall-to-wall with relief maps of Japan and mechanisms to accommodate detailed photography, that Roach mounted a more creative penance: *The Devil with Hitler*.

Alan Mowbray, as a somewhat pitiable Satan, regards Axis honchos George E. Stone, Bobby Watson and Joe Devlin in a publicity shot for *The Devil with Hitler*. (Photofest)

Roach's erstwhile colleague, Mussolini, comes in for a razzing in *The Devil with Hitler*, which starts with a vote among the assembled big shots of Hades to oust Satan (Alan Mowbray) and replace him with Adolf Hitler (Bobby Watson, who would reprise the impersonation in *Hitler—Dead or Alive* and Roach's own *That Nazty Nuisance*). Satan, determined to prove himself still the most malevolent character around, is allowed two days to catch Hitler in an act of common decency. Insinuating himself into Der Fuehrer's circle, Satan provokes the madman into a frenzy of mass-murder. In a sublimely absurd digression involving insurance policies on the lives of Hitler, Mussolini (Joe Devlin) and a Hirohito surrogate named Suki Yaki (George E. Stone), the three spend an inordinately hilarious span attempting to murder one another. Finally, Hitler is manipulated into a deed of near-clemency, and the devil's security is restored. After a bombing, Hitler finds himself a well-tormented inmate of hell.

Yielding easily a laugh a minute, this slight effort affords a clear if warped window into the mass American psyche during the war. The slapstick hilarity never undercuts the essentially embittered anger of the piece, which plays out like some top-notch newspaper's editorial cartoon come to life. The Axis villains are excellently well cast, and Alan Mowbray makes a peculiarly sympathetic Mr. Scratch. Douglas Fowley and Marjorie Woodworth supply a faint romantic relief, as prisoners of Hitler. The film provided more than yocks in its day, however: It vindicated the politically naive Roach in the eyes of those who still might have fancied him an Axis sympathizer.

"I remember those little pictures fondly," Roach said, "but none of the *Streamlined Comedies* turned out, really, to suit me. Probably because my studio wasn't really quite my own, all during the war, there—but we did the best we could under reduced circumstances. And United Artists never really had what it took to sell such a radical concept in short featuremaking." To his last days, Roach maintained that "most features, and especially most comedies, don't really need to be longer than 20, 30 minutes in length, 50 minutes at tops."

The first *Streamlined Comedies* entry, a likewise topical piece called *Tanks a Million*, had come along in 1941. A later *Streamlined*, called *That Nazty Nuisance*, was eventually recut into an expanded version of *The Devil with Hitler*. Roach's broad-stroke fantasy found itself echoed—probably unwittingly so, given the tribal amnesia that afflicts the culture—in 1999, when the animated satire *South Park: Bigger, Longer & Uncut*, portrayed the Mideastern dictator Saddam Hussein as a strange bedfellow for a sissified Satan.

CREDITS: Presented by: Hal Roach; Producer: Glenn Tryon; Director: Gordon Douglas; Screenplay: Al Martin; Treatment: Cortland Fitzsimmons; Photographed by: Robert Pittack; Special Effects: Roy Seawright; Art Director: Charles D. Hall; Assistant Director: Holly Morse; Editor: Bert Jordan; Set Dresser: W.L. Stevens; Wardrobe: Black & Royer; Musical Score: Edward Ward; Sound Engineer: William Randall; Makeup: Paul Stanhope; Running Time: 44 Minutes; Released: October 9, 1942

CAST: Alan Mowbray (Satan); Bobby Watson (Hitler); George E. Stone (Suki Yaki); Joe Devlin (Mussolini); Marjorie Woodworth (Linda); Douglas Fowley (Walter); Herman Bing (Louis); Sig Arno (Julius)

CRIMINAL INVESTIGATOR
(Monogram Pictures Corp.)

Our story so far: Hired as a news reporter only because his daddy is a big shot, arrogant young Bob Martin (Robert Lowery) boasts that he can snag an exclusive interview with a jailed killer named Black (Lawrence Creighton), who is known for stonewalling the press. Bob's editor (John Maxwell) takes the dare, certain that Bob will bungle the job. Bob finds out promptly that Black is deaf and mute—but trumps the deal by resorting to sign language. Black is so impressed with this show of resourcefulness that he leaks an encrypted message, giving Bob a banner story and leading to Black's release.

Bob is assigned next to interview a crooked beauty named Joyce Greeley (Vivian Wilcox). The circle begins drawing shut when Joyce is murdered by Miss Drake (Jan Wiley) and Soapy (Charles Hall), who are carrying out orders from Edward Judson—Black's lawyer. Coincidences start looking less coincidental when Bob rescues Joyce's sister, Ellen (Edith Fellows), from a kidnap attempt. Bob does not comprehend the kinship because Ellen refers to her sister by her christened name, Joan; Ellen is unaware of Joyce's murder. The complications build around a missing set of keys to a safe-deposit vault, and at length a cornered Judson is ready to confess the entire scam when he is killed by a thrown knife. Black proves to be the hidden killer. Joyce's will, naming Ellen as heir, is found in the deposit box.

The female of the species would emerge during the 1940s as a favorite Hollywood menace—a phenomenon that courses throughout our book *Human Monsters: The Bizarre Psychology of Movie Villains* (1995)—but in 1942 no such trend had yet dawned. It peeks through, all the same, in a nice show of murderous malice from Jan Wiley, as a thug enjoying equal status in crooked lawyer John Miljan's mob with such ominous heavies as Lawrence Creighton and Charles Hall. Robert Lowery is a determined greenhorn hero, who stumbles into one situation after another but improvises impres-

Robert Lowery is led to an interview with killer John Maxwell in *Criminal Investigator*.

sively well. Edith Fellows is just right as a wronged innocent who cannot imagine why she should have become a gangland target.

CREDITS: Producer: Lindsley Parsons; Director: Jean Yarbrough; Screenplay: George Jeske; Story: Arthur Hoerl; Additional Dialogue: Edmond Kelso; Photographed by: Mack Stengler; Technical Director: Dave Milton; Editor: Jack Ogilvie; Musical Director: Edward Kay; Sound Director: Glen Glenn; Production Manager: William Strobach; Running Time: 61 Minutes; Released: October 23, 1942
CAST: Robert Lowery (Bob Martin); Edith Fellows (Ellen); John Miljan (Edward Judson); Jan Wiley (Miss Drake); Charles Jordan (Charlie Brannigan); Gloria Faye (Belle); Paul Bryar (Stuart); George O'Hanlon (Powers); Vivian Wilcox (Joyce Greeley); Charles Hall (Soapy); John Maxwell (Brandt); Lawrence Creighton (Black); and Mauritz Hugo

BOWERY AT MIDNIGHT
(Banner Productions/Monogram Pictures Corp.)

Bela Lugosi delivers a chilling variant here on his work in the much better—and better-known—*Dark Eyes of London/The Human Monster* (England; 1939). Director Wallace Fox understands well the urgency of contrasting Lugosi's academic respectability, as an opinionated professor of criminal psychology, with a shabbier secret life as an outwardly benevolent Skid Row missionary. There is a third existence, as well: Lugosi's Prof. Brenner uses the shelter as a front for a campaign of robbery, using expendable thieves. The actor juggles the personalities effectively well, establishing beyond a

John Archer, left, and professor/missionary/ganglord Bela Lugosi in *Bowery at Midnight*.

doubt that, while the slum missionary, who goes by the name of Karl Wagner, is patently a masquerade, there is a dual-personality conflict raging between Brenner the questing intellectual and Brenner the murderous gangster.

Lugosi must have been grateful for this foray into more nearly cerebral territory, for he generously relinquishes the conventional mad-doctor business—and is there really any such thing as a *conventional* mad doctor?—to Lew Kelly, who plays a drug-addicted physician in the service of the Brenner mob. Taking charge of the bodies of all the hirelings whom Brenner has had murdered, Kelly's Doc Brooks sets out to prove himself a genius and secretly begins reviving the corpses. Never mind how.

These morbid complications form the backdrop for what seems at first a bright and adventurous struggle between sweethearts for control of their relationship. Judy Malvern (Wanda McKay) is an innocent helper at the mission, and Richard Dennison (John Archer) is an upper-crust collegian who tries vainly to persuade her to give up the charitable work.

For his class under Professor Brenner, Dennison proposes a study of the psychology of derelict men. Disguising himself as a bum, Dennison is astonished to spot his teacher posing as Wagner. Brenner feigns acceptance of his student's infiltration—and then orders the boy's murder.

Dennison's disappearance kicks the law into action, and at the Brenner home, Officer Pete Crawford (Dave O'Brien) recognizes a portrait of Brenner to resemble the missionary. Brenner's wife (Anna Hope), finally comprehending a reason for her many nights of neglect, is slain by Brenner before she can accompany the cops downtown. Judy, snooping about the shelter with Doc, is interrupted by Brenner, who demands her execution. Trigger man Mills (Tom Neal, three years away from the noir-ified triumph of *Detour*) is too much a gentleman to kill a dame. Mills is slain in a police raid.

Doc, leading Brenner to a hidden passageway, leaves the gang boss to the mercies of a roomful of walking corpses. Dennison, who turns out to have been merely wounded, recovers.

Dark by design and darker by attitude, this ostensible throwaway is yet another striking example of Lugosi's grace-under-pressure. Its tragic complications commence early and build on through the climax when even an outwardly happy ending seems compromised by the taint of evil. Had John Archer's character been written as more of a impulsively determined, modern-dress Beowulf and less as a bored and hapless buttinsky, the role would seem even more like an ancestor of Kyle MacLachlan's performance in David Lynch's masterful *Blue Velvet* (1986), a picture that owes its soul to the B-movie thrillers of the 1940s. Lugosi establishes the professor's confused depravity with a lethal efficiency, ordering the slaying of one trusting henchman after another, but he also underscores the performance with grave self-doubts. It is a performance to relish in a film to relish—a film of modest technical accomplishments but considerable emotional depth and intellectual curiosity. The fashionable sneers that *Bowery at Midnight* continues to inspire tell us, really, more about its critics than about the picture.

CREDITS: Producers: Sam Katzman and Jack Dietz; Associate Producer: Barney Sarecky; Director: Wallace Fox; Story and Screenplay: Gerald Schnitzer; Photographed by: Mack Stengler; Art Director: Dave Milton; Assistant Director: Arthur Hammond; Editor: Carl Pierson; Musical Director: Edward Kay; Sound Engineer: Glen Glenn; Running Time: 63 Minutes; Released: October 30, 1942

CAST: Bela Lugosi (Prof. Brenner and Karl Wagner); John Archer (Richard Dennison); Wanda McKay (Judy Malvern); Tom Neal (Frankie Mills); Vince Barnett (Charley); Anna Hope (Mrs. Brenner); John Berkes ("Fingers" Dolan); J. Farrell MacDonald (Capt. Mitchell); Dave O'Brien (Pete Crawford); Lucille Vance (Mrs. Malvern); Lew Kelly (Doc Brooks); Wheeler Oakman (Stratton); and Ray Miller

OUTLAWS OF BOULDER PASS
(Producers Releasing Corp.)

Sigmund Neufeld's lean-and-angry *Lone Rider* series takes a detour into backwater superstition with this quirky entry, which hangs on supporting player Dennis "Smoky" Moore's impersonation of a ghost—the better to flush out the *hombres* who have tried to kill him, and who long ago had split up his family with the murder of his father. The vigilante Lone Rider (played here by George Houston) and his ol'-duffer sidekick Fuzzy Jones (Al St. John) are more or less just along for the ride, here, with the Rider doing more observing than interfering. (If he's the Lone Rider, then how does he happen to have a sidekick? Just wondering.) Moore and the lovely Marjorie Manners (as an endangered rancher who has no idea of her real parentage) hold the plot in place, and those fine bad-guy players, I. Stanford Jolley and Karl Hackett, account for the villainy, past and present. The finale, where Moore pretends to be his long-dead father in order to spook a confession out of the bad guys, is a keeper.

CREDITS: Producer: Sigmund Neufeld; Director: Sam Newfield; Screenplay: Steve Braxton; Photographed by: Jack Greenhalgh; Assistant Director: Melville De Lay; Editor: Holbrook N. Todd; Sound Engineer: Hans Weeren; Production Manager: Bert Sternbach; Running Time: 61 Minutes; Released: During November of 1942

CAST: George Houston (Tom "Lone Rider" Cameron); Al St. John (Fuzzy Jones); Dennis "Smoky" Moore (Smoky Hammer); Marjorie Manners (Tess); I. Stanford Jolley (Gil Harkness); Karl Hackett (Sidney Clayton); Charles King (Jake); Ted Adams (Sheriff); Ken Duncan (Muley); Frank Ellis (Ringo)

HITLER—DEAD OR ALIVE
(Charles House Productions)

This tongue-in-cheek oddity takes its cue from an advertisement posted in May of 1940 in *The New York Times*: Dr. Samuel H. Church, president of the Carnegie Institute of Pittsburgh, offered a cool million smackers "to the person or persons who will deliver Adolf Hitler alive, unwounded and unharmed into the custody of the League of Nations..." No takers, of course, although Dr. Church reported many responses requesting expenses up front.

Nobody said anything about "dead or alive." That is a cheap-and-easy conceit of the film alone. The threadbare production values prevent such a story from achieving its potential, but dependable Ward Bond is excellent as the leader of a daringly lunkheaded bounty-hunter trio, and director Harry A. "Nick" Grinde proves himself as able a hand at boisterous satire as he had long been at crime melodramas and Westerns. The dark undercurrents are ever-present, even though *Hitler—Dead or Alive* clearly means itself a provocative amusement. A wrongheadedly self-serious curtain speech, probably an afterthought in the picture's long and troubled progress toward release, spoils much of the fun.

Ruffians Steve Maschik (Bond), Dutch Havermann (Warren Hymer) and Joe "The Book" Conway (Paul Fix), fresh out of prison, take up the challenge in short order, hijacking a Canadian Air Force plane and heading for a crash-landing in Germany, where they infiltrate Adolf Hitler's inner circle by posing, variously, as Nazi loyalists and entertainers. There are enough murders and threatened massacres here to establish the evils of the Third Reich beyond dispute, but the element of ridicule is broad to the point of slapstick. The forced irony of the finale involves the shaving of Hitler's famous paintbrush moustache: The dictator becomes a fair target for his own S.S. troopers, who do not recognize Der Feuhrer without the lip-fungus. Finally, the slain Hitler is acknowledged to have been merely a tin god, and the heroes come to understand that the Good Fight is far from finished.

Bond, Hymer and Fix weather the absurdities well, and Bobby Watson makes a convincingly loathsome Hitler, delighted with the suffering that follows his every move. Watson's transformation from arrogant world-beater to sniveling coward is a delight, and no red-blooded American of the war years can have resisted the spectacle of seeing even a fantasy-Hitler facing humiliation as a prelude to death.

Not that all that many Americans, red-blooded or otherwise, were ever treated to a look at the film. A Chicago opening late in 1942 was followed by a long silence, and the film was not even registered for copyright until a year later, when it landed a New York engagement. This commercial failure, coupled with critical notices that neglected to comprehend the joke but seized on every technical failing, must have been daunting to veteran director Grinde. He made only two more features—1943's *We've Never Been Licked* and 1945's *Road to Alcatraz*—and then became exclusively involved with television programs and commercials.

CREDITS: Producer: Ben Judell; Associate Producer: Herman Webster; Director: Nick Grinde; Story: Sam Neuman; Screenplay: Karl Brown and Sam Neuman; Photographed by: Paul Ivano; Art Director: Paul Palmentola; Assistant Director: Bob Farfan; Editor: Jack Dennis; Wardrobe: Emanuel Barton; Musical Score: Leo Erdody; Musical Supervisor: David Chudnow; Sound Engineer: Corson Jowett; Makeup: Harry Ross; Running Time: 70 Minutes; Released: Following Chicago Opening on November 12, 1942; New York Opening Delayed to March 31, 1943

CAST: Ward Bond (Steve Maschik); Dorothy Tree (Elsa); Warren Hymer (John "Dutch" Havermann); Paul Fix (Joe "The Book" Conway); Russell Hicks (Samuel Thornton); Bruce Edwards (Johnny Stevens); Felix Basch (Col. Hecht); Bob Watson (Hitler); Frederick Giermann (Meyer); Kenneth Harlan (Cutler); Faye Wall (Greta); George Sorel (Capt. Kuhn); Myra Marsh (Miss Grange); Eddie Coke (Jimmy); Jack Gardner (Lou)

VALLEY OF HUNTED MEN
(Republic Pictures Corp.)

A murderous rampage by fugitive Nazis propels this *Three Mesquiteers* series entry into a realm of higher interest. As the ringleader, Roland Varno effectively upstages the good guys—played this time out by Bob Steele as Tucson Smith, Tom Tyler as Stony Brooke and Jimmie Dodd as Lullaby Joslin. The venerable Edward Van Sloan stands out as a benevolent German scientist who runs afoul of bigoted mass hysteria.

Captain Carl Baum (Varno) engineers a breakout from a Canadian prisoner-of-war camp. Baum and two fellow goose-steppers promptly cross into Wyoming and begin their killing spree. Rancher Clem Parker (Hal Price) reckons that local Americanized Germans may be helping the war criminals, and suspicion falls on the refugee Dr. Steiner (Van Sloan) and his daughter, Laura (Anna Marie Stewart). Actually, the

Steiners are attempting to aid the Allied cause with their research. The Nazis' ranks eventually dwindle to Baum alone, who kills and then impersonates Steiner's visiting nephew. The complications run thick—what with Baum's abduction by a band of Nazi sympathizers, the disastrous contamination of one of Steiner's experimental formulas and a near-lynching for the good doctor—and the Mesquiteers find themselves relegated to almost a supporting status in their own show. Varno is so effective as the predatory German warrior that his mere capture and confession seem too lenient a resolution.

CREDITS: Associate Producer: Louis Gray; Director: John English; Screenplay: Albert DeMond and Morton Grant; From an Idea by: Charles Tedford; Photographed by: Bud Thackery; Art Director: Russell Kimball; Assistant Director: George Blair; Editor: William Thompson; Set Decorator: Otto Siegel; Musical Score: Mort Glickman; Released: November 13, 1942

CAST: Bob Steele (Tucson Smith); Tom Tyler (Stony Brooke); Jimmie Dodd (Lullaby Joslin); Edward Van Sloan (Dr. Heinrich Steiner); Roland Varno (Capt. Carl Baum); Anna Marie Stewart (Laura Steiner); Edythe Elliott (Elizabeth Schiller); Arno Frey (von Breckner); Richard French (Franz Toler); Robert Stevenson (Kruger).

The Living Ghost takes place amid a disappearance and within a household of grasping relatives and hangers-on. (Photofest)

THE LIVING GHOST
(Monogram Pictures Corp.)

This uneven fusion of horror and wisecracking wit is one of those films that threaten the very institution of Film Criticism simply by existing. A predictably petty backlash against *The Living Ghost* persists to this day, from avoid-at-all-costs tirades in 1942 to snide, review-at-a-glance labels

***The Living Ghost*'s charm today is its very survival as a relic of a time when horror and hokum could co-exist without corrupting one another. (Photofest)**

in the most fashionably ultra-booshwah movies-on-video books. Probably the scariest thing about *The Living Ghost*—as a film fully representative of its modest upstart kind—is that it comes prepared to jolt the assembled community of self-professed Film Critics into a state of inarticulate ridicule. Incapable of couching their dislikes in terms of thoughtful commentary, these ivory-tower snipers concoct meaningless gibberish terms—"BOMB" and "grade-Z" are favorites—to convey a contempt that they cannot be bothered to render eloquent. Which is pretty much what one might expect from a profession that has corrupted a perfectly valid industrial term, *B-movie*, from its truer B-means-budget context to suggest some schoolmarmish grading system.

That said, of course, *The Living Ghost* still has less going for it than even a tolerant viewer might desire. The picture's chief charm today is its very survival as a relic of a time when horror and hokum could co-exist without corrupting one another.

James Dunn is by turns annoying and annoyed as Nick Trayne, an unconventional private eye investigating the disappearance of banker Walter Craig (Gus Glassmire). Within a household of grasping relatives and hangers-on, Craig suddenly reappears—a zombie-fied shade of himself. A physician (Lawrence Grant) determines that Craig has deliberately been afflicted with brain damage. Craig's brother-in-law (J. Arthur Young) is found slain. Craig attacks Trayne, who traces a brain-paralyzing apparatus to the mysterious occupant of a desolate house nearby. Craig's former partner (George Eldridge) and Craig's second wife (Edna Johnson) attempt to kill Trayne as he nears a solution. He turns the tables on the crooks and betrays their scheme: The ex-colleague had posed as a doctor and administered the debilitating treatment, certain that the wife could keep the estate out of the hands of Craig's daughter (Jan Wiley) as long as Craig remained alive but incapacitated.

The picture would have fared better without Dunn's forcibly eccentric portrayal, which nevertheless does not compromise the severity of the investigation. A subplot involving Dunn's romance

James Dunn lays it on think as the excitable hero of *The Living Ghost*. Joan Woodbury wears those horizontal stripes most ably. (Photofest)

with the transformed banker's secretary (Joan Woodbury) exists primarily for the sake of giving the picture a happy ending—happy for the detective, that is. The members of the household are beyond happy endings, here, and so is an incidental victim of the mind-destroying experiment, discovered in an abandoned house during one of the more unsettling sequences. Director William Beaudine handles things with his usual steamroller efficiency, heedless of the ironies of Dunn's laughing-to-keep-from-screaming performance and more concerned with getting on to the next project than with nurturing such a strange yarn to its potential. *The Living Ghost* fails simply on grounds of its being an assembly-line production of a story whose twists deserve a more painstaking development. All the same, enough weirdness flourishes by accident to bear a look.

CREDITS: Producer: A.W. Hackel; Director: William Beaudine; Screenplay: Joseph Hoffman; Story: Howard Dimsdale; Photographed by: Mack Stengler; Assistant Director: Dick L'Estrange; Editor: Jack Ogilvie; Musical Director: Frank Sanucci; Recording Engineer: Glen Glenn; Production Manager: Ben Gutterman; Running Time: 61 Minutes; Released: November 27, 1942

CAST: James Dunn (Nick Trayne); Joan Woodbury (Billie Hilton); Paul McVey (Ed Moline); Vera Gordon (Sister Lapidus); Norman Willis (Cedric); J. Farrell MacDonald (Lt. Peterson); Minerva Urecal (Delta Phillips); George Eldridge (Tony Weldon); Jan Wiley (Tina Craig); Edna Johnson (Helen Craig); Danny Beck (Spieler); Gus Glassmire (Walter Craig); Lawrence Grant (Dr. Bruhling); Howard Banks (Arthur Wallace); J. Arthur Young (George Phillips); Frances Richards (Nurse); Harry Depp (Homer Hawkins)

SECRETS OF THE UNDERGROUND
(Republic Pictures Corp.)

Completing Republic's *Mr. District Attorney* trilogy—even though Republic deliberately removed the *Mr. D.A.* identity—is this weird tale of trunk murderers and human shop-window mannequins, all nicely entangled with Fifth Column intrigues. The picture stands on its own without the series connection, but it remains a mystery why the studio would have jettisoned its tie-in with a popular network-radio program, even though 1941's *Mr. District Attorney* and *Mr. District Attorney in the Carter Case* had not exactly provoked any stampedes to the box office. The pictures had already suffered from inconsistencies of casting, starting with Dennis O'Keefe in the lead and then picking up with James Ellison, and now comes John Hubbard as the star of a series heading smack into a *cul-de-sac*. Maybe no self-respecting B-movie leading man cared to be identified over the long haul with a character named P. Cadwallader Jones.

The film itself is another matter: It's a crackerjack-crisp murder mystery, long on chills with just the right comic-relief grace notes. Hubbard makes a wide-awake "Jonesy," the assistant district attorney who lands smack in the middle of a Nazi scam to flood the market with counterfeit war-tax stamps. Paul Panois (Miles Mander), a French artist, has been kidnapped and forced to create the fakes lest the Third Reich kill his daughter, Marianne (Robin Raymond). Father and daughter escape at about the same time, but Panois turns up croaked inside a trunk that was supposed to contain his counterfeit engravings.

Jones is promoted to D.A., but his news-reporter girlfriend, Terry Parker (Virginia Grey), starts causing trouble because Jones had neglected to clue her in on the murder. Terry is also jealous of Jones' attentions to Marianne Panois. Terry's snooping causes the death of a shipping depot attendant (Olin Howlin), who could have identified one of the racketeers. The reporter keeps up the pursuit, however, and her reckless manipulations finally place Marianne in peril. Dress-maker Maurice Vaughan (Lloyd Corrigan), the leader-in-secret of the gang, knocks out Marianne, wraps her in bandages and places her on view like a mannequin in a display window. Terry's recklessness finally places her own life in peril, and Vaugan and his cohorts make ready to bury Marianne and Terry alive in a silo full of grain. Jones comes to the rescue, then reconciles with Terry.

Lloyd Corrigan offers a splendid show of villainy as the Axis skulker, and Marla Shelton arouses suspicions nicely as an ever-so-patriotic chief of the Women's Defense Corps. John Hubbard and Virginia Grey make much of the antagonistic sweetheart roles in the midst of their competitive sleuthing.

Secrets of the Underground was shot during the autumn of 1942 under three titles, including the generic *Mr. District Attorney* and, invoking a war-boosterism slogan, *Mr. District Attorney Does His Bit*. A later intended title was *The Corpse Came C.O.D.*, without reference to the *Mr. D.A.* franchise. Title-card billing originally contained an acknowledgment of Phillips H. Lord's famous radio series, but this credit was withdrawn without explanation. The series' next screen version came in 1947 with a one-shot Columbia production called *Mr. District Attorney*, with Dennis O'Keefe returning to play the title character—wisely rechristened Steve Bennett.

CREDITS: Associate Producer: Leonard Fields; Director: William Morgan; Screenplay: Robert Tasker and Geoffrey Homes; Story: Geoffrey Homes; Photographed by: Ernest Miller; Assistant Director: Philip Ford; Art Director: Russell Kimball; Editor: Arthur Roberts; Set Decorator: Otto Siegel; Wardrobe: Adele Palmer; Musical Director: Walter Scharf; Running Time: 70 Minutes; Released: December 18, 1942

CAST: John Hubbard (P. Cadwallader "Jonesy" Jones); Virginia Grey (Terry Parker); Lloyd Corrigan (Maurice Vaughan); Robin Raymond (Marianne Panois); Miles Mander (Paul Panois); B. Olin Howlin (Oscar Mayberry); Ben Welden (Joe Martin); Marla Shelton (Mrs. Perkins); Ken Christy (Dave Cleary); Dick Rich (Maxie Schmidt); Neil Hamilton (Harry Kermit); Pierre Watkin (District Attorney Winton); Eula Morgan (Mrs. Calhoun); George Sherwood (Window Dresser); Herbert Vigran (Photographer); Nora Lane (Clerk); Charles Williams (Hypo); Bobby Stone (Messenger); Francis Sayles (Agent); Roy Gordon (John Perkins); Connie Evans (Switchboard Operator); George Chandler (Lynch); Eddie Lane (Bradley); Joey Ray (Harrison); Max Wagner (Baggage Handler); Pauline Drake (Receptionist); Eddy Chandler (Dan); Ben Taggart (Bob)

Afterword

Perfection, or the desire for same, is rather like Mr. Clemens' take on the weather: Everybody talks about it, but—yes, well, *you* know. In a more nearly perfect world, we'd have dragged this volume of *Forgotten Horrors* right on up through 1946 and the popularly acknowledged end of the second major cycle of talkie horror movies and kindred pictures, with (at the Poverty Row studios alone) the last gasps of the more earnest mad-doctor chillers, plus such benchmarks as Frank Wisbar's psychologically ambitious sequel to *The Devil Bat*, and the decisive assertion of an ideally hard-bitten film noir style from within the low-budget sector.

But we're the sort who like to allow our rediscoveries room to breathe and stir and flex their bony elbows. Our arbitrary cutoff with 1942 better serves the pictures individually and as a class, although it leaves the genre—broadly defined—hanging in a protracted state of World War and even divides one major bloc of films, Bela Lugosi's so-called "Monogram Nine," between the present collection and its forthcoming sequel. (And yes, I have wrapped and shipped the manuscript on *Forgotten Horrors III: Dr. Turner's House of Horrors*.)

The word on that next volume is that George E. Turner's exhaustive body of research and deathless enthusiasm for the subject matter will continue to lend style and substance on through our coverage of the 1940s. The third such book even contains some of George's earliest confident attempts at film criticism, as documented in a moviegoing journal he kept while on duty with the U.S. Navy during World War Twice. Which is, as we mentioned at the very beginning, a story for another day.

And shouldn't there *always* be stories for another day?

—**M.H.P.**

Recommended Video Sources

Film-commentary books used to require more faith than participation on the part of the reader. A Bill Everson or a Carlos Clarens could praise or trash this movie or that, given the advantage of those scholarly credentials that would get the bearer past the red tape of the great art museums' moving-picture collections and the studios' archives.

Video has been the great equalizer, starting with the movies-on-television breakthroughs of the post-WWII years and culminating in times more recent with the quick-change pageant of Betamax, CED, VHS and its permutations, laserdisc, CD-ROM and DVD; to say nothing of cable teevee's American Movie Classics, Turner Classic Movies, the Nostalgia Channel, the Western Channel, the Sci-Fi Channel, the Mystery Channel *et cetera, ad infinitum*.

The shirtsleeves movie buff is not only better informed as a consequence—but also more fairly equipped to carry on a dialogue with those of us who are fortunate enough to break into print. Informed disagreement is infinitely more fun than tacit assent, and any published author will tell you that a good argument beats a blank stare any day.

To that end, we encourage the reader to dash out and glom onto as many movies as can be glommed. Some of the choicer sources of B-picture obscurities follow herewith, and we don't really care to discriminate between pristine, supposedly definitive editions and just plain old watchable dubs. It is too easy, in the struggle for digital perfection-plus-commentary-tracks, to forget the simple pleasure of kicking back and watching some movie upon which one never expected to cast one's eyes.

Sinister Cinema—A continuing source of enlightenment in the retro (both -active and -spective) realms, and an early champion of the *Forgotten Horrors* project. Write to Sinister Cinema at Box 4369, Medford, Oregon 97501, or keyword Sinister Cinema on practically any Web search engine.

Bruce Tinkel—This personable mail-order and fan-convention dealer has turned up quite a few helpful reference dubs for the *Forgotten Horrors* books. A slender but impressive catalogue is available from Mr. Tinkel at Box 65, Edison, New Jersey 08818.

Grapevine Video—Continuing growth at this reliable resurrectionist label, with a particularly strong silent-films collection and a fondness for the Depression-into-wartime B-unit and indie pictures. Address: Box 46161, Phoenix, Arizona 85063. The company's name is its search-engine keyword—beats transcribing all those *http*'s and back-slashes.

Facets Multimedia—The massive catalogue is a delight all by itself, with strong concentrations on independents and imports. Address: 1517 W. Fullerton Ave., Chicago, Illinois 60614.

Video Yesteryear—Long-lived source of early-talkie and silent-screen rarities, including many of the *Forgotten Horrors* selections. Address: Box C, Sandy Hook, Connecticut 06482.

Nor should the enthusiast neglect to browse the video outfits that advertise in such magazines as *Filmfax* and *Psychotronic Video*—to say nothing of the innumerable eBay *et cetera* dealers in the cyberspatial arena.

—**M.H.P.**

About the Authors

Michael H. Price is director of movie-theatre operations and programming for the Sundance Square Entertainment District in downtown Fort Worth, Texas, where he presides over the Fort Worth Film Festival and broadcasts a weekly film-review and discussion program over KRLD NewsRadio 1080.

Price earned accreditation as a working film critic—back in the day when one actually had to *work* at becoming a film critic, rather than just contrive to imitate *Entertainment Weekly*'s pernicious name-dropping snark-isms—as an apprentice to George Turner during the preparation of Turner's seminal film-history book, *The Making of King Kong*, during 1968-75. The numerous Turner & Price ventures began in earnest during 1975-79 with the development of the *Forgotten Horrors* project—a groundbreaking volume whose 20th anniversary the authors marked in 1999 with *Forgotten Horrors: The Definitive Edition* for Midnight Marquee Press. From the springboard of Turner's rough notes and partial manuscripts, Price has carried on with the present sequels. He is at work on subsequent entries in the *Forgotten Horrors* series and meanwhile has retooled *The Making of King Kong* as a more expansive genre study called *Spawn of Skull Island*—forthcoming from Midnight Marquee Press.

George E. Turner (1925-1999) was the guiding force behind the original *Forgotten Horrors* collection during the 1970s. He graduated from there to a distinguished career in Hollywood as a cartoon animator, special-effects and scenic-design technician, storyboard artist and occasional character actor and scenarist—in addition to holding forth as editor of *American Cinematographer* magazine and abiding historical conscience of the American Society of Cinematographers. Turner's prior career had been no less distinguished but altogether less cosmopolitan, as a newspaper illustrator and writer, magazine publisher and art-gallery proprietor during 1950-78 in West Texas, where his work caromed wildly between the finer arts and thousands of gloriously lowbrow postal-card gag cartoons. His movie-town work is best represented by the rambunctious main-title sequence of Carl Reiner's *Dead Men Don't Wear Plaid*; the storyboarding and on-location supervision of many episodes of network television's *Friends*; and a starring role in the European-made superscreen-70mm horror film, *Dangling Death*. Turner had begun work on a contents list and a dozen chapters for *Forgotten Horrors II* and *Forgotten Horrors III* shortly before his unexpected demise.

INDEX

-A-
A.S. Barnes & Co. 11
Abbot, Anthony 197-198
Abbott & Costello 103, 118, 137, 144, 159, 189
Abel, Walter 137
Academy Awards (See Oscars)
Academy of Motion Picture Arts & Sciences, The 10, 167
Across the Plains 87
Acuff, Eddie 180
Acuff, Roy 184
Adams, Eadie 48
Adams, Ernie 154-155
Adams Film Exchange 205
Adams, Ted 93, 112, 126
Adler, Celia 59
Adventures of Captain Marvel 74, 150
Adventures of Chico, The 69, 160
Adventures of Kathlyn 74
Adventures of the Masked Phantom 94
Adventures of Superman, The (Teleseries) 215
Adventures of Tom Sawyer, The 124, 161
Africa Speaks 120
African Holiday 37
Alberni, Luis 215
Alexander, Ben 164
Alexander Bros., Arthur and Max 48, 112
Alexander, Richard 53-55, 118
Alias John Law 27
Alice in Wonderland 19
All That Money Can Buy 159
Allen, Judith 43, 60-61
Allwyn, Astrid 149
Almost Married 12
Aloha 20
Altman, Ben 203
Altman, Buck 203
Alvey, Glenn, Jr. 46-47, 106
Amateur Detective (See *On the Spot*)
Amazing Chan & the Chan Clan (See also *Charlie Chan* [Series]) 139
American Cinematographer, The 11, 47, 106-107
American Film Institute 11, 58
American Movie Classics (Network) 231
Amos 'n' Andy 107, 187-188

American Society of Cinematographers 106
Anders, Lynn 41
Anderson, Doris 41
Anderson, Eddie "Rochester" 189
Andromeda Strain, The 76
Angels with Dirty Faces 122
Angkor, or Forbidden Adventure (in Angkor) 13, 44-46, 58, 65
Angry Red Planet, The 58
"Any Bonds Today?" 200
Ape, The 77, 78, 81, 132-133, 138
Ape Man, The 202
Arabian Nights 28
Archer, John 157, 221-222
Armstrong, Robert 26, 77
Army Mystery (See *Criminals Within*)
Arnelo Affair, The 183
Arnon, Ceril 59
Arnt, Charles 148
Arsenic and Old Lace 16
Arson Gang Busters 121
Arthur, Johnny 43
Astor Pictures 155, 185
Atom Man vs. Superman 151
Atwill, Lionel 24, 59, 206, 215-216
Autry, Gene 12, 111, 112, 199-200
Ave Maria 204
Averill, Anthony 97
Awful Truth, The 68

-B-
B.F.'s Daughter 184
Back Street 159
Bad Boy 109
Bahama Passage 178-179
Baldwin, Alec 49
Baldwin, Robert 41
Ball of Fire 159
Bancroft, Henry 177
"Barbershop, The" 54
Barclay, Joan 32-33, 37-38, 56, 191-192
Bardette, Trevor 71
Barlow, Reginald 26, 43
Barnett, Vince 87, 123-124, 202
Barney Google & Snuffy Smith 12, 184
Baroness and the Butler, The 46
Barrat, Robert 83
Barrie, Wendy 136

Barrymore, John 163
Barton, Betty 166
Barton, Otis 83
Batcheller, George R. 164
Bates, Granville 39
Bates, Richard 135-136
Batman (Teleseries) 152
Bau, Gordon 78
Baxter, Alan 210
Baxter, Les 70
"Be Honest with Me" 200
Beast of Berlin (See *Hitler—Beast of Berlin*)
Beasts of Berlin (See *Hitler—Beast of Berlin*)
Beatty, Clyde 75
Beaudine, William 152, 189, 216, 226
Beck, C.C. 150-151
Beebe, Marjorie 61
Beebe, Dr. William 83
Beery, Noah, Jr. 84
Before Dawn 95
Beggars in Ermine 24-25
Behind the Mask 49
Bell, Rex 19
Bell & Howell 47, 106
Belle of Atlanta (See *Who Killed Aunt Maggie?*)
Bennet, Spencer Gordon 88
Bennett, Bruce (See Brix, Herman)
Bennett, Constance 35
Beowulf 222
Bergen, Edgar 61
Berlin, Irving 200
Bernard, Barry 197
Bertsch, Russell 107
Best, Willie "Sleep 'n' Eat" 137, 138, 158, 189
Bettison, Ralph 81
Betz, Mathew (Also as Matthew) 69
Bewitched 182
Biberman, Abner 176
Big Boy Rides Again 168
Billy Carson (Series) 88, 126
Billy the Kid (Series) 94, 125-126
Billy the Kid Outlawed 125-126, 127
Biograph (Studios) 46
Birds, The 76
Black Cinema Treasures: Lost & Found 136, 143
Black Doll, The 12, 62-63
Black Dragons 12, 190-193

Black Friday 137
Blackmer, Sidney 26, 51, 197
Blacks 'n' Jews 9
Blair, Joan 148
Blake of Scotland Yard 37-38
Blane, Sally 118
Blazing the Overland Trail 75
Bleifer, John 179
Blood of Jesus, The 142
Blue, Monte 32, 56
Blue Velvet 68, 222
Bond, Richard 144-145
Bond, Ward 223
Border Devils 19
Borg, Sven Hugo 112
Borg, Veda Ann 128
Borland, Barlowe 83
Bosworth, Hobart 62
Bow, Clara 124
Bowery at Midnight 220-222
Bowman, Laura 111
Boya, Billy 210
Box Office (Trade publ.) 188
Boyd, Wiliam "Bill" 159
Boys of the City 122
Boys Town 42
Bradley, David 165-167
Bradley, Grace 104-105
Bradshaw, Dorothy 90
Brady, Pat 127
Branded a Coward 88
Brandon, Edward 135
Brandon, Henry 113-114, 127
Breakston, George (Also as Georgie) 73
Breen, Joseph I. 45, 68, 69
Brent, Evelyn 33, 91
Bride Came C.O.D., The 56
Bride of Buddha 153
Bride of Frankenstein 10, 107
Brigati, Steve 16
Brincken, William von (Also as Brinken, William von) 57, 103
British Agent 95
Brix, Herman 38, 56, 74
Bromberg, J. Edward 175
Bromley, Sheila 89, 96-97
Bronze Buckaroo, The 109-110
Brooke, Hillary 143
Brooks, Jess 212
Brooks, Shelton (Also as Clarence) 168

Brother Orchid 46
Brown, Charles D. 175
Brown, Helen 148
Brown, Johnny Mack 129
Brown, Karl 148, 215
Browning, Tod 159
Brute Man, The 159
Bryan, Arthur Q. 141
Bryant, Howard 61
Bryant, Joyce 93
Bryar, Paul 130
Buchanan, Larry 143
Buell, Jed 38, 115-116, 186-187
Bufford, Daisy 111
Burgess, Dorothy 23
"Burglar to the Rescue, A" 48
Buried Alive 100-101
Burke, Kathleen 26, 28
Burnette, Smiley 41, 65, 179, 199-200
Burns, Edmond 19
Burroughs, Edgar Rice 28
Burrud, Billy 77
Burton, Frederick 194
Bush, James 51, 71
Bushman, Francis X. 167
Buster, Budd 93
Butterfield, Paul 131
Bwana Devil 184
Byrd, Ralph 37-38, 53-55, 74, 88
Byron, Walter 21, 90

-C-
CBS-TV 107-108
Cabot, Bruce 10, 26-27
Cactus Kid, The 24
Cagney, James 56
Callam, Alex 103, 105, 130
Cannibal Island (See *Gow*)
Cansino, Rita (See Hayworth, Rita)
Capra, Frank 56
Captain America 159
Captain Marvel (Franchise) 195
Carey, Harry 19
Carillo, Leo 18
Carleton, Claire 145
Carleton, George 152
Carmen, Jeanne 62
Carmen Jones 179
Carnegie Institute 222
Carney, Lt. Charles 35

Carr, Jack 179
Carr, Thomas 53
Carroll, Lewis 19
Carroll, Richard 32
Carter Case, The (See *Mr. District Attorney in the Carter Case*)
Carter, Jack 102
Carver, Lynne, 179-180
Cassidy, Ed 161
Castañeda, Movita 50-51
Castello, William 103
Caswell, Capt. Wallace 43-44
Cat and the Canary, The 123, 161
Catlett, Walter 87
Cavanaugh, Paul 23, 24, 177
Caviness, Cathryn 142
Censorship (See also Hays Office; Production Code Administration)14, 30, 45-46
Century of Fantastic Cinema, A 11
Chaffin, Glenn 84
Chaliapin, Feodor 87, 186
Chandler, Chick 199-200
Chandler, George 86
Chandler, Lane 25
Chaney, Creighton (See Chaney, Lon, Jr.)
Chaney, Lon, Jr. 24, 127, 206, 208
Chapin, Jack 25
Chapman, Marguerite 195
Charlie Chan (Series) 14, 79, 80, 132, 138, 160
Chase, Alden 123
Chasing Trouble 93, 103
Check and Double Check 108
Chee-Ak (See Mala, Ray)
Cheers for Miss Bishop 159
Chesebro, George 169
Chester, Hally 122
Children of the Wild (See *Topa Topa*)
Childress, Alvin 108
Chinese Ring, The 80
Chorniuk, Peter 83
Christie Studios (Christie, Al) 109
Chump at Oxford, A 46
Church, Dr. Samuel H. 222-223
Cianelli, Eduardo 41-42
Circus Shadows 25
Citizen Kane 74, 133, 159
City of Missing Girls 149
Clapton, Eric 131
Clarens, Carlos 231

Clark, Mamo 36, 57
Clark, Steve 169
Clarke, David 164
Clarke, Mae 51
Cleveland, George 103
Clifton, Elmer 149
Clive, Colin 15
Cinema of Adventure, Romance & Terror, The 11
Code of the Cactus 93
Cody, Bill and Bill, Jr. 26
Cody, Lew 21
Coffin, Tristram (Also as Tris) 130, 144, 201-202
Coghlan, Frank, Jr. 151
Cohen, Albert J. 137
Cohen, Emmanuel 41
Cohen, Octavus Roy 109
Coleman, Ruth 57
Collier's magazine 57, 79
Collins, Lewis D. 31
Colony Pictures 48, 112
Color Purple, The 142
Columbia Pictures 51-52, 75, 134, 151, 195, 227
Comics Code Authority 46
Compson, Betty 85, 154, 156
Connor, Allen 53
Consolidated Film Industries 75
Conway, Lita 169
Coogan, Jackie 84
Cook, Donald 27, 30
Cook, J.C. "Doc" 66
Cooper, Merian C. 24
Corio, Ann 211-212
Cornish, Dr. Robert 72-73
Corpse Came C.O.D., The (See *Secrets of the Underground* and *Mr. District Attorney* [Series])
Corpse Vanishes 200-204
Correll, Charles 107-108
Corrigan, Ray "Crash" 40, 129, 134, 169
Corrigan, Lloyd 227
Cortez, Ricardo 177, 213-214
Cortez, Stanley 63
Cosby, Bill 144
Costello, Willie 144
Courtney, Inez 33-34, 48
Cowan, Jerome 86
Coyle, John T. 152

Crabbe, Buster 75, 88, 94, 126, 172, 211-212
Crane, Lloyd (See Locher, Charles)
Creighton, Lawrence 219-220
Crime Club (Series) 12, 62-64
Crime Club Productions 62
Crime Doctor (Series) 52
Crime without Passion 66
Criminal Investigator 219-220
Criminal Lawyer 46
Criminals Within 164
Criner, John 135
Criner, Laurence 161
Criterion Pictures 117
Crocodile Dundee 57
Crosby, Bing 41, 131
Cross Country Cruise 12
Crowley, William X. (See Beaudine, William)
Cruze, James 18
Culp, Robert 144
Curry, Louise 126
Curtain at Eight 23
Curtis, Don 164

-D-

Dandridge, Dorothy 109, 136, 178
Dandridge, Ruby 135, 136, 178
Dandridge, Vivian 178
Danger Ahead 118
Danger Flight 84
Danger on the Air 63
Dangerous Lady 68
D'Arcy, Hugh Antoine 21
Darcy, Sheila 92-93, 172
Daredevils of the Red Circle 76
Darien, Frank 197
Dark Eyes of London 140, 220-221
Darkest Africa 75
Darmour, Larry 51-52
Darro, Frankie 13, 40, 91-93, 103, 118-119, 128, 130, 144, 160-161
Darrow, Clarence 18-19, 171
Darwinism 19
Daughter of the Tong 91
Davenport, Harry 86
Davidson, William 50
Davis, Bette 19, 56
Davis, Sammy, Jr. 109
Dawson, Coningsby 41
Day at the Races, A 68, 178

Day, Doris (Both of 'Em) 152
de Castro, Eduardo 70
de Cordova, Leander 96
de la Cruz, Jo 24
de la Falaise, Henri 35
De Maupassant, Guy 27
De Normand, George 38
Dead End 122
Dead End Kids (Series) 122
Deadly Game 164-165
Dealers in Death 97
Death Goes North 89-90
Death in the Air 85
Death Kiss, The 19, 33, 84, 87
Death Rides the Range 112
DeBeck, Billy 184
Defoe, Daniel 36
Dell, Gabriel 122
Deluge, The 60, 69, 74, 88
DeMond, Albert 215
Denny, Martin 70
Denny, Reginald 33-34
Dent, Vernon 98
Derleth, August W. 10
Detour 222
Desert Phantom 129
Devil Bat, The 139-141, 159
Devil Bat's Daughter 141
Devil Diamond, The 40
Devil of the Matterhorn 20
Devil Pays Off, The 174-176
Devil with Hitler, The 216-219
Devil's Daughter, The 8, 101-102
Devil's Mate 177
Devil's Rope, The (See **Devil of the Matterhorn**)
Devlin, Joe 219
Dick Tracy (Franchise) 36, 55, 74, 113
Dick Tracy Returns 74
Dick Tracy vs. Crime, Inc. 88
Dick Tracy's G-Men 96
Dickson, Gloria 169, 171
Dielmann, Henry, Jr. (Also as Harry) 107
Dillaway, Donald
Dilson, John H. 130, 139
Diltz, Charles 72
Disney Studios 76
Dixie National Pictures 116
Do the Right Thing 109
Docks of New Orleans 79

Dr. Christian (Series) 180
Dr. Cyclops 51
Dr. Jekyll & Mr. Hyde (1932) 46-47, 107
Dr. Jekyll & Mr. Hyde (1937) 12, 46-47, 107
Dr. Jekyll & Mr. Hyde (1941) 159
Dr. Rhythm 41
Dodd, Jimmie 223
Donovan's Brain 133
Doomed To Die 81-82, 139
Doran, Ann 164
Dorian, Ernest 210
Dorsey, Tommy 146
Douglas, Don 169
Douglas, George 95, 200
Downing, Joseph 77
Downs, Johnny 209
Doyle, Maxine 53, 55
Dracula (1931) 14, 15, 16, 118
Dracula's Daughter 95
Dragstrip Riot 167
Dream of a Rarebit Fiend 116
Drew, Roland 98, 99, 104-105
Drop Dead! An Exercise in Horror 184
Drums of Fu Manchu 74, 112-113
Du World Pictures 35
Duna, Steffi 32, 98
Duncan, Bud 184-185
Duncan, Ken (Also as Kenne) 126
Dunn, James 83, 225-226
Dunn, Linwood 10
Dwire, Earl 27
Dwyer, Marlow 195

-E-
E.C. Comics 19
Eagle-Lion Films (Also as **Eagle-Lion Studios**) **105, 183**
Eagle's Brood, The 159
East of Java 10
East Side Kids (Series) 122, 173-174
Eastman Co. 15
Eat 'Em Alive 23
Eburne, Maude 31
Eckhart, Alan 166
Edison, Thomas 74, 145
Edwards, Edgar 89-90
Edwards, Joaquin 197-198
Eldredge, Joan 179
Eldridge, George 225

Elfstrom, Katharine 166
Elite Pictures Corp. 182
Ellery Queen (Series) 26-27, 52
Elliott, John 169
Ellis, John 98, 140
Ellison, James 179-180
Elmer Fudd (See Bryan, Arthur Q.)
Emperor Jones, The 23, 158
English, John 196
Erwin, Ted 130
Escape 99, 182
Esper, Dwain 45, 66
Esso, Inc. 57
Evans, Dale 127
Everson, William K. "Bill" 11, 206, 231
Every Day's a Holiday 41
Exhibitor (Tradepaper) 122
Exile Express 86-87
Existentialism 118
Exposure 20-21
Exxon Corp. 57
Eyes Wide Shut 66

-F-

Face on the Barroom Floor, The 21
Facets Multimedia 231
False Faces 21
Famous and Poor 9
Fantomas 74
Farnum, William 19
Farrell, Charles 164
Farrell, William 37
Fatal Hour, The 80, 139
Father Sergius 73
Fawcett Publications 195
Fear 116
Featherstone, Eddie 51, 117, 130
Federal Fugitives 152
Fellows, Edith 219-220
Fenney, Walter 22
Feuer, Cy 159, 172
Field, Mary 134
Fields, Leonard 177
Fields, Stanley 73, 87
Fields, W.C. 54, 101, 179, 215
Fighting Deputy, The 38
Fighting Devil Dogs 74
Fighting Mad 118
Fighting Marines, The 75
Fighting Renegade, The 93

Film Bulletin, The 87
Film Daily, The 65
Film Encyclopedia, The 112
Filmo Topics magazine 47
Fine Arts Pictures 71-72
Finney, Edward 182
Fiske, Robert "Bob" 85, 191
Five 184
Fix, Paul 223
Flaherty, Pat 60
Flash, The (Comics Series) 46
Flash Gordon (*et Seq.*) 75, 150
Flash Gordon's Trip to Mars 15
Flavin, James 92
Fleetwood Mac 131
Fleischer Bros. 151
Fletcher, Bramwell 21
Flint, Sam 195
Flying Serpent, The 141
Foolish Wives 66
Fools of Desire (See *It's All in Your Mind*)
Forbidden Adventure (1931) 46
Forbidden Adventure (1938) 13
Forbidden Adventure (See also *Angkor*)
Forbidden Adventure in Angkor (See *Angkor*)
Forgotten Horrors 10-13, 15, 18-19, 23, 33, 45, 49, 51, 52, 68, 74, 88, 94, 101, 111, 144, 149, 159, 168, 177, 184, 199
Forgotten Mothers 59
Forgotten Silver 45
Forgotten Village, The 146-147
Forbes, Ralph 27
Ford, John 28, 96
Ford, Lee 53-54
Ford, Wallace 162-163
Forrest, Hal 84
Fort Worth Star-Telegram 9, 136
Foster, Norman 31
Foster, Preston 20, 177
Foulger, Byron 39, 67-68, 197-198
Four Shall Die 178-179
Fowley, Douglas 180, 219
Fox Film Corp. (See 20th Century Fox)
Fox, Gardner 46
Fox, Michael J. 119
Fox, Wallace 202
Foxx, Jamie 119
Fra Diavolo 46
Frankenstein (In concept) 194, 209
Frankenstein (1931) 14, 15, 16, 30, 51, 72,

78, 86
Frankenstein (1940) 12, 46-47, 105-107
Frankenstein (Hammer Series) 106
Franklin, Gloria 113-114
Frazer, Robert 164, 191
Freaks 159
Frenke, Dr. Eugen (Also as Eugene) 72-73, 86
Frey, Arno 212
Friedkin, Joel 121
Friedman, Josh Alan 9, 16
Frye, Dwight 77, 118
Fu Manchu (Franchise) 112
Fu Manchu Strikes Again 115
Fugitive Valley 169
Fung, Willis 169
Fury Below 69
Futter, Walter 12, 62, 153-154

-G-
G-Men vs. the Black Dragon 76
Gaines, William "Bill" 19
Gal Reporter 203
Gale, June 40
Gallagher, Lane 25
Gambling Ship 63
Gang's All Here, The 160-161
Gardner, Arthur 85
Gargan, William 31
Garrett, Otis 86
Garrett, Paul 181
General Motors Corp. 181-182
General Service Studios 35
Gentleman from Dixie 163
Georgia Rose 109
Gershwin, George 69
Gest, Inna 123-124
Ghost Creeps, The (See **Boys of the City**)
Ghost Fever 187
Ghostbusters 187
Ghostmasters 22
Ghosts in the Night (See **Spooks Run Wild**)
Ghosts on the Loose 173
Giblin, Charles 31
Gibson, Mel 144
Giermann, Frederick 98
Gillstrom, Arvid 109
Gilmore, Lynne 179
Girl from Scotland Yard, The 41-42
Glassmire, Gus 225

Gleason, Russell 69
Glover, Danny 144
Goff, Norris 184-185
Goldner, Dr. Orville 10
Goldwyn, Samuel 87
Gone with the Wind 56, 136
Goodbye, Mr. Chips 189
Goodbye, Mr. Creeps (See **Professor Creeps**)
Goodman, "Cousin" Herald 169
Goona-Goona: An Authentic Melodrama of the Isle of Bali 21
Goose Step (See **Hitler—Beast of Berlin**)
Gorcey, David 173
Gorcey, Leo 122-123, 173
Gordon, C. Henry 62-63
Gordon, Gavin 31, 162
Gordon, Huntly 27, 80
Gordon, Mary 122
Gorilla Ship 20
Gorilla Woman, The (See **Angkor**)
Gosden, Freeman 107-108
Gottschalk, Ferdinand 25
Gould, William 47-48
Gough, Michael 174
Gow 24
Gow the Head Hunter (See **Gow**)
Gow the Killer (See **Gow**)
Grand National Pictures 57, 71-72, 117
Grand Ole Opry 184
Grandstedt, Greta 60
Grant, Alfred 111
Grant, Lawrence 54, 225
Grapes of Wrath, The 146
Grapevine Video 126, 231
Gray, Linda 83
Gray, Lorna 130
Gray Shadow (Dog) 129
Grayler, Sydney 104
Great God Gold 26
Great Train Robbery, The (1903) 145
Great Train Robbery, The 145
Greed 74
Green, Anna Katherine 31
Green Pastures, The 160
Greenhalgh, Jack 97
Grey, Nan 63
Grey, Virginia 227
Grieg, Edvard 165
Griffith, D.W. 46

Grinde, Harry A. "Nick" 223
Gruenberg, Louis 159
Guhl, George 162
Gun Packer 83

-H-
Haade, William 60
Hackel, A.W. 182, 194
Hackett, Karl 129, 143, 222
Hadley, Reed 65
Hageman, Richard 159
Hagney, Frank 143
Hale, Alan 23
Hale, Rex 97
Hall, Charles 219-220
Hall, Henry 125
Hall, Huntz 122, 173
Hall, Jon (See Locher, Charles)
Halliburton, Richard 153-154
Halop, Billy 122
Halperin Bros., Edward and Victor Hugo 31-32, 62, 96-97, 100, 117, 118
Ham & Bud (Series) 185
Hamilton, John 78, 215-216
Hamilton, Lloyd 185
Hamilton, Neil 26, 64, 152
Hammerstein, Oscar 109
Hargrave, Clarence 188
Harolde, Ralf 177
Harrington, Hamtree 101
Harris, Robin 119
Harlem on the Prairie 110
Harlem Rides the Range 110
Harris, George F. 69
Harvey, Forrester 169, 171
Harvey, Paul 180
Hastings, Henry 186
Hatton, Rondo 159
Haunted House 124-125
Hawk of the Wilderness 76
Hayes, Bernadene 164
Hayes, George "Gabby" 127
Hays Office (Also Hays, Will) 14, 29, 68, 162
Hayworth, Rita 40
Hazards of Helen, The 74
Hearn, Lew 49
Hecht, Ben 66
Hei Tiki 25-26
Hell Bent for Frisco 19

Hell Bound 18
Hell Diggers (See *Fury Below*)
Hell's Angels 84
Hell's Devils (See *Hitler—Beast of Berlin*)
Hell's Headquarters 20
Hell's House 19
Hemsley, Sherman 187
Henderson, Evolution 44
Henderson, Jan Alan 16, 75-76
Heppell, Mitchell 89-90
Herbert, Holmes 63, 79
Herbert West, Reanimator 106
Here Come the Co-Eds 159
Herrmann, Bernard 159
Heston, Charlton 165-166
Heyburn, Weldon 47-48, 164, 172
Heymann, Werner 159
Hidden Enemy 103
High Noon 39
Hill, Harold 26
Hill, Herman 187-188
Hill, Jack 160
Hill, Robert S. "Bob" 33, 37
Hillbillies in a Haunted House (Also as *Hillbillys in a Haunted House*) 159
Hillbilly Blitzkreig 184
Hillie, Verna 27
Hincks, Reginald 90
Hit the Saddle 40
Hitchcock, Alfred 76
Hitler—Beast of Berlin 97-98, 105
Hitler—Dead or Alive 218, 222-223
Hitler's Reign of Terror 97
Hoarse Whisperer, The (See *Horse Whisperer, The*)
Hobart, Rose 22
Hobson, Valerie 73
Hodgins, Earle 129
Hoefler, Dr. Paul 120
Hoerl, Arthur 22
Hoffman, Gertrude W. 134
Hoffman, Max, Jr. 191
Hogan, Paul 57
Hold Back the Dawn 159
Holden, Gloria 182-183
Holden, Lansing C. 95
Hollywood Ho! 107
Hollywood Producers & Distributors 66
Hollywood Reporter, The 83, 88, 115, 136, 183, 189, 212, 214

Hollywood Stadium Mystery 64
Holt, Jack 51
Homans, Robert 47, 161
Home in Wyomin' 199-200
Hopalong Cassidy (Series)
Hope, Anna 222
Hopton, Russell
Horne, Lena 109
Horror, The (1933) 19, 22
Horror, The (Rajah Raboid) 22
Horror ban, British-European 11, 14, 30, 46, 132
Horrors of the Black Museum 174
Horse Whisperer, The 41
Hot Schlock Horror! 22
Houdini, Harry & Mrs. 85
House Committee on UnAmerican Activities 180
House of a Thousand Candles, The 52, 95
House of Dracula 73
House of Errors 68, 163, 196-197
House of Horrors 159, 196
House of Fear, The 63
House of Mystery, The 133
Houston, George 57, 128, 143, 222
How Green Was My Valley 96, 159
Howard, David 65
Howlin, Olin 199-200, 227
Hubbard, John 136, 227
Huber, Harold 51-52
Hughes, Charles 77
Hughes, Lloyd 38
Hull, Warren 50, 103, 121-122, 130
Human Monster, The (See **Dark Eyes of London**)
Human Monsters 11, 26, 219
Hurricane, The 28
Hussein, Saddam 219
Hutchison, Charles "Hurricane Hutch" 72
Hyer, Bill 33
Hymer, Warren 31, 60, 216, 223
Hytten, Olaf 113

-I-
I Conquer the Sea! 31-32
I Cover the Waterfront 46
I Escaped the Gestapo 12
I Killed That Man 177-178
I Spy 144
I Was a Captive of Nazi Germany 97

Ibsen, Henryk 165-166
Igloo 36
Igou, Joan 83
"I'm Thinking Tonight of My Blue Eyes" 200
Ince, Ralph 19, 20
India Speaks (See also **Bride of Buddha**) 153
Ingagi (See also **Son of Ingagi**) 21, 45, 58, 133
Ingram, Jack 214
Inner Sanctum (Series) 64
Inside Information 63
Inside Nazi Germany 97
International Crime 48-49
International Photographer magazine 182
Invisible Agent 28
Invisible Avenger 49
Invisible Ghost 124, 154, 215
Invisible Killer, The 104
Invisible Man Returns, The 63
Invisible Man's Revenge 28
Invisible Ray, The 55
Inyaah the Jungle Goddess and **Inyaah (Jungle Goddess)** (See **Forbidden Adventure** [1938])
Irish Luck 91
Irwin, Boyd 104, 149
Island of Lost Souls 19, 30, 202
Isle of Paradise 20
It Could Happen to You 33
It Couldn't Have Happened (But It Did) 33
"It Feels So Good" 109
It Happened in Chicago 77
It Happened One Night 56
It Happened Out West 33, 43
It's a Mad, Mad, Mad, Mad World 76
It's All in Your Mind 33, 66-68
It's Laughter We're After 107

-J-
Jack and the Beanstalk 159
Jack-the-Ripper 31
Jackson, Peter 45
Jackson, Selmer 47, 175
James, Gordon 130
James, Ida 101
Jamieson Film Co. 142
Jarrell, Edith 107

Jaws 83
Jazz Singer, The 109
Jeffries, Herb 39, 109-111, 115
Jenks, Si 146
Jewell, Isabel 130
Johann, Zita 24
Jolley, I. Stanford 133, 164, 193, 222
John Paul Revere (Series) 41
Johnson, Edna 225
Johnson, Frank (See Darro, Frankie)
Johnson, Lonnie 109
Johnson, Noble Mark 127-128
Jones, Dr. G. William 136, 143
Jones, James B. 142
Jones, Marcia Mae 124, 161
Jones, Thaddeus 183-184
Jordan, Bobby 122
Jory, Victor 49
Joseph in the Land of Egypt 20
Judell, Ben 97
Judge, Arline 185
Judge, Neoma 21
Judson, Edward 40
Julian, Rupert 98
Julius Caesar 166, 167
Jungle Bride 23
Jungle Gigolo, A 22
Jungle Girl 76
Jungle Goddess (See **Forbidden Adventure** [1938])
Jungle Gorillas (See **Angkor**)
Jungle Killer, The 22
Jungle Man 172-173
Jungle Siren 211-212

-K-

Kaaren, Suzanne 140-141
Kaiser, the Beast of Berlin, The 98
Kane, Joseph "Joe" 121, 145-146
Karloff, Boris 12, 13, 14, 15, 53, 59, 77, 78, 81, 107, 114, 132-133, 138, 206
Karloff, Sara 12
Karroll, Dot 95
Katz, Ephraim 112, 167
Katzman, Sam 33, 37-38, 55-56, 61, 93, 122, 124, 151, 203-204
Kay, Edward J. 134, 159
Keane, Edward 194
Keighley, William 56
Kelly, Lew 221

Kelly, Paul 43
Kemp, Matty 95
Keener, Hazel 163
Kendall, Victor 186
Kendis, J.D. 62
Kennedy, Edgar 63
Kent, Crauford 33-34
Kentucky Kernels 159
Kerr, Arthur 90
Kerr, Donald 140-141
Kibbee, Milton 182-183
Kidnapping Gorillas (See also **Love Life of a Gorilla**) 25
Kid's Last Ride, The 169
Kilburn, Terry 169, 171
Kilenyi, Dr. Edward 69, 70
Killer Bats (See **Devil Bat, The**)
Killers of the Sea 43-44
Killers of the Wild (See **Topa Topa**)
King Bros. (Production Company) 177
King, Charles 21, 38-39, 83
King, Claude 33
King, John "Dusty" 129, 169, 185
King Kong 10-11, 26, 51, 83
King, Max 182
King Murder, The 21
King of the Mounties 76
King of the Rocket Men 88
King of the Royal Mounties 76
King of the Zombies 141, 144, 157-160, 161, 186
Kingsley, Sidney 122
Kipling, Rudyard 69
Kirkwood, James 25
Kitchen, Maurice a.k.a. "Rajah Raboid" 22
Kliou, the Killer (See **Kliou [The Tiger]**)
Kliou (The Tiger) 27, 35
Kliou (See **Kliou [The Tiger]**)
Klondike 20
Knaggs, Skelton 96
Komai, Tetsu 19
Kosleck, Martin 175-176, 182-183
Krafft, John 48
Kruger, Otto 169, 171
Kubrick, Stanley 66
Krellberg, Sherman S. 29

-L-

La Roque, Rod 48-49
La Rue, Frank 38

La Rue, Jack 33-34
La Verne, Lucille 25
Lad and the Lion, The 29
Ladd, Alan 98, 99
Ladies in Retirement 159
Lady from Louisiana 178
Lady in the Morgue 63
Laemmle Award 12
Laemmle, Carl, Jr. 112
Laemmle, Carl, Sr. 48
Lane, Lola 18
Lang, Melvyn 81
Langdon, Harry 196-197
Lanning, Reggis 172
Larceny on the Air 39
LaRue, Frank 129
Lasswell, Fred 184
Last Alarm, The 121
Last Command, The 91
Last Days of Pompeii, The 60
Last Express, The 63
Last Mile, The 20
Last of the Redmen 28
Last Warning, The 63
Last Wilderness, The 26
Latell, Lyle 152
Lauck, Chester 184-185
Laughing at Danger 103, 128
Laurel & Hardy 118
Law of the Jungle 185-186
Law of the Sea 19
Lawrence, Marc 88
Lawrence, Martin 119
Lawson, Eleanor 194
Le Berthon, Helene 85
Lee, Spike 109
Leonard, Arthur 101
Leonard, Robert Z.
Leopard Men of Africa: An Exposé of Unrecorded Savage Rituals in the Congo, The 62, 120
Lease, Rex 19, 69, 214
Leavenworth Case, The 12, 30, 31
Lebedeff, Ivan 79
Lee, Christopher 106
Lelong (Dance of the Virgins): A Story of the South Seas 27, 35
Lem Hawkins' Confession 26
Leong, James B. 51
Leslie, Maxine 128

Lesser, Sol 43
Lester, Vicki 145
L'Estrange, Dick 71
L'Estrange, Jill 71
Let 'Em Have It! 26-27
Let's Go Collegiate 161
Lethal Weapon (Series) 144
Levine, Nat 39
Levinson, Mike J. 183
Lewis, Joseph H. 156
Liberty magazine 197
Liberty Pictures 75
Library of Congress, The 22
Life and Death of King Richard III, The 19
Life in the Congo (See **Kidnapping Gorillas**)
Life of a Gorilla (See **Love Life of a Gorilla**)
Life Returns 30, 72-73, 86
Lightnin' Bill Carson (1936) 27, 93
Lightnin' Bill Carson (Series) 93
Lightning Carson Rides Again 93
Lillian, Anna 59
Linaker, Kay 103
Linden, Eric 164
Lion Man, The 28
Little Foxes, The 159
Little Nemo in Slumberland 116
Little Tough Guys (Series) 122
Littlefield, Lucien 65, 84
Live Wire, The 68
Living Ghost, The 224-226
Livingston, Robert "Bob" 39, 40-41, 77, 83, 88, 143
Lloyd, Doris 62
Lobo, the Marvel Dog 29
Locher, Charles 28
Locke, Jack 107
Logan, Phoebe 38-39
London, Jack 96
Lone Bandit, The 25
Lone Ranger (Franchise) 143, 192
Lone Rider (Series) 126, 143, 222
Lone Rider Rides On, The 143
Lone Trail, The 19
Long, Lotus 79-80, 139
Loo, Richard 91
Lorch, Ted 61
Lord, Phillips H. 147, 227

Lorentz, Pare 69
Lorre, Peter 132, 147-148
Los Angeles Times 87
Lost in Alaska 159
Lost in Space 76
Lost Island of Kioga 128
Lost Ranch 61
Love Life of a Gorilla 13, 46, 58, 153
Lovecraft, Howard (Also as H.P.) 105
Lowell, Joan 203
Lowery, Robert 219-220
Lubin, Arthur 31, 137
Lucas, George 76, 207
Lucas, Wilfred 44, 46
Lucky Ghost 115, 186-187
Lugosi, Bela 12, 13, 14, 15, 52-55, 59, 79, 95, 111, 132, 139-141, 152, 154-156, 157, 173-174, 189, 190-193, 200-204, 206, 220-222
Luke, Keye 13, 132, 138, 161
Lum & Abner (Series) 185
Lund, Lucille 32
Lundigan, William 62
Lydecker Bros., Howard and Theodore 55, 75-76, 151, 196
Lydia 159
Lynch, David 68, 222
Lynn, Emmett 213
Lynn, Peter George 80, 84, 100-101
Lyon, Ben 20
Lyons, Harry Agar 114
-M-
MGM 32, 42, 99, 136, 154, 167, 182, 205, 216-217
MacArthur, Charles 66
MacKellar, Helen 146
MacLane, Willa 102
MacQueen, Scott 23
MacDonald, J. Farrell 51, 121-122
MacDonald, William Colt 40
MacLachlan, Kyle 222
Mad Doctor, The 30
Mad Love 154
Mad Monster, The 205-209
Madmen of Mandoras 167
Majestic Pictures 75
Major Pictures 41
Making of King Kong, The 10, 11
Mala, Ray 36
Malatesta, Fred 62

Man and the Devil (See **Phantom Killer**)
Man with Two Lives, The 194-195
Mander, Miles 227
Maniac, The (See **Invisible Ghost**)
Manners, Diane 33
Manners, Marjorie 222
Manors, Sheila (See Bromley, Sheila)
Marin, Edward 62
Mark, Bob 113
Marked Men 129
Markham, Dewey "Pigmeat" 9
Marlowe, John 33
Marsh, Marian 162-163, 197
Marshall, Alan 86
Marshall, William 213
Martel, Jeanne 61
Martin, Al 33
Martinelli, Arthur 83
Marusia 83
Marx Bros., The 178, 215
Mascot Pictures 75
Mason, Le Roy (Also as Leroy) 26, 43, 71, 129
Massen, Osa 175-176
Massey, Raymond 181
Matto-Grosso 23
Maugham, W. Somerset 9
Maxwell, John 219
Maynard, Ken 111, 112, 199
Mayo, Archie 109
Mayo, Frank 20
McCalla, Vernon 179
McCay, Winsor 116
McClennan, Frank H. 142
McClure's Ladies' World magazine 74
McCoy, Tim 93, 112
McCullough, Philo 133-134
McDaniel, Hattie 56
McGowan, J.P. 40
McGowan, Robert 124
McGrail, Walter 56, 126
McGuinn, Joe 126
McGuire, John 155
McKay, Wanda 221
McKee, Lafe 38, 61
McKenzie, Fay 199-200
McKinney, Nina Mae 101
Meaders, Paul 107
Meeker, George 84
Melancholy Dame, The 109

Mèliés, Georges 142
Melnik, Stephania 83
Mercader, George 69
Mercy Island 159, 169-172
Merton, John 69, 114, 126
Mescall, John 86
Metro-Goldwyn-Mayer (See MGM)
Metropolitan Pictures 91
Michael, Gertrude 210-211
Michael H. Price's Hollywood Horrors 11
Micheaux, Oscar 26, 110
Mickey Mouse 112
Middleton, Charles 74, 172
Middleton, Ray 169
Midnight Marquee Press 10, 11
Midnight Phantom 68
Midnight Shadow 134-136
Miles, Art 130
Milestone, Lewis 209
Miljan, John 164, 219-220
Miller, Charles 139
Miller, Ernest 200
Miller, Flournoy E. 115, 186-188
Miller, Ivan 175
Milliken, Carl E. 189
Mine with the Iron Door, The 43
Missing Lady, The 49
Mr. Broadway 23
Mr. Deeds Goes to Town 189
Mr. District Attorney 147-149, 227
Mr. District Attorney (1947) 149, 227
Mr. District Attorney Does His Bit (See *Secrets of the Underground* and *Mr. District Attorney* [Series])
Mr. District Attorney (Series) 147-149, 227
Mr. District Attorney in the Carter Case 149, 179-180, 227
Mr. Moto's Gamble 138
Mr. Washington Goes to Town 102, 115-116, 189
Mr. Wong (Series) 13, 14, 48, 53, 78, 132-133, 138
Mr. Wong, Detective 78-79
Mr. Wong in Chinatown 80
Mitchell, Irving 161, 191
"Modern Design" 200
Mohr, Gerald 151
Monogram Pictures 13, 31, 40, 47, 51, 60, 63, 75, 78, 84, 116, 117, 121, 122, 124, 154, 159, 163, 200-203, 215, 217

Monsters of the Deep 18
Moore, Clayton 191-192
Moore, Dennis (Also as Dennie and Smoky) 88, 92, 123, 173, 222
Moore, Tim 108
Moran, Frank 152, 201
Moran, Jackie 124, 161
Moreland, Mantan 9, 13, 91-93, 103, 115, 118-119, 128, 130, 144, 157-161, 168, 179, 185, 186-189, 215-216
Morgan, Dennis (See Morner, Stanley)
Morgan, William 171, 200
Morhart, Hans von 98, 164
Morley, Karen 41-42
Morner, Stanley 32
Morrison, Sunshine Sammy 124
Most Dangerous Game, The 95, 127
Motion Picture Academy (See Academy of Motion Picture Arts & Sciences)
Motion Picture Association (See Motion Picture Producers & Distributors Association)
Motion Picture Daily 188
Motion Picture Producers & Distributors Association 66, 97, 189
Motion Picture Herald, The 35, 71
Mowbray, Alan 218-219
Mower, Jack
Mulhall, Jack 20, 56, 169
Mummy, The 24
Mura, Corinna 210
Murder at Midnight 79
Murder by Invitation 161-163
Murder by the Stars (See *Invisible Ghost*)
Murder on the Yukon 118
Murphy, Eddie 119
Murphy, Maurice 84
Muse, Clarence 155-156
Music Hath Harms 109
Mussolini, Benito 217-219
Mutiny Ahead 26
Mysterious Bombardier (See *Death in the Air*)
Mysterious Dr. Satan 76
Mysterious Island, The 22
Mystery Channel, The (Network) 231
Mystery Man, The 26
Mystery Mountain 199
Mystery of Life: A Drama of Life as Told by Clarence Darrow 18

Mystery of Mr. Wong 79
Mystery of the 13th Guest, The 159
Mystery of the White Room 63-64
Mystery Plane 84
Mystic Circle Murders, The 84
Mystic Hour, The 68

-N-
N.A.A.C.P. (See National Association for the Advancement of Colored People)
NBC-Radio 147, 181
Nagel, Anne 209
National Association for the Advancement of Colored People 108, 160
Naughty Nineties, The 159
Nazis and Nazi Germany (In proliferation throughout)
Neal, Tom 222
Nelson, Bobby 29
New York *Times* 9, 114, 189, 222
Neufeld, Sigmund 93-94, 97, 99, 126, 129, 143, 205-206, 222
Neumann, Harry 134, 138
Newfield, Sam 38, 88, 93-94, 97, 99, 105, 126, 129, 206, 209
Newill, James 117-118
Newman, Alfred 159
Nigh, William 48, 79, 80, 133, 138, 190, 193
Night Hawk, The 77
Night Rider, The 129
Nollen, Scott 12
Normandy Pictures 28
Norris, Edward 194-195
Nostalgia Channel, The (Network)
Nothing Sacred 39, 56
Noval, Mykola 83
Nugent, Eddie 32-33

-O-
Oakman, Wheeler 20, 96, 100
Oboler, Arch 181-184
O'Brien, Dave 91, 117, 118, 123, 140-141, 163, 221
O'Brien, Florence 188
O'Brien, Pat 19
O'Brien, Willis H. 18
O'Brien-Moore, Erin 31
O'Connell, Arthur 185
O'Connor, Frank 85
O'Donnell, Gene 134, 141

O'Donnell, Joseph 104
Of Mice and Men 100, 146, 208-209, 217
O'Keefe, Dennis 148, 179, 227
OKeh Records 109
Oland, Warner 114, 133, 138
Oliver Twist 95
O'Malley, Pat 84
On the Prowl 13
On the Spot 103, 118-119
One Dark Night 160
One Million B.C. 70, 217
O'Neil, Nance 21
O'Neill, Eugene 66
Orphan of the Pecos 61
Oscars 159, 167, 169, 172, 189
Ouanga 101-102
Our Gang (Series) 43, 124, 216
Oursler, Fulton 197-198
Outlaws of Boulder Pass 222
Outlaws of the Orient 51-52
Outlaw's Paradise 93

-P-
PRC Pictures 12, 40, 94, 97, 105, 159, 164, 183, 196, 197-198, 205-209, 217
Padden, Sarah 162-163, 185
Page, Anita 23
Page, Bradley 179
Palange, Inez 62
Pangborn, Franklin 179-180
Panther's Claw, The 197-198
Paradise Isle: A Romance of the South Seas 50
Paramount Pictures 12, 19, 30, 35, 41, 107, 179
Parker, Jean 213-214
Parks, Gordon 109
Parshley, Prof. H.M. 18
Parsons, Milton 137
Pathé Laboratories 105
Patterson, Elizabeth 136
Pawley, William 49, 118
Pearson, Mr. and Mrs. Harry C. 37
Peer Gynt 165-167
Peer Gynt: A Dramatic Poem 166
Pembroke, George 100-101, 121-122, 177, 191, 193
Pendleton, Nat 21
Penitente Murder Case, The 111
Pepper, Barbara 65

Perils of Nyoka 76
Perils of Pauline, The 74
Perrin, Jack 24
Perry, Lincoln "Stepin Fetchit" 158
Phantom Cowboy, The 27
Phantom Creeps, The 55
Phantom Empire, The 55, 112, 144, 199
Phantom Killer (See also *Invisible Ghost*) 159, 215-216
Phantom Monster (See *Invisible Ghost*)
Phantom of Chinatown 78, 81, 133, 138-139
Phantom of the Opera, The (1943) 137
Phantom Patrol 27
Phantom Rancher 111-112
Phantom Ranger, The 112
Pichel, Irving 39, 53, 56-57, 87, 95-97
Pickford, Mary 70
Picorri, John 36
Piel, Edward, Sr, 191
Pilot X (See *Death in the Air*)
Piltz, George 50
Pine-Thomas Productions 12
Pink, Sidney 58
Pirrone, Johnnie, Jr. 32
Pitts, Michael R. 18
Pittsburgh *Courier* 187
Pitts, ZaSu 180
Pixilated Pictures 106-107
Playthings of Desire 25
Pocomania (See *Devil's Daughter, The*)
Poitier, Sidney 109
Pollard, Bud 19, 22
Popeye the Sailor Man 112
Porgy & Bess 179
Poverty Row 9, 10-12, 16, 19, 37, 39, 40, 56, 73, 86, 89, 93, 112, 117, 133, 134, 145, 153, 157, 203, 216
Powell, Lee 74, 143
Pratt, Sir John Thomas 78
President's Mystery, The 198
Pride of the Plains 41
Private Snuffy Smith 124, 184-185
Price, Babe 47, 106
Price, E. Humphrey 106
Price, Hal 88, 223
Price, Michael H. 9-12, 47, 106, 111, 136, 198, 206-207
Price, Roland C. 29, 111
Price, Vincent 30, 59
Prison Shadows 32

Prisoner of Japan 12, 210-211
Prisoner of Zenda, The 68
Private Live of Ingagi, The (See *Angkor*)
Producers Releasing Corp. (See PRC Pictures)
Production Code Administration 14-15, 45, 68, 69, 97-98, 171, 189
Professor Creeps 102, 111, 115, 186-190
Progressive Pictures (See PRC)
Prouty, Jed 87
Prowler (Comics Series) 13
Public Enemy, The 51
Puglia, Frank 80
Punsley, Bernard 122
Purcell, Dick 157, 159, 215-216

-R-
RKO-Radio Pictures 35, 42, 153
R. Crumb Comix 9
Rags to Riches 146
Rainey, Dr. Bill G. "Buck" 11
Rains, Claude 137, 182-183
Rajah Raboid (See Kitchen, Maurice and *Horror, The* [Rajah Raboid])
Ralston, Esther 51
Ramar of the Jungle 28
Randall, Jack 83, 88
Range Busters (Series) 61, 124, 129, 169
Ranger and the Lady, The 127
Rango 35
Rathbone, Basil 30, 59, 122
Rawhide Terror, The 87-88
Rawlins, Monte "Alamo" 94
Rawlinson, Herbert 37-38
Ray, Arthur 111, 186, 189
Ray, Bernard B. (Also as Ray, B.B.) 67-68
Raymond, Robin 227
Rebellious Daughters 159
Redd, Frances 135
Redford, Robert 41
Reed, Donald 56
Regal Productions/Regal Distributing Corp. 29
Regan, Jane 24
Reid, Dorothy 51
Religious Racketeers (See *Mystic Circle Murder, The*)
Renfrew (Series) 57, 117
Renfrew of the Royal Mounted 57, 118
Renfrew on the Great White Trail 118

Reptilicus 58
Republic Pictures 12, 18, 31, 36, 37-38, 49, 53, 55, 63, 74-75, 112-115, 127, 132, 147, 150, 159, 172, 178, 179, 184, 198
Rescue Squad 27
Return of Dr. X, The 32
Revier, Dorothy 21
Revenge of the Zombies 160
Revolt of the Zombies 32, 97
Reynolds, Craig 80
Reynolds, Marjorie 80, 103, 130, 139
Reynolds, Zachary Smith 23
Rhodes, Gary Don 16
Rice, Florence 148, 179
Richards, Addison 63
Richmond, Kane 29, 40, 195
Richmond, Warner 62
Riders of the Purple Sage 46
Ridges, Stanley 148
"Rikki-Tikki-Tavi" 69
Rin Tin Tin 29, 71
Rin Tin Tin, Jr. 89-90
Ripley, Arthur 201-211
Ritter, Tex 124
River, The 69
Roach, Hal 12, 43, 70, 114, 124, 216-219
Road to Alcatraz 223
Roadman, Betty 67
Roan Group, The 155
Robards, Jason 20
Roberts, Beverly 100-101
Roberts, Lynn 65
Roberts, Julia 55
Roberts, Oral 142
Robeson, Paul 158
Robinson Crusoe 36
Robinson Crusoe of Clipper Island 18, 36, 74
Robinson, Ollie Ann 135
Rochester (See Anderson, Eddie)
Rogell, Albert S. 20
Rogers, Roy 12, 127
Rogues Tavern, The 33, 71
Rohmer, Sax 112-115
Roosevelt, Franklin D. 198
Rose, Ruth 10, 83
Rosemond, Clinton 135
Rosen, Phil 34, 164, 177, 195, 215
Rossitto, Angelo 173-174, 201-202
Rosza, Miklos 159
Rouverol, Jean 31

Rowan, Don 100-101
Royer, Fanchon 85
Royle, William 80, 113
Rozan, Gerta 197
Rub, Christian 124
Ruhl, William
Russell, Elizabeth 201-202

-S-

S O S Coast Guard 15, 52-53, 74, 75, 132
S.O.S. Tidal Wave 88
Sack, Alfred (Also as Al) 109-110, 142
Saddle Mountain Roundup 168-169
Safari on Wheels 57
St. John, Al "Fuzzy" 38-39, 88, 126, 141, 143, 222
St. Polis, John 48, 50, 79
Salisbury, Capt. Edward 24
Salk, Dr. Jonas 134
Saylor, Sid (Also as Syd) 32-33
Scared to Death 202
Scharf, Walter 159, 172
Schary, Dore 41-42
Schechtman, Leo 59
Schoedsack, Ernest B. 10, 24, 35, 51-52, 83, 95
School Daze 109
School for Girls 25
Schorer, Mark 10
Schubert, Franz 204
Schumm, Hans 195
Schwartz, Julius 46
Sci-Fi Channel, The (Network) 231
ScienArt Pictures 73
Scopes, John 19
Scott, Fred 38-39
Scott, Wilton 106
Seay, James 199
Secret Agent K-7 (See *Special Agent K-7*)
Secrets of Billy the Kid 125
Secrets of the Underground 149, 227
Seidel, Tommy 210
Selig Studios 74
Selznick, David O. 42
Sennett, Mack 46, 53
Sgt. York 159
Serling, Rod 181
Shadow, The (Series) 48
Shadow, The (1940)
Shadow, The (1994)

Shadow Laughs, The 22
Shadow of the Eagle, The 196
Shadow Returns, The 49
Shadow Strikes, The 48-49
Shadows of the Orient 51
Shadows over Shanghai 83
Shaft 109
Shannon, Peggy 177
Shark Woman, The 160
Sharpe, Dave 151
She 95
Sheffield, Maceo B. 115, 168, 186, 188
She's Gotta Have It 109
Shelley, Mary W. 73, 105
Sherlock Holmes (Franchise) 122
Sheridan, Frank 31
Sherman, Lowell 21
Shirk, Adam Hull 133
Shock 30
Shores, Lynn 48
Short, Dorothy 91
Show Boat 158
Shurlock, Geoffrey 189
Silver Wolf (Dog) 71
Silverstein, David 177
Simmonds, Leslie 93
Sieg im Westen 99
Silly Billies 159
Simpson, Napoleon 135
Sin of Nora Moran, The 24
Sinatra, Frank 146
Sing Sing Nights 25
Sing Sinner Sing 23
Sinister Cinema 22, 126, 231
Sins of Bali (See *Wajan*)
Siodmak, Curtis (Also as Curt and Kurt) 133
Siren of the South Seas (See *Paradise Isle: A Romance of the South Seas*)
Six-Gun Trail 93
Sixteen Fathoms Deep 24
Skelly, Hal 22
Skinner, Frank 159
Sky Bandits 57, 117
Sky Patrol 84
Sky Racket 38, 55-56
Slaughter, Tod 141
Slave Ship 58
Sleep 'n' Eat (See Best, Willie)
Smalley, Phillips 20
Smith College 18

Smith, Sir C. Aubrey 23
Smoking Guns 112
Snazzy Sixteen 107
Snell, Earle 169
So Ends Our Night 159
Son of a Witch (See *Wajan*)
Son of Frankenstein 15, 53, 79, 107
Son of Ingagi 107-111, 142
Sothern, Hugh 194
Sound Masters, Inc. 182
South Park: Bigger, Longer & Uncut 219
Southern-Fried Homicide 111, 198
Southwest Film & Video Archive 168
Spanish Cape Mystery, The 26-27
Special Agent K-7 56
Sphinx, The 164, 215
Spider Baby 160
Spielberg, Steven 76, 142
Spooks Run Wild 172-174, 202
Spy Smasher 74, 195-196
Stahl, Walter O. 98
Stanley, Louise 83, 118
Stanley, Richard (See Morner, Stanley)
Star Packer, The 129
Star Wars Episode I—The Phantom Menace 207
Starrett, Charles 23
Steele, Bob 21, 27, 111, 126, 145, 223
Stefani, Joseph 118
Steinbeck, John 100, 146
Steiner, Max 159
Sten, Anna 86
Stepin Fetchit (See Perry, Lincoln)
Sternberg, Joseph von 91
Stevens, Eddie 23
Stevens, Onslow 73
Stevenson, Robert Louis 47, 148
Stewart, Anne Marie 223
Stewart, Peter (See Newfield, Sam)
Stoloff, Morris 159
Stone, George E. 219
Stone, Milburn 47-48, 84, 103, 118, 145-146
Storm, Gale 149
Story Teller magazine 112
Straight Shooter, The 94
Strange Adventure (See *Forbidden Adventure* [1938])
Strange Affair of Uncle Harry 116
Strange, Glenn 205-209
Strange Holiday 181-184

Beyond the Horror Ban   251

Strange Interlude 66
Strassberg, Morris 59
Streamlined Comedies (Series) 217-219
Stroheim, Erich von 59, 66, 74
Stuart, Malcolm 148
Stuchkof, Mischa 59
Stunt Pilot 84
Submarine Eye, The 22
Submarine Film Corp.
Sul-Te-Wan, Madame 157, 160
Sullivan, Ed 23
Sun Valley Serenade 178
Sundance Square 13
Sundown 159
Superman (Franchise) 112, 150-151, 215
Supernatural 32, 96-97
Suspicion 159
Sutton, Kay 128
Sutton, Paul 83
Svengali 21, 163
Swan, Buddy 133
Swamp Water 180
Swayne, Daniel 58
Sweeney Todd, the Demon Barber of Fleet Street 141

-T-

Tailspin Tommy (Series) 12, 84
Tailspin Tommy in the Great Air Mystery 84
Tait, Edward 70
Talbot, Lyle 20, 96-97
Tales from the Crypt 19
Tales of Times Square 9
Taliaferro, Hal (See Wales, Wally)
Talk about a Stranger 167
Tallichet, Margaret 175-176
Tanks a Million 159, 219
Tarzan (Franchise) 28
Tarzan (Horse) 112
Tarzan Finds a Son! 172
Taylor, Forrest 32, 61, 93, 122-123, 199
Tearle, Conway 21
Telephone Operator 60-61
Temple, Shirley 33
Terhune, Max 40-41, 61, 129, 169
Terror on Main Street (See *Strange Holiday*)
Terwilliger, George W. 101
Texas Wildcats 94
Thackery, Ellis "Bud" 55, 151
Thane, Dirk 62
That Nazty Nuisance 218-219
That Uncertain Feeling 159
That Woman Is Mine 159
Theatres, Blue Mouse (Seattle) 14
Theatres, Fine Arts (See Theatres, Regina)
Theatres, Interstate Circuit (Texas) 46-47, 105-107, 207
Theatres, Regina (Beverly Hills) 14, 15
Theatres, Rialto (Amarillo, Texas) 207
Theatres, St. Louis (St. Louis, Mo.) 15
Theatres, Victory (Salt Lake City) 15
These Are Strange Tales 198
These Three 124
They Made Me a Criminal 122
They Saved Hitler's Brain (See *Madmen of Mandoras*)
Third Reich (Everpresent herein)
Thirteen Steps 19
Thirteenth Guest, The 47
13th Man, The 47
Thirty Leagues under the Sea 22
This Precious Freedom (See *Strange Holiday*)
Thomas, Jameson 90
Thomas, Johnny 179
Thomas, Lowell 44
Three Mesquiteers (Series) 40, 61, 77, 88, 169, 223-224
Thunderbolt 29
Tinkel, Bruce 231
Titans of the Deep 83
Toch, Ernest 159
Todd, Thelma 20
Tolstoi, Leonid 73
Tomorrow We Live 213-214
Tonto Basin Outlaws 169
Toomey, Regis 51
Topa Topa 71-72
Toreña, Juan 57
Torres, Raquel 20
Torture Ship 95-97
Tower of London 63
Trail of the Silver Spurs 169
Travis, June 77
Trent, John 84
Trigger (Horse) 112, 127
Trigger Fingers 94
Trouble in Morocco 51
Trowbridge, Charles 80
Truman, Timothy 13
Tumbledown Ranch in Arizona 169

Tung Foo, Lee 139
Turner Classic Movies (Network) 231
Turner, George A. 141
Turner, George E. 9, 10-11, 13, 18, 72, 105, 117, 125, 141, 203, 206
Turner, Ray 83
Twain, Mark 118
Twardowski, Hans H. von 98, 99
"Tweedle-O-Twill" 200
Twelve to the Moon 167
Twenty Thousand Leagues under the Sea 22
20th Century Fox 12, 43, 58, 79, 132
21 Beacon Street 32
Two-Gun Man from Harlem 110
Twonky, The 184
Tyler, Tom 61, 150, 223

-U-
Ukrafilm Corp. 83
Ulmer, Edgar G. 20, 213-214
Ulrich, Charles 77
Umann, Emil 14
Uncertain Woman 41
Underworld 91
United Artists Corp. 62, 217
Universal Pictures 12, 14, 15, 18, 36, 53, 55, 64, 73, 75, 76, 78, 84, 86, 116, 122
Unwritten Law, The 21
Up in the Air 130
Up Jumped the Devil 115, 168
Urecal, Minerva 123, 201-202, 204
Usher, Guy 81, 128

-V-
Valley of Hunted Men 223-224
Valley of Vengeance 88
Vallin, Rick (Also as Ricki and Ric) 197
Vampires, Les 74
Van Peebles, Melvyn 109, 160
Van Sloan, Edward 15, 223
Van Zandt, Philip 149
Vanishing Riders 26
Varconi, Victor 152
Variety 22, 29, 35, 46, 56, 64, 65, 87, 88, 91, 97, 120, 136, 153, 154, 160, 161, 162, 194, 205-207
Varno, Roland 175, 223
Venable, Evelyn 64-65
Victor, Henry 157-160
Victory in the West (See *Sieg im Westen*)

Victory Pictures 37, 93
Video Yesteryear 231
Vigran, Herbert 162
Virgin of Sarawak, The (See *Forbidden Adventure* [1938])
Virginia Judge 109
Virgins of Bali 22
Vlahos, John 169
Voice from the Sky, The 18
Voice in the Wind 210-211
Voodoo 101
Vorhaus, Bernard 180
Voyage to the Bottom of the Sea 75-76
Vu Iz Mayn Kind? 59

-W-
Waggner, George 139, 209
Wahl, Evelyn 212
Wajan 72
Wales, Wally 18, 145
Walker, Mark 22
Walker, Mark Evan 198
Walker, Terry 155
Walker, Tish 107
Wallaby Jim of the Islands 57-58
Wallace, Edgar 41
Wallace, Emmett 102
Wallace, Morgan 79
Wallington, Jimmy 64-65
Walters, Luana 114, 129, 201, 203-204
Walthall, H.B. 43
Walton, Douglas 32, 57
War of the Worlds, The (Radio Dramatization) 88
Ward, Arthur Sarsfield (See Rohmer, Sax)
Ward, Edward 159
Warner Bros. 109, 134
Warner, H.B. 149
Warner, John 149
Warner-Allender Roadshow Attractions 66
Washburn, Bryant 33, 84
Waterfront 32
Watermelon Man 109, 160
Waters, Muddy 131
Watkin, Pierre 39, 50
Watson, Bobby 218-219, 223
Watson, Minor 148
Waxman, Franz 159
Wayne, John 19, 40, 77, 111
Weaver Bros. & Elviry 184

Webster, Pete 136, 179
Weiss, Louis 129
Welles, Orson 47, 74, 88
Wellman, William 39, 56
Wells, Carveth 22
Wells, H.G. 88
Wells, Jacqueline 96-97, 127
Wells, Ted 27
West, Joseph (See Waggner, George)
West, Mae 41
West of the Divide 19
Western Channel, The (Network) 231
Westland Case, The 63
Wetjen, Richard 57
We've Never Been Licked 223
Whales, James 158
What Happened to Mary? 74
What Price Decency? 23
Where Is My Child? (See *Vu Iz Mayn Kind?*)
Whipper, Leigh 157, 160
Whistler, The (Series) 52
White, Alice 60
White, Pearl 74
White Zombie 31, 54, 62, 96, 117
Whitten, Marguerite 157-158
Who Killed Aunt Maggie? 136-138
Wilcox, Robert 100-101
Wilcox, Vivian 219
Wild Horse Phantom 94, 141
Wiley, Hugh 79, 132
Wiley, Jan 219, 225
Wilkerson, Guy 173
Williams, Bert 109
Williams, Clark 84
Williams, Guinn "Big Boy" 168-169
Williams, Spencer Jr. 9, 13, 107-111, 142
Williams, Ted 121
Williams, Zack 111
Williamson, J. Ernest 22
Williamson, Lilah 22
Williamson, Sylvia 22
Willow Corp., The 167
Willson, Meredith 159
Wilson, Charles 152
Wilson, Grady L. 47, 203, 207-208
Wilson, Lois 73
Winstead, Col. Hubert 58
Winters, Roland 79
Wise, Ray (See Mala, Ray)
With Williamson beneath the Sea: Adventures

Among the Mysteries & Monsters of the Deep 22
Withers, Grant 60, 79, 80, 81, 91, 93, 139
Witney, William 196
Witness Vanishes, The 64
Wolf Man (Series) 133, 209
Wolf Man, The 209
Wolves of the Sea 62
Woman Alone, A 86
Wood, Edward D., Jr. 9
Woodard Bros., Horace and Stacy 69, 160
Woodbury, Joan 159, 177, 216, 226
Woods, Buck 135-136
Woods, Donald 62-63
Woodworth, Marjorie *219*
Wooley, John 16, 22
World War II (Throughout the work)
Worst!, The 9
Worth, Constance 164
Worth, Harry 27, 105
Wrangler's Roost 169
Wray, Fay 10
Wray, John 63
Wright, Harold Bell 43
Wright, William 174-176
Wrixon, Maris 133-134

-Y-

Yarbrough, Jean 141, 159, 186
Yates, Herbert J. 75, 148
"Yellow Mellow Moon" 39
Yellow Peril 19, 51, 83, 112, 115
Yiskor 20
York, Erskine Laurie 117
Young Blood 21
Young, Carleton 126
Young, J. Arthur 163, 164, 225
Young, Polly Ann 121-122, 155-156
Young, Victor 159
You're Out of Luck 144
Yukon Flight 118
Yukon Have It 117

-Z-

Zamboanga 70
Zenobia 46
Zorro's Fighting Legion 76
Zucco, George 59, 141, 205-206, 209

To learn more about those classic movies visit
Midnight Marquee's website at
www.midmar.com

or write for a free catalog
Midnight Marquee Press, Inc.
9721 Britinay Lane
Baltimore, MD 21234

www.ingramcontent.com/pod-product-compliance
Lightning Source LLC
Chambersburg PA
CBHW071228080526
44587CB00013BA/1533